Principles of Advertising
A Global Perspective

Second Edition

1

Monle Lee
Carla Johnson

Principles of Advertising
A Global Perspective
Second Edition

Pre-publication
REVIEWS,
COMMENTARIES,
EVALUATIONS . . .

"**A**ll marketing functions are affected by globalization, but nowhere are the challenges greater than with advertising. A globally coherent message has to account for differences in the legal and media environments and, most difficult of all, cultural variations, which can be very subtle. A global perspective is essential if we are to understand contemporary advertising and it is good to have a textbook that is packed with examples from around the world."

Tim Beal, PhD
Senior Lecturer,
School of Marketing
and International Business,
Victoria University of Wellington,
New Zealand

"**P**rofessors Lee and Johnson present a fresh, timely, and highly readable book that will provide students with a very comprehensive introduction to the dynamic world of advertising. The book's global perspective is crucial in today's academic environment where we are integrating a world-view into every course and concept. The book's focus on ethics also sets it apart—it is essential that our advertising and marketing students understand that consumers must be treated with exceptional care, not only for business and legal reasons but also because it is the right thing to do.

The authors have illustrated their concepts with marketplace examples that are compelling and current. This helps bring the material alive for students and allows them to see how agencies and clients apply advertising concepts in the United States and around the world. These authors have lived in both the academic realm and the real world of advertising—a potent and unique combination!"

Susan K. Jones, MSJ
Professor of Marketing,
Ferris State University

Principles of Advertising
A Global Perspective

Second Edition

Monle Lee
Carla Johnson

The Haworth Press
New York • London • Oxford

For more information on this book or to order, visit
http://www.haworthpress.com/store/product.asp?sku=5512

or call 1-800-HAWORTH (800-429-6784) in the United States and Canada
or (607) 722-5857 outside the United States and Canada

or contact orders@HaworthPress.com

The Haworth Press, Inc., 10 Alice Street, Binghamton, NY 13904-1580.

First edition published 1999.

Cover design by Marylouise E. Doyle.

Library of Congress Cataloging-in-Publication Data

Lee, Monle.
　　Principles of advertising : a global perspective / Monle Lee, Carla Johnson.—2nd ed.
　　　　p. cm.
　　Includes bibliographical references and index.
　　ISBN-13: 978-0-7890-2299-8 (hc. : alk. paper)
　　ISBN-10: 0-7890-2299-0 (hc. : alk. paper)
　　ISBN-13: 978-0-7890-2300-1 (pbk. : alk. paper)
　　ISBN-10: 0-7890-2300-8 (pbk. : alk. paper)
　　1. Advertising. I. Johnson, Carla, 1944- II. Title.

HF5821.L35 2005
659.1—dc22

2005002253

To the memory of our parents,
Mrs. Wuyao H. Lee
and
Mr. Harold P. Jackson,
in appreciation for their years of love and support

ABOUT THE AUTHORS

Monle Lee, DBA, is Professor of Marketing at Indiana University South Bend in Indiana and the co-author of *Principles of Advertising: A Global Perspective.* Her first book, *Advertising: Strategy and Management,* a Mandarin Chinese language advertising textbook, was released in Taiwan in 1998 for Taiwanese college students. Her research interests center on international marketing, ethics marketing, advertising, and ethical issues in different cultures. Her research has appeared in book chapters, business journals, and various conference proceedings. Dr. Lee was previously an international marketer in Taiwan.

Carla Johnson, PhD, is a professional writing specialist, Assistant Director of the Writing Proficiency Program, and Internship Program Coordinator for the English Department at Saint Mary's College in Notre Dame. She is the co-author of *Principles of Advertising: A Global Perspective* and the author of *21st Century Feature Writing,* and has presented at the International Society for the Study of European Ideas conferences and in advertising sessions of the Popular Culture Association's international meetings.

CONTENTS

Foreword

Forewords are strange animals. Sometimes they enhance the text to follow. Sometimes they simply summarize what the authors have said. Sometimes they are repayment for previous debts or favors between or among authors. Sometimes they are personal statements by the foreword writer. To understand a foreword and the value of it, I believe it is important for the reader to know how the foreword came about and why that particular person asked or was asked to write the comments.

When Carla Johnson called me about the text she and Monle Lee were writing, it was initially to get my permission to use some materials I had developed over the years on Integrated Marketing Communication (IMC) which they planned to use in Chapter 1. Since some of my views of IMC have changed over the years, Carla wanted to be sure that what she was quoting was how I now viewed the process. After all, some of my early writings are now about ten years old.

After reading Chapter 1, I called Carla and told her she and Monle had indeed captured the essence of IMC and what I have observed around the world. In fact, they had extended some of my own thinking, particularly in the global arena. That led to more discussions, and that led to this foreword. I wholeheartedly agree with what you will find in the pages that follow on IMC and advertising principles.

So now, as Paul Harvey might say, "You know the rest of the story."

I'm pleased to write this foreword for I believe that the approach which Carla and Monle have developed really does capture the concepts, practice, and spirit of Integrated Marketing Communication as we enter the twenty-first century. It is, to me, a unique principles text. It mixes the proven theory base of the academic community with the actual practice of IMC around the world. It is highly readable and easy to follow. It presents concepts and approaches in a logical, easy-to-follow sequence. It is filled with examples and case illustrations. But, then, one could say the same thing about a number of advertising principles texts. The real question is, "What makes this introductory text different?" In my view, there are four areas.

Integration

Integration and Integrated Marketing Communication (IMC) are "hot" topics in marketing and marketing communication today. Yet, many advertising and marketing text authors in the development of their approaches have treated IMC as a "bolt on" or "add-on" to their manuscripts. They've added a chapter or some timeworn examples here and there in the string of chapters and said, "Now, our text is integrated." That's not the case here. Lee and Johnson take a truly integrated approach to the development of advertising programs. IMC permeates this book. It is the basis for the entire approach to communication that they have developed. It is "integrated" in the best sense of the word. So, if you want to see an IMC process in action, this text personifies the process and the approach.

Global Perspective

Communication traditionally has been very culture-driven. That is, the approach to advertising or promotion has been based on the mores and structures of the economy or society in which it was written. Thus, a text written in Australia really wasn't too relevant to someone in Hong Kong. Or a text developed in Germany had little interest in South Africa. This book is, to my knowledge, the first text that takes a "global" approach to IMC. That is, it is boundary spanning and culture crossing. It is a horizontal view of the marketplace, across countries, across cultures, across economies. It is what has often been described as a "transnational" approach. Yet it is very practical for a student who never plans to go more than a couple of hundred miles from home. Global is a way of thinking and a way of doing advertising and communication that is as relevant in the local market as it is in a satellite-delivered Olympic venue which spans the globe. In short, *Principles of Advertising: A Global Perspective* practices what IMC is all about: the integration of marketing and marketing communication from the view of the customer, not just the view of the marketing organization.

Ethics

In most principles texts, ethics or ethical behavior in marketing and communication usually ends up somewhere near the end of the text.

Thus, the student or instructor can often "just not have time to talk about or cover the ethical considerations of an advertising or communication program" during the course. More critical, ethics is often separated from how the communication is either developed or implemented. In too many cases, authors treat ethics and ethical behavior by communicators as something that is added at the last moment. Lee and Johnson integrate ethics and ethical behavior throughout the book. Ethical communication and behavior is at the beginning and throughout the text. And, that's important. Too many consumers believe marketing communication and advertising is hucksterism or even worse, misleading or manipulative or just plain dishonest. In my view, ethical behavior by advertisers and communicators is one of the most critical issues of the twenty-first century. The increasing availability of individual customer information raises all the questions of privacy and marketers' "need to know" that consumer groups so legitimately challenge. Ethics is, to me, the cornerstone of effective communication, and this text is permeated with an ethical view. That's important for the student to learn and more important for the practitioner to implement.

Voices from the Industry

"What's it really like out there in the 'real world' ?" students often wonder. In this text, you will learn. Monle and Carla have asked their own students to tell, in their own words, their experiences. And, those experiences aren't the musings of a twenty-year veteran who foggily remembers what it was like to work in the 1970s and 1980s. These are "real-world," "day-to-day" experiences from new hires in the advertising and communication fields. They "tell it like it is, warts and all." Some of the experiences are good. Some are bad. But all are interesting and useful to a person who is considering a career in advertising, promotion, public relations, direct marketing, or IMC.

These are the four things that I believe differentiate this principles text from all the others on the market. It's integrated. It's global. It's focused on ethics and ethical behaviors by communicators. And, it's "real world." It's how IMC is being done today and will be done tomorrow.

Most of all, this text passes the four-C test I use to evaluate any text. In my system, Cs are good, not bad. The Cs I use are Clarity,

Conciseness, Completeness, and Currency. The book you are about to read passes all four of these tests with flying colors. So, rather than four stars, I give Carla and Monle four Cs. And that is about the best you can do in my classes.

Don E. Schultz
Northwestern University
Evanston, Illinois

Preface to the Second Edition

"It seems like every other day someone says, 'Well, since 9/11 . . .' It is almost that 9/11 started a new era."

This was one respondent's reply to a WPP Group's Lightspeed Online Research survey of 2,309 adults' feelings a year after the tragic terrorist attacks on New York and Washington, DC.[1] Lightspeed's results indicated that people have been significantly affected by the experience: "Psychological changes such as vulnerability and vigilance, gratefulness, xenophobia, a focus on 'today' and security now seem a part of our national fabric."[2]

Whether it's called a "new era" or the "new normal," 9/11 has changed the way Americans perceive themselves and their world. Every citizen was impacted by 9/11 in one way or another. Americans lost loved ones, lost their sense of security, lost hope, lost their jobs; the ramifications were extensive. The consequences were far-reaching, not only for individuals, but also for companies, corporations, and industries.

One industry transformed by 9/11 is the advertising industry. Granted, even before the Twin Towers fell, the advertising industry was standing on shaky ground. The economy was struggling after the economic boom of the late 1990s, causing businesses and corporations to cut back on advertising spending. The Enron scandal and the subsequent investigations of other corporations made consumers think twice about making purchases. So on September 11, 2001, an already depressed advertising market was suddenly faced with a whole new set of obstacles.

The advertising industry began to witness effects of 9/11 immediately. Airline and travel companies pulled their ads from newspapers. Advertising that had seemed inconsequential the day before was pulled off the air, to be rewritten according to the sensitive nature of the times. Many movies and video games scheduled for release in 2001 were held back because of questionable content. For instance, scenes in the movie *Spider-Man* had to be redone because the background featured the Twin Towers. The opening to HBO's hit series, *Sex and the City,* had to be reedited for the same reason.

Advertisers also faced ethical dilemmas in the weeks that followed 9/11. Many companies wanted to express their condolences but had to be careful so as to not appear to be cashing in on the tragedy. Some advertisers achieved sincerity while others seemed opportunistic. For example, Calvin Klein tastefully changed their slogan from "What you stand for is more important than what you stand in" to "What we stand for is more important than what we stand in," acknowledging the importance of solidarity as opposed to individuality. Less tasteful was Anheuser-Busch's national television commercial that announced its $3 million contribution to relief agencies. In a similar fashion, New York Sports Club promoted special introductory fees under the banner of "Keep America Strong." Critics have questioned the ulterior motives of some of these advertising campaigns that companies justified under the guise of patriotism.

Some of the companies that were hit most directly by 9/11, such as airline and travel, came back tentatively in the weeks and months after 9/11. Southwest Airlines was one of the first to resurface with an ad campaign that highlighted the strength of America. They distributed stickers that said, "Keep America Flying, I Flew Southwest Airlines Today." Other airlines promoted low-price incentives to coax nervous travelers into flying again.

Despite the many companies that continued to advertise, many other companies simply froze their advertising spending until they decided how to approach the fragile market. Depressing the market further in the year after 9/11 was the anthrax scare, which negatively impacted the $585.5 billion direct-mail industry.[3] Consumers feared unfamiliar direct mail that was being sent to their homes. Companies like Procter & Gamble and Nissan adjusted mailing programs in anticipation of consumer fear, and the Direct Marketing Association reduced its 2001 expenditure projections by $2 billion in response to the anthrax threat. All in all, 9/11 and its aftermath proved to be a difficult hurdle for the advertising industry to overcome in 2001.

On the one-year anniversary of the terrorist attacks, September 11, 2002, advertisers were faced with yet another ethical quandary. Some Americans were voicing the opinion that advertisers should go dark on 9/11, meaning that companies should withhold advertising for the day. This would cost advertisers as well as networks a lot of money, as the networks alone would lose $32 million in one day. Other Ameras the networks alone would lose $32 million in one day. Other Americans, however, had a "show must go on" mentality about the anniversary. Advertisers ended up making split decisions, with some choosing not to advertise while others ran commemorative ads.

After the anniversary, the industry began to focus on rebuilding. Public service announcements sponsored by the Advertising Council ran with the theme "Selling the USA," reminding Americans what we stand for. Both consumers and advertisers seemed to be coming to terms with what had happened and were forging forward in a new direction. Consumers were showing a resilience that was encouraging to the industry. Television ad dollars for broadcast networks were up 20.1 percent at the end of 2002, and other markets such as magazine ad revenue were growing as well.[4]

Although advertising seems to be surmounting the obstacles of 9/11, the industry will never be the same, just as Americans will never be the same. Americans have been made more vulnerable and, in turn, have become more self-aware. We understand in a new way that the decisions we make shape the world's opinion of us. This global awareness has become a crucial component of advertising strategy. 9/11 has forced advertisers to think more seriously about the way they portray America, realizing that these images not only affect Americans but also affect the way the rest of the world views Americans. Representing the United States is no small responsibility for the advertising industry to take on, but I am optimistic in thinking that after 9/11, the industry is up to the challenge.

Kate Dooley
Saint Mary's College
Notre Dame, Indiana

Acknowledgments

The authors wish to thank their families for their love, support, and patience: Dariush and Jennifer Behzadi, Wuchi Lee, Helen Jackson, Aaron H. Hoffman, Marie Remington, and James R. Jackson, and, of course, Sunny. We also wish to acknowledge with deepest gratitude the contributions of other special individuals: David R. Stefancic, our consultant for Eastern Europe; Stefan Horvath, who helped in countless ways throughout the writing of the first edition; Joyce Perry, Celia Fallon, Mary Beth Dominello, Tod Moorhead, Michael Rogers, and Star Staffing Services, Inc.; Eric Remington and Paula Winicur for ad design; and Dana Hanefeld, Tara Krull, Catherine A. Narbone, Amy Codron Randolph, Kathy Evans Wisner, Angela Saoud, and especially Arianna Stella for their invaluable contributions and assistance in obtaining permissions. We are also indebted to a number of Saint Mary's College students and alumnae, including Lauren Siegel, Mary Beth Broviak, and Sara Mahoney. Special thanks to Don E. Schultz and Kate Dooley for their willingness to write the Foreword and Preface, respectively.

Finally, the authors wish to acknowledge fellowships and travel support received from the Direct Marketing Educational Foundation, the Yellow Pages Publishers Association, the Saint Mary's College Center for Women's Intercultural Leadership (CWIL), and the International Radio and Television Society. In fact, the authors met at an IRTS seminar in New York City. Without that opportunity, this book would never have existed.

Chapter 1

Introduction to Advertising

Drive down any highway, and you'll see a proliferation of chain restaurants—most likely, if you travel long and far enough, you'll see McDonald's golden arches as well as signs for Burger King, Hardee's, and Wendy's, the "big four" of burgers. Despite its name, though, Burger King has fallen short of claiming the burger crown, unable to surpass market leader McDonald's No. 1 sales status. Always the bridesmaid and never the bride, Burger King remains No. 2.

Worse yet, Burger King has experienced a six-year 22 percent decline in customer traffic, with its overall quality rating dropping while ratings for the other three contenders have increased.[1] The decline has been attributed to inconsistent product quality and poor customer service. Although the chain tends to throw advertising dollars at the problem, an understanding of Integrated Marketing Communication theory would suggest that internal management problems (nineteen CEOs in fifty years) need to be rectified before a unified, long-term strategy can be put in place.

The importance of consistency in brand image and messages, at all levels of communication, has become a basic tenet of IMC theory and practice. The person who takes the customer's order must communicate the same message as Burger King's famous tagline, "Have it your way," or the customer will just buzz up the highway to a chain restaurant that seems more consistent and, therefore, more reliable. See Illustration 1.1 for an example of consistency in advertising.

According to Northwestern University advertising professor Don E. Schultz, the "father" of Integrated Marketing Communication (IMC), the concept of IMC starts with consumer needs and wants, and works back to the brand.[2] Today it is no longer enough for Burger King or McDonald's to come out with a new product and spend $75 million on television commercials. Advertising plans must not only

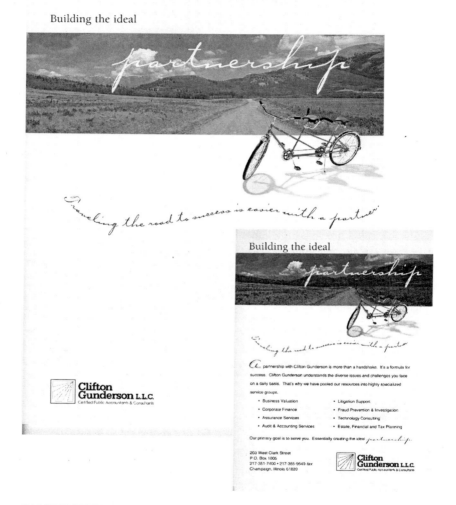

ILLUSTRATION 1.1. One sight, one sound. Clifton Gunderson L.L.C., one of the largest certified public accountants and consultants firms in the United States, employed a consistent image and message through integration of its public relations and advertising in Gunderson's "Building the Ideal Partnership" campaign. In the interest of consistency, the brochure (upper left) uses the same visual as well as the same tagline and headline as its print advertisement (lower right).

involve all the organization's communication systems but also the entire organization in total management of all brand contacts.[3]

Welcome to the world of Integrated Marketing Communications.

Integration of a mass media blitz with special product packaging and retail displays reflects the growing trend to "include and involve the channels of distribution in the communications mix" when an advertising campaign is launched.[4] The availability of consumer information, tracking, and electronic ticketing illustrates the wave of the future—the shift in marketplace power from the manufacturer or service provider to the consumer, or end user. That shift has impacted and will continue to impact the field of advertising.

Increasingly, those involved in the advertising profession recognize that future success depends on the ability to understand and use the tools of Integrated Marketing Communication. The evolution of IMC, or Integrated Communications (IC), will be discussed in this chapter. But first we must understand what advertising is and how it has evolved.

ADVERTISING DEFINED

Advertising is a paid, nonpersonal communication about an organization and its products or services that is transmitted to a target audience through mass media such as television, radio, newspapers, magazines, direct mail, outdoor displays, or mass-transit vehicles. In the new, global community, advertising messages may be transmitted via new media, especially the Internet. Online advertising spending has continued to recover from the slump it suffered after the September 11, 2001, attacks on the World Trade Center. During the fourth quarter of 2003, online ad spending was up 22.3 percent to over $574.2 million. This compares impressively to newspapers' 15.2 percent increase and network television's modest 3.8 percent increase.[5] Consumer media and business-to-business advertising spending hit close to $1 billion in the first quarter of 2003, a 7.4 percent increase over the same quarter in 2002.

Individuals and organizations use advertising to promote goods, services, ideas, issues, and people. For instance, Coca-Cola used a public relations-driven campaign to relaunch its Sprite brand that included a fifty-city sampling tour. The financial services industry, e.g.,

TABLE 1.1. Top U.S. advertisers.

Company	Previous rank	2003 dollars in billions
General Motors	1	3.43
Procter & Gamble	2	3.32
Time Warner	3	3.10
Pfizer	4	2.84
DaimlerChrysler	5	2.32

Source: Adapted from "Top U.S. Advertisers," *Advertising Age FactPack,* February 28, 2005, p. 12.

American Express, Merrill Lynch, and the New York Cotton Exchange, spends over $1 billion a year on advertising. Prescription-drug advertisements targeting consumers have became a booming new ad genre following the FDA's lifting of restrictions on TV ads for prescription drugs in 1997. The first television commercials for the prescription drug Prozac aired on September 14, 1998.[6] Lipitor, Pfizer's cholesterol-fighting drug, "the second-most frequently prescribed drug in the United States," netted record sales in 2002 that totaled just under $8 billion.[7] In 2003 Pfizer edged out DaimlerChrysler for the number four top domestic ad spender, with figures not far below number three—Time Warner (see Table 1.1).

Product categories continue to expand, creating challenges for advertisers and their agencies. Asian countries have become the trendsetters, launching products such as cell phone TV well ahead of the United States. However, Italy seems to be right up there with the Asian countries when it comes to innovative technologies. Telecom Italia Mobile initiated a cell phone TV service in late 2003. The cell phone products leader offered the new service free throughout the launch year. For the top-ten Asian product launches in 2003, see Table 1.2. Notice that Londoners discovered Chinese beer before their U.S. counterparts.

ADVERTISING CLASSIFICATIONS

There is not one clear, all-embracing term to describe advertising's complex character and multiple, interrelated functions. Advertising is frequently classified in several broad types.

THE GLOBAL PERSPECTIVE:
GLOBAL BRAND CREATION

"You have to know Japanese to work in most of the spas here," says Jessica, a Honolulu pedicurist. Hawaii has become a popular leisure destination for young Japanese career women who find the yen strong against the dollar at Honolulu hotels, shops, and spas. Spa owners know that, in today's competitive marketplace, the service industry must speak the customer's language.

In a smart IMC move, the Hilton Hawaiian Village in Honolulu tailors the vacation experience for this valued demographic. Nestled in a prime location on Waikiki Beach, overlooking the famous Diamond Head landmark, the village offers ninety retail shops, including a wide variety of designer boutiques. Sushi restaurants within the village offer familiar menus to Japanese guests. To accommodate its affluent clientele, the village maintains a tight security system; a security official posted at a bustling internal intersection controls the automobile and pedestrian traffic.

It is no surprise, then, that the Mandara Spa at the village also gives its visitor what she wants. Its menu lists a variety of massage styles, from Swedish to sports to Reiki. Spa guests are pampered with high-quality services and a plethora of amenities—sauna, jacuzzi, private lockers and showers, robes and slippers, and a private pool with a rock garden and waterfalls.

How do you create or reinforce a global brand? Traditional advertising is unlikely to reach Mandara's target, so the spa utilizes place-based communications. Hotel guests receive a coupon for a massage upgrade (upgrades may appeal more to the affluent than discounts). Coupons are also distributed in other upscale Waikiki hotels through guest-room placements.

To reach potential clients before they leave home, Mandara lists with Spafinder, the online purveyor of the world's renowned spas. The Spafinder Web site offers information, gift certificates, and subscriptions to its print publication, *SpaFinder Magazine*. Spafinder expands its reach by offering discounts to members of Victoria's Secret Escapes. The VS Escapes Web site and member services guidebook in turn advertise the indulgences of Spafinder's listed spas. Victoria's Secret's customers learn about the Mandara Spa by clicking on the Spafinder link.

Tailoring products, services, and messages to the customer must be part of a successful marketing plan, but global branding also requires brand exposure to the right customer.

TABLE 1.2. Top-ten Asian products/trends in 2003.

Product	Country	What it does
1. Cell phone TV	Japan	Phones save TV images
2. Amino acid drinks	Japan	Beverage with wide health claims
3. Ionic hair straightening	Japan	Permanently straightens hair
4. Electronic payment cards	Singapore	Single card that pays for anything and everything
5. Beer	China	Beer brands taking London by storm
6. Wrist gadgets	Hong Kong	Octo-phone by Nokia has electronic pay system
7. Designer pets	Singapore	Zebra fish glows red
8. Guo dong	China	Fruit jelly shots for children
9. PlayStation 3	Japan	Video game
10. Mortgages	South Korea	Finance luxury goods

Source: Adapted from "Products/Trends from Asia," *Advertising Age,* December 22, 2003, p. 30.

Product Advertising

The major portion of advertising expenditure is spent on product advertising: the presentation and promotion of new products, existing products, and revised products. For example, Apple Computer used advertising to launch its updated iPod and netted a 20+ percent market share in 2003; in 2004 the original iPod remained a contender in its category.[8] Chevy's GM division "launched an ad for its new pickup that featured kids getting soap stuck in their mouths for appearing to utter an incredulous expletive at the sight of the SSR pickup" on Super Bowl XXXVIII, creating controversy among viewers.[9]

Retail Advertising

In contrast to product advertising, retail advertising is local and focuses on the store where a variety of products can be purchased or where a service is offered. Retail advertising emphasizes price, availability, location, and hours of operation. Meijer, a Michigan-based superstore, which combines features of a discount store and supermarket, advertises frequently on local television and in local newspapers. Consumers are attracted to superstores by lower prices and one-stop shopping.

Corporate Advertising

The focus of these advertisements is on establishing a corporate identity or on winning the public over to the organization's point of view. Most corporate advertising is designed to create a favorable image for a company and its products; however, image advertising specifically denotes a corporate campaign that highlights the superiority or desirable characteristics of the sponsoring corporation. The Anheuser-Busch Clydesdale horses have made an appearance in the corporation's image ads at both Super Bowl XXXVII and XXXVIII.

Business-to-Business Advertising

The term relates to advertising that is directed to industrial users (tires advertised to automobile manufacturers), resellers (wholesalers and retailers), and professionals (such as lawyers and accountants). Advertising by professionals has gained momentum since U.S. Supreme Court decisions permitted such advertising.

Political Advertising

Political advertising is often used by politicians to persuade people to vote for them; therefore, it is an important part of the political process in the United States and other democratic countries that permit candidate advertising (see Illustration 1.2). Critics would like to see a limit placed on campaign spending. Other critics are concerned that political advertising tends to focus more on images than on issues, often referred to as selling a candidate's individual brand. During the 2004 Democratic presidential primaries, Vermont Governor Howard Dean hired a group of advertisers whose main goal was to portray his personal force. One possible reason for this change in the political arena is that it is easier to portray personalities than issues in a thirty-second time slot. President George W. Bush's $4.4 million ad campaign, launched in early 2004, used images of the U.S. flag and 9/11 devastation, generating protests from some of the 9/11 victims' families.

ILLUSTRATION 1.2. No negatives. Gary J. Bruce, candidate for District Judge in Berrien County, Michigan, bucked the trend toward negative political advertising with this newspaper ad designed by Eric Remington. The only "negatives" are the sections of reverse type on black.

Another common critique of political advertising is the negative tone it has developed in recent years. For example, although Governor Dean launched a history-making online campaign, it could not redeem his tainted image after outtakes of his Iowa concession speech showed the candidate in an apparent rage to the public.

Governments as well as individual politicians may employ advertising. Facing financial crises in 1998, Thailand and Malaysia launched ad campaigns to recover their tarnished reputations and lost investors. Print ads appeared in global business publications, and television spots aired on the cable network CNN. Likewise, in June 2003 the governments of Singapore and Hong Kong used TV and print ads to encourage tourism following the severe acute respiratory syndrome (SARS) scare.

Directory Advertising

People refer to directory advertising to find out how and where to buy a product or service. The best known form of directory advertising is the Yellow Pages, although today there are many different kinds of directories that perform the same function. Yellow Pages directories were added to phone books after World War II. By the 1950s and 1960s, directory fees were invoiced on the advertising company's phone bill. The dual market structure of Yellow Pages advertising evolved into 80 percent local listings and 20 percent national. In 1975 the Yellow Pages Publishers Association (YPPA) merged from two previous Yellow Pages publishers' associations. A unique feature of Yellow Pages directory advertising has been the ability to measure response. The advertising company may carry two different phone numbers, one given in Yellow Pages advertising, and the other used in alternative advertising channels, so that response to the Yellow Pages ad may be measured. Further, directory advertising is unique in that the user generally is ready to buy the product or service when the directory is consulted.

Direct Response Advertising

Direct response advertising involves two-way communication between the advertiser and the consumer. It can use any advertising medium (e.g., mail, television, newspaper, magazine), and the consumer can respond, often by mail, telephone, or fax. More and more companies now allow the consumer to respond online. The product is usually delivered to the consumer by mail.

For instance, *Time* magazine uses a television commercial for direct response advertising; the commercial urges viewers to call an 800 number to order a subscription to the magazine or to receive more information. Similarly, the company uses cards inserted into newsstand magazines which are, themselves, response mechanisms. The consumer need only complete the card and mail it, postage free, to initiate home delivery. *Time* often also advertises an "offer," such as a free camera or video, which serves as a "gift" should the consumer decide to subscribe. The "offer" and the list, if mail is the medium chosen, are said to be the most important criteria in direct response advertising success.

Public Service Advertising

Public service advertising is designed to operate in the public's interest and promote public welfare. These advertisements are created free of charge by advertising professionals, and the space and time are donated by the media. Management and staff at Bozell and Jacobs, a U.S. advertising agency, donate time, talents, and money to community service organizations such as the American Cancer Society, American Red Cross, and United Way. Many local television stations have cooperated with Mothers Against Drunk Driving (MADD), creating and airing free public service spots that urge young people not to drink and drive at prom time. The Partnership for a Drug-Free America produces antidrug advertisements.

Advocacy Advertising

Advocacy advertising is concerned with the propagation of ideas and the clarification of controversial social issues of public importance. A growing number of firms have applied advertising strategies to such social causes as conserving wildlife.

ADVERTISING FUNCTIONS

Definitions and classifications only provide a common language in which to develop an understanding of advertising. The effects of advertising on an organization may be dramatic and also need to be explored.

- Advertising performs an "inform" function; it communicates information about the product, its features, and its location of sale; it informs the consumers about new products. Apple used an ad blitz to inform the public of its new iMac computer and later for its updated iPod; the TBWA Chiat/Day ad campaign ("Yo Quiero Taco Bell") introduced television viewers to Taco Bell's new Gorditas taco (controversy about who actually created the spokesdog was settled out of court in 2003).
- Advertising performs a "persuasive" function; it tries to persuade consumers to purchase specific brands or to change their attitudes toward the product or company. Although Miller Beer has spent millions of dollars on ad campaigns designed to grab market share from Budweiser, Anheuser-Busch has kept control of the market with Budweiser and Bud Light, the world's top beer brands, through its humorous commercials. Sometimes advertising can be both informative and persuasive. As the Taco Bell ad campaign introduced the new Gorditas taco, it also encouraged viewers to choose Taco Bell for their fast-food purchases through the emotional appeal of the popular Taco Bell Chihuahua. Due to the success of past campaigns using spokesanimals, the trend has become an advertising staple. Ads featuring animals dominated Super Bowl XXXVIII (the Sierra Mist dog, Chevrolet elephant, Bud Light monkey, Pepsi bear, and Budweiser horses and a donkey).
- Advertising performs a "reminder" function; it constantly reminds consumers about a product so that they will keep buying the advertised product instead of the competitor's brand. Nielsen's listing is a good indicator of who's doing major advertising blitzes and how much support a marketer is putting behind a brand or advertising campaign. For years, McDonald's commercials have received top weekly exposure on television. Although the other top burger chains have put up a good fight, McDonald's remains number one. The purpose of McDonald's advertisements is to remind consumers that, when they get hungry, there is a McDonald's restaurant nearby.

Whether to introduce new products or to give consumers a brand reminder, the food and beverages category remains a big ad spender (see Table 1.3).

TABLE 1.3. Top global ad spenders by category (in millions of dollars).

Category	Total 2003 spending
Automotive	20,928
Personal care	15,294
Entertainment/media	9,431
Food	7,786
Drugs	5,599

Source: Adapted from "Global Marketing," *Advertising Age,* November 8, 2004, p. 36.

ADVERTISING AND MARKETING

Four years of free-market reforms and strong agricultural output in India are cracking open the mammoth market for everything from toiletries to television sets. Colgate-Palmolive India Ltd., a U.S. consumer goods company determined to draw more than half of its revenue from rural India by 2003, spent five times more on rural marketing than it had before. To get a foothold in rural India, consumer product makers can't rely on conventional Madison Avenue marketing techniques; more than half of all Indian villagers are illiterate, and only one-third live in households with television sets. So Colgate's marketers turned to half-hour infomercials carried through the countryside in video vans. Many Indians in rural areas have never handled such products as a bottle of shampoo or a toothpaste tube. Fewer than 15 percent of rural Indians regularly use a dentifrice, according to Colgate-Palmolive. For generations, they have used charcoal powder and indigenous plants to cleanse their mouths. Farmers and field workers were drawn to the video van where the infomercial was shown to them. The subtext was clear: Colgate is good for your breath and teeth. The audience was offered free samples. A Colgate marketer demonstrated how to use the toothpaste and toothbrush. To encourage parents to buy a tube, the company offered free Colgate brushes to a few children, only to leave many little hands grabbing for more.[10]

ETHICS TRACK:
HAS THE TOP PHARMACEUTICAL
ADVERTISER ABUSED ITS POWER?

An eighty-eight-year-old woman in Toledo, Ohio, takes Lipitor to keep her cholesterol levels down and Celebrex to make the pain of her arthritis bearable. These prescription drugs cost so much that she must choose between buying her medicine or buying groceries. Her fixed income, a Social Security payment of $800 a month, can't cover it all anymore. When she heard from friends about a bus taking senior citizens across the border into Canada to purchase the drugs at a fraction of the U.S. price, she no longer had to choose between enduring pain and having something to eat.

In an Associated Press-Ipsos poll, about one-third of Americans cited prescription drug costs as a problem, with many "cutting dosages to deal with the crunch."[a] Two-thirds of those polled favored fewer governmental restrictions on buying prescription drugs in other countries, including Canada, where they are cheaper because the government regulates brand-name drug prices.

Pfizer, the market leader in pharmaceutical ad spending, "posted revenue of $32 billion in 2002" with its top-selling drugs Lipitor, Norvasc (for high blood pressure), and Celebrex.[b] Pfizer used its clout to close off the pipeline to "lower-cost prescription drugs from Canada" when it sent letters to Canadian pharmacies in January 2004. Pfizer promised to cut off supplies of the popular drugs if Canadian pharmacies continued to sell to over one million Americans seeking to defray escalating health care costs. In another development, a U.S. Food and Drug Administration (FDA) survey of eight Canadian online pharmacies in 2004 cited violations that resulted in unsafe products being shipped to the United States, a charge denied by a Health Canada spokesman.

To further heighten controversy, Pfizer hired an Atlanta agency, Wanamaker Associates, that specializes "in marketing to medical professionals," according to a front-page *Advertising Age* story on October 13, 2003. Pfizer declined to comment on the hire. Do pharmaceutical companies commonly lobby doctors to prescribe their drugs? Why would Pfizer refuse to comment on the decision to hire an agency specifically focused on medical professionals?

It's a complex situation. American pharmaceutical companies say that they need the U.S. profits to fund research. As one of the top five ad spenders, could Pfizer's claim that the majority of its profits go to research fall under public scrutiny?

American senior citizens "reacted in anger and alarm to the news" that Pfizer had choked off their pipeline to cheaper drug prices in Canada.[c] Pfizer, the first pharmaceutical company "to make a total boycott succeed," left seniors with the option to do without the needed drugs or to switch to a different brand, perhaps a brand-name alternative or a generic. As Canadian pharmacies' supplies of Pfizer's drugs dried up, the American Association of Retired Persons (AARP) created a Web site to provide information on alternative brands and generics for the boycotted drugs. Pfizer took the risk of losing a part of its lucrative U.S. market, although prospects brightened for the pharmaceutical giant in late 2004 when Canadian Health Minister, Ujjal Dosanjh, announced plans to "prevent Canadian doctors from co-signing prescriptions for American patients they have not examined," a practice potentially unethical.[d] The decision could also be a reaction to the fact that Canadian drug prices have increased due to the growing American trade.

Is it right to charge higher prices to U.S. citizens than to buyers abroad? Some place the blame for prescription drug prices with U.S. government officials who rely on special-interest groups for campaign funds. Is the fault with politicians' resistance to campaign spending reform? Or are special-interest lobbyists, such as Pfizer, to blame?

[a]"Poll Shows Some Americans Find Paying for Prescriptions Difficult," *South Bend Tribune,* February 24, 2004, A3.
[b]Patricia Barry, "Crackdown in Canada," *AARP Bulletin,* February 2004, p. 18.
[c]Patricia Barry, "When the Pipeline Closes," *AARP Bulletin,* April 2004, p. 7.
[d]Julie Appleby, "Canada May Stop Over-the-Border Drug Sales," *USA Today,* December 29, 2004, USATODAY.com.

The Marketing Concept

This story about consumer product giant Colgate-Palmolive suggests that advertising is just a part of the total marketing effort. It also suggests that marketing strategies, including advertising, are not easily transferred from one culture to another. Individuals, businesses, government, and nonprofit organizations all develop products to satisfy customers, the people or organizations that purchase a product, and advertising helps persuade customers to select one product rather than another. However, marketing isn't just selling. The American Marketing Association defines marketing as "the process of planning and executing the conception, pricing, promotion, and distribution of ideas, goods, and services to create exchanges that satisfy individual (customer) and organizational objectives."[11]

According to the marketing concept, an organization should try to provide products that satisfy customers' needs through a coordinated set of activities that also allow the organization to achieve its goals. Today, manufacturers and service firms can produce more goods and services more efficiently than ever before, which means that supply is often greater than demand. Because people have so many product choices, an organization must give customers real reasons for choosing its products over competing products. Otherwise, the organization's profits will suffer as customers flock to rival products. Therefore, the key to success is to apply the marketing concept.

Three main components make up the marketing concept.

- *Meeting customer needs and wants*—An organization must find out what will satisfy customers and use this information to create satisfying products. The organization must also continue to alter, adapt, and develop products to keep pace with customers' changing desires and preferences.
- *Coordinating marketing efforts across the organization*—Marketing is only one of the functions involved in meeting customer needs. Research and development, manufacturing, finance, and other functions are also important, so coordinating these functions with marketing efforts greatly increases an organization's chances of success.
- *Achieving long-term goals*—A firm that adopts the marketing concept must not only satisfy its customers' objectives, but also achieve its own goals, or it will not stay in business long.

The overall goals of a business might be directed toward increasing profits, market share, sales, or a combination of all three. When organizations truly implement the marketing concept, they find that customers will continue buying the products that best meet their needs, which fuels sales and profits over the long term.

The Marketing Mix

The marketing mix consists of four major components: product, place, price, and promotion. Marketing mix variables are often viewed as controllable variables because a marketing manager can decide what type of each component to use and in what amounts in order to achieve customer satisfaction. Thus, promotion (marketing communication that includes advertising) must be balanced with product design and packaging, the method of distribution, and the price. Customers consider the overall marketing mix when they choose a product.

Product

The product is a "bundle of value" that meets customer expectations. For example, an Acer laptop computer is more than just the computer itself; it also includes an instruction manual, access to a customer service hotline, a warranty certificate, and other components. An airline ticket promises more than transportation; other components such as on-ground and in-flight services, and on-time and safe arrival to the destination are expected by consumers. Advertising these features and benefits helps customers choose products or services that fit their needs. Branding and packaging are two important features of a product. In order to translate the product's characteristics into something concrete that can be used to distinguish one product from another, many businesses advertise a distinctive brand, a name, a word, a phrase, a symbol, or a combination of these elements. For example, perfume companies invest a great deal of money in packaging their perfumes to distinguish them from competitors' perfumes.

Place

Place is also called channel of distribution or distribution channel. A channel of distribution refers to a group of individuals and organizations that directs the flow of products from producers to customers. Distribution activities include managing product transportation and storage, processing orders, and keeping track of inventory. The members of the distribution channel include wholesalers and retailers, and industrial buyers in the industrial market. Channel decisions are critical because they determine a product's market presence and accessibility to buyers. U.S. automobile manufacturers believe that their cars have been difficult to sell in the Japanese market because Japanese dealerships are controlled by the major Japanese automobile manufacturers.

Price

Price is the value that is exchanged for products in a marketing transaction. A product's price has to cover all the costs involved in its production, distribution, and promotion, as well as any expected profits. In addition, price can support a product's image, take sales away from competitors, or induce people to change the timing of their purchases. For example, marketers give discounts to the customers who are willing to purchase air conditioners during the winter season. Setting a high price for Chanel perfume helps build an exclusive image for that product.

Promotion

Promotion—marketing communication—covers the variety of techniques used to communicate with customers and potential customers. Along with personal selling, sales promotion, and public relations (publicity), advertising is one of the four elements of the promotional mix. Personal selling is personal, paid communication that attempts to inform customers and persuade them to purchase products in an exchange situation. Generally, personal selling is the most expensive element in the promotional mix. It is often used in the industrial market where personal contact is important to build relationships among industrial buyers. Sales promotion is increasingly important today for many organizations. Marketers often use free samples and coupons to reach consumers when they introduce new products. Public relations is a broad set of communication activities used to create and maintain favorable relations between the organization and its publics. These publics include customers, employees, stockholders, government officials, and society in general. Publicity is viewed as part of public relations. Organizations use media releases to gain free communication transmitted through a mass medium. Also, of course, advertising is paid, nonpersonal communication about an organization and/or its products, transmitted to a target audience through mass or alternative media.

THE EVOLUTION OF ADVERTISING

Advertising is hardly a new phenomenon. Even a hundred years ago, advertising was an integral if sometimes unwelcome part of daily life. The image of advertising has not improved over the years.

The very first U.S. newspaper, *Public Occurrences Both Foreign and Domestick*, appeared in 1690. In 1704 the *Boston Newsletter* was the first paper to carry an advertisement, which offered a reward for the capture of a thief. Two early colonial printers, James and Benjamin Franklin, started the *New England Courant* in 1721. By the time of the American Revolution, there were over thirty newspapers in the United States. Today, U.S. newspapers generally serve a specific geographic area such as a local community. *USA Today* bucked that trend when it was launched in 1982 as a colorful national newspaper with jazzy graphics and brief but punchy articles. After *USA Today* led the way, many newspapers added color printing, allowing advertisers to show their products more realistically and to use snazzier art to snag reader attention.

The mid-1800s marked the beginning of the development of the advertising industry in the United States. A number of social and technological developments associated with the industrial revolution had occurred during this period of time. The telegraph, the telephone, and the typewriter provided dramatic improvements in mass message delivery. Better printing technology and the ability to print photographs and detailed illustrations made magazine advertisements even more attractive to advertisers.[12] After the Civil War, *The Atlantic Monthly* and other U.S. magazines began carrying more advertisements. Advertising agency pioneer J. Walter Thompson prodded *Harper's Magazine* and other magazines to print advertisements for foods, soaps, and even patent medicines. By the dawn of the twentieth century, advertising had become a social and economic fixture in the United States. Magazines and newspapers were filled with advertisements for all kinds of products.

The first radio commercial in the United States was carried in 1922 by AT&T's station WEAF in New York. Within two years, radio expanded from a local medium to a national one, primarily because of the network, a group of stations that broadcast simultaneously in many markets. In 1926 AT&T sold its network of radio stations to the National Broadcasting Company (NBC).[13] The first FM radio station went on air on March 1, 1941, in Nashville, Tennessee. Today radio is unique among advertising media because about 80 percent of the stations are local, a factor that makes radio competitive with the digital media, such as iPods. Infinity Broadcasting research estimates that the average person spends 40 percent of his or her media time listening to one of the 5,000 AM and 4,000 FM radio stations operating in the United States.

The first commercial station was established in 1941. An early community antenna television system that started in Pennsylvania in 1948 was the forerunner of the cable systems that would pop up throughout the country during the 1970s and 1980s.[14] By 1954 NBC and CBS were the network leaders, trailed by ABC. In 1972 Home Box Office (HBO) began operation as a pay cable station. Today, cable networks such as MTV and CNN and local cable public access channels are widely available.

Advertising Phases

Advertising may be said to have evolved in phases. Until the early 1900s, advertising focused on product benefits with informational ads. These usually included the selling price and stressed product uniqueness and attributes. The 1920s saw the beginnings of status-conscious advertising. While the rich, upper classes enjoyed multitudes of luxuries, the so-called "Democracy of Goods" advertising formula promised that the lower classes could acquire at least some of these luxuries by purchasing certain products. For instance, a Chase and Sanborn's Coffee ad showed a butler serving coffee in an elegant home. The copy proclaimed that "no one—'king, prince, statesman, or capitalist'—could enjoy better coffee."[15] These ads frequently used such key words as "everyone," "anyone," and "any home."

By 1930 the focus of advertising messages had moved from the product to the user. Testimonials for various products, including tobacco, were common. Advertising themes included family, social status, and health.

Advertising shifted again following World War II. Wartime saw the cresting of America's producer economy, which necessarily shifted to a consumer economy after the war. As the unprecedented market created by the baby boom began to decline in the 1950s, manufacturers who had never geared down from wartime efficiency in mass production found themselves with product surpluses. To move these now stockpiled products, companies turned to the teams of psychologists who descended on Madison Avenue. Now advertising promised to transform the consumer. The 1960s saw a proliferation of guilt and fear appeals (some classic campaigns included "Ring-around-the collar" and "If she kisses you once, will she kiss you again? Be certain with Certs"). According to communication theorists Gary C. Woodward and Robert E. Denton, happiness, romance, and glamour would be possible for those who purchased the "prescribed product."[16] The image era of advertising has been attributed to David Ogilvy and his concerns with product image, long-term brand identification, and loyalty.

By the 1970s, products became emblems for group identification. Whereas the 1920s had been characterized by the elitist appeal of improved social status, advertising in the 1970s was characterized by populist appeals. According to Jack Solomon in *Rereading America,* the American dream "has two faces: the one communally egalitarian and the other competitively elitist."[17] The icons of populist commercials include "country music, small-town life, family picnics, and farmyards" as well as casual dress and an upbeat mood.[18] Thus, designer jeans defined particular groups of people, and a soft-drink commercial proclaimed the populist message, "I'd like to teach the world to sing/In perfect harmony . . ." .

The 1980s carried through with the upbeat, populist mood until, late in the decade, a new kind of elitist appeal emerged. This "narrative played on the worries of young corporate managers struggling up the ladder of success," representing the "elitist desire to 'arrive.'"[19] Meanwhile, McDonald's pioneered the strategically targeted commercial message. Resisting the "one size fits all" campaign, McDonald's simultaneously targeted various age groups, classes, and races.[20] From the Ronald McDonald fantasy spots targeted to children, to appeals to the adolescent need to belong, to the more sophisticated "Mac Tonight," to "the new kid" commercials aimed at senior citizens, McDonald's defied overall trends and differentiated specific market segments.

In the 1990s, a skeptical consumer climate grew in response to public saturation with commercial messages and hyperbolic, manipulative appeals. The "new consumer" found the Energizer bunny's interruption of "a rather pretentious Gallo campaign . . . pitched to the yuppie market" to be refreshing.[21] The anticommercial has become a familiar response to consumer cynicism. Today, products are still advertised as solutions to personal problems and needs. Advertising may still suggest that a product can define status and group membership, but the groups targeted have become more diverse, reflecting the variable lifestyles in contemporary society.

Phases of Integrated Communications

In his article "The Evolving Nature of Integrated Communications," Don E. Schultz has redefined Integrated Marketing Communication. More commonly referred to today as simply Integrated Communications (IC), Schultz says it is "not an activity or a field or an industry" but "a coordinated method or way of thinking about planning, development and implementation of communication programs for now and into the future."[22] He describes the following stages in the evolution of IMC, or IC.

Stage 1—"One Sight, One Sound" Approach to Integration

Prior to the mid-1980s, large, national brand marketing organizations, which had developed in the 1950s and 1960s, dominated the marketplace. Many communicators during this phase felt that they were practicing what has come to be called Integrated Communications by bringing advertising, sales, direct marketing, and public relations departments together to plan communications campaigns and programs. This first view of IMC brought together previously segmented components of the promotional mix in order to produce a consistent image and message, in other words—one sight, one sound.

Stage 2—Process of Alignment and Integration

By the mid-1980s, scanner data and the creation of massive retailers shifted power from the manufacturer to the retailer. The need and demand for integration shifted as well. Integration now needed to "include and involve the channels of distribution in the communications mix," according to Schultz.

The integrated campaign for Hewlett-Packard's Compaq TC 1000 actually began when the product was developed for very specific markets—education, pharmaceuticals, and health care. The price was set lower than the competition, and launched at a special event. Co-op programs were utilized to create awareness among the targeted segments, e.g., the product appeared on the covers of channel partners' catalogs and retailers' Web sites. Web marketing, including an e-mail campaign, included a "solid Web site" with 3-D illustrations.[23] In this campaign, a spectrum of audiences was reached through what Schultz calls a "coherent, timely, customer-oriented" communication program involving a number of distribution systems.

At the high end of this stage, developing and managing these communication programs involve the entire organization, Schultz contends. He believes that "IC has moved from a tactical activity which was practiced by Historical Marketers, to a more strategic, management-driven activity in the Current Marketplace."

Stage 3—IC in the Twenty-First-Century Marketplace

An Indiana college professor sent an overnight Federal Express package to a company in Boston. A call to the recipient revealed that the package had not yet been received by late morning. The professor phoned a toll-free FedEx number, provided the tracking number, waited a few seconds, and discovered that the FedEx van was heading toward the recipient's street in Boston, en route to deliver the package. The same tracking information was also available on the Internet. The reason for the later-than-usual delivery time was also discovered: the FedEx flight out of Chicago's O'Hare Airport had been delayed by early morning fog. While the professor was still on the phone, the recipient spotted the FedEx van pulling into a parking space on the street outside.

The evolution of IMC/IC has been driven primarily by the growth of information technology (computers, software, digital development, search engines, e-mail, Web sites, databases, etc.). The example of Federal Express tracking services illustrates one way that new media enable organizations to more fully communicate with their customers. Interactive communication systems are controlled by the consumer. In recent years, information technology has been tipping the balance of marketplace power increasingly toward the consumer.

In the coming years of the twenty-first century, Schultz predicts that consumers will no longer be "targets" but "compatriots," not the recipients of advertising messages as much as those to whom advertisers listen and respond. Message flow is already shifting from outbound to inbound, with "customers and prospects making known their needs, wants and wishes, and marketers and communicators listening and developing responses." This, Schultz says, "will likely be the toughest integration task of all."

Changes in the business world and technology have also placed new pressure on advertisers to be accountable, to show how the organization has benefited from a particular communication program. Although information technology makes "communication and IC more powerful and possible, the same sort of techniques are being offered as methods and manners in which to measure the *outcomes* of communication programs, not just the *output*," says Schultz.

Of course, some remain skeptical about the feasibility of integrated marketing. For example, Al Ries has said that integrated marketing agencies will "undoubtedly not" be the wave of the future.[24] A prolific author as well as owner of a marketing strategy firm, Ries argued for the primacy of public relations and the secondary role of advertising in his book *The Fall of Advertising and the Rise of PR*.

In addition to these challenges, advertisers must now communicate in a global marketplace. What may be an appropriate, effective channel or message at home may become impractical or culturally inappropriate in another part of the world. Colgate-Palmolive's attempt to market toiletries to villagers in rural India, mentioned earlier in this chapter, illustrates the challenges of advertising to people in another culture. The IMC/IC marketer must consider the different situations in which products may be used in other countries as well as which of the traditional and the new, alternative channels of communication will work best. As Schultz says, IMC/IC advertisers will need to learn "where, in what form, at what time, under what conditions, and at what level" customers want to hear from them.

SUMMARY

Classifications of advertising include product, retail, corporate, business-to-business, political, directory, direct-response, public service, and advocacy. Advertising may inform or persuade the consumer. In some cases, advertising serves to remind the consumer about a particular brand in order to maintain consumer loyalty. Advertising is just a part of the total effort carried out by the marketing mix (product, place, price, and promotion). The promotional mix includes advertising, public relations, sales promotion, and personal selling. Advertising in the United States has evolved in response to developments in the mass media and to other socioeconomic forces

:30 Spot:
Integrating an IMC Philosophy

Despite the vogue that Integrated Marketing currently enjoys, it lacks many full-fledged homes. Few companies have embraced the kind of organizational and philosophical approach that is taught in graduate programs and espoused in books. Instead, many marketing professionals believe that integration is simply using all available marketing communication tools such as public relations, advertising, direct marketing, and promotions.

As an alum of one of those graduate programs, I have come to find that the execution of the full arsenal of tools often touted as "integrated" is far less important than applying the overriding philosophies of Integrated Marketing in everyday business life.

In particular, I have long held the belief that customer focus—one of the primary tenets of IMC—should apply to a wide variety of groups: customers, consumers, employees, and shareholders, to name but a few. As an investor relations practitioner, it is paramount to expand this definition in order to meet the needs of the investment community while maintaining a consistent, effective message. Imagine the dilemma of telling a sizable shareholder one message and then having a trade magazine or business publication publish another, only to tell employees still a different story.

I suggest that treating every customer—broadly defined—as critically important and as a unique audience provides a powerful and necessary paradigm shift. Traditional business education says that businesses should be run to create shareholder value; thus, the shareholder's needs and satisfaction are at the forefront. Integrated Marketing generally teaches that the customer—narrowly defined—is the singular focus. Exploding these limiting definitions not only enhances the organization's potential for success, but it also gives the marketing or communications professional a philosophy of action that embraces all constituencies.

In my everyday world, I must recognize the importance of the needs of many audiences. Understanding what each requires represents a unique challenge. However, the payoff for successfully "integrating" the wants and needs of all customers is long-term prosperity for an organization, which is sure to make one's employer—yet another "customer"—quite happy.

Aaron H. Hoffman
Executive Director, Investor Relations
Sara Lee
Chicago, Illinois

that have affected manufacturers, wholesalers, retailers, and consumers or industrial users. Integrated Marketing Communication, now known widely as Integrated Communications, has responded to the ways that information technology has changed both the consumer and the ways we communicate with the consumer.

Chapter 2

The Advertising Environment:
Economy, Society, and Technology

A "privileged but awkward American teenager learns sensual Latin dancing from . . .a waiter."[1] If this sounds like the plot for the 1987 hit movie *Dirty Dancing,* you're both right and wrong. Lions Gate Entertainment's *Dirty Dancing: Havana Nights,* released February 27, 2004, brought the same story to the screen with pre-Castro Cuba and a Havana waiter substituted for the *Dirty Dancing* Catskills location and Patrick Swayze's dance instructor.

No longer is it enough to feature Andy Garcia, Cameron Diaz, Jennifer Lopez, or Antonio Banderas in Hollywood movies. Facing profound changes in the ethnicity of the U.S. population, Hollywood studios now hire "more Hispanic executives, consider a greater number of Latino-oriented films and TV shows and target Hispanics in their marketing."[2] The film industry has responded to the growing purchasing power of this ethnic group: Latino moviegoers buy more movie tickets per year, accounting for 15 percent of the box office revenue, and watch more television than non-Hispanics. Insiders admit that making more Latino-oriented films is just half the battle; regular films must be better marketed to Hispanics.

In addition, Unilever Bestfoods' Knorr brand launched its first bilingual campaign as a corporate sponsor for *Dirty Dancing: Havana Nights.* The campaign included traditional advertising in Spanish as well as movie ticket discount certificates and a Spanish-language Web site.[3] Recognizing that younger Hispanics "aren't cooking from scratch like their parents," Knorr also brought out a line of ready-to-serve Mexican cooking sauces.

According to a study released by Pew Hispanic Center, a Latino research group, the Hispanic population in the United States is expected to reach 60.4 million by 2020 (i.e., 18 percent of the U.S. pop-

ILLUSTRATION 2.1. "Wired." In addition to other changes in the advertising environment caused by economic and social forces, the impact of the computer revolution on the field of communications has been phenomenal. Photo © Dana Hanefeld.

ulation).[4] The Center based its prediction on the 1990s' Hispanic growth rate, about 1.2 million a year. In 2000 Hispanics numbered 35.3 million, 13 percent of the U.S. population.

The growing ethnic diversity of the United States is just one of a number of forces that create the advertising environment. This environment consists of external, or uncontrollable, forces that directly or indirectly influence advertisers, advertising agencies, media, and audiences. The advertising environment consists of economic, social, technological, and legal (and political) forces (see Illustration 2.1). The environment also involves ethical issues. Economic, social, and technological forces will be discussed in this chapter, and legal and political issues in Chapter 3. The ethical considerations are so important that ethics issues appear in the Ethics Track segments in each chapter of this book.

THE ADVERTISING ENVIRONMENT

Environmental forces are always changing. Changes in the advertising environment create uncertainty, threats, and opportunities for advertisers. Although the future is not very predictable, advertisers try to predict what may happen. We can say with certainty that advertisers continue to modify their advertising strategies in response to dynamic environmental forces. An advertiser can respond to the environment in two ways, reactively or proactively.

Reactive Response

When you believe you have no control over environmental elements, you will be reactive and simply try to adjust to them, many times after the fact. For example, a public relations consultant may be called upon to exercise damage control when an unanticipated crisis in a company occurs. The company must then react to what has already happened. Many crises could be averted if a company would proactively oversee all internal and external relations.

Proactive Response

When you think you have some control, you will be proactive and take steps to make changes that result in a more conducive environment for your activities. For instance, the number of immigrants coming into the United States has steadily risen in the past thirty years, resulting in a society that is becoming increasingly multicultural. The U.S. population has shifted from one dominated by whites to one consisting of three large racial and ethnic groups: whites, blacks, and Hispanics. Asians make up a fourth important group. Marketers recognize these profound changes in the U.S. population and the unique problems and opportunities they bring. A diverse population means a more diverse customer base, and advertising practices must be altered to fit it.

THE GLOBAL PERSPECTIVE:
KNOW WHEN TO BACK OFF

You would expect to see shop signs in Hebrew in Tel Aviv's new shopping mall. Instead, expect to see mostly English-language advertisements for Benetton and other trendy franchises. Don't expect businesses and restaurants to be closed on the Sabbath. But do expect Israel's ultra-Orthodox community to resent these artifacts of fast-spreading American consumerism. The young people who shop and work at the Tel Aviv mall may enjoy the freedom they feel these changes represent, but the older establishment wonders about the contradiction of having a Jewish homeland if it disregards "religious commandments to which other Jews were faithful, even on the point of death."[a]

The Israeli Embassy in Bangkok also reacted with indignation to a Thai television commercial which showed Adolf Hitler transformed into a "good person" after eating "X" brand potato chips. The ad's creator, Leo Burnett, immediately recalled the ad.[b] Tambrands has had difficulty selling Tampax tampons in Israel, France, South Africa, and Brazil, where women fear losing their virginity if they use the product, which is considered "unnatural."[c]

Culture includes all traditions, habits, religion, art, and language. It consists of beliefs, morals, customs, and habits learned from others. As in domestic markets, the advertiser who wants to communicate with foreign consumers must consider the environments that influence people's tastes, attitudes, and the way they think.

The impact of religion on international advertising has become apparent. McDonald's had to introduce a vegetarian burger when it opened restaurants in India. Kodak avoided beach scenes in commercials aired in Muslim countries in deference to local customs. A Saatchi & Saatchi, London, TV spot that showed the Virgin Mary giving birth on stage in a children's nativity play was pulled after UK audiences complained that the commercial was "blasphemous."[d]

Virginia Slims' classic tagline, "You've come a long way, baby," addressing female smokers, would be offensive in South Korea where smoking is "definitely a man thing."[e] South Korea's conservatism is reflected in the fact that women "hesitate to puff" cigarettes in public and a law prohibits cigarette ads targeted to women or young adults. Leo Burnett reversed genders for its Virginia Slims Korean campaign with the tagline, "The cigarette for the successful man."

International advertisers have become aware of global variations in cultural and religious barriers. Although Tambrands' sales "are increasing in some countries, such as Russia, Tambrands isn't targeting Muslim countries" at all.[f] Sometimes no ad blitz or advertising message can overcome cultural resistances, and a smart marketer has to accept that.

[a]Judy Peres, "A Human Mosaic," *Chicago Tribune Magazine,* Special Edition: Israel at 50, May 10, 1998, Section 18, p. 57.

[b]Pichayaporn Utumporn, "Ad with Hitler Causes a Furor in Thailand," *The Wall Street Journal,* June 5, 1998, p. B8.

[c]Yumiko Ono, "Tambrands Ads Aim to Overcome Cultural and Religious Obstacles," *The Wall Street Journal,* March 17, 1997, p. B8.

[d]"10 Ads We'll Never See in the U.S.," *Advertising Age,* December 22, 2003, p. 30.

[e]Namju Cho, "Korean Men Take a Drag on Virginia Slim," *The Wall Street Journal,* January 14, 1997, p. B10.

[f]"Tambrands Ads Aim to Overcome Cultural and Religious Obstacles."

ECONOMIC FORCES AND ADVERTISING

Economic forces in the advertising environment influence both advertisers' and consumers' decisions and activities. Advertising expenditures today account for a significant part of the U.S. economy. When the economy is expanding, consumers and businesses have the money and the inclination to buy, and higher sales fire up advertisers to increase their advertising budgets, which in turn fuels retail and industrial as well as media sales. For instance, ad spending skyrocketed during the economic expansion of 1976-1988. During most recessionary periods, profit pressures may cause some advertisers to cut back, despite studies suggesting that advertising during downturns can help firms increase sales and capture market shares from competitors who slow or stop advertising.[5] For example, in the recession of the early 1990s, retail bankruptcies, decreased real estate sales, and sluggish consumer spending dampened many advertising budgets. In turn, the reduced advertising spending set off a chain reaction that hurt the media, advertising agencies, and their clients.[6] The impact of this situation was so serious that in those years many people working on New York's Madison Avenue, where many large advertising agencies are located, lost their jobs. The negative economic environment following the 9/11 attacks also negatively impacted the media, ad agencies, and their clients.

Multinational corporations, in particular, are affected by financial crises in other countries. Concern in mid-1998 about a devalued Mexican peso and Venezuelan bolivar, weak commodity prices of Latin American exports, and dependence by such U.S. giants as Coca-Cola and General Motors on emerging Latin American markets for profit growth, reflected the extent to which economic conditions in one region or country impact others. "Latin America accounts for 21 percent of U.S. exports—compared with 14 percent for Asia, minus Japan."[7]

The link between advertising and the economy has traditionally been viewed in two ways. Some experts argue that advertising is the power in the hands of large firms with huge advertising budgets that create a barrier to entry. This condition makes it difficult for other firms to enter the market and results in less competition and higher product prices. Economists note that smaller firms already in the market find it difficult to compete against the large advertising budgets of the industry leaders and are often driven out of business. Defenders of advertising note it is unrealistic to attribute a firm's market dominance and barriers to entry solely to advertising. There are a number of other factors to consider, such as product quality, price, and distribution effectiveness. Other experts view advertising as a source of information for consumers, enabling them to choose among available products. The debate over advertising's roles in the economy continues. Economists, scholars, and practitioners are divided over advertising's influence on several economic elements, including pricing and competition. Does advertising raise or lower the price that consumers pay for products? Does advertising serve as a source of information or a barrier to enter the market?[8]

SOCIAL FORCES AND ADVERTISING

The role of advertising in society is controversial and has at times resulted in attempts at restricting or banning advertising of certain products or to certain groups. The controversy rages on over whether tobacco and alcohol advertising should be banned. These decisions involve very complex economic considerations as well as social issues. Distillers such as Seagram's, in defending the decision to advertise on television after a decades-old, voluntary liquor industry ban on television and radio advertising, promised not to advertise during prime time and other hours when children are most likely to watch television and not to use messages or symbols (including Santa Claus) especially attractive to children. The company also promised to push for "responsible consumption." However, antialcohol groups are foursquare against television ads for Absolut vodka, Johnnie Walker scotch, or any other liquor brands. They argue that, given the social harm already caused by alcohol—thousands of deaths caused by drunk driving, aggressive behavior such as rapes, spousal and child abuse, fire and other property damage—the last thing the United States needs is an increase in television advertisements promoting more drinking.[9] An American Legacy Foundation fake ad for "Shards O' Glass ice pops," aired during Super Bowl XXXVIII, ridiculed the tobacco industry for producing antismoking ads while cigarette manufacturers "soft pedal" the dangers of smoking and continue to flood the market with their products.[10]

ETHICS TRACK:
INVASIVE TECHNOLOGIES

In the past I never considered myself a technology person. Now, I would say that both my husband and I are on the brink of technology, since our jobs require that of us. It never ceases to amaze me how closely advertising is linked with advancements in technology.

A few years ago, if asked where was advertising headed, the response would have been the Internet. Yet, those flash ads, once so promising, have become the *National Enquirer* of advertising. Unsavory companies are most likely to rely on pop-up ads to advertise their usually unsavory products.

Overall, Internet advertising is viewed as invasive by most computer users. As a computer trainer, I have the opportunity to talk to people across a wide spectrum of computer knowledge and employment positions. In the past two years, I have not met one person who appreciates or trusts pop-up ads. Rather, I find one of the first questions I am asked is how they can be turned off. What surprised me the most was people's dislike for Web sites that remembered their last purchases and made suggestions for their next purchase based on earlier choices. To me, that is marketing at its finest.

Across the board, America is turning off advertising. Digital television recorders such as Ultimate TV and TiVo allow viewers to skip through commercials. This has upset advertisers who pay top dollar for prime time spots. Some advertisers are turning to product placements in programming as an alternative to buying commercial time.

Marketing has recently tried a new avenue, advertising to people's cell phones. This is not the telemarketing of the twentieth century, but rather SMS (short message service) marketing. Advertisers utilize the mobile messaging feature on cell phones, similar to e-mail, for direct marketing. One of the first companies to do so, the United Kingdom McDonald's began an SMS marketing campaign in June 2002. One of the mobile marketing campaigns, a text club, sent restaurant promotions to cell phones. Although initially successful, the company decided to end all mobile marketing campaigns by April 2003.

Advertising outlets have changed, but consumers remain skeptical of advertising messages. That makes free newsletters one of the most effective ways to advertise online. Since the user subscribes to the newsletter, the advertising is not viewed as intrusive. This may also be the key to opening up the mobile marketing arena. As cell phone users sign up for free news and weather, more advertisers can sponsor these free services.

America's perception of advertising has changed. We like companies that can laugh at themselves. We like companies that do something good for our country. We don't want companies to invade our privacy.

Do you think online advertising is invasive? What other examples of invasive advertising can you identify? How has technology impacted the privacy of U.S. citizens?

Erin Deschene,
Marketing
Cincinnati, Ohio

Criticism of Advertising

Advertising is claimed by its practitioners to be largely responsible for the good things in life and is criticized by its opponents as the cause of much of what is bad. Advertising copy is accused of playing fast and loose with the rules of language (e.g., twisting words or using incorrect spelling and grammar to make a point), which encourages the audience to do the same. A classic example of this is the 1954 tagline, "Winston tastes good, like a cigarette should." The correct phrasing would be "as a cigarette should." More recently, Apple Computer used the slogan "Think different" instead of "Think differently," which would be grammatically correct.[11] Sara Lee's classic tagline, "Nobody doesn't like Sara Lee," has endured almost a century despite its grammatically incorrect double negative.

Another criticism is that advertising causes people to buy products or services that they do not need. The defenders acknowledge that the whole reason to advertise the product or service is to persuade consumers to purchase the right products. Another common criticism of advertising is that it perpetuates stereotyping, the process of categorizing individuals by predicting their behavior based on their membership in a particular class or group. The problem, critics say, is that advertisements often portray entire groups of people in stereotypical ways, for example, showing only women as homemakers and only elderly people as senile. These advertising stereotypes can reinforce negative or undesirable views of these groups, and this can contribute to discrimination against them.[12]

Advertisers have gradually realized stereotyping is not acceptable because it alienates potential customers. Moreover, by presenting minorities and women more realistically, advertisers can significantly expand their market segments for a wider variety of products. In looking for ways to make advertisements seem more realistic, some advertisers and advertising agencies have used real-life people in their ads rather than professional models or actors.[13]

The society in which we live and our own social standards influence advertising—the way it works and the ideas it uses. For example, before 1959, no women were depicted in liquor advertisements in *Time* magazine, even though U.S. prohibition was repealed in 1933. This was because society did not approve of women drinking, and women were not allowed to drink in public places. Advertisements after 1959 showed the beginnings of a standard practice of including women in liquor advertisements. As society's attitudes changed, advertisers reacted and found that it was acceptable to put women in liquor advertising.[14] However, advertisers have generally been slow to reflect societal attitude changes toward women.

A 1996 Saatchi & Saatchi study made it clear that women did not feel advertisers were keeping up with the times in the 1990s. For the most part, women still found most advertising to be sexist, especially ads for beauty products, clothing, and food intended to keep women thin. Failure to "get the message right" carries consequences more serious than just not making a sale—it can "interrupt the consumer's connection with the brand."[15] When focus groups revealed that

Kellogg's Special K ads offended the women targeted, the company's ad agency created a new ad campaign. Baby boomers couldn't relate to the models who "squeezed their drop-dead perfect bodies into clingy dresses and tight jeans" to preen in front of a mirror, so the new campaign, launched in February 1998, used women who projected a heavier, healthier look.[16] One ad in the campaign even pokes fun at men. A man gathered with friends at a bar worries about his too-large thighs, while another laments his big butt. The tagline says it all: "Men don't obsess about these things. Why do we?" According to Cheryl Berman, chief creative officer for Leo Burnett, "Women want respect, understanding, help," and they control "80 percent of U.S. purchases and 75 percent of consumer electronics purchases."[17]

Advertising, in turn, affects society. Berman encourages women to enter the advertising profession. Women in advertising, she believes, can have a positive impact in reshaping culture: "We have the power to influence how women are talked to and portrayed." Because as much as 40 percent of our information comes from advertising, Gloria Steinem argues that advertising "gives us our idea of normalcy and affects the environment and the future of our planet. We've all been created by the images we see."[18]

Advertising pays many of the costs of the mass media and almost all the costs of the broadcast media. Criticism has especially been directed toward the incestuous relationship between the advertising and magazine industries. In her book, *Decoding Women's Magazines,* Ellen McCracken, a critic of mass culture, levels major criticism at what the magazine industry calls the problem of "separation of church and state," i.e., editorial content and related advertisements logistically placed.[19] The willingness of magazines to allow advertisers to dictate where, when, and in what context their ads will be placed has evolved from the origins of women's magazines—they were originally merchandise catalogs. In 2003 the Magazine Publishers of America initiated industry self-regulation and began citing magazines that violated its new edict to separate "church and state." Some big players received the first citations: *Rolling Stone* apologized for an infraction, but the industry continues to worry about the increasing demands of advertising media buyers in a climate of magazine publishers' resistance.

As with any controversy, the debate about the influence of advertising on society is not likely to come to a quick conclusion.

TECHNOLOGICAL FORCES AND ADVERTISING

Technological developments provide important opportunities to advertisers who can use them to meet customer needs. For example, because of technological changes in communications, marketers now can reach large masses of people more efficiently through a variety of media. Quantum, a pay-per-view cable service developed by a division of Time Warner Inc., uses fiber optics and coaxial cables to offer fifteen movies starting every half hour, twenty-four hours a day. For less than $5 a film, viewers can select a movie and the time it will air by pressing a remote control button to activate the on-screen guide. With fiber optics in place, Quantum is ready to offer HDTV (high-definition television) and voice interactivity when these become available.[20] As a category, technology products and services now show a decided presence among the top-ten megabrands (see Table 2.1).

The Internet and Advertising

When HotWired, a Web site about Web technology and culture, was launched on October 27, 1994, it pioneered the most explosive new advertising medium since the start of cable television. In the years since then, an entire infrastructure has sprung up to support the

TABLE 2.1. Top megabrands by measured 2003 ad spending.

Rank	Megabrand	Parent company
1	Verizon (telecommunications)	Verizon Communications
2	AT&T (phone services)	AT&T
3	Ford (vehicles)	Ford Motor Co.
4	Sprint (telecommunications)	Sprint Corp.
5	Nissan (vehicles)	Nissan Motor Co.
6	Toyota (vehicles)	Toyota Motor Co.
7	Chevrolet (vehicles)	General Motors Co.
8	Cingular (wireless services)	SBC Communications
9	Sears (stores)	Sears, Roebuck & Co.
10	McDonald's (restaurants)	McDonald's Corp.

Source: Adapted from "Top U.S. Megabrands," *Advertising Age FactPack,* February 28, 2005, p. 13.

online advertising industry: companies create advertisements, buy advertisements, sell advertisements, measure advertising success, and manage advertisements. An industry group now promotes Internet advertisements. Furthermore, marketer efforts on the Web have moved beyond the experimental stage. Many marketers make Web advertising a line item in their ad budget alongside magazines, television, and radio. The September 1996 Forrester Research survey of forty-four marketers found that 54 percent intended to spend less than $250,000 a year for Web advertisements, 38 percent planned to spend $250,000 to $1 million, and 8 percent more than $1 million.[21]

The Internet is a reality that advertisers and marketers can no longer choose to ignore (see Illustration 2.2). The Commerce Department's first major study of the economic effect of the Internet in the 1990s revealed that Net traffic doubled every hundred days.[22] The report found that, while "radio took 30 years to reach an audience of 50 million, and TV took 13, the Internet took just four years" to reach 50 million. By 2003, with 120 million people "wired" and the digital economy doubling the growth rate of the overall economy, online ad spending hit $3.1 billion.[23]

ILLUSTRATION 2.2. Driving the traffic. This ad by Eric Remington gives alternatives to the customer who wants to order flowers for Valentine's Day: Phone the florist or visit the florist's Web site. Including the Web page address in print advertising has become commonplace; it encourages customers to visit Web sites, i.e., drives the traffic to the Internet.

One clear-cut advantage the Internet holds over other advertising media is its accountability (see Table 2.2). The Internet makes it possible not only to record the number of "hits," or visitors, but also "to project the specific costs of bringing targeted visitors to sites."[24] Nevertheless, as late as 1996 many of the biggest advertising spenders still were not sure where, or if, Internet advertising fit into their plans. The head of promotion services at Campbell Soup Co. didn't see the Internet as an efficient delivery system for advertising soup, which largely sells for about a dollar a can. Internet ad spending just seemed more justifiable for big-ticket items.[25]

However, by 1998, the Campbell's Web site became a wonderland of advertising and promotions. On the home page, a brick road wound through a colorful town, each building modeled from a Campbell's soup can, and leading to the site menu. Other corporations followed suit. Hershey's Web site includes a variety of options designed to appeal to its customers, including recipes. The Sara Lee Web site meets the needs of its customers, investors, and employees with a wide-ranging menu; site visitors can even watch the corporation's commercials.

What may not have seemed possible or likely two years ago may have become a reality today in the wild world of Internet advertising.

Data-driven marketers and media buyers rely on comScore and Nielsen to measure search engine effectiveness. Table 2.2 shows the top comScore sites.

Special Effects

Much video animation and most special effects, such as moving titles and whirling logos, can be done with a joystick. All major video

TABLE 2.2. Top search engines.

Search engine	Visitors (in thousands) during April 2004
1. MSN-Microsoft sites	97,241
2. Yahoo! sites	93,049
3. Microsoft	90,941
4. AOL	69,760
5. Google sites	65,379

Source: Adapted from "Hot Property," *Advertising Age,* June 7, 2004, p. 3.

production companies today use dedicated digital video effects units (DVEs) that can manipulate graphics on the screen in a variety of ways—fades, wipes, zooms, rotations, and so on. BBDO Agency has introduced computer-generated M&M/Mars candies. A recent trend has combined old clips of such classic film stars as Fred Astaire and John Wayne with new footage of such products as vacuum cleaners and soft drinks. For the 108th anniversary of the birth of "Kentucky Colonel" Harland Sanders, founder of the Kentucky Fried Chicken (KFC) fast-food restaurant chain, the company decided to make its founder's image more visible. Instead of hiring an actor to portray the Colonel, as the company did in its unsuccessful 1994 campaign, or using clips of the real Harland Sanders—who made personal appearances until his death in 1980, KFC decided to create an animated likeness of the goateed gentleman in the white suit.[26] The company hoped the animated image would be less offensive to those who remembered the real Colonel rather than using an actor.

Special effects entertain viewers and win advertising awards. However, if the sales message is complex or based on logic, another technique might be better. No technique should be so enthralling to viewers that they pay more attention to it than to the product being advertised. Although disputed by Energizer's (which used the mnemonic device—bunny) parent, Ralston Purina, some industry figures suggest that Duracell still outsells Energizer batteries.[27] The Energizer bunny may be lovable, but the public's affection does not necessarily lead to sales.

The level of available technology affects the way companies advertise their products and services in foreign markets. In 1991, seven of the world's ten fastest-growing ad markets were in Asia. Hong Kong's satellite television, StarTV, launched the first pan-Asian network that year. With 2.8 billion people in 38 countries under a "footprint" that runs from the Mediterranean through Southeast Asia and up to far eastern Russia, StarTV offers advertisers a new way to think regionally (advertisements aimed at more than one country). Broadcasting across eight time zones allows StarTV to target its programming to a particular country's prime time.

Forget regional efficiencies—in Taiwan and India, penetration is deep enough to make advertising on StarTV as cost-effective as local television. When Lipton, a division of Unilever, launched its iced tea in Taiwan in 1992, its advertisement on StarTV was a hit. In addition,

StarTV's ability to evade government broadcast regulations makes it an even better buy for some companies. Both United Distillers and Hennessy cognac used StarTV to target Taiwan, which limits advertisements for imported liquor.[28]

Advertisers, agencies, the media, and audiences are all part of a larger environment, influencing and being influenced by the economy, society, and technology. The impact of these complex environmental elements can be positive or negative, sometimes even both. Advertising is a source of information for consumers and a source of market power for advertisers. Advertising has been accused of harming society because it seems to go beyond merely selling products. It can also shape social trends and attitudes in powerful ways. With the Internet, a firm can present consumers with a combination of advertising, information, and entertainment related to its product. Consumers are able to control their exposure to a product and ultimately decide whether they want to learn more about it or even place an order. Advertising budgets became increasingly tighter in the 1990s and were negatively impacted by 9/11. In the twenty-first century, accountability has become more important than ever. Internet advertisers are able to record the number of people who have actually viewed their ads and know in advance how much each Web site visit will cost them.

SUMMARY

Advertising is affected by economic, social, and technological forces. These forces are constantly changing. Advertising is inextricably linked to the economy, and the relationship between the two remains controversial. Just as controversial is the role that advertising plays in society. Advertising is also affected by technological change. The Internet has become a viable advertising medium.

(:60) :60 SPOT:
THE TIMES THEY ARE CHANGIN'

Market fragmentation, media segmentation, and diversity are key words in advertising today. Mass media is not what it used to be. Thirty years ago an advertiser could purchase a "roadblock" (a thirty-second commercial on the three networks at the same time) with the potential to reach 93 percent of the viewing audience. The same technique today barely delivers 50 percent of the viewing audience. Advertisers seek to spend each dollar as efficiently as possible to reach the desired audience. This is the concept that has made Integrated Marketing Communication (IMC) a major topic. Consumers and their attitudes have changed also. Not only do they want more value, they want more convenience. They can shop twenty-four hours a day from retail stores, home shopping channels, infomercials, the Internet, and catalogs. The old idea of considering each communications element separately no longer applies from the consumer standpoint. A 1992 consumer survey by Leo Burnett U.S.A. revealed that consumers consider all messages, whether public relations, sales promotions, direct mail, billboards, event marketing, point-of-purchase signs and displays, Internet banners, product placements in movies and videos, etc., to be advertising.

In an effort to reach and accommodate these consumers, advertisers, with advanced technology and capability, continue to define their target audience more and more precisely. Demographics and the traditional ethnic minorities are not enough. There is no longer a "majority." Hispanics and African Americans are part of most major advertising campaigns. Asian Americans, the fastest-growing segment, are also targeted. In addition, key segments such as women and the over-fifty market (including the burgeoning baby boomers) are further defined by lifestyles and attitudes. Gays and lesbians and the disabled are now targeted separately by advertisers. Computers allow for further analyses and segment identification than ever before, and media allow advertisers to reach them directly.

Whereas mass marketing and mass media produced more product alternatives and lower prices, consumer loyalty to brands and products eroded. In one sense, the advertising challenge has come full circle. Key objectives for national advertisers now focus on building long-term relationships, offering real value, and creating brand loyalty. This was the initial purpose of most national television commercials and magazine ads in the 1960s. Watching commercials on top-rated television events such as the Super Bowl, the Olympics, and the final episodes of popular series such as *Seinfeld* and *Friends,* reveals the importance of entertaining viewers as part of advertising strategy.

Both advertisers and consumers have more choices for products, services, and media than ever before. Indications are that these choices will increase rather than decrease in the future. As they say on the news, stay tuned, whether it be our television sets, or our computers.

Jon A. Shidler
Associate Professor,
School of Journalism

Chapter 3

Legal and Political Forces
and Advertising

"*Kaash agar mera beta hota* (If only I had a son)," laments a down-on-his-luck dad in a television commercial for Hindustan Lever Ltd. (HLL). HLL, London-based Unilever's Indian subsidiary, had to pull its commercials for Fair & Lovely fairness cream following a complaint lodged with the National Human Rights Commission in New Delhi.

Suntanning may be trendy in Western countries, but "skin lightening products have been historically popular in Asia."[1] The commercial shows the advertised cream as a solution to the dilemma faced by the dad's dark-skinned daughter. After the product lightens her skin, she is transformed into a successful career woman who can afford the luxuries the dad desires. The All India Women's Democratic Association filed the complaint, arguing that the product may be "safe for the skin, but not for society"; the commission subsequently directed its satellite and network channels not to air it, citing violation of the Cable Television Networks Act of 1995. The Act prohibits advertisements that negatively portray any race, caste, color, creed, or nationality and, further, that depict women in subordinate roles. This incident "underscores changing social mores in India and highlights tensions between the government and the Advertising Standards Council of India, an autonomous industry group, over how to regulate Indian broadcast content, including advertising."[2]

Of course, not all legal issues in advertising are as important as this one. In the United States, Chicago consumers filed lawsuits against Illinois-based Classic Cinemas and national theater chain Loews Cineplex Entertainment, alleging fraud, false advertising, and breach of contract. Theater owners were taken by surprise when the Cook County consumers took them to court because the theaters claimed

ILLUSTRATION 3.1. Outlawed. This billboard for Doral cigarettes with its cartoon dog has become a historical artifact. The tobacco industry's settlement with forty-six states in November 1998 included the agreement to no longer advertise tobacco products on billboards or to use cartoon characters in tobacco advertising. Photo © Dana Hanefeld.

their films would start at a certain time, when in actuality on-screen commercials for Coca-Cola, Cingular Wireless, Fandango, and the NAACP delayed advertised start times by three to four minutes.[3]

Welcome to the legal and political environments of advertising.

No one in the advertising business can afford to ignore government policies and the legal system. Many laws and regulations may not be designed specifically to address advertising issues, yet they can have a major impact on a firm's opportunities, both locally and abroad. This chapter will deal with the political and legal environments in the United States as well as other parts of the world.

THE POLITICAL AND LEGAL ENVIRONMENTS IN THE UNITED STATES

Several government agencies regulate U.S. advertising. Since 1895 the U.S. Postal Service has regulated direct-mail advertising; the Food and Drug Administration (FDA), created by the Pure Food and Drug Act of 1906, regulates food, cosmetic, drug, and health care advertising; the Federal Trade Commission (FTC), established in 1914, "protects against false advertising and unfair business practices"; since 1934 the Securities & Exchange Commission has regulated the advertising of stocks and bonds and the Federal Communications Commission (FCC) has regulated political advertising in the broadcasting industry. "When the government doesn't intervene, individual consumers have access to the courts," resulting in lawsuits.[4]

Although advertisers feel they should be protected by the First Amendment's promise to protect free speech, they continue to feel pressure from various constituencies regarding the truth and fairness of advertising content and its effects, especially its effects on children.

Advertising and the U.S. Constitution

Although advertisers refer to the U.S. Constitution's First Amendment to defend themselves, the Constitution sometimes works against advertising. A U.S. Court of Appeals decision in October 2003 declared that the $600 million "Pork: The Other White Meat" campaign launched by the pork industry was unconstitutional. Earlier in the

THE GLOBAL PERSPECTIVE:
THE IMPACT OF ADVERTISING ENVIRONMENT ON INTERNATIONAL ADVERTISING

Like other countries, the United States has its political sensitivities. Zirh International, licenser of the French Connection U.K. fragrance, placed its FCUK Him and FCUK Her fragrances in U.S. stores but had to revise the labels when the largest U.S. retailer, Federated Department Stores, pulled the brand from shelves. It also misguidedly placed its "Scent to Bed" print ad in *Seventeen* magazine, prompting protest from "such groups as the Mississippi-based American Family Association and Minnesota-based Catholic Parents OnLine."[a] The offending print ad showed an obviously teenaged girl wearing only her underwear and clutching her pillow as a bare-chested young man clutched her from behind. A school committee in Tennessee reviewed its subscriptions to *Seventeen,* even though the FCUK brand was not sold in the state.

Now *that's* upset. Zirh responded that it had not understood how young the *Seventeen* readers actually were. The licenser had thought they were targeting college-aged women. Zirh continued its campaigns in sixty-one other countries.

On the other hand, a U.S. commercial that had no problem in other countries got the boot from a Greek television network. Pepsi had created the ad, which showed two chimps drinking cola—one guzzling Pepsi, the other Coca-Cola—specifically for the international market. Because many countries, including Greece, ban or restrict comparative ads that name a rival's product, Pepsi prepared different versions for different countries. In another version, which ran successfully in twenty countries, one of the chimps drinks Pepsi, the other Brand X.[b]

Following the growing influence of Muslim fundamentalists in many parts of the world, Malaysia, a country with a large Muslim population, outlawed ads showing women in sleeveless dresses and pictures showing underarms. These were considered offensive by strict Muslim standards. Obviously, this caused considerable problems to marketers of deodorant products.[c]

When India banned feminine hygiene product advertisements on terrestrial TV, Procter & Gamble used Hong Kong's StarTV, the first pan-Asian satellite television network, as a way to reach women in India.[d]

As these advertisers discovered, a country's political system, national laws, regulatory bodies, and interest groups all have a great impact on international advertising.

---

[a]Jack Neff and Jon Fine, "Magazines, Retailers Ban Racy FCUK Scent," *Advertising Age,* October 13, 2003, pp. 1, 69, and "10 Follies," *Advertising Age,* December 22, 2003, p. 42.

[b]Pat Guy, "Chimp Ad's Appeal Isn't Quite Global," *USA Today,* February 1, 1994, p. 2B.

c"Curbs on Ads Increase Abroad As Nations Apply Standards of Fairness and Decency," *The Wall Street Journal,* November 25, 1980, p. 56.
dJonathan Karp, "Medium and Message," *Far Eastern Economic Review,* February 25, 1993, pp. 50-52.

year, the Cattlemen's Beef Promotion and Research Boards' campaign, "Beef: It's what's for dinner," was also ruled unconstitutional by a U.S. court. In both decisions the marketing assessments placed on meat producers were believed to "force producers who don't want advertising to pay for it."[5] The assessment represents "forced," not free, speech. These cases raise questions about constitutional protections and the "long legal process" in the United States.

Alcohol and Tobacco Advertising

Since 1948, there has been a voluntary ban on hard liquor advertising on U.S. broadcast and cable television. After bans were rescinded in the United Kingdom and Canada, Seagram's Beverage Company was the first hard liquor company to jump on this opportunity. TBWA Chiat/Day, New York, pitched a television campaign for Absolut vodka with a number of cable networks, including CNN and Bravo. Bravo's lawyers, however, were very concerned that the ads might generate problems with cable subscribers in American cities and towns. Another reason cable networks were afraid to touch the ads was that Congress had only recently passed the new telecommunications bill and no one wanted the switchboard on Capitol Hill lit up by pressure groups because of the ads. Other liquor marketers are not looking to stir things up with changes. Spokespersons for the industry say that they would have to be certain that public officials, regulators, and the public itself would go along with broadcast advertising of hard liquor before they would seek any changes in the Distilled Spirits Council code regarding the voluntary ban on broadcast advertising.[6]

One of the more contentious areas in regulating alcohol and tobacco advertising has been the effects of these advertisements on children. Responding to criticism of the industry for marketing alcohol products to children, "alcohol marketers agreed to advertise only in media that reached an audience consisting of 70 percent adults."[7] However, the Marin Institute, an antialcohol group, has accused the industry of violating its own guidelines when Coors tied into Miramax's PG-rated *Scary Movie 3* with TV ads and in-store displays. The Coors' "busty and ubiquitous" spokestwins also make a cameo appearance in a party scene in the film. A $4 billion lawsuit filed against Anheuser-Busch and SABMiller in early 2004 alleged that the companies advertised to minors.

In 1997, the tobacco industry settled antitobacco litigation with a deal that restricted tobacco advertising and sales in the United States (see Illustration 3.1). Subsequently, Senator John McCain sponsored a bill that, among other things, would have further restricted tobacco advertising and marketing. In June 1998, the McCain bill met defeat in the U.S. Senate. Senate supporters of the bill failed to win the sixty votes needed to clear procedural hurdles, and the bill was dropped. President Clinton blamed the bill's defeat on an aggressive advertising campaign waged by tobacco companies.

Comparative Advertising

In 1938 the U.S. Congress passed the Wheeler-Lea Act, which prohibits unfair and deceptive acts or unlawful practices, regardless of whether they injure competition. It specifically prohibits false and misleading advertising of food, drugs, therapeutic devices, and cosmetics. The Wheeler-Lea Act also provides penalties for violations and procedures for enforcement. In 1946, Congress passed the Lanham Trademark Act. It, and a subsequent revision, the Trademark Law Revision Act of 1988, allows companies to challenge a competitor's false advertising claims about its own product and, in comparative ads, false claims by the competitor about the other company's product. Since the latter remedy was added, most of the litigation has involved Company A suing Company B to halt B's advertising campaign on the basis that B was making false claims relative to B's own product.

For instance, Tropicana aired a television commercial using Bruce Jenner, a celebrated athlete, as its spokesperson. The athlete squeezed an orange while saying, "It's pure, pasteurized juice as it comes from the orange." He then poured the juice he squeezed into a Tropicana carton. In the advertisement, a voice-over claims that Tropicana's Premium Pack orange juice is "the only leading brand not made with concentrate and water." Coca-Cola, one of whose products is Minute Maid orange juice, sued to halt the advertisement on grounds that it was making false claims about Tropicana's orange juice. Coca-Cola requested an injunction to prevent the continuation of the advertising campaign.

Whether the plaintiff will suffer irreparable harm if the advertising campaign is not halted is an important factor in a court's determination as to whether an injunction will be issued. Marketing research studies can be critical in making such determinations. If consumers are misled into believing that Tropicana's product is more desirable, since it contains only fresh-squeezed juice, then it is likely Coca-Cola could lose a portion of the chilled juice market and thus suffer irreparable injury.

Comparative advertising remains a "hot button" issue among advertisers.[8] MTD Corp.'s Yard-Man and John Deere & Co., Virgin Atlantic, and British Airways were all hit with comparative advertising lawsuits in 2003; Procter & Gamble was hit with four suits in that year. As a result, representatives of the National Advertising Review Council (NARC) and the National Advertising Division (NAD) of the Council of Better Business Bureaus have called for industry self-regulation. Sparing and judicious use of comparative ads and bringing complaints to the NAD instead of the courts have been suggested as solutions to the growing number of lawsuits.

Industry Self-Regulation

Self-regulation refers to actions taken by advertisers themselves rather than by governmental bodies. Several industry and trade associations and other organizations have voluntarily established guidelines for advertising within their industries. For instance, in 1936, makers of distilled spirits agreed collectively not to air ads on radio, and a decade later followed suit for television, which was just becoming popular in American homes. However, after a twenty-year drop in liquor consumption and a huge upswing in revenues to the beer and wine industries, Seagram's, the country's number two distiller, aired an advertisement for its Crown Royal whiskey on a local television station in Corpus Christi, Texas, in June 1996, breaking the industry ban honored over several decades.

Self-regulation by the NAD and National Advertising Review Board (NARB) has been the most publicized and perhaps most effective. Complaints received from consumers, competitors, or local branches of the Better Business Bureau are forwarded to the NAD. After a full review of the complaint, the issue may be forwarded to the NARB and evaluated by a panel. Any unresolved cases may be forwarded to the appropriate government agency, such as the FTC, FDA, and FCC. For instance, NAD ruled in favor of Papa John's Pizza in a substantiation claim initiated in 1998 by Tricon Global Restaurants, owners of the Pizza Hut chain. At issue was an ad that declared Papa John's pizza had bested Pizza Hut's pizza in a taste test. Papa John's struck back at Pizza Hut in full-page ads run in national newspapers on August 21, 1998. The ad featured a drawing of the biblical character David holding a slingshot and wearing a Papa John's shirt as he faces the towering Goliath (with Pizza Hut emblazoned on his shield) and an army of lawyers. The headline said it all: "What's The World Coming To? Now Goliath Is Suing David For Pain and Suffering." The ad's text reiterated Papa John's claims that its advertising is truthful and accurate and that consumers prefer Papa John's over Pizza Hut. Although Papa John's substantiated the taste tests, the council did recommend that future ads be modified to only compare Papa John's pizzas to Pizza Hut's.[9]

The motion picture industry also has a history of self-regulation that has led to the current rating system (PG—Parental Guidance, R—Restricted, etc.). The motion picture academy instituted Oscar night advertising rules in the early 1980s to decree that ads may not show feminine hygiene products, Oscar nominees or presenters, or clips from nominated films.

Government Regulation

At the national level, the primary instrument in the regulation of advertising is the independent regulatory agency, the Federal Trade Commission (FTC). In 1914 the FTC was given regulatory authority in both the antitrust and advertising areas. It exercised the latter under directions to halt "unfair methods of competition." The Wheeler-Lea Act in 1938 significantly broadened the FTC's authority by authorizing it to prevent "unfair or deceptive acts and practices." As amended, the law now states, "unfair methods of competition . . . and unfair or deceptive acts or practices . . . are hereby declared unlawful."[10] The major difference between the Lanham Act and the Federal Trade Commission Act is that the former only strikes at "false" advertising claims, whereas the latter is broader in scope by sweeping "deceptive" ads within the FTC's regulatory purview. It is considered deceptive for an advertisement to

1. offer two for the price of one, if both items were not sold at a normal price of one unit prior to the advertising campaign;
2. offer buy one, get one free, if the price of the former is marked up to compensate for the cost of the "free" item;
3. engage in "bait and switch" sales tactics; utilize a celebrity endorser for a product if the celebrity does not actually use or prefer the item; or
4. use a mock-up in the advertisement while telling the viewer that the real item is being used.

The FTC regards an advertisement as deceptive if it contains a representation, practice, or omission likely to mislead consumers acting reasonably and the representation, practice, or omission is material to a consumer's choice. The FTC also regards as deceptive an advertising claim that is made without *prior* substantiation. Thus, if when challenged by the FTC, the advertiser conducts tests that prove the validity of the claim, those facts will not provide a safe harbor from the legal storm. The FTC requires that an advertiser have a reasonable basis, or substantiation, for the claim prior to their assertion in an advertisement. This substantiation requirement applies to both expressed and implied claims. The FTC also monitors the advertising practices and rating systems of the film, music, and electronic games industries. Although the music industry has taken steps to self-regulate, the FTC has still found adult-themed entertainment in music marketed to teenagers.[11]

As the regulator of food, cosmetic, drug, and health care advertising, the FDA oversees these industries' compliance with federal law and their legal pricing and marketing. The FDA has authority over certain other areas of food products. The agency made major news in August 1995 with its proposed widespread regulation of cigarette advertising. By declaring nicotine a drug, and tobacco a drug delivery device, the FDA proposed to ban brand-name advertising at sporting events and on products that are not tobacco related, such as T-shirts; forbid outdoor advertisements of tobacco within 1,000 feet of schools and playgrounds; limit advertising in publications that reach a significant audience of children; and require tobacco companies to fund a $150 million advertising campaign to stop young people from smoking (see this chapter's Ethics Track). Cigarette advertising is now limited to in-store promotions and print ads.

The FDA halted advertising of Aventis' best-selling drug, Allegra, when the agency determined that two TV spots, a print ad, and a fulfillment letter made false or misleading statements.[12] AstraZeneca Pharmaceuticals paid $355 million for a violation of a federal drug marketing law in June 2003. The company pleaded guilty to giving free samples of Zoladex to urologists who then submitted claims for close to $40 million "for the prescriptions to Medicare, Medicaid and other federally funded insurance programs."[13]

The FCC extends its reach beyond the broadcast media to fax machines. An American Advertising Federation government report on July 23, 2003, noted the FCC's revision of a rule governing facsimile advertising to require fax marketers to receive written consent from recipients before sending facsimile ads.

In 1995, the U.S. Supreme Court handed down an important ruling dealing with the power of the Bureau of Alcohol, Tobacco, and Firearms (BATF) to regulate advertising on beer labels (*Rubin v. Coors,* 63 LW 4319 [1995]). The Agriculture Department possesses authority over certain aspects of food products. Under that authority, it issued a rule that, effective August 1996, poultry cannot be labeled and sold as fresh if it has been frozen.

Other governmental agencies that have become involved in advertising regulation include the Department of Transportation, which regulates airline industry ads, and the Federal Bureau of Investigation (FBI) and U.S. Department of Justice, which launched an investigation in 1995 of a controversial Calvin Klein campaign that featured the nude body of model Kate Moss in erotic poses. The FBI and Justice Department questioned whether the ads violated federal pornography laws. Although the investigation was dropped, Klein pulled the offending ads.

Such gutsy campaigns are said to have "attitude," a term that refers to a disposition or tone of hostility. Advertising with attitude generally reflects a view that conflicts with most people's perceptions of what is politically correct or appropriate. For instance, Gucci ran a double-paged ad in European editions of *Vogue* "showing model Louise Pedersen displaying her pubic hair shaved into the letter G as a man kneels before her."[14] The ad's creator, Tom Ford, called the ad the ultimate in branding.

THE POLITICAL AND LEGAL ENVIRONMENTS IN OTHER SELECTED COUNTRIES

The U.S. Lanham Trademark Act (1946) provides protections and regulation of brand names, brand marks, trade names, and trademarks. Yet copyright laws and violations are becoming an increasing concern for international executives. Many Asian countries have been problematic for international firms due to a lack of copyright protection. For instance, a Taiwanese manufacturer that had been producing running shoes for a U.S. shoe company decided to market itself to other shoe companies. The manufacturer advertised in an international magazine displaying the U.S. firm's brand name on the product. Although this was an honest mistake made by the Taiwanese manufacturer, it clearly violated the copyright law set by the United States. The manufacturer was subsequently sued by a major U.S. shoe company. U.S. trade representatives often watch over trading partners to ensure they are protecting intellectual property.

In another incident, a globally distributed Gap apparel ad featured unauthorized use of the "ultra-hip" eyewear of New York designer

ETHICS TRACK: TOBACCO'S WOES

A number of ethical issues are linked to advertising. Among the topics debated today are advertising to children and minority audiences and advertising controversial products (e.g., alcohol and tobacco).

Since 1966 tobacco manufacturers have put warning labels on cigarette packs. Nevertheless, makers of alcohol and tobacco products have frequently employed billboards and other advertising media to target brands to African Americans and Hispanics. Billboards advertising alcohol and tobacco were disproportionately more likely to appear in inner-city areas.[a] On November 21, 1998, tobacco companies settled a lawsuit with forty-six states in a landmark deal that included the agreement to no longer advertise tobacco products on billboards and to cease using cartoon characters in their ads.

The loss of billboard advertising challenged tobacco manufacturers' agencies to become more creative. For example, Bates Worldwide ran an "urban-targeted" program for the third-largest cigarette manufacturer that played on a "key lifestyle activity" of the target, playing cards.[b] The "Play on the House Spades Slam" featured a sixteen-city tour that ended in a national card-playing final at Caesars Palace, Las Vegas, with a $50,000 grand prize. The tours were promoted through magazine ads in minority-targeted publications such as *Urban Latino* and *Essence*.

Perhaps the most controversial advertisement was R. J. Reynolds' character spokesperson, Joe Camel. Nine years after a campaign featuring the cool, sax-playing, cigarette-smoking camel first appeared, the company was forced to retire Joe to settle an onslaught of lawsuits. Research showed that Joe Camel had become as recognizable to children as Mickey Mouse, and critics believed that the cartoon character's appearance on such diverse public venues as billboards and racing cars encouraged children to smoke.[c]

A Rand Corp. study released in 2004 indicated that African-American youths are more likely to smoke by age thirteen (62 percent of African Americans compared to 52 percent of whites and 36 percent of Asian Americans), although by age fifteen, "just 7 percent of African-Americans had become regular smokers, compared to 20 percent of whites and Latinos and 8 percent of Asian-Americans."[d]

How might cigarette advertising to children and minorities be curtailed? In April 1999, the Supreme Court agreed to hear the Clinton administration and the tobacco industry argue whether or not the Food and Drug Administration (FDA) has the authority to restrict cigarette advertising and sales. What did the Supreme Court decide? What should the advertising industry's responsibility be regarding controversial products?

[a]"Fighting Ads in the Inner City," *Newsweek,* February 5, 1990, p. 46.
[b]Cara B. Dipasquale, "Kool Tries Card-Playing Promo," *Advertising Age,* September 2, 2002, p. 8.
[c]Christian Thompson, "Joe Camel Dies: Victim of His Own Success," *USAToday,* July 11-13, 1997, p. A1.
[d]"Diversity Factoids: Feb. 13," *DiversityInc.,* www.diversityinc.com, 2004.

On Davis.[15] The designer filed a lawsuit seeking $10 million in punitive damages and additional compensation of more than $2 million, saying that the Gap just wasn't "hip enough" to qualify for free product placement of his high-priced spectacles in their advertising.

Business does not function strictly by its own set of rules. It has to answer not only to its customers but also to the government, which sets the rules in the political-legal environment. This dimension of the marketing environment includes laws and regulations. The rapidly changing nature of the international political scene is evident to anyone who regularly reads, listens to, or watches the various news media. Political upheavals, revolutions, and changes in government policy occur daily and can have an enormous effect on international business, for example, international advertising strategies. A country's political system, national laws, regulatory bodies, national pressure groups, and courts all have great impact on its marketing and advertising. A government's policies regarding public and private enterprise, consumers, and foreign firms influence marketing/advertising across national boundaries. In this section, we will discuss the political and legal environments in selected regions and countries.

Asia

China

Since 1979, the year of the thirtieth anniversary of the People's Republic of China (PRC), authorities have permitted foreign advertising to influence how the vast country communicates, both internally and with the rest of an increasingly interdependent world. Although interest in China has begun to pay off for international advertisers and advertising agencies, questions about the effects of advertising have been raised.

In May 1998, China announced "a ban on all forms of direct marketing, including Chinese versions of pyramid sales schemes and conventional direct-selling practices used by Amway and other U.S. companies," such as Mary Kay cosmetics and Avon products. Chinese authorities worry that the sales methods of these multinational companies—door-to-door selling "conducted by individuals who generally work with little supervision"—may be a potential "breeding ground for social unrest and economic havoc."[16]

Closer scrutiny is also given to tobacco and pharmaceutical promotion and the link to poor public health. Spirits advertising—including corporate image campaigns for liquor products—has been banned from 7 p.m. to 8 p.m. (during prime time) on China's only national television station (CCTV). Spirits advertising had brought CCTV $36.8 million in revenues during 1997.[17]

China's domestic advertising agencies' concerns about competition from foreign joint venture advertising agencies resulted in the 1993 Interim Regulations. The regulations clearly defined the roles of media and advertising agencies. The Interim Advertising Censorship Standards were promulgated at the same time as the Interim Regulations of 1993. The standards address emotional responses aroused by advertising. The second article of the standards is devoted entirely to visuals and images displayed in ads. Use of sex appeal, fear appeals, and visuals that may lead to dangerous or negative behavior are forbidden.[18]

Despite the need for official approvals, the country has opened up considerably. Heinz launched Growing Up Oats, the country's first oat-based baby cereal, on the Chinese mainland before introducing the product to other Asian countries. Coty and L'Oreal have been owners of two of China's largest department store skin-care brands, Yue-Sai and Mininurse. L'Oreal also sells its L'Oreal Paris, Maybelline, and Lancome brands in China.

Besides Japan, Hong Kong has had the liveliest, most competitive advertising and commercial environment in Asia. As a British colony, Hong Kong had historically served as a center of foreign trade and communications. Many transnational advertisers, advertising agencies, and media have had offices in Hong Kong. Agencies such as Ogilvy & Mather and Leo Burnett used the colony as a base from which to try to expand into neighboring China. In 1997, when Hong Kong reverted to China after Britain's ninety-nine-year lease expired, many were concerned that Hong Kong might lose its Western-oriented commercial and communications services, including advertising. That didn't seem to be the case when, in late 2003, WPP Group relaunched its Hong Kong–based Bates Asia, a specialist network that serves a broad region of Asian markets.[19] Furthermore, Shantel Wong, a Hong Kong marketing director, now oversees brand leadership at McDonald's China Development Co. Since the acquisition of Hong Kong, China, "a previously undeveloped market," has become McDonald's Corp.'s "fastest-growing market in the world."[20] However, in the first decade of the twenty-first century, marketers and agencies have tended to locate in Shanghai, a major mainland city in China, rather than in Hong Kong. The lure is mainland China's 1.2 billion consumers.

Japan

In April 1998, the tobacco industry ceased television, radio, movie theater, and Internet advertising in Japan. That limits tobacco advertising to print and outdoor media.[21] The restrictions on tobacco advertising will primarily affect foreign tobacco companies. Regulation of online communications that are viewed as pornographic or political is also under consideration.[22] New media and tobacco have been hot regulation issues throughout Asia as highly developed and regulated countries such as Japan and newer advertising markets such as Vietnam seek to protect their diverse cultures and religions.

Taiwan

To maintain fair competition among sellers and to protect consumers, the government of Taiwan ratified the Fair Trade Law on February 4, 1991. The law went into effect a year later, creating the Fair Trade Commission. Under this act, vertical price fixing is prohibited. Also, it makes resale price maintenance, a common practice in Taiwan, illegal. Under the previous law, producers were not penalized if they attempted to control retail prices. It is now illegal for manufacturers and wholesalers to force retailers to accept a suggested retail price. The law specifies that sellers cannot engage in price discrimination unless there are provable differences between selling costs. Basically, this is an antitrust law that restrains unfair methods of competition.

While the Fair Trade Law protects competitors from one another, Article 21 of this law addresses the issue of false or misleading advertising. This article states that

> an enterprise shall not make, on goods or in ads relating thereto, any false, untrue or misleading presentation which may likely cause confusion to or mistake by consumers such as their price, quantity, quality, content, manufacturing process, date of manufacturing, validity period, use method, purpose of use, place of origin, manufacturer, place of manufacturing, processor, and place of processing.[23]

Furthermore, an enterprise shall not sell, transport, export, or import goods bearing false, untrue, or misleading presentations referred to in the preceding statement.

The Consumer Protection Law was promulgated on January 11, 1994, and became effective on January 13, 1994. This law was enacted for the purpose of protecting the interests of consumers, facilitating the safety of and improving the quality of the consumer life of the Taiwanese nationals. Because this second law is new, there may be some jurisdictional conflict between the Fair Trade Commission and the Consumer Protection Commission regarding deceptive advertising. Nevertheless, it is clear that consumers who seek damages from a company should go to the Consumer Protection Commission. Consumers may also complain to the Fair Trade Commission about deceptive advertising. If the Fair Trade Commission's investigation finds an advertisement deceptive, the commission has the power to fine the company.

It took more than ten years for these two laws, first envisioned in 1981, to be enacted. In the meantime, consumers endured misconduct from businesses, such as deceptive advertising and a low level of product quality.

Online theft led to additional legislation in Taiwan. To alleviate the problem of Web-based purchasing fraud, the government "launched an advanced online payment system in October 2003 that enables customers to submit their data directly to banks and provides online merchants with delivery information only."[24]

Malaysia

Although there are numerous situations in which differing customer needs require tailor-made advertising campaigns, in many instances, the particular regulations of a country prevent multinational corporations from using standardized approaches. Malaysians prohibit jeans, for example, which they consider to be Western and decadent. In countries such as Malaysia, regulations are a direct outgrowth of culture and changing political circumstances.

The Malaysian government does not have an overall or comprehensive policy regarding advertising practices. In theory, the main set of regulations controlling advertising ethics is the Malaysian Code of Advertising Practice. This code is not a piece of legislation introduced by the government; it is a purely voluntary set of guidelines drawn up and administered by a private-sector organization, the Advertising Standards Authority (ASA). Although no comprehensive advertising legislation exists in Malaysia, the Trade Descriptions Act (1972) empowers the Ministry of Trade and Industry to act against companies that give misleading statements or suggestions in advertisements. The Radio Television Malaysia (RTM) Code of Advertising is not too different from the Code of Advertising Practice. Since it was first issued by the Ministry of Information on December 27, 1972, it has been updated several times. Several distinguishing features of the RTM code are bans on the following types of ads: alcoholic beverage ads; ads that use children to promote products not intended for them; ads for women's products, such as sanitary napkins, that are screened before 10 p.m.; and cigarette ads.[25]

Singapore

Advertisers, media, and advertising agencies find it in their own best interest to support self-regulatory bodies rather than wait until the government has to step in and take measures that might adversely affect the advertising industry. One of the best-organized self-regulatory bodies in Asia is in Singapore. The Advertising Standards Authority of Singapore (ASAS) has ties to consumer and trade union groups and includes representatives of agencies, advertisers, and the media. It sets standards, publishes a code of ethical advertising practice, and deals with complaints from the public and from within the industry. In a number of developing countries, however, codes either do not exist or are difficult to enforce.

First as a British colony, then as part of Malaysia, and now as an independent republic, Singapore has thrived as a regional commercial and communications center for foreign businesses. Transnational advertising agencies and their clients have flocked to Singapore because facilities for communications are excellent and there are no regulations against wholly owned subsidiaries.[26] Nevertheless, Singapore has become one of the "most policed" of the Asian countries, especially when it comes to new media. "The government has established the Proxy, a central master server and screening service for material on the Internet."[27]

Indonesia, Thailand, and Vietnam

Concern about growing advertising markets has led to tighter regulations—regarding tobacco and alcohol in particular—in Indonesia, Thailand, and Vietnam. Although Indonesia allows cigarette advertising on television, spots cannot show the cigarette packs or scenes that involve actual smoking. A ban on all cigarette advertising has been under review. A change in Thai Censorship Board regulations permits television advertising of alcohol, but only after 10 p.m., and restricts the content of liquor advertisements from making claims about quality.

Whereas advertisers view Thailand as "modern" and receptive, Vietnam presents a hostile climate. Ad agencies, restricted to representative offices, must conduct financial transactions outside the country. Media buying may eventually be restricted to Vietnamese-owned agencies. Although currently there are no such regulations, and policies change often, the general atmosphere has been anti-Western.[28] An advertising ordinance, introduced in 2002 and implemented the next year, "clarified specific regulations on advertising outdoors, in printed materials, and on television."[29] This ordinance regulates billboard placement and the number of continuous days that ads may air, and restricts front-page print ads to newspapers that specialize in advertising.

Europe and the United Kingdom

Advertisers do not so much fear the diversity of European laws as they fear not knowing the laws. For example, a marketer cannot advertise on television to children under twelve in Sweden or Germany, cannot advertise business chains in France, and cannot advertise at all on Sunday in Austria. Issues facing the European Union's highest executive body, the European Commission, have included new media, protection of children, privacy, and tobacco bans. In late 2002 the European Union decided not to allow prescription drug advertising.

Some European countries have taken action to prevent the medical consequences and long-term effects of obesity caused by junk food. The British Parliament introduced a bill in 2003 to prohibit celebrity endorsements of junk foods, and the Italian and British medical associations placed a "fat tax" on these foods.[30] Perhaps anticipating such legislation would spread to the United States, the U.S. McDonald's restaurants ended supersized portions in 2004.

The British advertising regulatory regime is a unique combination of case law, statutory law, and self-regulation. It differs from the regulatory systems of continental Europe and the United States in two major respects: (1) the absence of general statutory laws prohibiting misleading and unfair advertising, and (2) the central role of voluntary self-regulation in the control of specific advertising abuses. The centerpiece of the British scheme is the self-regulatory system. Most complaints about advertising content are generally directed, in the first instance, to the nongovernmental Advertising Standards Authority or Independent Broadcasting Authority. The courts and the law provide legally enforceable alternatives when self-restraint does not succeed or when the abuse is beyond the scope of self-regulation. The scope of the law differs to some extent from the scope of the self-regulatory system. Self-regulation focuses principally on the content of ads, whereas the law has a much wider scope, including the behavior of the advertisers and agencies.

Although some countries are still dealing inadequately with public and industry complaints, the United Kingdom Advertising Standards Authority (ASA) instituted advertising regulations in 1994. These regulations banned the use of humor in tobacco ads and led to tobacco industry agreements to cut its poster advertising budget by 40 percent, to stop putting posters within 200 meters of schools, and to increase the size of health warnings in advertising by 20 percent. TV advertising regulations were relaxed in 2003 when the Office of Communication replaced other broadcast watchdogs; complaints now are dealt with "on a voluntary basis."[31]

The United Kingdom's Direct Marketing Association became subject to government regulation in 1999. Canada and Australia, "telecom-savvy countries with ample infrastructure," are working to regulate outbound telemarketing.[32] Total UK telemarketing expenditures have been as high as $4.9 million (2001). Canada's $12 billion telemarketing industry has a voluntary do-not-call program for its Canadian Marketing Association members. Australia's $8 billion call center industry plans to self-regulate.

The British Commonwealth of Nations

Many members of the British Commonwealth of Nations have adopted political and legal systems patterned on the English system. Industrialized Commonwealth countries, including Canada, Australia, and New Zealand, have also adapted many aspects of the British advertising regulatory scheme to their national situations. All these countries have central self-regulatory bodies somewhat comparable to the British Advertising Standards Authority, with the exception of

New Zealand, which has established a less extensive system of voluntary restraints.

Although advertising in Canada is closely tied to U.S. industry, the regulatory system is independent. Canada pioneered a system of self-regulation in 1957. Today, the Advertising Standards Council (ASC) is the self-regulatory arm of the Canadian Advertising Foundation (CAF). The ASC cooperates with the government. The CAF was the first to outline educational guidelines for sex-role stereotyping and to establish a Broadcast Code for Advertising to Children, which it jointly administers with the Canadian federal government.[33]

Since outdoor advertising was banned in 1995, there has been no cigarette advertising in Australia. As the most regulated, Westernized country in its region, Australia has a number of regulatory agencies. For example, a commercial can be aired in Australia only if it is shot with an Australian crew. The Australian Competition and Consumer Commission is a governmental regulatory body with codes governing, among other areas, the portrayal of women and children in advertising. These codes are administered by the Media Council. Other regulatory agencies include the Australian Association of National Advertisers and the Advertising Standards Council (which represents the public as well as the advertising industry).[34]

Russia

Reflecting a worldwide concern about advertising alcohol to minors, Russia has banned prime-time beer commercials "and the use of people or animals in beer ads" since 2002.[35] Ad spending for beer in Russia exceeds $90 million annually.

South America

Venezuela

Venezuela's congress has already banned tobacco advertising on radio and television. Advertising agencies, in what has been described as a hard-line country, are represented by the Venezuelan Federation of Advertising Agencies. Chile and the Dominican Republic represent a less restrictive advertising environment in which marketers, advertising agencies, and the media practice self-regulation, pulling ads with "questionable content."[36] Silec, an ad trade group, resolves a high percentage of advertising conflicts in Mexico, Argentina, Nicaragua, and Venezuela. In Colombia, the lobbying group Asomedios represents advertisers.

Brazil

In the hope of avoiding governmental regulations, Brazil has been self-regulatory since the early 1980s. However, in the early 1990s, a strong pro-consumer sentiment mandated visual and audio health warnings in tobacco advertising and banned the link of tobacco and alcohol products to such healthy situations as sports.

Chile

After eight years of negotiations, the free trade agreement between the United States and Chile became effective in 2004. Although Chile, with a population of 15 million, is "one of the smallest markets in South America," it is also "one of the most economically and politically stable."[37] This agreement, the first between the United States and a South American country, eliminates consumer and trade taxes. Furthermore, the agreement represents an opening into Latin America, an attractive market to U.S. interests for decades.

Argentina

In April 2004, Argentina banned commercial breaks during movies on pay TV. Channels such as Cinecanal, Space, and TNT had been preferred venues for such multinational corporations as Coca-Cola and Unilever because cable reaches 50 percent of Argentine homes. Ad spending on cable had increased 70 percent in 2003, reflecting the country's recovering economy.[38]

Africa and the Mideast

For decades, advertisers have had to be sensitive to cultural issues in Arab countries and racial divides in South Africa. Reducing tariffs and opening markets have presented other challenges. In 2001, the United States reached a free-trade agreement with Jordan. In 2004 a similar trade agreement was reached with Morocco in North Africa, the second such deal to be cut with an Arab country, although similar agreements had already been reached with Australia and Central

American countries such as Guatemala, El Salvador, Nicaragua, Honduras, and Costa Rica.[39]

Before a company enters a foreign market, it must thoroughly analyze the environment. If an advertising strategy is to be effective across national borders, the complexities of all the environments involved must be understood. In 1998, Asian economic problems adversely affected both the U.S. trade deficit and the stock market. The overthrow of the government in Indonesia in May 1998 also created a sense of caution among international marketers. Any change in the political and economic climate of a country will eventually impact the world of marketing and advertising.

Fortunately, these days, multinational corporations are paying more attention to the uncontrollable environments (e.g., political and legal issues) in foreign markets when they design their ads. For instance, few advertising and public policy issues have attracted more attention in recent years than the international controversy over the marketing of infant food. Infant formula manufacturer Nestlé has been boycotted and its activities in developing countries closely scrutinized. To improve its company image, Nestlé has gone out of its way to support social development efforts by emphasizing that teaching is satisfying work in ads created by Ogilvy & Mather in Kuala Lumpur. Gradually, in Malaysia and elsewhere, advertisers are becoming aware of the social value of reinforcing cultural traditions and the political value of supporting government policies.[40]

SUMMARY

Advertising businesses cannot afford to ignore government policies and the legal system. Many laws and regulations may not be designed to address advertising issues, yet they can have a major impact on a firm's opportunities, both locally and abroad. The political and legal environments in the United States are influenced by federal government regulation, especially Congress and the Federal Trade Commission. In Taiwan, the Fair Trade Law and Consumer Protection Law have affected advertising. In other countries, the political system, national laws, regulatory bodies, national pressure groups, and courts all have great impact on international marketing and advertising. Before a company enters the international marketplace, it must thoroughly analyze each country's political and legal forces.

:30

:30 Spot:
The Benefits of a Graduate Degree

The decision to go forward and earn my master's degree in Integrated Marketing Communication right after completion of my bachelor's degree was one of the best decisions of my life. Whether to join the "real world" after college or continue on with graduate school is a scary, tough decision for a young person. Many circumstances need to be considered, including the state of the economy. It was an employee's economy the year I graduated college, but it shortly turned into an employer's economy with scandals at Enron and Nortel Networks.

There are advantages to having a graduate degree. A master's degree gives a candidate for employment an edge over other applicants for the same position, but the master's degree must be coupled with some sort of practical experience in the respective field. If possible, a student should try to work in his or her respective field while pursuing an advanced degree. For example, a student pursuing a public relations career should try to work as a PR assistant while in school. This kind of experience will make the person stand out when looking for the perfect job to begin a career. Employers want to see practical experience, so internships or prior experience are crucial to keep the edge. Employers respect applicants who had the initiative to go to graduate school. This extra effort shows that the person has drive and perseverance, and took the extra step to make himself or herself more marketable.

The graduate degree also carries disadvantages. Many companies have been forced to cut costs, and one of the first cuts is the advertising budget. As a result, agency employees and in-house advertising and public relations staffs have been laid off, especially in areas that rely heavily on tourism, such as Florida and California. Not all employers can afford to pay people who have earned master's degrees and command higher salaries. As a result, an employer may choose a less-qualified applicant to avoid insulting an advanced-degree holder with a low salary offer.

A master's degree is an accomplishment. Recently, more and more people are deciding to go the extra step to earn a master's degree, making the marketplace more competitive. The work involved in earning an advanced degree can be tedious and at times seem never-ending, but when you walk across that stage and receive the degree, it is one of the best feelings. Once you have earned a master's degree, nobody can ever take it away from you.

Jacqueline V. Ader
Associate Marketing Manager
U.S. Airways Vacations, and
Marketing Instructor
Columbia College
Orlando, Florida

Chapter 4

The Advertising Business and Advertising Agencies

"I want the ball," growls a suited-up Ty Law; "Come and get it," responds Jake Delhomme, quarterback for the Carolina Panthers. As the two face off, the New England Patriots' cornerback holds a glass of milk in his gloved hand, and both wear milk mustaches. Just in time for Super Bowl XXXVIII, Lowe, New York, featured the two football players in its MilkPEP campaign for America's Dairy Farmers and Milk Processors. Maybe Delhomme didn't get the Bowl, but as the classic tagline says, he "got milk." Lowe is part of Interpublic Groups of Cos.

Goodby, Silverstein & Partners was named Agency of the Year by *Advertising Age's Creativity* for a "Got milk?" spot during its ten-year-running campaign for the California Milk Processors Board. BSMG Marketing Communications Chicago launched a public relations campaign for U.S. milk processors (see this chapter's Sixty-Second Spot).

Each agency has milked the mustache concept for its own campaigns.

Of course, there is more to running an agency than milking a known commodity. Lauded for its successful Taco Bell campaigns, in 2003 Foote Cone & Belding Worldwide got the white on its face with a $200 million KFC campaign that promoted fried chicken as health food. This was not good news for the embattled agency that lost the $1.2 billion DaimlerChrysler account in 2001 and shaved its staff by almost a third in 2002.

There is more to an advertising agency than creating ads. Bozell International has helped clients find qualified local personnel in global marketplaces, prescreened potential distributors, and even put clients in touch with plant acquisition opportunities. Bozell's philos-

ILLUSTRATION 4.1. Creative people. Agency employees develop and prepare advertising plans and produce advertisements and other promotional materials. Account executives must have writing and computer skills to communicate via mass and new media. Catherine A. Justak has been an account executive for Golin/Harris Communications Inc. and is now Program Manager–Education for The American Academy of Periodontology. Justak stresses the importance of writing skills in her Sixty-Second Spot: Writing the Road to Success (Chapter 7) and defines the function of public relations in Chapter 18's Sixty-Second Spot.

ophy is that by helping clients open up networks of distribution and marketing, the agency may create an unlimited partnership with them.

As Bozell and its clients know, creating an ad campaign, whether for a local market or a multinational market, involves a partnership between the advertiser and the agency. There are two other key players in the advertising business. The first is the media, which sell time in electronic media and space in print media to carry the advertiser's message to the target market. The second, the suppliers, includes the illustrators, photographers, printers, typesetters, video production houses, and other intermediaries who assist both advertisers and agencies in preparing advertising materials.

This chapter examines the advertisers and agencies—what they do, who they are, and how they work together.

THE ADVERTISING BUSINESS

The large and complex business of advertising involves many types of organizations and people. The 1990s saw a surge in international revenues. According to *Advertising Age,* 1994 international advertising agencies' billings increased 9.1 percent over 1993 billings.[1] However, after 9/11, international revenues inched up, increasing only .4 percent in 2002 to $19 billion in worldwide revenue.[2] In addition to 9/11, the Enron scandals, recession, and war in Iraq negatively impacted agency revenues. A 2.2 percent decline in 2001 was "the worst year and only negative reading recorded since the industry dropped 4.4 percent in 1987."[3] However, by 2003 revenues for the top global agency brands increased as much as 29 percent over 2002 (see Table 4.1).

TABLE 4.1. The global perspective: Top ten ad agencies (ranked by 2003 worldwide revenue, rounded).

Agency	Location	Revenue (in millions of dollars)
1. Dentsu	Tokyo	1,860
2. BBDO	New York	1,230
3. McCann-Erickson Worldwide	New York	1,220
4. J. Walter Thompson	New York	1,180
5. Publicis Worldwide	Paris	1,020
6. DDB Worldwide Communications	New York	940
7. Leo Burnett	Chicago	890
8. TBWA Worldwide	New York	780
9. Euro RSCG Worldwide	New York	760
10. Ogilvy & Mather Worldwide	New York	706

Source: Adapted from "World's Top 10 Core Agency Brands," *Advertising Age FactPack,* February 28, 2005, p. 51.

THE GLOBAL PERSPECTIVE:
"I'M LOVIN' IT" IN CHINA

Justin Timberlake is "Lovin' It."

An increasingly competitive global marketplace led some U.S. corporations to go agency shopping. "In a competition among ad agencies all over the world" for the best idea for a youth-oriented campaign for McDonald's Corp., the surprise winner was Leo Burnett China.[a] The "I'm Lovin' It" campaign was launched worldwide in the winter of 2003 and continued into 2004 with a commercial featuring teen idol Timberlake.

Once characterized as drab and propagandistic, Chinese advertising is now characterized as lively and edgy. Chinese agencies' local creative staffs are winning international awards, including their first Clio in 2002. China could overtake Japan as the second-largest ad market, according to Nielsen Media Research.

As the nabbing of the McDonald's account suggests, the Chinese bring a fresh new perspective to the marketplace. This is true whether the Chinese are creating the advertisements or responding to them. Youths between the ages of fifteen and twenty-eight in China, a cynical, hard-to-reach market elsewhere, have already demonstrated Western brand loyalties. WPP Group's Ogilvy & Mather Worldwide and the research firm Synovate surveyed 202 youths from affluent families in south China's Pearl River Delta.[b] The research showed that 94 percent of the group drink Coke, and Nike scored a 7.79 on a scale of 10 in rating sneaker superiority. Young people tend to think independently, favoring international brands over such Chinese brands as Li Ning and Jianlibao. Ogilvy's planning director for Hong Kong and southern China concluded that the market has as much potential as other markets, if not more. McDonald's China, "a hip hangout for Chinese teens," gave out free hamburgers on the day China's selection for the 2008 Olympic games was announced. Adidas launched a campaign featuring "China's leading football star," marking the first time it created a TV spot specifically for the Chinese market."

Levi's chose to pursue this desirable demographic via a Web campaign. After all, Chinese youths ages eighteen to twenty-four account for 37 percent of the Asian online population, according to OgilvyOne-MDigital.

An ad campaign tagline for Hong Kong's *Financial Times* said it all: "Independent. Inspired. Indispensable." That's China.

[a]Geoffrey A. Fowler, "China's Edgy Advertising," *The Wall Street Journal,* October 27, 2003, pp. B1, B4.

[b]Normandy Madden, "Study: Chinese Youth Aren't Patriotic Purchasers," *Advertising Age,* January 5, 2004, p. 6.

What Advertising People Do

Advertisers or the advertising agencies they hire must perform certain basic tasks. These include planning, budgeting, coordination, and ad creation (see Illustration 4.1). In a large firm, the advertising manager is the person who is in charge of all the advertising tasks. In the advertising agency, the account manager generally pursues these tasks.

Planning

Planning is a constant, ongoing process of defining and redefining goals and objectives, performing advertising research, developing and scheduling advertisements, and evaluating results.

Budgeting

The advertising manager, the person who is in charge of all the advertising tasks, or the account manager (or other personnel) formulates the annual budget and presents it to top management. The person then sees that the staff (either the advertiser's or the agency's) adheres to the budget.

Coordination

Business activities usually fall into three broad, functional areas: production, finance, and marketing. Advertising is a marketing activity. The person in charge of the advertising process must coordinate advertising activities with other marketing functions (e.g., sales) as well as with production and finance activities. Advertising agency personnel also need to coordinate the advertising activities with other marketing, production, and finance functions within their client's company.

Creating Advertisements

The creative tasks consist of three main elements: copywriting, art direction, and production. The advertising manager or other personnel need to be sure that the finished advertisements will fulfill the company's goals.

The Advertisers

Advertisers hire many people to create advertisements and buy ad time and space. Advertisers may be international, national, regional, or local; they may be global corporations such as Coca-Cola, or small businesses. These advertisers range from one-person certified public accountant (CPA) offices that advertise only in the local Yellow Pages to national chain stores that advertise on television and in national newspapers. In fact, the *Standard Directory of Advertisers* (known as the advertiser's "Red Book") lists roughly 25,000 advertisers in the United States alone and includes their budgets and their advertising agencies. Virtually every company has an advertising department. Large companies may have a separate advertising department which employs many people and is headed by an advertising manager who reports to a marketing director or marketing services manager. Smaller companies may have just one person who performs all the advertising tasks and reports to the top management. In these smaller companies, this person may also be part of top management.

THE ADVERTISING AGENCY

The American Association of Advertising Agencies defines an advertising agency as an independent organization of creative people and businesspeople who specialize in developing and preparing advertising plans, advertisements, and other promotional tools. The agency purchases advertising space and time in various media on behalf of its clients—various advertisers or sellers—to find customers for the clients' goods and services.[4]

Advertising agencies range in size from small to giant businesses that hire thousands of employees. The smaller agencies usually have up to a dozen employees and handle accounts of up to $10,000. Medium-sized agencies bill an average of $10,000 to $100,000,000 annually. In 1997, J. Walter Thompson pulled up from number two to top the *Advertising Age* U.S. brand rankings with a gross income of $387.8 million, replacing Leo Burnett which occupied the top spot in 1996. J. Walter has remained on top (see Table 4.2). Brand agencies

TABLE 4.2. Top U.S. agencies (revenue rounded).

Rank in 2003	Rank in 2002	Agency	Location	Revenue (in millions of dollars)
1	(1)	J. Walter Thompson Co.	New York	456
2	(2)	Leo Burnett Worldwide	Chicago	404
3	(3)	McCann-Erickson Worldwide	New York	300
4	(4)	BBDO Worldwide	New York	279
5	(7)	Grey Worldwide	New York	252
6	(5)	DDB Worldwide Communications	New York	251
7	(8)	Ogilvy & Mather Worldwide	New York	235
8	(6)	Foote, Cone & Belding Worldwide	New York	221
9	(10)	Y&R Advertising	New York	215
10	(9)	Publicis Worldwide	New York	201

Source: Adapted from "Top 25 U.S. Agency Brands by Core Advertising Revenue," *Advertising Age,* April 19, 2004, p. S-2, and *Advertising Age FactPack,* February 28, 2005, p. 50.

do not handle their clients' specialty advertising and non-media components such as public relations. Dentsu is one of the world's largest brand agencies with worldwide gross income approaching $2 million (see Table 4.1).

Advertising agencies may be organized into departments based on functional specialties (account services, creative services, marketing services, and administration) or into groups that work as teams on various accounts. Advertising agencies can be classified by the range of services they offer and the types of business they handle. The two basic types are full-service agencies and specialized service agencies such as creative boutiques and media-buying services.

Types of Advertising Agencies

Full-Service Agencies

A full-service agency performs at least four basic functions for the clients it represents: research services, creative services, media services, and account management. In addition to these functions, some advertising agencies are expanding their services by offering direct marketing, public relations, and even sales promotion services in the spirit of becoming Integrated Marketing Communication agencies. DDB Needham Worldwide's subsidiary, DDB Needham Marketing Communications, deals with sales promotion, direct response, and other marketing services.

Specialized-Service Agencies

Creative boutiques. Creative boutiques are limited service advertising agencies. These relatively small agencies concentrate entirely on preparing the creative execution of client communications. The focus of the organization is entirely on the idea and the creative product. There is no staff for media, research, strategic planning, or other services, which a full-service agency can offer. McDonald's Corporation surprised the industry when it hired Fallon McElligott, Minneapolis, basically a creative boutique, to handle its $75 million introduction of the Arch Deluxe in May 1996. It also went beyond its core advertising agencies (Leo Burnett USA and DDB Needham Worldwide) for creative resources for its other products (see Illustration 4.2).[5]

Health/medical agencies. This special type of agency concentrates on advertising for pharmaceutical companies such as Merck, Pfizer, and Upjohn. The health/medical agency carries out most of the functions a full-service agency performs but concentrates on the medical field. Health care is one of the fastest-growing segments in advertising in the United States today. Prescription and over-the-counter drugs account for much of this advertising. Many full-service agencies and holding companies have been buying health/medical agencies. In 1996 McCann-Erickson Worldwide bought Torre Renta Lazur Healthcare Group, one of the United States' leading health agencies. Large U.S. agencies have also made consumer health advertising a priority. For instance, Saatchi & Saatchi Advertising in New York has created a separate division called Healthcare Connection to keep up with its competitors.[6]

Direct marketing agencies. These agencies specialize in strategic planning, creative solutions, and execution as well as database management for direct-response advertising. However, some direct mar-

ILLUSTRATION 4.2. Mucho successful. Leo Burnett China came up with a campaign idea for McDonald's that allowed the Chicago-based corporation to span the globe with culturally diverse commercials, print ads, and billboards.

keting agencies have expanded to become full-service agencies. Such an agency is Rapp Collins Worldwide, New York, a direct marketing pioneer, founded in 1965, and now part of Omnicom Group Inc. The agency has more than 2,000 professionals in seventy offices in thirty-eight countries, servicing over 5,000 clients in over 100 countries. Relationship marketing and interactive communication have always been the special domain of direct marketers. Today, direct marketing agencies offer such services as Web site creation, e-commerce, Internet marketing, and data mining and modeling, along with traditional direct-response services.

Ethnic agencies. Another example of a specialized agency is the ethnic agency. In the United States, multicultural agencies may even further specialize and focus on major ethnic populations, such as Hispanics, African Americans, and Asian Americans (see Table 4.3 for the top multicultural agencies).

- *The Hispanic Market:* The Dallas-based Hispanic agency Dieste, Harmel & Partners, named Agency of the Year by *Advertising Age* in 2004, launched PepsiCo's Frito-Lay Cool Guacamole potato chips. The campaign brought $65 million in first-year sales. Even though it had targeted largely urban, Hispanic consumers, the product went mainstream and far exceeded the expected $12 million sales return. Over 37 million strong in 2003, Hispanics have replaced African Americans as the largest U.S. minority. As noted in Chapter 2, the Hispanic population is expected to reach over 60 million by 2020, representing enormous buying power considering it already represented $240 billion a year in 1995. Hispanic magazines and television and radio stations have emerged to specifically serve what has officially become the largest U.S. minority population. Many blue-chip marketers recognize the importance of this fast-growing consumer group, such as IBM, General Motors, AT&T, and Revlon, and now place ads in Hispanic magazines.[7] American Honda Motor Company's Hispanic agency, La Agencia de Orci & Associates in Los Angeles, created advertising campaigns for fifteen Latin American countries. The advertising, designed for all markets, allowed for alterations as needed in each country.[8]
- *The African-American Market:* Based on a population of 34,658,190 in that year, Census 2000 projected that African

Americans will be 12 percent of total U.S. population by 2007. Other projections put the African-American population at 39 million by the year 2010. By 2003 the Census Bureau reported the population had reached 36.1 million. Spending by this group already exceeds $300 billion. Agencies have worked to aggressively diversify their ranks with full-time minority employees for their own benefit and for the good of the nation's top brands. George Fisher, former CEO of Eastman Kodak, has noted that customers do not all want the same things and cannot all be treated the same way. One of Kodak's four advertising agencies is Uniworld, a minority-owned agency whose advertising primarily targets African Americans.[9] Some companies even have an in-house agency to create advertisements aimed at African Americans.

• *The Asian-American Market:* The U.S. Census showed that the Asian Americans numbered 10,242,998 in 2000, less than the previously projected 12 million by that year. However, Census 2000 showed that Asian Americans continue to be better educated, have higher incomes, and to occupy more prestigious job positions than any other segment in American society. According to Diversity Inc. <www.diversityinc.com>, Asian Americans are "affluent, educated, and young." Some firms successfully market to specific Asian groups by customizing marketing programs specifically to their values and lifestyles rather than merely translating Anglo programs. Understanding the popularity of chicken-based dishes among the Chinese, Perdue Farm Inc. advertised in *World Journal,* a New York City Chinese-language newspaper. Often, an Asian agency is used by these advertisers. Muse Cordero Chen, a Los Angeles agency, specializes not only in marketing to Asian consumers but also to African-American and Hispanic markets.

AGENCY COMPENSATION

To survive, an agency must make a profit. Basically, agencies make money from three sources: media commissions, fees, incentive payments, and markups.

TABLE 4.3. Top U.S. multicultural agencies 2003.

Agency	Cultural specialty	U.S. revenue (in thousands of $)
1. Bromley Communications	Hispanics	32,937
2. Bravo Group	Hispanics	31,775
3. Burrell Communications Group	African Americans	26,072
4. Carol H. Williams Advertising	African Americans	25,000
5. Dieste, Harmel & Partners	Hispanics	23,000
6. UniWorld Group	African Americans	20,148
7. Zubi Advertising Services	Hispanics	16,400
8. La Agencia de Orci & Assoc.	Hispanics	14,160
9. Lapiz Integrated	Hispanics	12,432
10. Lopez Negrete Communications	Hispanics	12,095

Source: Adapted from "Top Multicultural Agencies," *Advertising Age,* April 19, 2004, p. S-13, and *Advertising Age FactPack,* February 28, 2005, p. 58.

Media Commissions

The media channel may allow an agency to retain a 15 percent commission on the time or space purchased for clients. For example, a television station bills an agency $10,000 for airing a commercial. The agency bills the advertiser $10,000. The advertiser pays the agency in full, and the agency submits $8,500 to the station, keeping $1,500 (a 15 percent commission). An agency typically provides creative, media, research, and account management services to earn its 15 percent commission for its largest accounts. For outdoor advertising, the commission ranges from 15 to 16.67 percent.

The 15 percent commission has been a matter of some controversy between the advertisers and agencies. Agencies argue that a 15 percent commission does not cover their costs; smaller advertisers must sometimes pay additional fees. On the other hand, many advertisers feel that a 15 percent compensation is too much. The disagreement has spurred the growth of other compensation systems. In fact, a 1995 study by the Association of National Advertisers revealed that only 14 percent of advertisers still pay a 15 percent commission. According to the study, the most common compensation method is a reduced commission system (less than 15 percent commission). Forty-five percent of the advertisers surveyed indicated that they use this form of compensation. An Andersen Consulting study revealed that most advertisers using agencies for full-service advertising pay commissions ranging from 8 to 15 percent, with larger advertisers paying an average of 13 percent. Other studies show an even lower range, from 8 to 10 percent.

Another controversy regards hidden costs extracted from advertisers by the media, especially television. Agencies say these fees further cut into their profits. For instance, the broadcast networks charge a $125 to $550 "integration fee" each time an ad runs. Networks say the fee covers the costs of ad screening and on-air placement. Agencies view the fees as unnecessary.[10]

Labor-Based Fees

A labor-based fee system has become popular in recent years. Thirty-five percent of advertisers surveyed compensated agencies on time commitment. An hourly fee is negotiated between the advertiser and the agency. The agency then monitors the labor and bills the client on the time spent. This system is also used for special services the agency renders for its clients. For example, an agency arranges a focus group study for its client. The client will receive a bill from the agency based on an agreed-on hourly rate. A survey of Association of National Advertisers' members revealed that the use of billings-based compensation had already fallen to 35 percent by 1997 while labor-based compensation had increased to 53 percent.

Incentive Payments

In the late 1990s, Ford Motor Co. was the first of the Big Three automakers "to dump the old commission system" and join a nationwide trend.[11] Ford initiated a new payment system that began with a base fee for all the work, followed by payments tied to "specific performance goals, including the profitability of the Ford unit involved."

Markups

The agency may need to purchase photographs, illustrations, or other services from outside suppliers for its clients. The agency pays these suppliers a set fee and adds a markup, typically 17.65 percent,

ETHICS TRACK:
THE CANADIAN CONUNDRUM

The so-called "sponsorship scandal" became news on February 10, 2004, when Canada's Auditor General Sheila Fraser released audit results of the federal Public Works Department. Fraser found that a reported $100 million in government funds were misspent in forms of fees and commissions to advertising and communications agencies since 1995. The scheme apparently generated commissions for the agencies instead of the funds' intended purpose, to benefit Canadian taxpayers. In one instance, $1.6 million in federal government contracts was just handed to a Montreal advertising agency.[a]

More specifically, the audit report found that five major agencies—the Royal Canadian Mounted Police (RCMP), Via Rail, Canada Post, the Business Development Bank of Canada, and the Old Port of Montreal—allowed advertising agencies to collect money without doing the work intended or signing a contract. For example, a $3 million government sponsorship of RCMP's anniversary celebration was found to be wasteful; the display of the "Canada" trademark was already required. Furthermore, government funds were misused when contracts worth $101 million were used to buy two VIP jets to transport high government officials when the Canadian Department of Defense was already satisfied with the condition of the old jets.[b]

However, while some agencies and private companies benefitted from these government dealings, the Canadian citizens were penalized. Because of the misuse of funds, the Canadian government had less money to spend on its people and on other programs that would benefit Canadians. Since the money was channeled elsewhere, Canadian parks and heritage documents were neglected. For example, some important heritage documents began to rot because of improper storage, while private collectors bought others. Also, according to Fraser, the 170-year-old Fort Henry in Kingston, Ontario, was near collapse.

After the scandal broke, former Public Works Minister Alfonso Gagliano and fourteen other Canadian government workers were either fired or reprimanded. In addition, Canadian Prime Minister Paul Martin appointed a special counsel to recover some of the misused funds. This counsel began an independent query to further investigate the scandal.[c]

Arianna Stella

[a]"Federal Sponsorship Scandal," CBC News, <www.cbc.ca/news/background/groupaction>, February 11, 2004.
[b]"Auditor General's Report 2004," CBC News, <www.cbc.ca/news/auditorgeneral/report2004>, February 11, 2004.
[c]Gail Chiasson, "Canada Reports on Misused Funds," *Advertising Age*, February 16, 2004. p. 13

to the client's bill. For example, ABC Advertising Agency purchased illustrations from XYZ services for $1,000. ABC would add $176.50 to its client's bill, which becomes $1,176.50. This additional $176.50 earned by the agency would become 15 percent of the final bill ($1,176.50) to the client. Therefore, the agency still earns the traditional 15 percent commission.

An American Association of Advertisers' study showed that 7 percent of member advertisers compensate their agencies on the basis of a prearranged incentive-based system. Incentive payments came out of the trend toward nontraditional payment systems, which often include a combination of payment methods. In this system, agencies are compensated based on the extent to which a client's advertising objectives are accomplished. The agency earns more if the campaign attains specific, agreed-on goals. The increased emphasis of top management in the 1990s on measurable results and accountability has placed added pressure on agencies to show *outcomes,* not just *output.*

As mentioned in Chapter 1, the need for greater accountability is one of the driving forces in the evolution of Integrated Marketing Communication. Agencies now struggle with ways to bill for services and to quantify *outcomes* when the client's goal is long-term relationship marketing.

CLIENT-AGENCY RELATIONSHIPS

Many advertisers employ a combination of the different advertising options (e.g, in-house agency, boutiques, and outside advertising agency) rather than using one of them exclusively. However, due to intense competition, the recent trend has been for advertisers to use the services of full-service agencies, moving away from in-house agencies. Some have also reviewed their relationships with advertising agencies they have used for years and welcomed other advertising agencies to compete for accounts. These agency reviews have created an area of both opportunity and contention between the advertiser and the agency. Advertisers have even begun asking agencies pitching an account to offer creative ideas, which can later be used by the advertiser even if another agency gets the business. For example, to update its image, BankAmerica, the third-largest bank in the United States, invited six advertising agencies to compete for its account, valued at $45 to $55 million. BankAmerica chose one agency to do all of its creative work and a second shop that specializes in media buying to decide where to put its advertisements.[12]

Agency shake-ups represent a change in the attitude of the advertiser. It is no longer enough for an agency to have a good, long-term relationship with its clients; to survive, the agency must also document not just *output* but *outcomes*. A client-agency relationship may end if the advertising does not meet client sales expectations. Lowe & Partners/SMS, creators of the "Pardon me, would you pass the Grey Poupon?" ads for Nabisco's high-class mustard, ended its relationship with the manufacturer rather than participate in an agency review. Nabisco said it wanted an advertising breakthrough with measurable results, and the "Pardon me" campaign had not met sales objectives.[13]

Because advertising may have become too narrowly defined by its *output,* agency clients are "increasingly handing over their strategic-thinking chores to marketing consultants."[14] Consultants are perceived as providers of strategic advice, while advertising agencies have been perceived as producers of "clever commercials, amusing animated spokescharacters, and punchy promotions."[15] Despite these perceptions, advertising industry leaders argue that the advertising profession and its agencies do understand the various consumer groups and know how and where to best connect with them—the industry just needs to work on reshaping these perceptions.

The "Total Communications" Agency

In the late 1980s, spending on public relations and other areas of promotion "surged ahead" of traditional ad spending. A philosophical shift among major ad agencies reflects the endurance of Integrated Communications thinking in the business world. Agencies now focus more on campaigns that are low in cost but high on measurable effects by auxiliary use of traditional media and strategic blending of special events, sponsorships, sales promotion, direct marketing, targeted radio, and new media.[16] That branding solutions *involve* but are no longer necessarily *about* advertising has led to the creation of special, integrated units within major agencies (e.g., J. Walter Thompson's Total Solutions Group and DDB Needham's Beyond DDB).

The Merger Boom

From the 1960s through the 1980s, Wells Rich Greene was known as one of Madison Avenue's "most glittering jewels."[17] The agency famous for its creation of ads for Alka-Seltzer ("Plop, plop, fizz, fizz") and Benson & Hedges ("Oh, the disadvantages") has now become famous for the speed of its dissolution. Wells Rich Greene became Wells BDDP when it was purchased for an exorbitant $130 million in 1990. BDDP failed to keep ad legend Mary Wells Lawrence involved after the sale to assure a smooth transition. A series of leadership problems and bad decisions plagued the agency throughout the decade, and Wells' parent company GGT was sold to the giant ad-holding company, Omnicom.

In 1997 "agencies gobbled up one another to the tune of more than $1.25 billion," according to AdMedia.[18] Furthermore, only 6 percent of respondents to an AdMedia survey predicted a merger and acquisition slowdown in the next few years. About 21 percent of those surveyed work for "Goliath" agencies with revenues above $150 million. One force driving the merger boom is the demand of large advertisers for greater marketing efficiency, with their global ad dollars distributed to fewer agencies. Another force has been identified as "Wall Street's hunger for steady earnings growth," which has led such companies as Omnicom and Interpublic Group to acquire smaller firms. Larger is not always better, however. Some Goliaths have been less progressive than smaller agencies in developing such top-expansion interactive marketing areas as direct marketing, multimedia advertising, and database management. Mergers often lead clients to cut down their agency rosters.[19]

Another drawback of the large agency is that clients do not like to share their agency with a competitor. To remedy this problem, Britain's WPP Group created an entirely new company, Intuition Group, out of its J. Walter Thompson agency. The parent company will keep its Unilever and Warner-Lambert accounts while the new company will handle the Bristol-Myers account in product categories that do not currently overlap. All three companies compete as drug and consumer-product makers.[20]

In its own effort to minimize a disadvantage of the large-sized agency, Leo Burnett has decentralized its U.S. operations. Late in 1997, the Chicago agency created seven small agencies—mini agencies—within the large one. The mini agencies, which remain within Burnett's headquarters but are responsible for their own profit and loss, represent the agency's interest in communicating more closely with its clients.[21]

SUMMARY

Advertisers range from small, local businesses to large, multinational corporations. Those hired by advertisers to create and place advertisements are involved in planning, budgeting, coordination, and creative tasks. Many advertisers are the clients of advertising agencies that provide the services of specialists in developing and preparing advertising plans, advertisements, and other promotional tools as well as purchasing advertising time and space. In addition to full-service agencies, which provide research, creative, media, and account management services for their clients, advertisers may choose from other types of agencies—creative boutiques (limited service agencies), health/medical agencies (which specialize in health care), and ethnic agencies (which specialize in communications with specific ethnic groups). Agency compensation, agency reviews, and mergers are areas of controversy.

:60 Spot:
:60 THE MILK MUSTACHE STORY

Campaign Background

Facing three decades of declining consumption, the U.S. milk processors joined forces to reposition milk as a contemporary beverage and get more people drinking milk. Market research was conducted to identify barriers to milk drinking. It revealed several, including health concerns, age appropriateness, and an "uncool" image. To reverse the situation, an integrated marketing campaign of advertising, public relations, and promotion was developed to give milk a more positive and compelling image to spur milk sales.

The cornerstone of the campaign is a series of ads featuring high-profile celebrities sporting their badge of milk enjoyment—a milk mustache. Instead of trying to break through the clutter of beverage advertising on television, the agency made a radical decision to focus the bulk of ad dollars in national magazines and utilize public relations to extend the campaign into other media.

Public Relations Campaign Strategy

Four audiences are targeted in the milk campaign: teens; college-aged men and women; women aged twenty-five to forty-nine; and men aged twenty-five to thirty-four. Ad celebrities are selected based on their appeal to a specific target and their credibility in delivering relevant health messages about milk.

The role of public relations is twofold: (1) to educate and extend audience reach of the print ad campaign, and (2) to partner with leading health professionals and organizations such as the National Osteoporosis Foundation (NOF).

Public Relations Campaign Tactics

In the beginning, the program was tailored to each target market's needs in order to educate about the benefits of milk.

Programs targeted to women were designed to communicate the target's need for constant bone replenishment through intake of calcium-rich milk—specifically, fat-free milk since women tend to be more diet/weight conscious. For example, a "3-A-Day" campaign led by milk-mustache celebrity Florence Griffith-Joyner encouraged women to add an extra glass of fat-free milk to their daily diet to meet the RDA of 1,000 mg. The campaign kicked off with a press conference in Washington, DC, hosted by then Secretary of Health and Human Services Donna Shalala.

For men, programs showcased recent research that proved calcium can reduce hypertension, and positioned milk's high potassium and high protein content over that of the leading sports drink. The campaign also gained endorsement from winning sports teams like the Denver Broncos and Chicago Bulls.

The hard-to-reach teen audience was literally taught the benefits of milk through a classroom program, "Crash Course on Calcium," featuring an MTV-style video with young actors telling teens—in "kid speak"—why they should drink milk. Campaign celebrities and the nation's calcium and health experts endorsed the campaign to add an extra punch.

To capture the attention of the college community, milk mustache photo booths were set up on fifty campuses to get attention and create a venue to teach kids "Calcium 101" and bring the campaign to life. It also gave students an opportunity to see what they look like with a milky upper lip. Winning photos were placed in school newspapers, and one finalist appears in an actual milk ad in *Rolling Stone* magazine.

Evolution Through Integration

At the start of its fourth year, the campaign faced new challenges. Although awareness continued to grow, milk messages were mixed through the popularity of the "Got Milk?" campaign. Consumers often confused the "Where's *Your* Milk Mustache?" campaign with the "Got Milk?" campaign, only remembering the visual of one and the tagline of the other. The two campaigns, running simultaneously, fragmented the efforts and did not affect milk sales as much as in the first year of the campaign. Also, it is a challenge to keep the media's interest in a long-running campaign and maintain the campaign's positive image of milk to consumers.

As a result, integration became a healthy solution for the two campaigns. Thus, the Milk Processor Education Program or MilkPEP ("Where's *Your* Milk Mustache?" campaign) and the National Dairy Council/Dairy Management Incorporated ("Got Milk?") began the integration by replacing the "Where's *Your* Milk Mustache?" tagline with "Got Milk?" on print advertisements. By doing this, they maintain the powerful milk mustache as an icon with the equity of the "Got Milk?" line.

Campaign Results

Research was conducted at the beginning of the program to provide a baseline and, at the end of each year's programming, to evaluate the effort. The results of the first three years indicate a change in attitude toward milk and milk drinking, especially among women, the key target. Overall milk consumption increased 1 percent, the largest increase in a decade, and low-fat milk products showed increases of 4 to 6 percent.

Thus far, the integration has proved to be a success as consumer awareness of the importance of drinking milk in promoting strong, healthy bones continues to grow with the campaign.

Brandee Carlson and Angela Cataldo Tocci
Account Executives
BSMG Marketing Communications
Chicago

Chapter 5

Market Segmentation, Target Marketing, and Product Positioning

Barbie entered the world of market segmentation in 1968 with Mattel's introduction of her African-American friend Christie. Ken gave Barbie lovers a doll of another gender, and Kayla became the first in the Barbie collection to represent "various ethnic groups," including Asians and Hispanics, when she debuted in 2002.[1] Thus Mattell "pioneered diversity marketing in the toy industry." Mattell brought Kayla out after Census 2000 showed a viable market for a doll for racially mixed girls ages three to eight. Baby boomers who grew up with Barbie and have tremendous brand loyalty provide another market. By 2003, to appeal to a lucrative market of aging baby boomers, Mattell brought out Grandma and Grandpa, "a slim pair of semi-gray-haired folks who will *not* be sold separately."[2]

A market segment consists of individuals, groups, or organizations with one or more similar characteristics that cause them to have relatively similar product needs. This market segment can be an ethnic group, a geographical region, or a specific country. To create one of the largest global food brands and secure the company's lead in the multibillion-dollar global snack food market, PepsiCo Inc.'s international snack-food division made a series of marketing and operations changes that ranged from new packaging and advertising campaigns for Lay's potato chips to overhauled manufacturing techniques to higher quality standards for all PepsiCo products sold abroad.

To market the brand overseas, the company more than doubled its advertising spending—to $50 million. To satisfy the new consumers' culturally determined tastes, PepsiCo came up with a shrimp chip for the Korean market, a squid-peanut snack for Southeast Asia, and "cheeseless" Cheetos for China. The company also built plants in tar-

ILLUSTRATION 5.1. Culturally determined tastes. To tap into the lucrative global snack-food market, companies like PepsiCo and Coca-Cola adapt their products and promotional images to meet the wants and needs of overseas consumers. Photo © Dana Hanefeld.

geted countries to assure the quality of its international potato chip products.[3]

According to Pride & Ferrell, marketing is "the process of creating, distributing, promoting, and pricing goods, services, and ideas to facilitate satisfying exchange relationships in a dynamic environment."[4] The Lay's potato chip story exemplifies this definition. Just as Mattell created a diversity of dolls for a diverse market, PepsiCo created different flavors of potato chips for its foreign markets (see Illustration 5.1). Advertising can't do it all in attracting consumers to buy a product.

MARKET SEGMENTATION

Marketing and advertising people constantly scan the marketplace to see what needs and wants various consumer groups have and how they might be better satisfied. One of the techniques they use is market segmentation. PepsiCo Inc. realized that the overseas snack business brings in more than $3 billion in annual sales and, in the long term, would be a very important business venture for the company. It also realized that not all consumers have the same tastes, especially in the global markets. PepsiCo went on to develop a paprika-flavored chip for Poland and Hungary. The company saw each country as a different market and offered a different product to each different country, or market segment.

The purpose of using market segmentation is to enable a marketer to design a marketing mix that more precisely matches the needs of consumers in a selected market segment. In the United States, target marketing of different ethnic groups is now common practice, as the example of Barbie illustrates. Toyota designed a campaign specifically for the African-American market and launched it in February for Black History Month. A print ad showed a car's blueprint with the headline, "There's a part of black history in every automobile." The text recognized "that African American automotive inventors have always been a big part of our success." The blueprint labeled car parts credited to African-American inventors, e.g., turn signal invented by Richard B. Spikes, 1913, and two-cycle internal combustion engine invented by Frederick M. Jones, 1950. The ad's text mentioned Toyota's sponsorship of the Los Angeles Urban League Automotive

Training Center and explained the reason for the sponsorship: "Because our past is the blueprint for our future."

A marketer using segmentation to reach a market can choose one or several methods. As Table 5.1 shows, the segmentation methods for a consumer market can be grouped into four categories: demographic, geographic, behavioristic, and psychographic. For the industrial market, segmentation methods can be grouped into three categories: geographic, type of organization, and product use.

Methods for Segmenting the Consumer Market

Demographic Segmentation

Demographic segmentation involves dividing the market on the basis of demographic variables such as age, sex, family size, stage of family life cycle, income, occupation, religion, race, and nationality (see Illustration 5.2). Marketers rely on these demographic characteristics because they are often closely linked to customers' needs and purchasing behavior and can be readily measured. Time Inc. is one of several publishers that has expanded its child-oriented titles. Such publications have included *Time for Kids,* aimed at high school students, and *Sports Illustrated for Kids.* ABC Radio Networks

TABLE 5.1. Segmenting consumer and industrial markets.

Methods	Variables
Consumer markets	
Demographic	Age, sex, family size, stage of family life cycle, income, education, occupation, religion, race, nationality
Geographic	Region, population size, density, climate
Behavioristic	Benefits sought, volume usage, brand loyalty
Psychographic	Lifestyle, personality
Industrial Markets	
Geographic	Location
Type of organization	SIC Code/NAICS
Product use	Where used, how used

THE GLOBAL PERSPECTIVE:
A WEEK IN MARKETING

In just one week in January 2004 *Advertising Age* reported on a number of international campaigns that involved market segmentation and product positioning. The German manufacturer of Volkswagen and Audi pitched its cars in Spain with an $83 million media buying account. Two UK publishers tried to differentiate their new weekly "lad titles" to a marketing segment of males sixteen to thirty years old.[a] Chinese home appliance manufacturer Guangdong Midea sought to position its products against the Japanese Panasonic brand and rival Chinese brands.

In the same week, Western marketers sought to tie into the Chinese New Year festivities. In targeting the Chinese segment, Western advertisers need to be aware of China's cultural norms, according to "The Rules of the Game," an article written by Normandy Madden, dateline Hong Kong.[b] Madden urged "warm, sincere and courteous ads" for this special celebration, "steering clear of humor." Societal "taboos become stronger at this time of the year, so advertisers should be especially sensitive to images that could convey bad luck," avoid "anything related to death," and develop a color scheme utilizing red not white (white signifies death in Chinese culture).

In the process of positioning a product, marketers and advertisers have to be aware of cultural norms and taboos lest they insult the segment they are trying to engage.

[a]"The World," *Advertising Age,* January 12, 2004, p. 14.
[b]*Advertising Age,* p. 11.

launched its first Radio Disney outlets on AM stations in four U.S. city test markets in 1996. The twenty-four-hour children's station format included programs such as *ESPN for Kids* and *ABC News for Kids.* Advertisers have earmarked more dollars for Hispanic advertising in the United States in recent years, especially in major markets such as Los Angeles, New York, and Miami.

Geographic Segmentation

Geographic variables such as region, population size, density, and climate also influence consumer product needs. People in one region of the country—or the world—have needs and purchasing behavior that differ from people in other regions. For instance, a large market for suntan lotion exists year-round in Florida, but only seasonally in

ILLUSTRATION 5.2. Diversity. This Rapp Collins Worldwide/Chicago print ad for Lions Clubs International was part of a campaign that used images of people with different ethnic backgrounds and ages to show that the organization helps all kinds of people, all around the world.

northern states. Internationally, marketers compare the needs and preferences of various geographic segments in order to look for differences. Marketers have noted post-Soviet Central Asia as an attractive source of sales growth. Multinational corporations such as Coca-Cola Co. and Procter & Gamble built Central Asian plants and introduced their brands to 55 million people in this area, previously occupied by the Soviet Union, who had never heard of these brands or product categories before. In 2004 Coca-Cola "consolidated its estimated $10 million media planning and buying business in Hong Kong" and put $30 million into media buying for mainland China.[5]

Behavioristic Segmentation

Firms can divide a market into groups according to the benefits they seek, volume usage of the product, and brand loyalty. As an example, time is an important commodity for working mothers. Thus, this group seeks such product benefits as ease of use in appliances and quick preparation in microwavable meals. Parents comprise a multibillion dollar market. Recognizing that working mothers seek quick, nutritional meals for their children, Boston Market introduced its first-ever "kids' meals" with ads focusing on the meals' wholesomeness.

Psychographic Segmentation

Dividing the market on the basis of lifestyle and/or personality is referred to as psychographic segmentation. The determination of lifestyles is usually based on an analysis of the activities, interests, and opinions (AIOs) of the consumers. One of the more popular studies of lifestyle is conducted by the Stanford Research Institute's Value and Lifestyle Program (VALS). The VALS program places American consumers in three broad groups: outer-directed, inner-directed, and need-driven consumers. The VALS studies have been used to select advertising media and determine advertising content. A VALS 2 classification categorizes consumers into five basic lifestyle groups—strugglers, action oriented, status oriented, principle oriented, and actualizers.

SRI International also conducted psychographic studies of the Japanese market; broader-scope studies have been conducted by such global advertising agencies as D'arcy Massius Benton & Bowles (DMB&B) and Young & Rubicam (Y&R).[6]

Methods for Segmenting the Industrial Market

Geographic Segmentation

In some cases, marketers find it beneficial to segment an industrial market geographically. Like those who segment geographically in consumer markets, industrial firms can concentrate their efforts on areas with high population growth rates. Or due to differences in the climate and needs of markets in various countries, companies might target countries whose needs best fit into the company's product lines.

Type of Organization

Another way to segment industrial markets is by type of organization. For almost seventy years in the United States, the Department of Commerce used the Standard Industrial Classification (SIC) system to segment industrial markets. These codes, used by business-to-business marketers, were based on broad industry categories. The North American Free Trade Agreement (NAFTA) outdated this system in 1994; it was subsequently replaced by the North American Industry Classification System (NAICS). The new industry-wide classification system was "designed as the index for statistical reporting of all economic activities of the U.S., Canada, and Mexico." The index identifies NAICS industries by a six-digit rather than the SIC four-digit code.[7]

Product Use

The way an organization will use a particular product is another basis for segmenting industrial markets. Basic raw materials, in particular, may be used in numerous ways. How an organization uses products affects the types and amounts of products purchased and business purchasing procedures. Computers, for example, can be used at an advertising agency for designing graphics or used in a university environment for word processing or accounting purposes. A computer producer may segment the computer market by types of use because companies' needs for computers depend on the purpose for which computer products are purchased.

TARGET MARKETING

Once marketers group consumers or possible product users by shared characteristics (demographic, geographic, or other variables), they can proceed to the next step: target marketing. The way this is accomplished determines the content, design, and implementation of the company's advertising.

Selecting the appropriate target market(s) is the key to implementing a successful marketing strategy and important to a company's survival. Failure to appropriately target can lead to low sales, high costs, and severe financial losses. A careful target market analysis places an organization in a better position to serve customers' needs and to achieve its own objectives. For instance, Meredith Corp., publisher of *Ladies' Home Journal* and *Better Homes and Gardens,* spotted a market for a new fashion, beauty, and health magazine targeted to women ages forty to sixty-four. Meredith reasoned that, by 2012, this would be the largest, richest group of females. The publisher also determined that this group has felt "abandoned and unrepresented by glamourous publications such as *Vogue, Harper's Bazaar,* and *Elle,*" yet is extremely interested in beauty and health topics.[8] In this case, the company created a product which would be highly appropriate for a specific target market when it launched *More* magazine in September 1998.

Once a company defines its target market, it knows exactly where to focus its attention and resources. It can shape the product concept (e.g., special features for its product); establish proper pricing; determine the need for location of stores; and prepare the most convincing advertising messages. In other words, the marketing mix can be aimed at making the product attractive and accessible at the right time and place to the target market. When Sears, Roebuck & Company noticed that almost a fifth of its stores had a strong Hispanic customer base, the company began airing ads on *Sabado Gigante,* a four-hour Saturday night show which reaches 20 percent of the U.S. Hispanic population. Colgate-Palmolive Co. has also advertised on the show with a targeted commercial in which the audience sang an upbeat

ETHICS TRACK:
MARKETING COSMETIC SURGERY

Cosmetic surgery procedures increased a staggering 198 percent from 1992 to 2000, and it seems that more and more of these procedures are being performed not only by qualified physicians but also by plastic surgery quacks.

According to the American Society of Plastic Surgeons (ASPS) Web site, the number of liposuctions, breast augmentations, and eyelid surgeries had increased 386, 476, and 190 percent, respectively, so it is easy to see why cosmetic surgery has become big business and why untrained physicians might pick up the scalpel in an effort to line their pockets. It is dangerous if these surgeries are not performed by qualified physicians. In 2003, New York State prosecutors brought charges against a couple impersonating physicians who had been injecting patients with an illegal drug they falsely portrayed as BOTOX.

N. David Saddawi, MD, FACS, FICS, a practicing plastic surgeon in South Bend, Indiana, believes that physicians not certified by the American Board of Plastic Surgery are performing procedures outside of their expertise solely for economic payback. "Doctors are affected by commercialism today," he said.

When it comes to finding a competent surgeon, Saddawi said that it is up to patients to do their homework on the surgeon, and it is vital that they know as much about surgeons and their work as possible. "Prudent behavior is for consumers to look into the surgeon and to then make informed choices and to be sure they know what they are getting into before they jump in."

Saddawi has been in practice for three decades. Despite the impression given by reality television shows such as *Extreme Makeover* and *The Swan,* Saddawi by no means performs surgery on every consultation he has. He states that out of 100 consultations he performs about 40 procedures. The major issue that Saddawi has with the increase in cosmetic surgery advertising is that "some doctors are concerned with quantity over quality and that can lead to problems very quickly." When doctors are concerned with economic issues, they may sacrifice their ethics and morals.

The best advice Saddawi can offer consumers is to talk with the doctor's former patients, know that doctors cannot be perfect, and realize that doctors have their own specializations. He says, "Make sure that you seek a second opinion, be knowledgeable about the experience the surgeon has, and be sure there is chemistry between you and the surgeon."[a]

In the end, when it comes to cosmetic surgery, consumer beware!

Sara Mahoney

---

[a]<www.plasticsurgery.org>.

tune while a hip-swinging company spokeswoman extolled the virtues of Colgate Tartar Control toothpaste in Spanish (for a print example, see Illustration 5.3).[9] Other companies, such as Nike, have also joined the trend toward spending more on niche programming. Some advertisers contend that network television "just doesn't deliver the way it used to," but it might be more accurate to say that it's just more difficult to meet today's target marketing goals using the mass media.[10]

A particularly hard group to successfully market to has been "Generation X." This group, also referred to as "baby busters" or "twentysomethings," is usually defined as people born between 1965 and 1981 and makes up about 18 percent of the U.S. population.[11] Because this group grew up in front of a television set, it is unusually media savvy and especially cynical about advertising. Members of Generation X characteristically value honesty and are unmoved by slick, glitzy ad campaigns. A new genre of advertising was been created to embrace Generation X's skepticism—the "antiadvertisement advertisement."[12] For instance, Coca-Cola's Sprite campaign carried the tagline, "Image is nothing. Thirst is everything. Obey your thirst." One spot in the campaign used a voice-over which declared, "Trust your taste buds—not commercials."

The latest marketing challenge is "Generation Y." This group, 68 million strong, was born between 1981 and 1995 and represents "the largest demographic bulge since that of their baby boomer parents."[13] This group has "whimsical" tastes and, like Generation X, is media savvy and "immune to most sales pitches."[14] What they don't want to see are baby boomers using the products advertised to them.

The habits of the younger generations have made U.S. senior citizens a lucrative market for the music industry. While young people increasingly pirate their music through illegal Web site downloading and CD burners, senior citizens continue to pay for their CDs. Because of this, performers such as Josh Groban and Harry Connick Jr., who appeal to all age groups, have been able to rise quickly to the top of the industry.

Internationally, those sixty-five and older have become an important target market for advertisers in the twenty-first century. Table 5.2 shows that, in some countries, senior citizens will eventually constitute almost a third of the population. One of the effects of the trend toward generational target marketing has been that fewer ad campaigns

NUEVA
Colgate Total

Protege tu boca aún cuando no te estás cepillando.

¡La nueva COLGATE TOTAL, con su avanzada fórmula de acción prolongada sigue trabajando después de cepillarte y te ayuda a proteger tu boca contra las caries, el sarro, la placa, la gingivitis y el mal aliento, hasta por doce horas! Colgate Total es una pasta tan avanzada que sigue trabajando entre cepilladas mientras te diviertes, mientras trabajas y hasta cuando duermes. ¡Hora tras hora tras hora!

NEW   HELPS PREVENT CAVITIES · GINGIVITIS · PLAQUE
Colgate Total
ANTICAVITY FLUORIDE AND   ANTIGINGIVITIS TOOTHPASTE
LONG LASTING FRESH BREATH PROTECTION · FIGHTS TARTAR

La cepillada tan avanzada que trabaja entre cepilladas.

ILLUSTRATION 5.3. Target market ad. Colgate has been aggressive in targeting the growing U.S. Hispanic market by printing ads in Spanish. Reproduced with permission of Colgate-Palmolive Company.

TABLE 5.2. Senior population growth in the top six world economies (in percent).

Country	1990	2010 (projected)	2030 (projected)
Italy	15	21	28
Germany	15	20	28
Japan	12	21	26
United Kingdom	16	17	23
France	14	16	23
United States	13	14	22

Source: Derived from Anne R. Carey and Elys A. McLean, "Aging Industrial Societies," *USA Today,* August 12, 1998, p. A1.

can reach all the income levels within these demographics. *USA Today* reviewed more than sixty campaigns in its "Ad Track" feature to determine how these campaigns scored with various income groups. The newspaper's analysis suggests that "the link between income and ad tastes can often determine a campaign's success."[15] Two commercials spanned all age and income levels to rank among the 1990s' most popular—the Budweiser Lizard campaign and the Taco Bell Chihuahua. Although other ads' popularity differed among age groups, the Budweiser and Taco Bell spots were unusually successful with "runaway hits" in all categories. For instance, while young consumers liked Levi's Wide Leg Jeans ads, which featured the 1970s nostalgia of Partridge Family tunes, older consumers preferred the sentimental, multigenerational family pitch of Hallmark Cards.[16]

Once the target market has been selected, a company must find a way to fit the product to the selected market and to sell the product to that market. This is no small feat. Product positioning is one method marketers use to sell the product by setting it apart from competitors.

PRODUCT POSITIONING

Product positioning has been defined as "the art and science of fitting the product or service to one or more segments of the broad market in such a way as to set it meaningfully apart from competition."[17]

Clearly, product positioning refers to the decisions and activities intended to create and maintain a certain concept of the company's product, relative to competitors' brands, in consumers' minds. For instance, Volvo employed a positioning strategy founded on safety. The company used the strategy whenever it advertised in the media, whether in print or on television. Chief Auto Parts Stores, a top-ranked U.S. retailer in aftermarket auto parts, steered away from everyday low pricing and repositioned itself around quality with a $3 million campaign.[18] Marketers sometimes analyze product positions by developing perceptual maps. Perceptual maps are created by questioning a sample of consumers regarding their perceptions of products, brands, and organizations with respect to two or more dimensions.

Product differentiation is the competitive strategy of creating a product difference that appeals to the preferences of a distinct market segment. In advertising, nothing is more important than informing prospects how your product is different. The idea of consumer perception is critically important in differentiating products because the differences between products can be either real or perceived. Real differences might include features, price, or quality. Differences created by perceptions are typically based on a product's image. When an ad shows Michael Jordan eating Wheaties, the consumer may assume that eating Wheaties contributes to athletic performance whereas consuming other cereals does not. Whether a teenager believes a clothing label is "cool" or "uncool" depends not so much on the product as on the consumers' perception of that product. Celebrities influence what consumers see as "cool" or "hot" (see Table 5.3).

Whether the differences between products are real or extrinsic to the product or service, all marketers/advertisers take steps to ensure that these differences do exist. Coca-Cola has long positioned itself as the all-American choice, while Pepsi has attempted to portray itself as "hip" and "cool" to make Coke seem "dull."[19] However, Pepsi targeted too narrowly with its "Generation Next" tagline, designed to appeal to the emotions of a very specific market segment—that tagline was dropped.

Product positioning is a customer's perception of a product's attributes relative to those of competitive brands. To position a new product or reposition an existing one, marketers need to know how consumers or industrial buyers in its target market perceive products in that category.

TABLE 5.3. Most wanted celebrity-driven products.

Product	Who made it "hot"
Miravision	Demi Moore and Ashton Kutcher
UGG boots	Oprah Winfrey and Sarah Jessica Parker
Desperate Housewives	Nicolette Sheridan on commercial during *Monday Night Football*
Monday Night Football	Madden franchise
Maurice Malone denims	Paris Hilton and Nicole Richie
Revlon makeup	Halle Berry

Source: Some of the above was adapted from "10 Must-Have Products for 2004," *Advertising Age,* December 22, 2003, p. 12; "10 Must-Have Products for 2005," *Advertising Age,* December 20, 2004, p. 8; "10 People to Watch in 2005," *Advertising Age,* December 20, 2004, p. 12; and Cotton Timberlake and Shobhana Chandra, "Revlon Profit First in More Than Six Years," *USA Today,* March 9, 2005, p. 6B.

Advertisers often use comparative advertising to claim superiority to competitors in some aspect (see Chapter 3 for a discussion of the legal issues in comparative advertising). Avis Rent-A-Car's positioning campaign is probably the most famous example. When Avis "was a small force in the market compared to category leader Hertz," Avis' tagline, "We're only number two. We try harder," made it a major contender in the field.[20] Such advertisements are legal so long as the comparison is truthful. In addition to being truthful, comparative advertisements must also make the comparison in terms of some objectively measurable characteristic of a product or service. For example, an American Express ad campaign positioned its travel service with this print ad copy: "When the grind gets to be too much, American Express has the world's largest travel agency to get you out of here. Not to mention over 1,700 travel service locations worldwide to help you while you're there." In fact, American Express did operate the world's largest travel agency and did have 1,700 worldwide offices.

SUMMARY

A company must be able to locate possible customers, wherever they are, and then be able to understand and communicate with them. Marketing, the process of creating, distributing, promoting, and pricing goods, services, and ideas to facilitate satisfying exchange relationships, is the answer. Advertising alone cannot do it all. The consumer market segmentation process differs from the segmentation process for the industrial market, but each market must be segmented if a company's advertising is to be successful. Once a target market has been segmented, advertising must position and differentiate the product or service from its competitors.

:30 Spot:
"Paws-itively Hilarious"

I started at Edelman Public Relations Worldwide in July and was promoted to account executive in April. I never knew life at age twenty-two could be so hectic!

So, you ask, what do I do? You better be sitting down for what I am about to tell you. I am currently going across the country looking for North America's best singing pet! Yep, you read right—singing pets. If you have seen the commercials for Advantage flea control for cats and dogs, then you might have an idea of what I am talking about. Cats and dogs are so happy to be flea free, they are literally singing the praises of Advantage!

I do the event planning and media relations for Advantage—which is made by Bayer's animal health group. Last year we generated over 300 million media impressions with our program, increased sales, and had superior placements on *The Tonight Show with Jay Leno, Regis and Kathie Lee,* and many other syndicated shows. People *love* the cute animals and are already asking us when our 1998 winner will be announced! We even got a placement on the front page of *The Wall Street Journal.* If you are interested in checking out what these singing cats and dogs are all about, you can visit our Web site at <www.nofleas.com> or call our help line at (800) NOFLEAS. It is "paws-itively" hilarious!

I also had the honor of representing Taco Bell Home Originals and Kraft Foods, Inc. as a six-foot dancing Taco. I traveled the East Coast for a week to launch the new taco kits that are in grocery stores. We appeared on *The Today Show* and several local market television stations teaching the anchors the "Two-Step Taco"—two steps to the left, two steps to the right, and you do the taco! The fun never ends for me.

I never knew the "real" world would be so adventurous.

Diane Grant
Account Executive
Edelman Public Relations Worldwide
Chicago, Illinois

Chapter 6

Buyer Behavior and Advertising

Japanese consumers weren't supposed to want refrigerators like the big General Electric model in Hiroshi and Yukie Tanaka's living room. The refrigerator's journey to the Tanakas' Yokohama apartment from a GE factory in Kentucky broke all the rules: that exporters must tailor their products to Japanese tastes; foreigners must find Japanese partners to negotiate the distribution system; big American home appliances will not sell in Japan at any price. For years, many U.S. marketers tried hard to tap into the Japanese market without much success. But in the mid-1990s, more Japanese women worked after marriage and could not shop for food daily as their mothers had. Big, inexpensive, two-door refrigerators suddenly made sense.[1]

Consumers' needs and wants are constantly changing. To be successful, marketers need to make considerable effort to determine their customers' current needs. In this way, they may get a better grasp of their customers' buying behavior, as GE did when it defied convention and offered American refrigerators to the Japanese market. Many foreign manufacturers, makers of everything from computers to cars, have done well by changing products to suit Japanese tastes. However, American marketers have come to realize that economic and social factors continue to change Japanese consumers' needs.

Understanding consumers' product needs has become increasingly important in the twenty-first century. Already Levi Strauss has employed computer technology to custom fit women's jeans with its Personal Pair Program. Infrared scanners precisely measure the customer's foot in Custom Foot stores. A Japanese bicycle manufacturer uses the customer's instep measurement to construct a made-to-fit bicycle. Burger King has long been savvy to the consumer appeal of customized products and messages with its enduring tagline, "Have it your way." The tagline, first used in the early 1970s, made a surprise comeback with a 2004 Crispin Porter & Bogusky ad campaign.

ILLUSTRATION 6.1. Customized products and messages. When your target market is a discerning, theater-going segment of the public, advertising that is too "commercial" might offend. This print ad for Stratford Festival gift certificates uses the old-fashioned, nostalgic image of Feste the holiday bear to appeal to a consumer more interested in the artistic than the mass-produced Christmas gift. The text stresses the customized features of this gift choice with the wording "something for everyone" and "Any way you package them . . ." Illustration and design by Karen Garratt, headline and copy by the Stratford Festival Marketing Department, Stratford, Ontario, Canada.

Marketing involves developing and managing a product that will satisfy certain needs. It also focuses on making the product available in the right place and at a price that is acceptable to customers. By knowing customers' buying behaviors, marketers can create marketing mixes that satisfy customers and lead to success in the marketplace. GE found that price was a deciding factor for Japanese consumers in the market for a refrigerator. The company then emphasized that its refrigerators cost half the price of a Japanese model. Constant research on buyer behavior and the factors influencing buying behavior is definitely important for marketers of any products. Chapter 7 will focus on the important topic of research methods.

The goal of advertising is to persuade the consumer to do something, usually to purchase a product. If advertising is to attract and communicate to audiences in a way that produces this desired result, advertisers must first understand their audiences. They must acquaint themselves with consumers' ways of thinking, with those factors that motivate them, and with the environment in which they live (see Illustration 6.1).

In this chapter, we will first examine the buyer decision-making process as it goes through the various stages of problem solving. We will discuss what occurs at each stage and how advertising and promotion can be used to influence buyer decision making. We will also examine the influences of various personal (such as demographic) and psychological factors (such as perception, motivation, attitudes, lifestyle, and personality) on the buyer decision process as well as the influence of external influences (such as social factors). The chapter will finally take a look at the importance of understanding consumer behavior.

THE BUYER DECISION PROCESS

All customers can be split into two general groups: business and consumer buyers. The business market consists of manufacturers, resellers, governments, and nonprofit institutions. The consumer market is made up of individuals and households who buy goods and services for personal use. The ways in which the two groups respond to advertising and make purchase decisions are similar in many respects but are quite different in others.[2]

THE GLOBAL PERSPECTIVE:
WE CAN CREATE IT, BUT WE CAN'T SHOW IT

Madonna and Britney Spears share a kiss at a televised awards presentation. A stepfather and his daughter talk openly about their incestuous relationship on the *Jerry Springer* show. Part of the American character seems to be moral contradictions. Americans may tolerate—and even enjoy—salacious confessions on television talk shows and turn on the nightly news to hear about politicians' sexual sins, but when it comes to advertising, they are conservative and critical. An *Advertising Age* headline called it "The New Puritanism."[a]

To promote a new line of self-tanning lotion, The Body Shop displayed posters in its stores that showed a man with a bottle of the lotion tucked inside the front of his bathing suit. The words "Fake it!" spanned the poster.[b] The man pictured in the poster was generously exposed, but the poster itself had a short exposure time in the United States. The London-based international cosmetics retailer had to remove the image that offended American men from its U.S. shops.

A number of commercials created by U.S. agencies and honored at the Cannes International Advertising Festival could never air in the United States.[c] For example, a popular BBDO/Canada beer commercial featured two women kissing, but the spot was considered too racy to be aired or printed at home. American agencies can dish up the sexy stuff that generates sales overseas, but they can't show it in their own country.

Culture is an integrated pattern of behavior shared by people in a society. Some believe that the mainstream American attitude toward sexual explicity in advertising derives from the social importance of traditional family values. A spokesperson for the American Family Association expressed the view that there's too much that's sexually explicit in American advertising already. The number of single-parent and other nontraditional households has been increasing (single-person households increased from 10.9 percent in 1950 to 26.3 percent in 2002), and American society has changed "from the days of *Donna Reed* to the 1960s counterculture. The Pill. Feminism . . . the roaring '90s."[d] Yet Americans still consider a family with mother, father, and children to be the norm.

A survey published in the *American Journal of Public Health* indicated that, while Americans surveyed were more critical of premarital and extramarital sex than their British counterparts, higher percentages of Americans reported having multiple sexual partners—13 percent of American men had twenty-one or more partners over a lifetime. On the other hand, a lucrative segment of American society—younger, more sophisticated consumers—reject the conservatism that has pressured the Federal Communications Commission (FCC) and TV networks. They opt "for cable, satellite radio, the Internet, pay-per-view," sending "hundreds of millions of ad dollars" from broadcast to cable.[e] This educated population segment desires luxury brands and entertainment to match their high standards. And they aren't squeamish about sex.

U.S. marketers sensitive to segmented consumer values considered parallel G- and R-rated campaigns after Janet Jackson rocked mainstream America at the 2004 Super Bowl. The House of Representatives raised the indecency fine from $27,500 to $500,000, and the Clean Airways Act had already addressed what conservatives viewed as the FCC's laxity. The act banned specific words from being uttered on broadcast channels.

In the United States, marketers think twice about "edgy" advertisements that might work abroad but raise eyebrows at home.

[a]Eric Gillin and Greg Lindsay, "The New Puritanism," April 5, 2004, p. 1.
[b]Craig Wilson, "Tanning Lotion Ad Display Leaves Some People Burning," *USA Today,* May 30, 1997, p. D1.
[c]Shannon Reilly and Sam Ward, "One-Person Households Rising," *USA Today,* December 30, 2003, p. A1; and Melanie Wells and Dottie Enrico, "U.S. Admakers Cover It Up; Others Don't Give a Fig Leaf," *USA Today,* June 27, 1997, p. B1.
[d]Ann Oldenburg, "The Family Unit Changes," *USA Today,* February 10, 2004, p. 5A.
[e]Gillin and Lindsay.

The buying decision process for both business and consumer markets is viewed as a series of stages through which the buyer passes in purchasing a product or service. The process includes five stages: need recognition, information search, alternative evaluation, purchase, and postpurchase evaluation.

Need Recognition

A buyer's first step toward a purchase decision is recognizing a need, which means that the buyer perceives a discrepancy between an actual state and a desired state. This discrepancy can be as simple as thirst for a drink or realizing that a company needs a faster computer to process its orders. At this stage of the decision-making process, the advertiser can try to influence buyers by helping them recognize needs that the advertiser's products can satisfy.

Information Search

When buyers have identified a need, they may look for information about how to satisfy that need. This information search is both internal and external, and the buyer's memory can be a key aspect of the process. If a buyer has satisfied a similar need in the past, he or she is likely to start the search for information by recalling how that need was satisfied. Often the buyer consults with other people in his or her reference group (e.g., relatives and friends). Buyers also acquire information from marketers through advertisements, packages, salespeople, and the like.

Alternative Evaluation

Based on the information gathered, the buyer identifies and evaluates ways to meet his, her, or a company's need, looking for the best choice in terms of quality, price, delivery time, and other factors deemed important. In this stage, the rational and emotional appeals of advertising play an important role.

Purchase

After considering the possible options, the buyer makes a purchase decision. This step includes deciding whether to buy and, if so, what to buy, where to buy, and when to buy. With large purchases in the business market, the buyer and seller must also work out delivery time, payment terms, installation, and so forth. At this stage, advertising continues to play an important role to prevent the buyer from changing his or her mind.

Postpurchase Evaluation

After buying a product, customers formally or informally evaluate the outcome of the purchase. Although consumers tend to be much less formal with their evaluations in that they do not have set criteria to properly evaluate their purchases, organizational customers usually use standardized performance criteria to evaluate key suppliers.

In the case of large-ticket items, a common response is for the consumer to have doubts about the choice after the purchase. This feeling is called cognitive dissonance—a state of anxiety brought on by the difficulty of choosing from among several alternatives. Advertising can help buyers overcome dissonance if it continues to reinforce the reasons for making a particular choice.

FACTORS INFLUENCING THE BUSINESS MARKET

Relatively few business purchase decisions are made by just one person; mostly, they are made through a buying center. These persons include the user, influencer, decision maker, gatekeeper (e.g., secretary), and purchaser. Identifying the roles in a buying center is a key step in planning effective advertising because people in the various buying center roles have different information needs and purchase criteria.

The user: Users are the people in the organization who actually use the product.

The influencer: Influencers are people who affect the buying decisions. For example, an engineer may help to develop product specifications.

Decision makers: These are the people who actually choose the products.

Gatekeepers: Those in the organization who control the flow of information into the buyer center are called the gatekeepers. Such people may include secretarial and technical personnel.

Purchasers: The authority and responsibility to select suppliers and negotiate purchase terms resides in the person whose title is the purchaser or, in some cases, director of purchasing.

Derived Demand

Of all the differences between consumer and business buyer behavior, perhaps the most important is the idea of derived demand, which means that the demand for industrial products derives from the demand for consumer products. When consumer demand for a product changes, a wave is set in motion affecting demand for all firms involved in the production of that consumer product. A tire manufacturing company may need to stimulate demand for cars in its advertisements so the company can sell tires to the automobile manufacturers.

Supplier Selection

Supplier selection is often a formal process among business buyers, as customers try to find the best suppliers for each type of product they need. Many companies have "approved supplier" lists, and employees are prohibited from purchasing goods or services from anyone not on the list. This encourages advertisers to convince potential customers (e.g., members in the buying center) that they are capable and reliable sources of products. In turn, the buying organization may invite suppliers to submit formal proposals for buyers' purchasing evaluation purposes.[3]

Business-to-Business (B2B) Advertisements

Businesses may advertise services or goods (products). Of the two, advertising for services lends itself more to the use of emotional appeals in order to develop a "service personality."[4] However, a research study conducted by Turley and Kelley found that only 4.4 percent of service ads studied employed emotional appeals. This reveals that "emotional appeals are rare in the business-to-business context," even where they might be expected—in service ads. Business-to-business advertising generally employs rational appeals, perhaps because business buyers "are believed to use a more rational decision-making process than final consumers."[5]

FACTORS INFLUENCING
THE CONSUMER MARKET

Unlike the buying decision process in business markets, which is influenced by buying center personnel or other factors (e.g., derived demand and company policy), the buying decision process in the consumer market is mostly influenced by personal, psychological, and social factors.

Personal Factors

Personal factors are those that are unique to a particular person. Numerous personal factors influence purchasing decisions. Demographic factors are individual characteristics, such as age, gender, educational level, occupation, and income. Given such differences, people tend to make different choices regarding their uses of a car, their choices of media, and their patterns of spending. For example, researchers have discovered that, while red violet is a popular fashion

ETHICS TRACK:
MARKETING TO MEN

Special K's classic commercial spoke to women who worry about looking fat with the tagline, "Men don't obsess about these things: reshape your attitude." However, feminists fear that men do, in fact, worry about "these things." Men have sought to be physically transformed by reality shows such as *Extreme Makeover, Queer Eye for the Straight Guy,* and MTV's *I Want a Famous Face.* These shows communicate the idea that hair on a man's chest is gross, having a sprayed-on tan is better than naturally white skin, and men's wardrobes must be color coordinated and fashionable. As women already know, that's a lot of pressure.

According to the American Society of Plastic Surgeons, almost half a million eighteen- to twenty-four-year-olds fed the $7 billion-a-year plastic surgery industry in 2001. That demographic accounts for about 30 percent of plastic surgeries. Of 8.3 million surgical and nonsurgical cosmetic procedures performed in 2003, men accounted for 1.1 million of those procedures. Teenaged twins Mike and Matt Schlep, featured on *I Want a Famous Face,* declared that they were ugly and needed surgery to look like Brad Pitt. They talked about the capacity of a surgical makeover to bring personal happiness now and their intentions, later in life, to have brow lifts and face-lifts.

A 2004 issue of *GQ* featured makeup for macho men in hard hats, while ads for Viagra and Levitra implied that outward physical appearance is not the only concern men should have. Celebrities from politician Bob Dole to football coach Mike Ditka have pitched drugs that offer a cure for "erectile dysfunction." Viagra and Levitra's 2004 advertising budgets reached $50 million each.[a] A Jaguar campaign appealed to males with the tagline, "Born to perform."

A new male group, especially concerned about image and, thus, susceptible to advertising, has emerged—the "metrosexual," a straight urban man in touch with his feminine side. He may shop as much as his girlfriend, take as long to dress for a date, and have as many shoes. He is willing to pay for his impeccable fashion sense, whether it be Diesel jeans or stylish smokes. Some say advertising has shaped metrosexuals' expensive tastes. Designer Tom Ford, worried about the pressure on men to be what they are not, chose a hairy model for his M7 ads "because he wanted a man who hadn't tweezered and shaved every hair on his chest," going for a natural male image.[b] And isn't that what women have wanted for so long—a natural, easy-to-live-with image?

· Feminist writer Astrid Henry believes ads that play on gender stereotyping are not beneficial to men or women: "House cleaning products are still marketed to women because men are portrayed as dumb, goofy, and can't cook." Advertising "can profit from the insecurities of both sexes equally." Does advertising pressure women to look like size one models (or worse, the now-popular size zero)? The days of buying the same skirt that Britney Spears is wearing are gone, and buying a body that looks like hers is here. Some blame the fitness culture, advertising in general, or youth-driven consumerism. In February 2004 CNN broadcast Melissa Rivers' satellite media tour designed to convince women that their partners needed makeovers (see more about the Brawny makeover competition in Chapter 17).

Consider the part gender should play in understanding consumers. Review the five stages of the buying decision process. Which stages should concern advertisers and make them aware of appropriate and inappropriate ways to pitch products and services to both women and men? Does advertising place unrealistic pressure on both men and women to sell products, or does advertising simply reflect society's views?

Mary Beth Broviak
Lauren Siegel

[a]Theresa Howard, "Viagra Faces Competition," and "Levitra Ads Challenge Viagra, but Viewers Aren't Impressed," *USA Today,* January 26, 2004, pp. 5B, 8B.
[b]"Ads Show Men Hairy and Proud of It," *The South Bend Tribune,* February 16, 2003, p. F5.

color with women, men are indifferent to the color. If an advertiser determines that a product is most likely to appeal to members of certain groups, a marketing mix can be developed that takes these differences into account.

Psychological Factors

Psychological factors operating within individuals partly determine people's general behavior and thus influence their purchasing behavior. Each individual consumer is influenced by his or her perception, motives, attitudes, and personality (see Illustration 6.2).

Perception

One reason that consumers respond differently to the same situations is that they perceive those situations differently. Perception refers to the way people gather and record information. Although marketers cannot control people's perceptions, they often try to influence them. In recent years, advertisers have found that men perceive athletes as "perfect," a quality to which most men aspire. In response to

ILLUSTRATION 6.2. Boss. Advertisements play on gender stereotypes, as does this signage placed in a public square in Fuengirola, Spain. The men of the Costa del Sol are encouraged to fulfill their macho image in a Hugo Boss blazer.

this perception, advertisers have been featuring more male athletes, rather than male entertainers, in their ads.[6]

The efficacy of subliminal messages, embedded material in advertising designed to "reach the consumer below the threshold of consciousness," has been an area of controversy since the famous study in which messages to eat popcorn and drink Coca-Cola were projected on movie screens (sales of popcorn increased 57 percent and Coke 10 percent).[7] Opinion has been divided. Skeptics, often academics, do not believe embedded material permeates the subconscious mind at all, and proponents, usually practitioners, may exaggerate the effects.

Motivation

When consumers perceive that they have a need, the inner drive that propels them to fulfill the need is called motivation. Psychologist A. H. Maslow developed a theory that characterized needs and arranged them in a hierarchy to reflect their importance. In his 1970 book, *Motivation and Personality,* Maslow identified five levels of needs: physiological needs, safety needs, social/belongingness needs, esteem needs, and self-actualization needs. Other researchers have proposed other motives. In his 1974 book, *The Uses of Mass Communications,* W. J. McGuire organized motivation into sixteen categories. Basic human needs range from comfort and convenience to social acceptance to the need for love, sex, and power.

Advertisers want to know what motivates consumers so that they can appeal to those motives. A DDB Needham lifestyle study sought to discover the motivation that drives today's consumer. The results were expressed in three words: "Gain without pain."[8] The study indicated that Americans are motivated by the need for comfort and traditional values—but only so long as those traditional values did not interfere with convenience, practicality, or individualism. The consumer desire for the continuity and consistency of traditional values also prompts revivals of old advertising themes and jingles.[9] Just as Burger King every so often goes back to its famous tagline, "Have it your way," Johnson & Johnson has reprised its "I'm stuck on Band-Aids" tune, nearly a quarter of a century old; commercials for Ralston-Purina's Cat Chow periodically feature a silver tabby doing the cha-

cha; and the Meow Mix kitten has made encore performances of its "Meow, meow, meow" song.[10]

Attitudes

When people are motivated to meet a need, the way they meet that need depends on their attitude toward the various alternatives. An attitude is an individual's enduring evaluation, feelings, and behavioral tendencies toward an object or idea. Consumer attitudes toward a company and its products greatly influence success or failure of the firm's marketing/advertising strategy. Therefore, marketers should carefully measure consumer attitudes toward advertisements, package designs, price, and other product features to assure success in the marketplace.

One of the most impressive attitude-change advertising campaigns of the twentieth century was launched by the National Fluid Milk Processor Promotion Board. When American attitudes toward milk became tepid, the "MILK: Where's *your* mustache?" campaign's bold, full-page ads featured celebrities with dramatically white milk mustaches above their lips. The celebrities—among them Super Bowl champion John Elway, country singer LeAnn Rimes, talk show host Conan O'Brien, and child star Jonathan Lipnicki—were chosen to gain the interest of an array of specific target groups and to change their indifference into positive attitudes toward milk. The mustache campaigns have continued into the twenty-first century, as detailed in Chapter 4.

Lifestyle

Consumers' attitudes can influence the lifestyle they adopt. A lifestyle can be defined as a person's activities, interests, opinions, and consumption patterns.[11] Marketers use lifestyle information to tailor the marketing mix to meet customers' needs. When the Atkins diet swept the United States as an unprecedentedly popular fad diet, low-carb foods hit the market. High heart attack rates have also changed American lifestyles and created consumer interest in heart-healthy foods. In response, Masterfoods USA launched CocoaVia, a cholesterol-lowering candy, with print ads in magazines such as *Prevention* and *Cooking Light,* direct mailings, Internet marketing, and trial shipments at reduced prices.

Personality

Another psychological element that has attracted the attention of advertising researchers is personality, a person's characteristic and consistent patterns of behavior.[12] A number of marketers are convinced that consumers' personalities do influence types and brands of products purchased.

Social Factors

External forces that impact individual buying behavior are called social factors. Most notable is the broad grouping of forces generated by culture, reference groups, and social status.

Culture

The beliefs, values, and symbols that a society shares and passes from generation to generation constitute its culture. Value differences in different cultures (e.g., the United States and Japan) can be especially notable in international marketing and advertising. For instance, the Domino's pizza chain offers squid and tuna toppings in Japan. Mos (mountain, ocean, and sun) Burger, one of McDonald's competitors in Japan, even offers shrimp cutlets and rice burgers. In response to the scares about mad cow and bird flu diseases, McDonald's introduced Fish McDippers, similar to Chicken McNuggets, to its Asian markets.

Reference Groups

In addition to culture, buyer behavior can be influenced by a reference group, including family, friends, and professional organizations. This group may consist of one or more persons who have a direct influence on the buyer's decision making. Reference groups influence people's decisions by providing information or by pressuring them to conform to group norms. Reference groups have the most impact when consumers are unfamiliar with a product. Advertisers need to find a way to gain the support of various reference groups in their efforts to sell their products to consumers.

Social Status

Social status is another important factor in buyer behavior. Consumers in every country are of different social classes. A social class is a group of individuals with similar social rank (e.g., similar education and skills). Social class determines to some extent the type, quantity, and quality of products that a consumer buys and uses. In some instances marketers attempt to focus on certain social classes through advertisements, personal sales efforts, pricing, and other strategies.

CONSUMER BEHAVIOR

Automobile manufacturers such as Porsche, Mercedes-Benz, and BMW now cater not only to the wealthy as a group but also to individuals within that target market. Porsche upholstered a sports car for an American rancher with hides from his herd. Mercedes' Designo and BMW's Individual offer an array of options, including a pop-up television screen and a VCR for back-seat passengers.[13] General Nutrition Centers (GNC) customizes vitamins, shampoo, and lotions. Consumers can e-mail personalized greeting cards from countless Web sites.

American Demographics has said that there is no longer a typical American consumer: "There is no average family, no ordinary worker, no everyday wage, and no middle class as we knew it."[14] Mass customization of both products and messages is as important in the twenty-first century as mass production was in the twentieth. Marketers understand that consumers no longer want choices—they want what they want. Factors that have contributed to this consumer attitude include the growing diversity of the American public and the transition from the Industrial Revolution to the Information Age. Today, database technology allows marketers to store and retrieve precise details about individuals. The Internet allows for two-way communication and interactive relationships between the supplier and the consumer.

Computer technology, especially the database, has enabled marketers to gather more information than ever before about consumers' buying habits. Not surprisingly, information breeds insight.[15] Consumers have become increasingly skeptical about the millions of new products and commercial messages that inundate them daily, and marketers hope that individualizing products and messages will better meet consumer needs and wants.

Transforming the Agency: The Role of the Account Planner

In response to the challenge to gain the deepest possible understanding of the consumer, advertising agencies have begun to employ account planners. The account planner's job is to convey insights about the consumer to other members of the traditional agency.

The role of the account planner originated in J. Walter Thompson's London office in 1967. Jay Chiat of Chiat/Day, then a small West Coast agency, imported the practice to the United States because he believed that British advertising was superior to American advertising. Although some traditional American agency researchers view account planners as simply qualitative researchers, in reality the difference between the two is the role each plays, not the research tools each uses.[16] Agencies have become increasingly interested in people who can discover and express consumer insights. Understanding consumer behavior is crucial for advertisers in the competitive marketplace and in the recently flagging world economy.

SUMMARY

Buyer decisions in business are made collaboratively. The biggest difference between the business and consumer buyer is that the demand for industrial products derives from consumer demands (derived demand). Business buyers generally purchase through a formal process. Consumers' wants and needs are constantly changing, affecting both business and consumer buyer behavior. If advertisers are to attract and communicate with audiences, they must acquaint themselves with consumers' ways of thinking, with those factors that motivate them, and with the environment in which they live. The buyer decision-making process involves various stages of problem solving.

Consumer behavior is also influenced by various personal (such as demographic) and psychological factors (such as perception, motivations, attitudes, lifestyles, and personality). External influences, such as social and economic factors, affect this process. Computer technology, from the Internet to computerized production machinery, has also affected business and consumer buyer behavior as well as those who study it. With customized products and messages, marketers have begun to market to the differences among people, not just the similarities. Some agencies now employ account planners who attempt to better understand consumer behavior in today's challenging marketplace.

:60 Spot:
"Marketing Professional Services"

The job of marketing professional services in the twenty-first century holds tremendous challenges and opportunities. Professional services marketing has been important to the overall growth of marketing for several decades. The late 1970s marked the period when certain professional organizations began to realize that marketing had become a critical factor in determining an organization's success or failure. This movement led to the American Institute of Certified Public Accountants (AICPA) slowly lifting its ban on advertising and marketing the profession. In addition, the landmark Supreme Court case *Bates v. State Bar of Arizona,* 433 U.S. 350 (1977) gave attorneys the constitutional right to advertise under the First Amendment.[a]

Marketing is the process or technique of promoting, selling, and distributing a product or service. However, as the marketing function continues to grow and expand, so does the need to define the intricacies involved in the processes and techniques used in marketing professional services versus the marketing of consumer products.

Marketing professional services requires the targeted market to make an investment in the intangible. It involves creating superior value in something that lacks physical attributes, taste, or smell. Unlike product marketing, service marketing is a science that requires detail and precision in its technique. There is a large level of uncertainty associated with an intangible service. This leads to the current service marketing challenge of creating ways to erase uncertainty with value.

As marketing coordinator for a regional accounting and consulting firm, I struggle with this challenge every day. For example, one of our marketing strategies is built on the concept of "clients first." Since characteristics of services (i.e., trust, competence) can only be assessed during or after the process, it is critical that clients feel that their goals and ideas are being valued and will never be compromised during or after the process. "Clients first" helps build stronger relationships with clients and will lead to additional revenue through additional services provided and referrals from these clients in the future.

Marketing is a concept that is here to stay. Your ability to add value to the service being marketed will determine your success. The challenge for professional service marketers in the twenty-first century is defining, through focus and creativity, what marketing strategies will best provide profitability and success for each particular segment of the service industry.

The challenges are your opportunities. As General George S. Patton once said, "Accept the challenges, so you may feel the exhilaration of victory."

Amy Randolph
Marketing Coordinator
Clifton Gunderson L.L.C.
Champaign, Illinois

[a]*National Public Accountant,* July 1996, Volume 41, p. 22.

Chapter 7

Marketing and Advertising Research

During February 2004 sweeps CBS "won its fifth consecutive crown" in the ratings race, while NBC captured the young adult audience with its airing of the "finale-nearing" episodes of *Friends*.[1] In the jargon of the mass media, "sweeps" is not something you do with a broom. The term refers to a "ratings period, used by many local stations to set future ad rates."

The February 2004 sweeps showed that the Academy Awards telecast topped the ratings. It was watched by 43.5 million viewers overall and by 19.7 million viewers in the age group eighteen to forty-nine. Advertisers are especially interested in the younger viewers, particularly men eighteen to thirty-four whose TV viewing fell from the mid-1990s to the early years of the twenty-first century, with typical yearly declines about 2 percent.[2] Even though NBC captured the younger audience (see Table 7.1), ratings showed the network down 2 percentage points from the previous year. Compared to February 2003, CBS was up 1 percentage point over the previous year. With over $60 billion annually riding on advertising revenue, TV executives have had a "long-simmering feud" with Nielsen, claiming that the ratings service makes mistakes.

Nielsen conducts the survey "sweeps" four times a year in major market areas and publishes "sweeps books" that provide the basis for network and local station advertising rates. But it all began with the British People Meter.

In 1984 the People Meter was introduced in the United States by Audits Great Britain (AGB Advertising Research). Shortly thereafter, Nielsen Media Research followed with its own people-meter system. The meter records the viewing habits of family members and visitors by automatically recording the programs watched, the number of households watching, and which members of the household are watching. This viewing information is combined with each

ILLUSTRATION 7.1. Measures of emotion: Research shows that ads which are better liked and which elicit positive emotions are more likely to be remembered and to persuade. This Children's Memorial Hospital ad, created by Rapp Collins Worldwide/Chicago to promote the hospital's corporate holiday cards, features the original work of a young artist, drawn during a stay at the Chicago pediatric hospital. The ad uses a combination appeal. The visual offers the emotional appeal of the child's drawing, and the copy offers the rational appeal of factual information.

TABLE 7.1. Network viewer averages per week (first quarter 2004).

Network	Average no. viewers (in millions)	Average no. viewers ages 18-49
CBS	14.1	5.2
NBC	12.2	5.5
ABC	10.3	4.5
Fox	9.3	5.2

Source: Adapted from "Prime-Time Nielsen Ratings," *USA Today,* March 3, 2004, p. 4D.

household's pertinent demographic profile to provide a single source of data. So what about the viewer who watches television in a bar or airport lounge? With the cooperation of Nielsen, Arbitron introduced a "portable people meter" the size of a pager that "picks up encoded signals in the media."[3]

Networks depend on big shows such as the Academy Awards and Grammy presentations. In the past, NBC got a boost from its popular series *Seinfeld* and *Friends* in its Thursday night lineup. CBS got a ratings boost from its reality show *Survivor,* while ABC had success with its reality show *Super Millionaire.* Rival network Fox found itself fueled by *American Idol.* On Cable, MTV's *Real World* spanned a decade of popularity. The Nielsen ratings let the networks and their advertisers know whether or not they successfully reach a specific audience with specific programming.

Marketing and advertising research employs a variety of techniques for a multitude of purposes. Employing another research method, an agency may use focus group research to come up with a campaign that addresses the interests and lifestyles of the target market and speaks the target's language.

Hundreds of billions of dollars are spent annually worldwide to market products and services. Sound business practice requires that efforts be made to determine whether these expenditures are justified. Accordingly, a significant amount of time and money are spent on testing marketing, including advertising effectiveness. Therefore, this chapter will describe many of the research techniques used in the marketing and, especially, the advertising research business.

MARKETING RESEARCH

Companies use research to identify and uncover problems with their market share, evaluate their competitive strengths and weaknesses, and measure consumer attitudes. Marketing research consists of all the activities that enable an organization to obtain the information it needs to make decisions about its environments (e.g., social, regulatory, and economic), its marketing mix (product, price, place, and promotion), and its present or potential customers. The marketing research process consists of five steps:

1. defining problems;
2. designing the research project;
3. collecting data;
4. interpreting research findings; and
5. reporting research findings.

Defining Problems

Problem definition is a statement of the topic to be looked into via marketing research. A good problem definition directs the research process to collect and analyze appropriate data for the purpose of decision making.

Designing the Research Project

Once the problem is defined, there must be an overall plan to obtain the information needed to address it. The objective statement of a marketing research project should include a hypothesis drawn from both previous research and expected research findings. A hypothesis is an informed guess or assumption about a certain problem or set of circumstances. When marketers need more information about a problem or want to make a tentative hypothesis more specific, they may conduct exploratory studies to gain ideas and insights, and to break broad, vague problem statements into smaller, more precise statements. Once an issue is clarified, marketers rely on conclusive research—the structured collection and analysis of data pertaining to a specific issue or problem such as survey, observation, and experiment.

THE GLOBAL PERSPECTIVE:
CONSUMER INTELLIGENCE

Despite the continuing popularity of cold war spy movies such as *The Manchurian Candidate* and the James Bond sequels, the Western world may see things quite differently from its cinematic nemesis. Beijing authorities considered early marketing research, "such as interviewing shoppers," to be a form of spying until 1989, when China opened its market to foreigners' consumer data collection.[a] Nevertheless, restrictions have not abated on consumer research, such as prohibiting questions about politics and sex, and governmental prescreening of opinion poll questions.

Marketing/advertising research plays the same important role in the development of international advertising and promotion strategies that it does in one's home country. However, many companies do not conduct advertising research in international markets. The difficulty of acquiring accurate data about China's market of 1.3 billion consumers is obvious. Marketing research may also come with a high price tag (e.g., the likelihood that research methods will have to be adapted to local environments) and a lack of basic data (e.g., demographic information). Although the United Nations does offer some secondary demographic and economic data on more than 200 countries, many advertisers prefer primary data.

But don't be discouraged. Primary data may also be available from companies and/or advertising agencies located in foreign cities as well as in the United States. A. C. Nielsen acquired Asia's largest supplier of consumer market intelligence, Survey Research Group (SRG), in 1994. Hong Kong-based SRG also operates in Australia, Canada, China, Indonesia, Japan, Korea, Malaysia, New Zealand, the Philippines, Singapore, Taiwan, Thailand, and Vietnam.[b]

SRG also operates in the United States. By 2002 over a third of the top U.S.-based research firms collected global revenues; however, at least half of these firms were acquired by non-U.S. owners during a "trend toward foreign ownership [that] accelerated in 2003."[c] One of the earliest and most notable of these was the 2001 acquisition of A. C. Nielsen, a company founded in the United States in 1923, by VNU Inc., Haarlem, Netherlands.

[a]Gabriel Kahn, "Chinese Puzzle: Marketing Data," *The Wall Street Journal*, October 15, 2003, pp. B1, B10.
[b]Ronald E. Yates, "A. C. Nielsen Grabs Asian Data Giant That IRI Had Sought," *Chicago Tribune*, July 6, 1994, pp. B1, B3.
[c]Jack Honomichl, "Revenues Up, but Little Real Growth," *Marketing News*, June 9, 2003, pp. H6, H10.

Collecting Data

If the project warrants continued investigation, the researcher must determine what additional information is needed and how to gather it. Secondary data, primary data, or both can be used in an investigation. Secondary data consist of information not collected for the issue or problem at hand but for some other purpose. This information is available within a firm (e.g., sales reports) or externally (e.g., trade organizations, private research firms, and university libraries). Primary data consist of information gathered to address a specific issue or problem at hand. Such data are needed when a thorough analysis of secondary data is insufficient for a proper marketing decision to be made.

The three widely used methods of gathering primary data include survey (mail, telephone, and person-to-person interview), observation (human and mechanical), and experimentation (laboratory and field). Since the 1980s, focus groups have been widely used as a technique to gather primary data. The focus group is a special type of one-on-one interview conducted through survey panels. A moderator leads a group discussion of panelists' opinions in order to determine buying habits or perceptions of a specific product or idea. Panelists are drawn from the group targeted by the research. Sessions are usually videotaped and followed up with questionnaires.

Interpreting Research Findings

After collecting data to test their hypotheses, marketers interpret the research findings. Data require careful interpretation by the marketer. If the results of a study are valid, the decision maker should take action. Valid and reliable results depend upon a sufficient sample. Differences or distinctions determined by analysis must be large enough to offset the unavoidable margin of errors. Incorrectly worded questions may also invalidate the data.

Reporting Research Findings

The end product of the investigation is the researcher's conclusions and recommendations. Most projects require a written report, often accompanied by an oral presentation to management. At the end, researchers should follow up their studies to determine whether their results and recommendations are being used.

Many standardized marketing information services are available for marketing researchers in the United States and other countries, although developing countries may lack these services. The top fifty research organizations had collective revenues of $5.5 billion in 1997. Business activities outside the United States accounted for $2.2 billion (39.5 percent) of these revenues. Research organizations are increasingly challenged to become more "worldly" in accommodating their multinational clients' interest in overseas markets.[4] A.C. Nielsen Marketing Research is by far the most widespread with operations in eighty-eight countries.[5]

Marketing information services are available at some cost to the users and, in this respect, are a more expensive source of secondary data than published (e.g., government) information. However, such services are also typically much less expensive than it is for a company to gather its own primary data because, with the services, a number of companies share the costs incurred by the supplier in collecting and analyzing data. The main disadvantage of using secondary data from services is that they do not always ideally fit the needs of the user.

In today's increasingly competitive environment, firms must have an accurate assessment of how they are doing. A common yardstick for that assessment is sales and market shares. Historically, measurements have been handled in several ways, including the use of diary panels of households (e.g., the National Purchase Diary consumer panel, which is the largest in the United States) and the measurement of sales at the store level (e.g., A.C. Nielsen Company's Nielsen Retail Index). The NPD Group Incorporated's Syndicated Tracking Service also provides database information on store movement and consumer purchasing.[6] Another area in which there is a great deal of commercial information available for marketers relates to the assessment of exposure to, and effectiveness of, advertising.

ADVERTISING RESEARCH

Advertising is often the largest single cost in a company's marketing budget. No wonder its effectiveness is a major concern! Testing is the primary tool advertisers use to ensure their advertising dollars are being spent wisely. It can give the advertiser some measure (besides sales results) of a campaign's value.

Advertising research can be divided into two types: Media research concerns information about the circulation of newspapers and magazines, broadcast coverage of television and radio, and audience profiles. Message research addresses how effectively advertising messages are communicated to people and how well those messages influence people's behavior.

Media Research

A variety of resource materials are available to advertisers for determining the potential audience size for specific media vehicles (e.g., *Time* and *Life* magazines). The following techniques measure media audience.

Television Audience Measurement

A.C. Nielsen is one of the oldest, largest, and most influential research companies in the world. It is best known for its Nielsen National Television Index, which is responsible for determining the ratings that network television (e.g., ABC, CBS, NBC, and Fox) shows receive. Nielsen uses the People Meter, an electronic device that records the daily network, cable, and home video viewing members and guests in the 5,100 households that make up the U.S. market sample. It also measures television audiences through paper diary surveys in the fifty-four largest local markets. With a high rating on the Nielsen National Television Index, a television program can command a high advertising rate. For example, advertisers are willing to pay more to reach the hard-to-get younger audiences. Thus, based on agency and media-buying company estimates, a thirty-second spot on *Friends* cost $473,500 during the 2003 season, considerably more than any other prime-time show.

Survey Research Group (China) Limited (SRG), an A.C. Nielsen unit, has been in China since 1984. It derives television ratings from fourteen cities, with 300 households in each city recording their viewing habits every quarter for a two-week period. After 1996, SRG had data from electronic people meters in Beijing, Shanghai, and Guangzhou.[7] In most countries, television stations pay for 70 to 90 percent of ratings research—a cost that can run into millions—because they use the ratings to price commercial air time.

As the accuracy of Nielsen ratings has been questioned by the networks and a number of agencies, an alternative method to establish the size of the viewing audience will continue to be explored.

Radio Audience Measurement

Arbitron Radio is the dominant radio audience research service, measuring audience sizes in more than 286 local markets in the United States. Arbitron researchers provide data on network radio audiences through two national rating services: RADAR and Radio Nationwide.[8] RADAR provides thirty-seven networks with audience size for radio programs and commercial programming. Radio Nationwide surveys radio audiences twice a year to provide local and regional market network ratings.

Magazine Audience Measurement

Simmons Market Research Bureau's (SMRB) *Study of Media and Markets* is a major resource for consumer advertisers. It combines magazine and newspaper readership data, statistics on television viewing, product purchase data, demographic data, and other research results. The report helps advertisers in such tasks as profiling buyers in specific product categories and assessing the readership of a given magazine. Media Research Incorporated (MRI) provides advertisers and agencies with an alternative magazine-readership source. MRI interviews 13,000 adults per year and, similar to SMRB, obtains readership statistics for over 100 magazines along with product/brand usage and demographic information.

Like television's feud with Nielsen, magazine audience measurement also has become contentious. The Audit Bureau of Circulations accused *Rosie* magazine of overstating its 2002 newsstand sales. The incident caused advertisers to question how magazines represent their sales and circulation figures.

Internet Audience Measurement

Media Metrix uses personal computer technology to provide new media audience measurement. In addition to determining audience reach and frequency, the company provides information on "online media use, visitor demographics, and buying power for the home, work, and university audiences across local U.S. markets and for dozens of countries."[9] VNU Media Measurement and NetRatings Inc. (NR) also provide Internet audience measurement and analysis as well as online advertising intelligence.

Message Research

Advertising effectiveness is measured in terms of achieving awareness, conveying copy points, influencing attitudes, creating emotional responses, and affecting purchase choices. Based on these objectives, message research methods can be divided into five different forms of response to ads: measures of recognition and recall, measures of emotions, measures of physiological arousal, measures of persuasion, and measures of sales response.[10]

Measures of Recognition and Recall

Recognition refers to whether a respondent can recognize an advertisement as one he or she has seen before. The most widely known service in measuring print advertising recognition is Starch INRA Hooper. Roper Starch Worldwide was acquired by New York-based NOP World U.S. in 2001. In a typical Starch test, respondents are taken through a magazine and, for each advertisement, asked whether they remember seeing it in the issue. The following four measures are generated for each advertisement as follows: noted readers (the percent of readers of the issue who remember having seen the advertisement); associated readers (the percent who saw any part of the advertisement that clearly indicates the brand or advertiser); read-some readers (the percent who read any part of the advertisement's copy); and read-most readers (the percent who read half or more of the copy).

Recall refers to measures of the proportion of a sample audience that can recall an advertisement. There are two kinds of recall—aided recall and unaided recall. In aided recall, the respondent is prompted by being shown a picture of the advertisement with the sponsor or brand name blanked out. In unaided recall, only the product or service name may be given. The best-known recall method in television is called the Burke's day-after-recall method (DAR). The DAR procedure tests commercials that have been aired as part of normal television programming. The day following the first airing of a new commercial, employees of the Burke Marketing Research Division conduct interviews with a sample of 150 consumers. The sample includes individuals who watched the program in which the test commercial was placed and were physically present at the time the commercial was aired. These individuals receive a product or brand cue, are asked whether they saw the commercial in question, then are asked to recall all they can about it.

IPSOS-ASI, known for its copy testing services, delivers advertising material (perhaps a videotape) directly to the consumer's home to test multiple measures of recall and persuasion in the natural viewing environment. IPSOS-ASI also offers advertisers a global copy testing service in North America, Europe, Latin America, and Asia.[11]

Measures of Emotion

Research has shown that advertisements that are better liked—often because they elicit positive emotions—are more likely to be remembered and to persuade (see Illustration 7.1).

A commonly used measure of consumers' feelings toward advertisements is a technique called TRACE that is used by the Market Facts, Incorporated, research firm. TRACE enables consumers to reveal their feelings toward what they are seeing in a television commercial by pressing a series of buttons on a handheld microcomputer.

Measures of Physiological Arousal

Several kinds of instruments are used to observe consumers' reactions to advertisements. In general, they attempt to capture changes in the nervous system or record emotional arousal during the exposure sequence. The eye camera is a device that photographs eye movements, either by photographing a small spot of light reflected from the eye, or by taking a motion picture of eye movement. Pupillometrics deals with eye dilation. The pupils dilate when something interesting or pleasant is seen, and constrict when confronted with unpleasant, distasteful, or uninteresting things.

PreTesting Company Inc., Tenafly, New Jersey, provides copy testing services that include "commercial zapping, ad wear out, impulse purchase selection in a virtual supermarket/pharmacy, eye tracking, and change in competitive imagery."[12]

Measures of Persuasion

Advertising Research Services (ARS) runs theater tests. Precommercial brand preferences are taken from a total sample of 400 to 600 persons in four cities in the United States. Viewers then watch a thirty-minute television program with three sets of two commercials embedded in the program. A second thirty-minute program is then shown, with six additional commercials included. Although only one of the twelve commercials is the test commercial, the measure of brand preference change is based on responses to all twelve commercials.

Measures of Sales Response

Information Resource, Inc's. (IRI) BehaviorScan pioneered single source data collection in 1979. Panel members provide IRI with information about the size of their families, their income, number of televisions owned, the types of newspapers and magazines they read, and which household member(s) does most of the shopping.[13] IRI then combines all of these data into a single source databank to determine which households purchase what products/brands and how responsive they are to advertising and promotional techniques.

IRI's InfoScan Advantage retail tracking service records consumers with a checkout scanner and tracks the purchases of a national panel of 70,000 households supplied with handheld scanners. It also provides "granular consumer behavior insights" through an alliance with Europanel, the European panel operator.[14] This is similar to A.C. Nielsen's worldwide consumer panel service which tracks actual consumer purchases through a panel of 155,000 households in twenty-two countries. In the United States, 61,500 panel households use handheld scanners located in their homes to record every barcoded product purchased. Panel members also use their handheld scanners to enter any coupons used and to record all store deals and in-store features that influenced their purchasing decision. Panel members transmit purchases and other data back to the Nielsen company every week by calling a toll-free number and holding up their scanner to the phone. The data are then recorded via a series of electronic beeps through the phone.

RESEARCH TRENDS

Although traditional research methods still form the backbone of marketing and advertising research, marketers now look for ways to get beyond statistics and what consumers can articulate and to get inside the consumer's mind. Focus groups became trendy in the 1980s, but the 1990s saw widespread use of alternative research methods. Some of these unconventional research techniques included approaches as creative as asking people to color with crayons. In 1997, the Minneapolis agency Fallon McElligott employed this technique in its efforts to revamp a United Airlines ad campaign. "Frequent fliers got eight colors and a map showing the different stages in a long-distance airplane trip and were told to let their emotions do the drawing—hot colors for stress and anger, cool ones for satisfaction and calm."[15] The research led the agency to create a tagline which would be responsive to passengers' desires for overall improved service: "UNITED RISING."

Because researchers suspect that focus group panelists may be influenced in what they say by peer pressure, including dominant and opinionated people who overwhelm other group members, marketers have begun to employ other methods similar to Fallon McElligott's coloring exercise. In order to better understand consumers' feelings, Chicago-based Leo Burnett has asked people to create collages using pictures from magazines.

Marketers have also borrowed techniques from anthropologists' practice of ethnography, the study of comparative cultures that employs observation to learn about various people and their characteristics. Research that includes observation of the consumer has extended from the focus group into the consumer's home. Home surveillance involves filming paid participants in their homes as they go about their daily rituals, including bathroom routines. In some cases, marketers even move in with the consumer. "Honda and Toyota have

ETHICS TRACK:
JANET JACKSON EXPOSED

Janet Jackson is no stranger to controversy. Throughout her career she has often been criticized for using sex to sell records. However, during the 2004 Super Bowl the controversy surrounding this pop star reached new heights. During the halftime show sponsored by MTV, a duet featuring Jackson and pop sensation Justin Timberlake ended with Jackson exposing a breast to the Super Bowl audience. The incident, described as a "wardrobe malfunction," shocked the audience, CBS, and the Super Bowl's advertisers. Furthermore, many parents were upset by the event. The FCC received a record number of complaints about the halftime show from angry viewers. Although MTV initially assumed no responsibility for the incident, it later confessed prior knowledge of the conclusion to the performance.

The exposure has been described as a successful publicity stunt put together by Jackson's promoters to create awareness on the eve of the release of the pop star's new album. However, not all media factions were impressed with the "wardrobe malfunction." The Federal Communications Commission (FCC) launched an investigation into the incident. Many networks now enforce a delay with live shows in an attempt to detour a future "wardrobe malfunction" from being aired on television and possible FCC action. The delay did not stop the broadcast of a goodaddy.com ad in Super Bowl XXXIX in 2005, though. Alarmed because the straps of a woman's T-top slipped off her shoulders in the ad, Fox pulled the ad that had been scheduled for a repeat later in the show, even though it had already aired once.

Also, advertisers found Jackson's stunt to be less than advantageous to their own campaigns. The average Super Bowl advertising spot cost around $2.5 million for thirty seconds. However, once the halftime show aired, the advertising, once the main event of the Super Bowl, became secondary, back-page news. Media research firm Carma International reported that Janet Jackson received a record number of U.S. press mentions in the four days following the Super Bowl, 1,153 mentions compared to 596 mentions of the advertisers, including favorite Anheuser-Busch whose Budweiser and Bud Light brands received 183 mentions.[a] Clearly, the publicity stunt was a commercial success.

Ethics refers to moral principles that define right and wrong behavior. The complexity of ethical issues in advertising requires the advertiser to make a conscious effort to deal with each situation. This presumes personal standards of what is right and what is wrong. However, what is or is not ethical is a judgment call made by imperfect individuals. When stunts are intentionally performed by celebrities looking for free press, does the media have an obligation to serve as its own ethics watchdog of the advertising it airs or prints?

Advertisers have long been criticized for being deceptive, untruthful, and offensive. Critics also contend that advertising influences people to do things they would normally not do and helps to perpetuate stereotypes. Should the advertiser be responsible for the ethical content of its advertisements?

Arianna Stella

[a]Claire Atkinson, "Bodice-Ripper Raises PR Bar," *Advertising Age,* February 9, 2004, p. 49.

sent staff to live with families and observe how they use their vehicles—a tactic that Honda says confirmed its decision to add backseat room to the 1988 Accord."[16] Live-ins allow researchers to observe consumer behavior in a natural setting and even to learn the target market's lingo—information that is often quite useful in creating taglines and copy for advertising campaigns. The consumer of the twenty-first century is increasingly regarded as an individual person.

SUMMARY

Advertisers and their agencies can take advantage of a wide range of commercial research services. The firms that offer these services deal with broadcast, print formats, and the media (who is watching, listening, or reading?) and messages (are the advertisements effective?). Some of these services are syndicated, whereas others are conducted on a custom basis for individual advertisers. Each research technique has advantages and disadvantages. The type of research employed must be determined by the client's purposes and needs. Advertisers need to analyze facts and statistics, but they also need to discover insights into their consumers' minds.

:60) :60 Spot:
WRITING THE ROAD TO SUCCESS

Internships can play a pivotal role in determining one's career path. An internship, essentially "on-the-job" training, allows one to learn the foundation of the industry from researching media to writing client memos.

Internships differ at every agency; however, all agencies look for strong writing and communication skills in intern candidates, especially in public relations. A formal interview, writing test, and/or review of writing samples are a part of the intern interview process. As the internship progresses, other skills or values, such as time management and initiative, will be considered for a full-time, entry-level position at the organization.

"One of the main qualities I look for in an intern is an eagerness to learn as much as possible about the organization with which she or he will be working," says Kimberly Suda-Blake, director of public, practice, and scientific affairs at the American Academy of Periodontology.

When an intern is given a writing assignment, it is often considered a sign of the intern's progress and the agency's trust in his or her ability. Because writing is a critical skill, typically all writing assignments must be approved by a senior member of the team. These writing assignments build a portfolio and are a great display of the intern's accomplishments.

"Write as much as possible—be proactive about keeping up creative thinking skills during the first few years when most of the work will be tactical," says Arlana Boone, communications manager at a Chicago nonprofit organization. "Also, if possible, it would be helpful to intern at a couple of places, allowing you to compile a variety of writing assignments. Displaying the real work will give you an edge over entry-level candidates."

Time management is another critical skill. As an intern, responsibilities will increase week by week and managing time will be a priority. Organization factors into time management; thus, taking an assignment and finishing it in a timely manner shows dedication to the task at hand.

"To be successful in public relations, particularly as an intern, individuals need to learn how to prioritize. Because 'unscheduled' projects often develop on any given day, it's important to stay calm, be flexible with your schedule, and tackle the most important and time-sensitive projects," comments Kelly Thornicroft, senior account executive at GCI Public Relations.

Thornicroft also acknowledged that when an intern is in doubt about a task, she or he should ask for clarification. This will help the individual learn more about the business and gain a better understanding of the scope of the work.

In addition, an intern should take the initiative to be imaginative and find new opportunities to maximize the internship experience. Foresight, resourcefulness, and the ability to look at the "big picture" shed light on an intern's creativity as well as his or her comprehensive training as an intern. The ability to take pieces of a puzzle and put them together to reach a solution is a valuable asset.

"Treat the job as if it was a permanent position . . . you never know what the hiring needs of an organization will be when the internship ends," comments Suda-Blake.

Many factors can lead to a successful internship, but only you can determine the combination of these factors and utilize them to the best of your ability.

Note: The opinions expressed herein are my own, and do not reflect those of The American Academy of Periodontology, or the Academy's officers, members, or employees.

Catherine A. Justak
Program Manager—Education
The American Academy of Periodontology

Chapter 8

The Marketing and Advertising Planning Process

What if Andre Agassi, Lance Armstrong, Randy Johnson, Marion Jones, Brian Urlacher, Michael Vick, and Serena Williams stepped outside of their sports, for which they are already known as world-class athletes, and displayed their talents in boxing, baseball, hockey, volleyball, gymnastics, and bowling? Nike's six-week spring 2004 ad campaign featured the famous sports figures, translating their talents to other sports, in realistic vignettes for the "What If?" television spots created by Wieden & Kennedy.

"Basketball players want to be like Mike, but shoe companies want to be like Nike," the world's number one shoemaker.[1] Since the late 1980s, Nike has worked to transform its image from a brand of sneakers to a dynamic reflection of the booming sports entertainment industry itself—from pro sports arenas to inner-city basketball courts refurbished through Nike's P.L.A.Y. program, from Foot Lockers in shopping malls to the latest Niketown in New York City. Nike's advertising has depicted the vast scope of its business as well as the unifying spirit of sports. The Nike name ranks, with Coca-Cola and McDonald's, among the world's top brands.

According to Hoover's Online, Nike owns a 20 percent share of the American athletic footwear market, far ahead of adidas-Salomon, Fila USA, and Reebok. Nike's marketing formula has been to integrate its swoosh logo into the emotional and cultural tapestry of sports. The formula has proven successful, as Nike's growth has coincided with the growth in sports—at least until the summer of 1998 when Asian economic woes brought Nike its first loss in a decade, a fiscal fourth-quarter loss of $67.7 million.[2] Since then, Nike has counted its vice president for Asia Pacific among its top five positions.

TARGET MARKETING PLAN
FOR
LIFELINE PLANNING℠ SERVICES

LIFELINE

LIFELINE PLANNING SERVICES
TARGET TOWN CSC

FY ENDING 5/31/98

Clifton Gunderson L.L.C.
Certified Public Accountants & Consultants

ILLUSTRATION 8.1. Beneath the covers. This title page opens to a marketing plan that includes among its goals concentrating the majority of its marketing efforts on existing clients. Such documents usually include strategies for accomplishing each goal along with action plans, team members' responsibilities, and due dates. Courtesy of Clifton Gunderson L.L.C., Champaign, Illinois.

Nike was named the *Advertising Age* Marketer of the Year in 1996. Its strength across diverse sports segments has been clearly illustrated in its advertising campaigns. The "If you let me play" campaign underscored Nike's push into women's sports; "Nike vs. Evil," in which Nike's soccer endorsers do battle with Satan, reflects Nike's belief that it must dominate soccer to have global credibility. Nike's worldwide brand marketing and advertising strategy has been to take a global point of view, but with individual, country-by-country plans. For instance, responding to the Asian downturn of 1998, Nike dealt with Japan's inventory-reduction slowdown by shifting 540,000 sneakers from Japan to the faster-paced U.S. market.

Lee Jeans and Levi Strauss & Co., the two largest jeans manufacturers, engaged in a battle for the jeans market by launching new advertising campaigns in May 1998. Lee, with two-thirds of its customers women, decided to target seventeen- to twenty-two-year-olds with a new line of dungarees. To reach this target, Lee invested $13 million in a three-minute film reintroducing the company's seventy-six-year-old promotional doll, the dungaree-wearing Buddy Lee, on cable television's E! and Comedy Central.[3] The company conducted research to determine how the target perceived its brand. Research revealed that younger consumers thought of Lee as the brand their mothers wore. Lee hired Fallon McElligott to create a campaign to change that perception.

These vignettes illustrate how companies analyze their situations before developing a marketing plan. The marketing plan will outline objectives prior to the creation of advertising campaigns.

THE MARKETING PLAN

The Nike story demonstrates that marketing success depends on careful planning. It also shows that advertising is just a part of the total marketing effort. Nike's Web site, segmented by continents and further subdivided by countries, illustrates the fact that marketing strategies, including advertising, are not easily transferred from one culture to another.

While Integrated Marketing Communication theory suggests that a new, outside-in process may be more advantageous in the future, traditional marketing begins inside the organization, and works out

THE GLOBAL PERSPECTIVE:
WHEN COKE MAY NOT BE "IT"

A "wave of anti-Islamic jingoism" following 9/11 took a bite out of Western brands when Muslims responded "with their wallets."[a] One of the brands boycotted was Coca-Cola.

Zahida Parveen, a businesswoman from Derby, England, analyzed the situation. Then she developed a product and a marketing strategy. She would target Muslims with a politically correct cola alternative. Her product would come in red cans and bottles bearing Arabic text. Using the tagline "Liberate your taste," she launched a marketing campaign for Qibla Cola in the United Kingdom, Canada, the Netherlands, Norway, and Bangladesh.

Abdul Kahume Jamal, owner of several Arab grocery stores, reported that both Muslims and non-Muslims bought cases of Qibla Cola each day to express their frustration with major world brands.

Particularly appealing to the target market was Parveen's decision to give 10 percent of the profits to "groups dedicated to alleviating the plight of Palestinian children" and another 10 percent "to local charities in all 54 [targeted] countries ranging from Australia to Cameroon."[b] Marketed as the "ethical cola," Qibla Cola "probes business-partners' undertakings before signing a licensing agreement."

Qibla Cola and other "political and ethical" alternatives to the big soft drink brands sold particularly well in the aftermath of the invasion of Iraq, which generated a global tide of anti-American sentiment. The Pew Research Center for the People and the Press polled adults in nine countries in early 2004 to determine attitudes toward the United States regarding the war in Iraq. Only 3 percent of those polled in Turkey, 7 percent of Pakistanis, and 8 percent of Moroccans had a favorable opinion of President George W. Bush; opinion in Germany wasn't much better, with a 14 percent approval rating.[c] A stunning 70 percent of Jordanians felt that suicide bombings carried out against Americans and other Westerners were justifiable.

In the context of these sentiments, the Qibla Cola story suggests that political messages can translate into product benefits.

[a]Indiantelevision.com Team, "Qibla Cola signs agreement for Bangladesh distribution," Indiantelevision.com, <www.indiantelevision.com>, March 14, 2004, and CBC News Online Staff, "Qibla-Cola, the real thing for Muslims," Canadian Broadcasting Corporation, <www.cbc.ca/stories> August 8, 2003.

[b]Arundhati Parmar, "Drink Politics," *Marketing News,* February 15, 2004, pp. 11-12.

[c]"Rating Iraq Conflict and War on Terrorism," *USA Today,* March 17, 2004, p. 7A.

toward the consumer. The traditional, inside-out marketing planning process generally involves three steps, detailed as follows.

Step One: Conduct a Situation Analysis

A situation analysis presents all relevant facts about a company's history, growth, products and services, sales volume, market share, competitive status, strengths and weaknesses, and any other pertinent information. The situation analysis also includes information on key factors outside the company's control—for example, the social, technological, economic, political or legal environments in which the company operates.

A situation analysis is sometimes referred to by the acronym SWOT, which stands for strengths, weaknesses, opportunities, and threats. The analysis of strengths and weaknesses focuses on internal factors; opportunities and threats analysis focuses on factors that are external to the organization. Through analysis of external factors, Lee Jeans and Levi Strauss recognized that, while they were both competing for the jeans market share, they appealed to different consumer groups.

SWOT analysis prompted PepsiCo to spin off its three fast-food chains, Pizza Hut, Taco Bell, and KFC, in 1997. The breakup allowed PepsiCo to concentrate on its core soft drink and snacks businesses, free of the headaches that plague fast-food restaurants. Fast-food ventures are especially vulnerable to mutable consumer preferences, slow growth, and managerial difficulties.[4] As noted in the opening vignette of Chapter 1, Burger King's problems with product quality and customer service led to a drop in its overall quality rating. Responding to consumer concerns about childhood obesity, McDonald's dropped its super-size portions in 2004.

Step Two: Develop Marketing Objectives

The next step in marketing planning is to determine the marketing objectives of the organization's management. Marketing objectives must be designed so that their achievement will contribute to the corporate strategy and so that they can be accomplished through efficient use of the firm's resources. Marketing objectives must consider the amount of money the company has to invest in marketing and production, its knowledge of the marketplace, and the competitive environment. Marketing objectives should relate to the needs of target markets and to specific sales goals. In order to sell to a new target market—men ages seventeen to twenty-two—Lee Jeans had to change the consumer perception that only older women wore their jeans.

Step Three: Develop Marketing Strategy

The third major step of marketing planning is to develop the marketing strategy—the company's plan to accomplish its marketing objectives. In marketing terms, the objectives are what the company wants to accomplish, and the strategy is how the company will accomplish these goals. To achieve its marketing objectives, an organization must develop a marketing strategy, or a set of marketing strategies. The organization's marketing program refers to a set of marketing strategies simultaneously implemented. Through the process of marketing planning, an organization can develop marketing strategies that, when properly implemented and controlled, will contribute to the achievement of its marketing objectives and its overall goals.

The first step in strategy development is to select the target market. Marketing managers use the processes of market segmentation and research to define their target market. Ohio-based regional bank KeyCorp defined its customer groups as small business, emerging affluent, mainstream, and upscale, then targeted small business owners with one of its four magazine titles, *Business Vision*. Rather than communicating generic information to all its audiences, KeyCorp chose communication channels appropriate to each constituency.[5]

The second step in developing the marketing strategy is to determine a marketing mix (product, price, place, and promotion) for each target market the company pursues. For example, to differentiate its Gap, Banana Republic, and Old Navy brands, Gap Inc. "steered toward classic pieces such as corduroys and jeans," Old Navy "aimed at casual lower-priced items for the whole family," and Banana Republic revamped "business casual and dressy weekend wear for 30-something professionals." These so-called covetable items were featured in print and outdoor ads, direct-mail pieces, in-store displays, and on the company's Web site.[6]

Companies have a wide variety of marketing strategy options. These include finding new uses for an old product, implementing discount pricing, increasing the number of stores that sell the company products, or expanding into new markets, local as well as foreign. The four marketing-mix elements (product, price, place, and promotion) are interrelated; decisions in one area affect actions in another. Selection of each option depends on the product's position in the market and its stage in the product life cycle (introduction, growth, maturity, and decline).

Ultimately, management must select a combination of elements that will satisfy target markets and achieve organizational and marketing goals. For example, an industrial market company focuses more on personal contact than advertising. Distribution channels for the industrial market are also more direct. The company may need to decide whether to use one marketing mix to serve all its market segments or to change parts of the marketing mix for various segments of the total market.

A company's marketing strategy has a dramatic impact on its advertising. Even though the company may have the best product, lowest price, and appropriate distribution channel, success is unlikely without effective communication with target audiences. Today's most successful consumer goods brands were built by heavy advertising and marketing investments years ago. In 2002, the top twenty-five U.S. advertisers put $42 billion into U.S. advertising, promotion, and direct marketing campaigns, with top U.S. advertiser General Motors Corp. spending $3.65 billion.[7]

The marketing strategy affects the amount of advertising used, its creative thrust, and the media employed. A new strategic trend has been the ad blitz, increasing the number of ads in a campaign from a few to over a dozen. The "What If?" Nike campaign ran ninety-, sixty-, and fifteen-second spots on sports broadcasts and youth-oriented television shows in a variety of broadcast outlets from late February through early April 2004. Marketers who favor ad blitzes argue that money can be saved by airing more ads fewer times, and that such expenditures make a company appear larger and more dominant. However, ad blitz critics say these campaigns are creating malaise among ad-weary consumers.

Marketing strategy also affects the creative thrust of an ad. To reach senior citizens and newly retired baby boomers the Wyoming

Office of Travel and Tourism chose a series of retro print ads with fonts reminiscent of 1950s' movie posters and images of natural wonders framed by romantic images, such as bucking broncos and traditional couples hiking or horseback riding. The copy-heavy ads featured the hyperbolic messages associated with mid-twentieth century advertising: "CREST THE RIDGE *as the* CHOW BELL CLANGS, CALLING YOU HOME FROM THE RANGE. JUST ONE DAY IN THE SADDLE *and* ANOTHER COWBOY IS BORN IN WYOMING." Despite the nostalgic colors and images of the ads, an 800 number and a Web site address invited the target market to contact the tourism office, using the latest technologies, "FOR A FREE WYOMING VACATION PACKET."

See Illustration 8.1 for an example of a marketing plan document.

The Outside-In Planning Approach

Ideally, Integrated Marketing Communication's outside-in planning approach requires an exhaustive amount of consumer information. According to Don E. Schultz and Beth E. Barnes in *Strategic Advertising Campaigns,* the steps include the following:

- *The business review:* Similar to the situation analysis in internal and external examinations, the business review includes analysis of "what the organization might become," with an eye toward future development.
- *Consumer analysis:* This process uses database information on individual customers.
- *Behavioral segmentation:* This is the area that most differs from the traditional process. It involves breaking down groups that appear to be homogeneous based on such demographic information as gender, age, and income. This is done using individual market behavior such as purchase history, volume of use, place of purchase, and product use available through in-store scanners, telephone records, airline flight data, and banking, financial, or credit card transactions.
- *Customer valuation:* Information on purchase loyalty, occasional buyers, price-reduced buyers, etc., allows marketers to determine which customers are most profitable.

- *Behavioral objectives:* When marketers know what the customer does and what the customer is worth, then they can work to change current behavior to become more profitable.
- *Communications objectives:* This is the message, incentive, or activity needed to maintain or change consumer behavior.
- *Spending levels:* A budget is developed based on what needs to be done.
- *Tactics:* This compares to the step in the traditional model in which decisions are made about message, distribution, and so on.[8]

The emphasis on the consumer and the organization's long-term future are two features which distinguish this process from that of traditional marketing planning.

THE ADVERTISING PLAN

The advertising planning process is a distinct process within the marketing function. It consists of the six major steps that are detailed in the following material.

Reviewing the Marketing Plan

The advertising manager first reviews the marketing plan to understand where the company is going, how it intends to get there, and the role advertising will play in the marketing mix.

Analyzing the Company's Internal and External Situations

The internal and external situation analyses briefly restate the company's current situation, target market(s), short- and long-term marketing objectives, and decisions regarding a product's position in the market and its stage in the product life cycle, and its related marketing mix.

Setting Advertising Objectives

The advertiser's next step is determining what the firm hopes to accomplish with advertising. Advertising objectives should be stated clearly, precisely, and in measurable terms. Precision and measurability allow advertisers to evaluate advertising success at the end of the advertising campaign, assessing whether or not objectives have been met. The advertising objectives can be sales oriented or communication oriented. If an advertiser defines objectives on the basis of sales, the objectives focus on raising absolute dollar sales, increasing sales by a certain percentage, or increasing the firm's market share.

Even though an advertiser's long-term goal is to increase sales, not all campaigns are designed to produce immediate sales. Some campaigns are designed to increase product or brand awareness, make consumers' attitudes more favorable toward the product or brand, or increase consumers' knowledge of product features. Chapter 4's opening vignette and Sixty-Second Spot, "The Milk Mustache Story," detail campaigns designed to reverse decades of declining milk consumption in the United States.

Developing and Executing Creative Strategy

The advertising objective(s) declare(s) where the advertiser wants to be with respect to market share or consumer awareness. The creative strategy describes how to get there. This strategy consists of the following elements:

- *Target audience.* The target audience is the group of people at which advertisements are aimed.
- *Product or service concept.* A product can be an idea, a service, a good, or any combination of these three. This definition also covers supporting services that go with goods, such as guarantees and maintenance. When writing the advertising plan, the advertising manager must develop a simple statement to describe the product concept—that is, how the advertising will present the product. To create this statement, the advertiser first considers how the consumer will perceive the product and then weighs this against the company's marketing strategy.
- *Advertising media.* The creative team describes the appropriate media channels for the proposed campaign.
- *Advertising message.* What the company plans to say in its advertisements and how it plans to say it—verbally and nonverbally—make up the advertising message. Each advertisement needs a headline or opening to create consumer interest and

ETHICS TRACK:
OLYMPIC SPONSORSHIP AMBUSHED

General Electric and its NBC unit spent $2.2 billion to acquire sponsorship rights to the 2010 and 2012 Olympic Games.[a] The corporation would not be pleased if another corporation that hadn't contributed a dime toward sponsorship used the Olympic logo in its advertising campaign. Unfortunately, such unethical behavior occurs.

The need for companies to financially support the Olympic Games dates back to 1826. The fund-raising efforts of the first three Olympiads in Athens, Paris, and St. Louis were poorly run. As the Games grew, so did the costs, and financial burdens escalated. The 1976 Games in Montreal raised $4.18 million, yet left Quebec with a debt as high as $1 billion. Had cities lost incentive to host the Games, the Olympians would have nowhere to compete.

To establish incentive, The Olympic Partner Programme (TOP) was created in 1985. Under TOP, companies pay an entrance fee and in turn receive certain rights, entitlements, and privileges to which other companies do not have access, including the right to advertise to a large, diverse audience. During the twentieth century, the Olympic Games became a popular worldwide event. According to the Atlanta Committee for the Olympic Games, corporate sponsorship was its single greatest benefactor, providing about $628 million, or 40 percent of the money needed.

As sponsorship became advantageous, many nonsponsors have used every possible technique to associate themselves with the Games and gain these advantages. These "ambush advertisers," though they do not possess any sponsorship rights, still referred to Olympic themes in their advertisements during the 1996 Centennial Games. Some of the ambushers who played significant roles in the Atlanta Games were Reebok, Nike, Honda, and Lucent Technologies.

The goal of both official sponsors and ambushers is to associate themselves with the positive themes of the Olympics, and each has used different tactics to do so. Official sponsors have tied themselves to the Games by using their right to show the Games' logos—the rings, torch, etc. Ambushers have also suggested Olympic themes in a variety of ways, some of which were within acceptable limits. In essence, ambushers used Olympic-related imagery to sell their products without using the word Olympic and saved the multimillion-dollar price tag assumed by official sponsors.

Most ambushers used Olympians (or athletes who represented Olympians) and sporting events in their advertising. Reebok chose non-Olympian Emmitt Smith of the Dallas Cowboys to portray an Olympic hopeful. Another method of association exploited the wide spectrum of

Olympic-related sporting events. Nike used this strategy in its sixty-second mini-Olympiad, blending events such as boxing, pole vaulting, discus, and swimming into "Nike Medley." Nike took advantage of soccer's global popularity (more than 300 million play worldwide) and featured the sport in two spots, "Nike Medley" and "Women's Soccer."

Ambushers also associated with the Olympics through the use of various symbols. Reebok's logo consists of two horizontal lines and a third line dissecting them. Reebok cleverly flipped the position of the logo from horizontal to vertical, and added a flame at the top. Obviously, Reebok turned the logo into its own version of the Olympic torch, a meaningful symbol that dates back to the Games' ancient origins. One Nike ad featured a female soccer player with interlocking rings on her uniform. Ambushers also used easily identifiable symbols such as the awards platform and gold medals.

Ambushers also used terminology, an extremely powerful strategy. Lucent Technologies' ads mentioned previous host cities of the Games. The spots showed a letter being typed on a computer screen from Lucent Technologies to the next host city, Nagano. The voice-over read, "Dear Nagano (Japan), Heard you're hosting next Games. Would like to build your communication network. Have experience. For references, call Atlanta (or Barcelona, Albertville, Lillehammer)." Reebok and Honda incorporated event-related words in their spots. For instance, the Smith campaign used phrases such as "an official event" and "U.S. Football Hopeful" (as opposed to "U.S. *Olympic* Hopeful"). In addition, Honda's spot saluted "all the athletes who have traveled so far to reach their goal," avoiding the word "Olympians."

Finally, ambushers strategically aired their ads between coverage of Olympic events to further enhance the association between the spot and the Games. Nike's "Slow Motion Swimmer" and "Female Soccer" were ordinary commercials that could be aired at any time but were strategically placed to make Olympic associations. When viewers saw "Slow Motion Swimmer" immediately after swimmer Janet Evans' last Olympic event, the connection was obvious.

The Olympics have turned into a marketing extravaganza, the ultimate global event sponsorship opportunity. Unlike ambushers, sponsors own rights to all Olympic slogans and logos. Ambush advertisers do not pay for these rights, but instead use techniques of association to link their products to the positive image of the Olympics.

Cynthia L. Dietz

[a]"GE Talks to Shops About Global Games Sponsorship," *Advertising Age,* April 12, 2004, pp. 1-2.

copy that presents the message. Content decisions also involve the use of color and illustration, advertisement size or length, the source, the use of symbolism, and the adaptations needed for foreign markets. The role of these factors depends on a firm's goals and resources.

Developing and Executing Media Strategy

Advertisers need a systematic method of determining which media to use, how to use them, when to use them, and where to use them to effectively and efficiently deliver their advertising messages. Media planning helps answer such questions as: What audiences do we want to reach? When and where do we want to reach them? How many people should we reach? How often do we need to reach them? What will it cost to reach them? The media include traditional methods such as newspapers, magazines, television, radio, or billboards, and supplementary media such as Yellow Pages advertising, Internet advertising, and specialty advertising. Table 8.1 shows the 2003 ad spending figures for the top U.S. advertisers. The top two U.S. advertisers were also the top spenders in three media categories. The breakdown of the top three's expenditures by medium also appears in Table 8.1.

Evaluating Advertising Effectiveness

In managing its advertising campaign, a company should carefully evaluate the effectiveness of previous campaigns. Top executives

TABLE 8.1. Top advertisers by media in 2003.

Marketer/medium	Marketer's spending (in millions)	U.S. overall/ medium (in billions)
Procter & Gamble/consumer magazine	$582.3	11.44
Verizon Communications/ newspaper	513.7	44.84
AT&T/newspaper	510.4	44.84

Source: Adapted from the *Advertising Age FactPack 2005,* pp. 14-15, and TNS Media Intelligence/CMR.

want proof that the advertising they buy is worthwhile. They want to know whether dollars spent will produce the same sales volume as they would if the revenue were spent on other marketing activities. An advertisement's effectiveness may be tested before it is presented to the target audience, while it is being presented, or after it has completed its run. Chapter 7 detailed the methods used to measure advertising effectiveness.

MAKING BUDGET DECISIONS

After setting objectives and defining creative and media strategies, an advertiser faces the next advertising challenge: figuring out how to pay for it. The advertising budget is, in many respects, the most important decision made by advertisers. If too little money is spent on advertising, sales volume will not achieve its potential, and profits will be lost. If too much money is spent, unnecessary expenditures will reduce profits. Of course, the dilemma faced by advertising or marketing managers is determining what spending level is "too little" or how much is "too much."

Several methods and formulas for setting advertising budgets have been developed over the years, but none is adequate for all cases, and many advertisers try to employ several methods to help them arrive at the right figures. Following is a quick look at the most commonly used methods.

Percentage of Sales Method

The percentage of sales method defines the advertising budget as some predetermined percentage of past or expected sales. Assume, for example, that a company allocated 5 percent of anticipated sales to advertising and that the company projects next year's sales of a particular brand to be $50 million. Its advertising budget would be set at $2.5 million. Although this method's major advantage is that it is easy to apply (once an advertiser has arrived at the right percentage, that is), the major flaw in the percentage of sales method is that it does not rest on the premise that advertising can influence sales. An advertiser could spend too much (on products that may not need that much advertising) or too little (on products that could benefit from an advertising boost). In practice, most sophisticated marketers do not use percentage of sales as the sole budgeting method. Instead, they employ the method as an initial pass, or first cut, for determining the budget and then alter the budget forecast depending on the objectives and tasks that need to be accomplished.

Objective and Task Method

The objective and task method is used by two-thirds of the largest advertisers.[9] This method looks at the objectives set for each activity and determines the cost of accomplishing each objective: What will it cost to make 60 percent of the people in your target market aware of your product? How many people do you have to reach and how many times?

Competitive Parity Method

Another budgeting method is to adjust the advertising budget so that it is comparable to competitors' budgets. The logic is that the collective minds of the firms in the industry will probably generate advertising budgets that are somewhat close to the optimal.

All You Can Afford Method

Firms with limited resources may decide to spend all that they can reasonably allocate to advertising after other unavoidable expenditures have been allocated. This method and the competitive parity method are most frequently used by smaller firms. However, some larger firms also use this method, particularly those that are not marketing driven.

The budgeting decision is one of the most important advertising decisions and also one of the most difficult to manage. Perhaps the most important point to learn about budgeting is that there is no magic formula that will deliver the right answer every time. Instead, experts recommend a logical process that can help identify minimum and maximum values. However, like most business decisions, setting the budget requires judgment and experience.[10]

SUMMARY

Marketing success depends on careful planning. The marketing plan involves three steps: situation analysis, development of marketing objectives, and development of market strategy. The advertising plan involves analysis of the company's internal and external situations, setting advertising objectives, developing and executing creative strategy, developing and executing media strategy, and evaluating advertising effectiveness. Of course, budget decisions are, in many respects, the most important decisions made by advertisers.

:30 Spot:
(:30) A Day in the Life of an Evolving Brand

Most see only the physical and monetary growth of a company. I see the daily struggles of a brand that continues to grow and evolve in a state of constant fluctuation.

When I joined Qwest Communications in January 1998, the company had been public for several months, consisted of 1,500 employees, had acquired two small companies, and had just launched its first comprehensive corporate brand advertising campaign. As the proverbial end-of-the-year books close for 1998, Qwest will log a stock split, over 6,000 employees, a four-billion-dollar acquisition of LCI International, and a joint venture with a European telecommunications company that consequently creates the world's largest interconnect network. To most Qwest employees, the general public, many of the company's stakeholders, and even some industry analysts, Qwest has had a successful and rather amazing year. It's hard for me to disagree with that, but my role as corporate marketing communications manager has enabled me to see the past ten months in an entirely different light.

Qwest's overall business position is the construction of a high-capacity fiber optic network poised to reliably deliver high-speed broadband services and the framework necessary to empower businesses with the next generation of multimedia communications. Qwest's is the first network designed with enough capacity to send multimedia content—data, images, and video—as seamlessly as voice is carried on traditional networks. To communicate this, Qwest unveiled a new corporate identity as a public company along with its first corporate advertising campaign in October 1997.

The entire identity and branding campaign was intended to communicate, in a single phrase, the benefits of Qwest's unprecedented network technology—designed to erase the constraints of time and distance. Qwest's tagline, "ride the light," was inspired by Albert Einstein's teachings about the Theory of Relativity (see Illustration 8.2). The tagline represented a clarion call to individuals and businesses to begin enjoying the benefits of twenty-first-century digital communications. The branding campaign and its respective advertising was designed to make Qwest synonymous with the simple yet powerful attributes of light, such as speed, clarity, simplicity, illumination, and enlightenment. To deliver these branding messages, Qwest rolled out a national print advertising campaign to communicate the power and possibilities of the Qwest vision and network. Later we introduced additional print ads and corporate television spots to the media plan.

Qwest successfully emerged through a cluttered marketplace. Its brand evolved throughout 1998, reaching its target audiences with consistent messages about the network benefits. However, Qwest's merger with long-distance provider LCI International in June 1998 posed the brand's greatest challenge. The Qwest brand, so carefully positioned as a high-tech, multimedia network, was suddenly forced to integrate with LCI, a brand that communicated "simple, fair, and inexpensive" long distance service—at odds with Qwest's benefits: speed, reliability, accuracy, and security. Fortunately, Qwest's overall business direction did not change as a result of the merger. Qwest continues to position itself as the company building a network for the next century. Because the Qwest network has been more fully deployed, enabling the company to offer more products and services than when the brand was first launched, and because we have acquired a massive customer base and additional product and service functionality from LCI, Qwest has much more to add to its story in 1999.

What's next? We don't have a firm response. This is a crucial time for the Qwest brand as it enters a new year with its new constituents. The magnitude of changes that the brand has incurred during the past year make it seem only natural that some confusion would exist about its future evolution. Although it is critical that corporate marketing's number one objective is to determine where we take the brand next, it is equally important to the brand's evolution that we acknowledge the company as a "player"—meaning that it can't be ignored. Neither can we, as builders and protectors of the brand, ignore the fact that our brand is now visible and recognized around the world, not only because of a record-breaking year of successful business transactions but also because of the successful first year of a comprehensive, integrated campaign.

Tara J. Krull
Manager, Corporate Marketing Communications
Qwest Communications
Denver, Colorado

ILLUSTRATION 8.2. Riding the light. This print ad is part of Qwest Communications' corporate identity and branding campaign. Tara J. Krull, Qwest's corporate marketing communications manager, discloses Qwest's marketing plan in this chapter's Thirty-Second Spot. Photo © Tony Stone Images. "Gymnast" © Qwest Communications International, Inc., 1998.

Chapter 9

The Creative Aspect of Advertising

"From the Moment they met it was Murder!" was the tagline that pitched the 1944 film *Double Indemnity*. A classic of film noir, the movie pits femme fatale Barbara Stanwyck against insurance agent Fred MacMurray when she talks him into a murder/insurance fraud scheme. This would be the perfect film for an insurance company commercial to spoof. Aflac seized this opportunity for its 2004 "film noir" spot.

"She was beauty and brains," says the ominous voice-over that sets the scene in a dimly lit office. We see a woman in the low-key dark and gloomy light, her eyes downcast and illuminated by some skewed source. Wearing stylish 1940s attire—a hat and fur-trimmed coat—she implores the hard-boiled private eye, "You have to help me. I'm afraid I'm gonna get hurt, and I need cash." The voice of the private eye cuts through her paranoia: "You have that insurance," he reminds her. "What insurance?" she asks. "Go ask about it," he says.

Shot in black and white, the commercial cuts to a rain-slicked city street with the deep shadows and wet asphalt characteristic of film noir, the French critics' term for the dark style and themes of American crime and detective films that became popular during World War II.[1] "Ask about what?" the woman shouts from the bleak street to the private investigator in a window above her. She can neither hear the private eye's response nor that of the Aflac duck who stands beside her and quacks repeatedly, "Aflac, Aflac." This film noir spoof featuring the Aflac spokesduck earned a 267 on Intermedia Advertising Group's recall index for the last week of February 2004, making it "the most memorable ad of the period."[2]

The best television commercials are mini movies that use the techniques (vocabulary), stock characters (the woman in the Aflac spot is a femme fatale, a beautiful but duplicitous, desperate woman who leads men astray), and types (genre, e.g., war, epic, western, sci fi) of

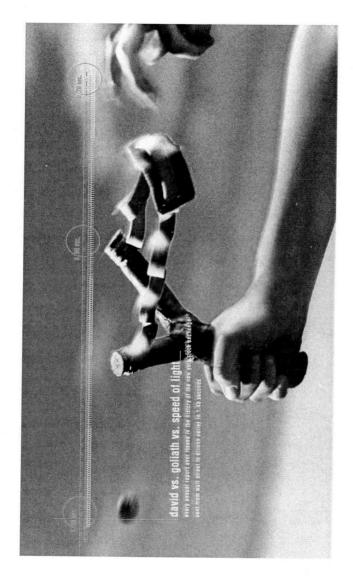

ILLUSTRATION 9.1. The Big Idea. To make concrete its abstract "product," one of the world's most advanced fiber networks, Qwest, employs visual representations of the speed of light in an advertising campaign. For instance, one of its television commercials shows the dramatic image of a lightning strike and ends with the tagline, "Ride the light." The print ad above recalls one of the most memorable displays of unexpected, unseen power in history—David striking down Goliath—in its visual of a youthful hand and a slingshot, and its headline: "David vs. goliath vs. speed of light." "Slingshot" © Qwest Communications International, Inc., 1998.

their feature-length cousins. Legendary ad creator George Lois, who worked for Doyle Dane Bernback in the 1960s, firmly believed that advertising is an art. What separated Lois from the rest was not that he strived so fervently for success—many do. Instead, he mastered the unexpected, the bold, the outrageous—in other words, he recognized the Big Idea when he stumbled on it. His definition of advertising flouts the scientific aspects of the business—advertising is an art, and the process is intuitive. His famous Braniff Airlines campaign ("If you've got it, flaunt it") tripled Braniff's business. It's hard to argue with success like that.[3]

What is the Big Idea? Don E. Schultz and Beth E. Barnes describe it in their book, *Strategic Advertising Campaigns,* as "usually very simple, but it brings a realism, an understanding of the marketplace, and an empathy with the target market that literally makes the advertisement jump off the page or television screen and into the life of the reader or viewer."[4] As an example, they offer a Cheer detergent ad that showed a man washing his clothes in ice water. The Cheer ad got across the detergent's long-time "all-temperature" message in a fresh, memorable way. For one thing, to see a man—instead of a woman—washing clothes in a detergent ad is unusual in itself. Beyond that, what is the probability that *anyone* would wash the laundry in ice water? Since 2000 Aflac ads have featured the spokesduck whose quacked outcries of the company name carry the Big Idea, that Aflac is continuously ignored by people needing the insurance company's help.

CREATIVE CONCEPTS
OR CREATIVITY IN ADVERTISING

Behind every good advertisement is a creative concept, a Big Idea that makes the message distinctive, attention getting, memorable (see Illustration 9.1). Really great ideas may be hard to come by, but some advertising experts argue that for an advertising campaign to be effective, it must contain a "big idea" that attracts the consumer's attention, gets a reaction, and sets the advertiser's product or service apart from the competition's. The Energizer bunny's "It keeps going and going" Big Idea resulted in memorable, effective advertising with endless applications (the cultural icon of the bunny popped up in cartoons, conversations, and political campaigns, and was even reproduced as a mechanical toy).

Another icon, the Morton salt girl, first stood beneath her umbrella and said "When it rains, it pours" in 1912.[5] The Aflac duck brought a tremendous amount of exposure to Aflac's products and services when it appeared on numerous talk shows over the years. In 2001 the duck enjoyed a positive debut in Japan, the company's first U.S. ad campaign to travel overseas.

It is often difficult to pinpoint the exact source or inspiration for a Big Idea or to teach advertising people how to find them. However, several methods can guide the creative team's search for a major selling idea and offer alternative solutions or options for developing effective advertising. These methods include the "incubation" technique of James Webb Young, the process of lateral thinking, and the storytelling process.

A Technique for Producing Ideas

In *A Technique for Producing Ideas,* James Webb Young proposes a process for idea generation. A creative executive with J. Walter Thompson, Young developed this process in 1940.[6]

1. *Gather information:* To begin, gather specific information (elements and information directly related to the product or service) and general information (observed information about life and events). Then, digest this material and give it a mental workover.
2. *Incubate:* Next, in the "incubation" period, forget about it and let the subconscious mind go to work. Young predicts that the idea will appear "out of nowhere."
3. *Mull, develop, adapt:* Finally, shape, develop, and adapt the idea to advertising. The idea of consciously forgetting about the project and letting the subconscious *mull* ideas over time is typical of the creative writing process. Insights may come from the subconscious mind as mental pictures. For instance, the American playwright Arthur Miller said that his play, *Death of a Salesman,* initially came to him as images, many derived from his observations of people and their lives—the image of "a little frame house on a street of little frame houses, which had once been loud with the noise of growing boys, and then was empty and si-

THE GLOBAL PERSPECTIVE:
HARD SELL IS A HARD SELL OVERSEAS

"Akiko is late, isn't she?" a young woman says to her friend as they wait in a theater lobby for the missing Akiko. In the boredom of waiting, conversation turns to hair. It seems that one of the women attributes her beautiful, "supple" hair to Rejoy hair rinse: "It's much better than before." The spot concludes with an announcer's voice-over, "A much better rinse. Single-step Rejoy. You'll feel the difference when you touch [your hair]. From P and G."[a]

The Rejoy commercial may not seem very remarkable unless one considers the stereotypes of Japanese commercials as frequently humorous, emotional, and less than informative. Japanese creatives are said to employ indirect, emotional advertising appeals (soft sell) as opposed to the direct, hyperbolic hard sell that characterizes Western advertising. A study of 464 American and 863 Japanese commercials in 1993 confirmed suspicions that Japanese commercials were less informative with their "soft sell" approaches than American commercials.

This characteristic of Japanese commercials may have led an Australian beef wholesaler to protest the Japanese parliament's increase in its tariff on Australian beef through a humorous ad depicting the Japanese flag as a round orange.[b] The print ad's text asked and answered its own question: "Why Does Japan Put a 50% Tariff on Our Beef? Because It's the Best in the World." Now that's pretty direct.

However, Michael L. Maynard's qualitative, interpretive analysis of the Rejoy commercial suggests that the persuasive strategy in Japanese advertising is more complex than initially thought. The Rejoy commercial presents product information (the rinse has been improved, it makes hair feel supple, yet it is light), and its dialogue employs repetition of the product name and its attributes (the selling points). In fact, the Rejoy commercial's slice-of-life format presents the mini drama of two ordinary people in an ordinary situation. What makes the commercial interesting to the viewer, in this case, cannot be attributed to humorous or emotional appeals. The viewer becomes drawn in as an "eavesdropper" to a private conversation—a casual, friendly "story." The spot's complexity blends "hard-" and "soft-"sell characteristics, reflecting Japan's cultural norms.

[a]Michael L. Maynard, "'Slice-of-Life': A Persuasive Mini Drama in Japanese Television Advertising," *Journal of Popular Culture,* 32(2), Fall 1997, pp. 131-142.
[b]*China Times,* July 22, 2003, p. B1.

lent," images of futility—"the cavernous Sunday afternoon polishing the car," images of aging—"so many of your friends already gone," and the image of a private man "in a world of strangers."[7] From these mental pictures, Miller understood his main character, Willy Loman, and wrote his masterpiece play.

Lateral Thinking

Another process for idea generation widely used today is lateral thinking. This process explores new relationships, breaking established thought patterns to generate new ideas and escape old ways of thinking. Since ideas are turned upside-down and looked at in new ways, this concept is also called out-of-the-box thinking. In his book, *Lateral Thinking for Management,* Edward deBono contrasts vertical ("traditional logical thinking") with lateral thinking.[8] Some of these contrasts are depicted in Table 9.1.

The Cheer ad showing a man washing his clothes in ice water broke "out of the box" in which detergent ads generally operate to present a surprising, improbable picture—most likely born from lateral thinking. A 1998 Leo Burnett campaign for Kellogg's illustrates out-of-the-box thinking that led to a surprising approach to the campaign's execution. Burnett chose to use a generic approach—usually

TABLE 9.1. Differences between vertical and lateral thinking.

Vertical	Lateral
Selective	Generative
Analytical	Provocative
Sequential	Makes jumps
Has to be correct	Does not have to be correct
Uses negatives to block pathways	Recognizes no negatives
Excludes the irrelevant	Welcomes chance intrusions
Follows most likely path	Explores least likely path
Finite	Probabilistic

Source: Adapted from Edward deBono, *Lateral Thinking for Management,* New York: American Management Association, 1971, cited in Don E. Schultz and Beth E. Barnes, *Strategic Advertising Campaigns,* Fourth Edition, Lincolnwood, IL: NTC Business Books, 1995, pp. 18-181.

employed to increase sales in an entire product category, not for just one brand. For instance, the National Pork Producers Council ran generic ads to jump-start sales in a declining product category. Since cereal sales figures had been flat in the United States, Burnett decided to hype the general health benefits of eating any brand of cereal with the tagline, "Cereal. Eat it for life."[9]

Storytelling

Advertising at its best is a form of storytelling. The most compelling advertisements have all the components of a short story. They introduce characters, identify tensions and problems, develop toward a conflict, and then offer a resolution that is usually provided by the product or service. Some of the best television commercials could be called lyrical; they have the poetic quality of condensing legendary and mythic stories familiar to the target's culture into spots as brief as fifteen seconds.

For instance, an award-winning Australian commercial for Levi's 501 jeans alludes to both the myth of the American cowboy and the legendary rebelliousness of the 1950s. With no dialogue, the spot uses the classic rock single "Be My Baby" as the musical backdrop for a sixty-second fantasy. Employing the familiar journey motif of American film, the commercial begins with an establishing shot of an isolated stretch of desert highway. A dark car travels the highway, down a sun-drenched hill, into a valley, where it breaks down. The driver, a bespeckled young man in a conservative suit, disappoints his wholesome-pretty, girl-next-door companion when he is unable to fix the car. Rescue comes as another young man arrives in a pickup truck. The first image of him shows his dusty cowboy boots hitting the sand as he jumps from his vehicle. The car is overheated, so the handsome rescuer, bare chested except for an open denim jacket, takes off his Levi's jeans, an action observed with admiration by the young lady. In the closing sequence, using the legs of the jeans as a towing rope, the hero and the girl drive off into the sunset. As they drive away, the jeans split in two, leaving the "square" behind. The splitting of the jeans' legs is reflected in the commercial's clever tagline, "Separates the men from the boys." For a product targeted largely to young men, this story taps into that group's interest in the Old West, in the rebel characters of the 1950s, such as Marlon Brando and James Dean, and in winning the heart of a pretty girl.

To create effective advertisements, ad creators must be familiar with the target's cultural interests, e.g., the music, books, and magazines they enjoy; the movies they are likely to have seen; the problems that typically occupy their minds. For instance, lists of the all-time best movies periodically appear. Those who aspire to create great ads by tapping into the American psyche should familiarize themselves with American movies that typically appear on these lists, such as *Gone With the Wind* (1939), *Casablanca* (1942), and *The Godfather* series (1972/1974/1990).

Familiarity with these classics and with various film genres allows creatives to envision memorable commercial spots, such as Aflac's "film noir" and a Saatchi & Saatchi, Frankfurt, commercial spoof of *The Graduate,* the film that launched Dustin Hoffman as a star. In the spot, Hoffman himself reprises his mad dash to the altar to stop his girl from marrying someone else, the gripping conclusion to *The Graduate.* In the commercial, it's his daughter he rescues as the movie's theme song, "Mrs. Robinson," recalls the movie's twists and turns of plot. The agency launched the commercial for Volkswagen's Audi A6 on March 13, 2004, for German eyes only; Hoffman, like other celebrities who do foreign commercials, cut a contract to prohibit the commercial's appearance in the United States.[10]

The tie-in to a famous film allows the commercial to deliver a full story line, by allusion, in just a few seconds. As another example, an award-winning Australian television commercial for bolle alludes to the famous 1953 American film *From Here to Eternity.* A scene in the movie that shows its stars, Deborah Kerr and Burt Lancaster, making love on a beach pushed the envelope in the amount of sexual intensity that was considered acceptable in American film. In the Australian commercial, two lovers, clad similarly to the film's stars in black bathing suits, appear in the same prone position on the sand, washed by a raging surf, as they commence lovemaking. The only dialogue is the young woman's question, "Do you have any protection?" In response, the man puts the bolle (the advertised brand) sunglasses on his face. Although the black-and-white film used a day-for-night filter to suggest its lovers met at night, the commercial is shot in full color, in blazing sunlight. This difference is key to the man's response to the woman's question; he needs the sunglasses to protect his eyes.

By tapping into viewers' existing perceptions of the classic film, the spot resonates with associations and meanings far beyond what it could otherwise present in thirty seconds.

Creative giants in the United States today include partners Rich Silverstein and Jeff Goodby (the "Got Milk?" campaign), Dan Wieden of Wieden & Kennedy (Nike's "Just Do It"), Mike Byrne and Hal Curtis of Wieden & Kennedy (Nike's "What If?"), and TBWA Chiat/Day's Lee Clow who sees advertising as "an uplifting social force, as a way not only to persuade but to inspire and entertain."[11] In May 1998 Clow launched his agency's first campaign for Levi Strauss & Company by opening a box conspicuously placed outside Levi's San Francisco headquarters. "Inside the container was . . . nothing," illustrating that Levi's "now thinks outside the box."[12]

Of course, however creatively the Big Idea may be conceived, the ad must do more than resonate with the consumer. It must also be grounded in sound strategy. The consumer who views the ad must be able to understand, among other things, the product benefit and selling message.[13]

DEVELOPMENT IN CREATIVE STRATEGY

Similar to any other area of the marketing and promotional process, the creative aspect of advertising is guided by specific goals and objectives that require development of a creative strategy. A creative strategy focuses on what the advertising message will say or communicate and guides the development of all messages used in the advertising campaign. Some of the best-known and most discussed approaches include the following:

- *Unique selling-proposition approach (USP).* With this approach, developed by Rosser Reeves of the Ted Bates agency, an advertiser makes a superiority claim based on a unique product attribute that represents a meaningful, distinctive consumer benefit. Many of the successful USPs, such as "M&M candies melt in your mouth, not in your hand," result from identifying real, inherent product advantages.[14] When research showed that Las Vegas had a distinctive liberating capacity as a vacation spot, R&R Partners launched a "$58 million, 20-month campaign for the Las Vegas Convention and Visitors Authority" using the tagline "What happens here, stays here."[15] By the end of the first year, the "'Vegas Stories' campaign was the seventh most likeable" of 2003, according to *USA Today's* Ad Tracker, and its tagline became a pop culture catchphrase.

- *Brand-image approach.* Whereas the USP approach is based on promoting physical and functional differences between the advertiser's product and competitive offerings, the brand-image approach popularized by David Ogilvy, founder of the Ogilvy & Mather agency, involves psychological rather than physical differentiation. Advertising attempts to develop an image identity for a brand by associating the product with symbols. Perhaps the most successful image advertising of all times is the Marlboro campaign. The campaign has focused on western imagery (cowboys, horses, ranching). Since the United States is said to have two major myth systems—the Old West and the Old South—the cowboy is a strong and compelling image.

- *Positioning approach.* The concept of positioning as a basis for advertising strategy was introduced by Jack Trout and Al Ries in the early 1970s. According to this approach, successful advertising must implant in the customer's mind a clear meaning of what the product is and how it compares to competitive offerings. One of the most famous advertisements using the positioning approach was that of the Avis rental car company—"We're only number two. We try harder."

- *Generic brand approach.* When you are the number one brand, you have no need to acknowledge the competition or claim superiority. Such an approach can be used only as long as a product or service truly does dominate the brand category. A 1998 television commercial for the Gap shows numerous couples, all wearing khaki pants, executing the popular 1940s dance, the swing. The tagline makes no mention of any brands. It simply says, "Khakis swing," followed by "The Gap." There is no claim of superiority; for instance, a less dominant brand might claim, "Khakis swing better." As already mentioned, Leo Burnett chose to use a generic approach for Kellogg's "Eat it for life" campaign, a surprising but innovative choice.

- *The resonance approach.* This approach requires that the creative team has a deep understanding of the target audience's world, including their experiences and emotions. Advertising created with this approach "does not focus on product claims or brand images, but rather is designed to present situations or emotions that evoke positive associations from the memories of the respondents."[16] For example, Hallmark uses this approach in appealing to the emotions of those who buy greeting cards with their familiar tagline, "When you care enough to send the very best."

The copy platform, or creative brief, is the written document that specifies the basic elements of the creative strategy. The format of the copy platform varies from agency to agency, but it generally contains some variations of the following: a profile of the target audience; the problem, issue, or opportunity that advertising is expected to address; the advertising objective; the key customer benefit; supportive benefits; and a creative strategy statement (a campaign theme or Big Idea, an advertising appeal, and the creative execution style to be used). Kathy Evans Wisner of Rapp Collins Worldwide elaborates on the importance of the creative brief in the thirty-second spot in this chapter.

The basic content and form of an advertising message are a function of several factors. Characteristics of the people in the target audience (income, age, race, gender, occupation, etc.) influence both content and form. An advertising campaign's objective(s) also affects the content and form of an advertising message. If an advertiser faces the problem of low brand awareness and its advertising objective is to increase brand awareness, the message may need to repeat its brand name many times. In order to persuade consumers to buy its product, the key and supportive customer benefits should also be included in the advertising message.

Advertising Appeals

Advertising appeal refers to the basis or approach used in the advertisement to attract the attention or interest of consumers and/or to influence their feelings toward the product, service, idea, or cause. Advertising appeals can be broken down into two categories—informational/rational appeals (hard sell) and emotional appeals (soft sell).

ETHICS TRACK:
ADVERTISING AS PROGRAMMING?

Argentine ad agency Agulla & Baccetti creates more than ads for its clients. The agency created "a TV program in which crime victims confront their perpetrators."[a] The idea takes advertisers beyond product placement (see Chapter 15) and corporate sponsorship to actually creating, producing, and marketing a television series. As a way to boost brands, the Argentine agency was not the only one that looked to programming as "a livelier alternative to traditional advertising." To "build their brands in consumer psyches," General Motors, Unilever, and Coca-Cola also wrote themselves into dramatic and comedic scripts, Procter & Gamble initiated a televised version of its United Kingdom online feature HomeMadeSimple, Chrysler's Jeep partnered with NBC Sports' "Jeep World of Adventure Sports," and Kraft launched "Food & Family Live," a TV program based on its custom-published *Food & Family* magazine and Web site.[b]

Is this taking the creative aspect of advertising too far?

The viewers of the Argentine show *Asuntos Pendientes* didn't think so. The hour-long show gained a "solid following" on the country's second-ranked Canal 13. One episode put a victim's sisters face to face with their brother's alleged murderer. Advertisers bought into the concept, and Agulla & Baccetti followed up with "El Once," a humorous police show "set in a busy Korean and Jewish neighborhood in Buenos Aires."

What would you say should be the ethical considerations of the Argentine ventures? Of a General Motors-backed show that stars "its Chevrolet Meriva five-door family car"? Or a Coca-Cola beverage "written into the script of a comedy set in an ad agency"? How does this compare to and/or contrast the controversial product placements in movies and television programming? Should agencies and their clients be the forces behind the creation of mainstream entertainment?

[a]Charles Newbery, "Argentine TV Show Pits Victims, Culprits," *Advertising Age,* March 8, 2004, p. 6.
[b]Stephanie Thompson, "Kraft Unveils Syndicated TV Programs," *Advertising Age,* April 26, 2004, p. 3.

Informational/Rational Appeals (Hard Sell)

These appeals focus on the consumer's practical or functional need for the product or service and emphasize features of a product or service and/or the benefits or reasons for using or owning a particular brand. Many rational motives can be used as the basis for advertising appeals, including comfort, convenience, and economy.

Emotional Appeals (Soft Sell)

These appeals use an emotional message and are designed around an image intended to touch the heart and create a response based on feelings and attitudes (see Illustration 9.2). Advertisers can use emotional appeals in many ways in their creative strategy. Humor and sex appeals, or other types of appeals that are very entertaining, upbeat, and/or exciting, affect the emotions of consumers and put them in a favorable frame of mind. Fear appeals can be equally dramatic in arousing emotions but have an opposite effect on the viewer's frame of mind.

Humor appeals. Consumers have historically given high ratings to humorous advertising (see Illustrations 9.3 and 9.4). Among consumers' all-time favorite ads are the Energizer bunny that "just keeps going and going"; the hip, singing-and-dancing California raisins; and the Taco Bell Chihuahua with its meaningfully raised eyebrows and suave style.

Sex appeals. The old adage "sex sells" may not always be true. For instance, men gave high ratings to Special K ads featuring nearly nude, extremely thin women copping sexy poses in front of a mirror, but the ads did not appeal to the group targeted—women. An Anheuser-Busch ad that showed a wife luring "her husband to their bedroom with the promise of a Bud Light" was rated the top ad of 2002 by *USA Today's* Ad Meter number one hall of fame.[17]

Fear appeals. Long a staple of advertising, these appeals have heightened consumer fears about social acceptance and isolation (expressed in ads for anti-itch creams and diarrhea remedies), personal hygiene (advertisers originated the term "athlete's foot" and made "halitosis" a household word), and motherhood (ads for cheese and peanut butter products commonly consumed by children have used such guilt-producing slogans as "Choosy mothers choose Jif"). The high-tech phone service category has also employed fear appeals. A 1998 Iridium ad for its worldwide, mobile phone service played to the universal fear of being out of touch, and a Nextel commercial appealed to financial worries. In the Nextel spot, a cellular phone user driving out of his local calling area is stopped at a "border" on a bleak

ILLUSTRATION 9.2. Soft sell. Rapp Collins Worldwide/Chicago designed its message around a dominant, emotional image of a child for this Lions Clubs International print advertisement. Even the headline appeals to the heart in a clever play on the duality of the word vision: *Our vision is a world where no one loses theirs.*

We interrupt your Year 2000 project to offer you a little piece of advice.

Run!

from all the half-baked Year 2000 solutions out there. The "quick fixes" that don't really fix anything. The products that lock you into long-term consulting. Take cover with PLATINUM TransCentury solutions, instead. Our easy-to-learn tools work well, get any job done fast, and come with consulting services only if you want them. Whether you need a single tool or a complete "find-it, fix-it, test-it" solution, call us at 1-800-890-7528, ext. 40160. Or log onto www.platinum.com/y2k

PLATINUM
TECHNOLOGY

You're Not Alone.™   ©1997 PLATINUM technology, inc. All rights reserved.

ILLUSTRATION 9.3. High ratings: Humor appeals score high with consumers. In this Rapp Collins Worldwide print advertisement for PLATINUM technology, the childlike drawing sets a lighthearted tone for the two-part headline: *We interrupt your Year 2000 project to offer you a little piece of advice.—Run!*

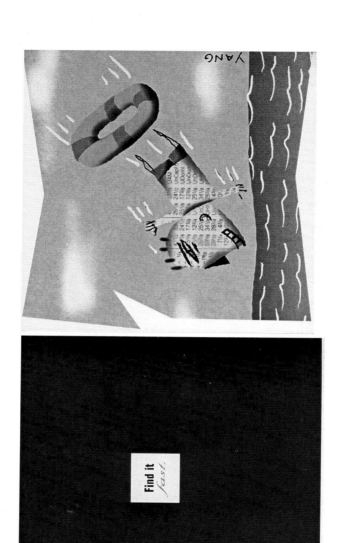

ILLUSTRATION 9.4. Integration for even higher ratings: Rapp Collins Worldwide/Chicago created a direct mail piece for PLATINUM technology which coordinates in image and tone with the print ad shown in Illustration 9.3. The same picture and the first half of the ad's headline appear on the mailing's cover. Inside, a figure drawn in the same style, by the same artist, dives through a tube into the water while minimal text proclaims, "Find it *fast.*"

landscape where a crazed guard vacuums all the money from the cell phone user's pockets and even sucks up the coins in his penny loafers. The ad creates a terrifying image of being fleeced by cell-phone roaming charges.

Fear appeals have also been heavily used in campaigns designed to combat drug addictions and other health-related problems. In 1998 the Hepatitis Foundation International ran a print ad showing a young woman wearing a bright bathing suit and eating a salad. The advertisement resembled a travel ad for a tropical resort. The travel industry claimed that the headline, "She just picked up a virus to bring home to her family and friends," and a color-coded map, which showed most parts of the world as danger zones for hepatitis, inflamed travelers' fears about diseases. Although the ad raised the ire of tourist offices and travel agencies, it also successfully raised the demand for hepatitis vaccinations, which was the purpose of the campaign.

Combination Appeals

These appeals combine informational/rational and emotional appeals. In many advertising situations, the creative specialist does not choose an emotional over a rational appeal, but rather decides how to combine the two. Consumer purchase decisions are often made on the basis of both emotional and rational motives, and copywriters must give attention to both elements in developing effective advertising. For instance, the success of Pepsi's Super Bowl advertising has combined product focus with the use of humor, minimal dialogue, and an underlying universal truth. Some of the commercial spots have been directed by Joe Pytka who has used the appeals of animal magnetism (e.g., the goldfish and chimps) and big stars (e.g., Cindy Crawford) in thirteen of Pepsi's highest-scoring ads.[18] Pepsi's Super Bowl XVI spot featured a bear that "clawed its way" to become the Bowl's second most popular spot.[19] The bear disguised "itself as a grizzled bear hunter to pass a check for Pepsi at a convenience store."

Rational and emotional appeals have been further differentiated by Foote Cone & Belding. In 1978 the advertising agency developed a model based on the assumption that consumer buying decisions are affected by their degree of involvement in the decision. The model, shown in Table 9.2, provides a matrix with each quadrant detailing

TABLE 9.2. Foote Cone & Belding model.

Level of involvement	Thinking	Feeling
High	Products: Cars, house, furnishings	Products: Jewelry, cosmetics, clothes
	Message variables: Long copy, informational demonstration, comparative	Message variables: Emotional, visual
Low	Products: Food, household items	Products: Liquor, candy, cigarettes
	Message variables: Coupons, samples	Message variables: Creativity, lifestyle

Source: Adapted from Richard Vaughn, "How Advertising Works: A Planning Model," *Journal of Advertising Research,* October 1980, pp. 27-33.

how the purchasing decision relates to consumer involvement. In this matrix, "thinking" refers to rational appeals, and "feeling" refers to emotional appeals.

- *High involvement/thinking.* This type of appeal can be successful when advertising a product of high importance to the consumer, such as a car or computer. Long, informational copy would be appropriate.
- *Low involvement/thinking.* This appeal applies to products or services that are routinely purchased; rational appeals that encourage trial purchases (such as cents-off coupons) will be more effective than long copy.
- *High involvement/feeling.* Emotional appeals work best for products or services related to the consumer's self-esteem, such as makeup, fashion accessories, and clothing (e.g., see Illustration 9.5). The emotional value of some types of clothing has been illustrated by the length to which some teenagers have gone—including theft and violence—to acquire name-brand athletic shoes. Teenagers are especially vulnerable to esteem appeals.
- *Low involvement/feeling.* Emotional appeals also work well for products and services that satisfy desires for personal gratifica-

tion, such as soft drinks, beer, liquor, and tobacco products. Since such purchases are often enjoyed socially, appeals to the desire to be accepted by a certain group can also be a factor. For instance, the circular argument "Coke Is It" has no valid logic but implies social acceptance.

It is clear that most advertising works. It is also clear that not all advertising works equally well. What is unclear is what makes one campaign more effective than another. For years, experts have tried scientifically to pinpoint the ingredients that make an exceptionally effective campaign. However, these efforts have seldom been conclusive. Opinions about what works and what does not generally fall into two schools: the straightforward and the creative.

BE AN ANGEL.
Buy Our Cards.

LIFT THE SPIRITS OF OUR
YOUNG PATIENTS, JUST BY BUYING
OUR CORPORATE HOLIDAY CARDS.

Ah, a breath of fresh air in a world of computer-generated holiday cards. It's the Children's Memorial Hospital Collection, and it features only original works of art created by children during their stay with us. There's a watchful angel...a festive city scene...even a holly-adorned "Chicago Bull." Each design is reproduced on a high-grade paper and printed large to capture every precious detail. But beyond the charm and quality of these cards lies the best reason of all to buy them—a full 100% of the net proceeds will go toward our Child Life program, which sponsors creative and therapeutic activities for our young patients and their families. So this holiday, be a messenger of hope to our children. And get some wonderful one-of-a-kind cards in return.

ILLUSTRATION 9.5. High involvement/feeling. Another Rapp Collins Worldwide/Chicago print ad, this one for Children's Memorial Hospital's corporate holiday cards, responds both to the motivation of desired self-esteem associated with greeting card buyers and to the high importance to the corporate consumer of purchasing the right holiday cards to send to clients and customers. While the angel drawn by a hospitalized child appeals to emotion, the long copy satisfies the need for information in making an important decision.

Those who prefer straightforward, no-nonsense, factual advertisements like appeals that deliver relevant facts in support of the product. They want presentations to be professional, but they do not believe it is important for the advertisements to be artistic. Others favor a creative, emotionally based approach. They believe that advertisements focusing heavily on information are likely to be ignored, and that focusing on emotion is more likely to create the desired response.

Evidence suggests that one of the approaches is quantifiably more likely to bring success. The Effie Awards, sponsored by the American Marketing Association's New York Chapter, measures results rather than creativity alone. Analysis of a slate of Effie Gold Award winners revealed that a wide majority employed emotional appeals. Indeed, humor seems to improve a campaign's chance for success. Next to humor, the most successful element seems to be an empathetic understanding of the customer. In the end, the advertisements that achieve exceptional results more often communicate a deep understanding of how consumers feel rather than what they think.[20]

Creative Execution Styles

Once the specific advertising appeal that will be used as the basis for the advertising message has been determined, the creative specialist or team must then turn its attention to execution. Creative execution refers to the way in which an advertising appeal is carried out or presented. In addition to using humor, an advertising message or appeal can be presented in numerous ways.

- *Testimonial.* Also called word-of-mouth advertising, this approach uses well-known figures or an unknown, "typical" person to provide product testimonials.
- *Problem-solution.* This tactic presents the viewer with a problem to be solved and the solution is provided by the advertiser's product.
- *Demonstration.* This is designed to illustrate key advantages or benefits of the product or service by showing it in actual use or in some contrived situation.
- *Slice-of-life.* A variation of the problem-solution approach, this technique portrays a real-life situation involving a problem or conflict that consumers face in daily life. The ad then focuses on

showing how the advertiser's product or service can resolve that problem.

- *Fantasy.* This approach uses special effects to create an imaginative place, events, or characters.

Advertising Format and Copy Elements

Once creative strategy, appeals, and execution styles have been decided, it is time to create the actual advertisement. The three basic components of a print ad are the headline, body copy, and visual or illustration. The headline and body copy portions of the advertisement are the responsibility of the copywriters, while artists—often working under the direction of an art director—are responsible for the visual presentation of the ad. Artists also work with copywriters to develop a layout. The layout involves the arrangement of the various components of the ad, such as headlines, subheads, body copy, and taglines. The tagline is a memorable saying or slogan that conveys a selling message, such as the tagline for the Las Vegas campaigns, "What happens here, stays here."

Television copy consists of two elements—the audio and the visual. The video (visual elements) is what the viewer sees on the television screen. The visual generally dominates the commercial so it must attract the viewer's attention and communicate a key idea, message, and/or image. The audio includes such elements as voices, music, and sound effects. Broadcast commercials are demanding to make. They must be credible and relevant. Research shows that the following techniques work best: the opening should be a short, compelling attention getter; demonstrations should be interesting and believable; the content should be ethical, in good taste, and entertaining; and the general structure of the commercial and copy should be simple and easy to follow.[21]

Radio copy presents a particular challenge to advertisers and their agencies because it lacks the visual aspects of both print and television. Successful radio spots usually enable listeners to visualize the product or something related to it. For this reason, radio advertising is often referred to as "theater of the mind." A radio spot for Kruse Farm Supply in Bristol, Indiana, shown in Exhibit 9.1, illustrates how a radio advertising spot can evoke images and associations in the listener's mind. This particular spot alludes to Alfred Hitchcock's fa-

EXHIBIT 9.1. Kruse Farm Supply radio ad.

Kruse Farm Supply
:60 radio
"The Birds"

SFX: MUSIC SIMILAR TO THE SOUNDTRACK OF ALFRED HITCHCOCK'S "THE BIRDS"

MAN: Aahh . . . this is so relaxing . . . watching the birds eat at the bird feeder . . . I hope it's enough . . . it's the last of the bag. Why are they looking at me like that? I don't have any more seed. Hey, guys, the show's over . . . the buffet's closed . . . don't hurt me. I'm the hand that feeds you . . . what about my fine feathered friends . . . this is not an Alfred Hitchcock movie . . . AHHHH!

SFX: MUSIC FADES UNDER

ANNCR: Don't let another senseless bird attack happen. Be prepared for fall feedings—stop by Kruse Farm Supply during their sale going on Monday through the 4th. Save 20 percent on bird feeders and accessories. Thistle seeds are only 79 cents a pound. Fifty pound bags of black oil sunflower seeds, just $10.50, and premium ear corn is a low $5.50 for a 50 pound bag. Sign up to win 100 pounds of free bird seed at Kruse Farm Supply—no purchase is necessary! And see Kruse's bird room . . . a section dedicated to bird enthusiasts. Keep your flock of birds a happy one—with bird seed and feeders from Kruse Farm Supply . . . stop by during their sale starting Monday. Kruse Farm Supply. On County Road Six in Bristol!

Source: Michelle Egan, South Bend, Indiana. Printed with author's permission.

mous film, *The Birds,* to gain attention and to generate mental pictures. Also, the writer covers all the copy points (specific details about the product, price, and place—the retailer's location) that the retailer requested.

One of the most challenging aspects of writing for radio is making the script fit the time slot.[22] The copywriter should read the script out loud for timing. With electronic compression, recorded radio advertisements can now include 10 to 30 percent more copy than text read live.[23]

To appear professional and to be easy to produce, copy must adhere to the appropriate industry format. Exhibit 9.1 shows the correct format for radio copy. All copy begins with the name of the advertiser in the upper left-hand corner. The size of the print ad or length of the broadcast script followed by identification of the medium to be used appears on the second line—for example, "Full page, magazine" or ":60 radio." The name given to the advertisement appears on the third line. Often a series of advertisements are created for a specific advertising campaign. In this case, all the ads created for the campaign may have one name, which unifies the series.

SUMMARY

Advertising is both an art and a science. The art comes from writing, designing, and producing exciting messages. The science comes from strategic thinking and planning, including research. The creative specialist or team must first deal with the problem of coming up with a concept. Then the specialist or team must develop a creative strategy, determine appropriate appeals, and select a style of execution. The ad must then be cast into a print, television, radio, or other format. At this stage, copywriters generally collaborate with artistic or production teams to create the actual advertisement. From start to finish, the process of ad creation involves a multitude of decisions that require understanding of both the product and the consumer as well as knowledge of the various formats and media.

:30 SPOT
(:30) THE KEY TO GREAT CREATIVE

In advertising, there are "Suits" (account people) and "Creatives" (copywriters and art directors). The creative brief is the document that the Suits provide the Creatives so that the Creatives can do their job (i.e., create advertising). The better the creative brief, the better the advertising—plain and simple.

So, what exactly is a creative brief? It's a document that describes an assignment that is given to an advertising agency by one of its clients. Usually, account people from the agency work with the client to put together an initial draft of the brief, and then they pass it on to the Creatives for their input. All parties must agree to the brief before any creative is done.

Each agency has its own version of the creative brief, but the contents are generally the same. A typical brief starts with some background information about the company, marketplace, and competition, and goes on to describe the benefits of the particular product or service (not just the features) including the key benefit that the advertising should focus on.

Next, the target audience is defined along with relevant information about their attitudes and past behaviors. A key insight about the audience is given to help further focus the creative. Finally, the purpose and scope of the specific assignment is spelled out, including the tone, media, offer (if any), deadlines, budget, legal copy, and desired end result.

What makes a good creative brief? Simple language (not a lot of marketing jargon). A lot of details about the target audience. A good key insight. And a leverageable point of difference for the product or service. Deliver these, and you're bound to get some really great advertising!

Kathy Evans Wisner
Associate Creative Director
Rapp Collins Worldwide
Chicago, Illinois

Chapter 10

Advertising Production

United rose above the clutter. It's not unusual for an airline to rise; airplanes do that every day. But it isn't every day that an airline's commercial is said to be the most charming film clip among the many film clips shown at an Academy Awards telecast. United Airlines' "Interview" received such praise.[1] As George Gershwin's "Rhapsody in Blue," United's long-time theme song, played in a "lovely, inspiring, understated piano rendition," Oscar-nominated animators Wendy Tilby and Amanda Forbis provided the visuals. The spot substituted music and visuals for dialogue to tell the story of a young job applicant's misadventures when he flies to an interview. It lifted United above the clutter and even soared above the clips of the nominated films with its unique look and rapturous conclusion—after the interview, the man's cell phone vibrates as the important call comes in, his face lights up, he celebrates his success.

Crushed by the 9/11 attacks, the recession, and rising fuel costs, United decidedly needed the lift.

For decades, art directors have searched for ways to break through the clutter of competing advertisements. Typography is another way to break through the clutter of competing print and Internet advertisements. Long one of advertising's humblest tools, typography has taken on new importance in the Information Age. The most eye-catching new face on Madison Avenue in 1996 appeared in a Nike advertisement showing a little girl in a swing and the slogan, "If you let me play." That face was Bell Gothic, a clean, streamlined typeface with elegantly curved edges and the suggestion of cyberspace. A similar typeface adorned a UPS campaign as well as ads for Epson, Discover Card, Chrysler, Budweiser, Citibank, Samsung, and Compaq. Bell Gothic and similar lean, simple typefaces balance the visual chaos of collagelike advertisements intended to look like computer screens. Furthermore, designers say that such typefaces suit the con-

ILLUSTRATION 10.1. Visual interest enhancement using varied typefaces. Karey Welde and Paige Inglis designed this ad for *The Elkhart Truth* using interesting typefaces and reverses. Because color is expensive and not always reliable in newspaper advertising, ad designers occasionally use reverses to add visual interest. The black banners with the reversed type create a top and bottom "frame" which helps lead the eye to the dog's poignant face.

tradictory corporate image that Madison Avenue has been selling for a decade: strong yet sensitive, technologically sophisticated yet back-to-basics.

The search for unique typefaces reflects a larger concern for advertisers: how to grab attention when more advertisements than ever are crammed onto billboards, sports arenas, television, magazines, and the Internet. Although computer graphics have enlarged the art director's bag of visual tricks, the simple ad or simple typeface can reach burnout. Even the greatest message can be perceived as too trendy or overused if the end result seems typecast, like an actor identified with just one part. Then the purpose of creating a distinct, fresh identity could be defeated.[2]

Production is what happens between the approval of the Big Idea and an ad's appearance time in its proper medium. Broadcast production involves audio tapes, sound effects, recordings, film or videotape, camera operators, directors, performers, and editors. Production of print advertisements embraces the separate technical skills of typography, reproduction, and printing. Producing advertisements for the Internet involves all the skills of Web site creation as well as knowledge of typography, graphic design, and the latest multimedia software.

PRINT ADVERTISING PRODUCTION

Every print advertisement (both newspaper and magazine) represents the outcome of a highly complex process: reproduction of visuals, precise specification and placement of type, and the checking, approving, duplicating, and shipping of printing materials to newspapers and magazines in time to meet their deadlines. This production process requires good planning, and those involved must understand layout and design, typography, and desktop publishing.

Layout and Design

Once headlines and body copy have been written, copywriters prepare rough sketches to convey their concept to the art directors. These sketches rough out the desired placement of headlines, subheads, body copy, the company logo, and visuals. Basic advertising layouts include these types: Copy Heavy (ad space dominated by text), Frame (graphics or other images frame the copy), Grid (space divided by squares of equal size), Mondrian (space divided into boxes or sections, not necessarily of equal size), Picture Window (space largely occupied by art—a photo, drawing, or other image), and Type Specimen (space dominated by the headline which substitutes for art). Subheads are often used to break up long copy. Italicized copy and reverses (white print on black) should be used sparingly.

THE GLOBAL PERSPECTIVE:
WHEN THE BIG IDEA GOES ABROAD

The *Seinfeld* television show began with a whimper in 1989, but it went out with a ratings bang in 1998. It went on to become the number two syndicated TV show in 2003-2004 with a :30 spot averaging $186,632.[a] However, in the beginning, American television viewers didn't find the "show about nothing" very funny. As the show persisted throughout the 1990s, a cross-section of the American public began to identify with the show's depiction of the everyday frustrations of life in an indifferent culture.

Stand-up comedians such as Jerry Seinfeld are painfully aware that comedy is difficult to pull off. If the punchline doesn't resonate with the audience, the whole business falls flat. Nevertheless, as the *Seinfeld* show demonstrates, if humor does work, the payoff can be big. When it showed fifty national print and television advertising campaigns to 11,000 U.S. adults, *USA Today* discovered that the top choices for likability and effectiveness had one common characteristic: they were funny.[b] The benefits of humorous appeals were discussed in Chapter 9.

Of course, humorous appeals that are effective in one country may not be in another. Ireland's Guinness brand has generated some of the world's wittiest advertising. However, at least one verbal innuendo in a Guinness tagline might raise eyebrows in the United States. A Guinness billboard depicted a man's briefcase opened to show a pair of undershorts and a bottle of Guinness. The tagline said, "I'm packed." Advertisements created in the United Kingdom have employed other puns about male sexual prowess that Americans have found offensive.

Of course, the Big Idea of the Guinness ad is that a real man is not complete without his Guinness. The problem for American men would not be the Big Idea but its execution. The creative team must have a clear idea of the characteristics of the audience to be exposed to the message. The advertiser must determine the targeted consumers' needs, motivations, and attitudes. Then the Big Idea can be developed, and specific appeals and execution styles chosen.

Let's face it. Americans laughed at the idea of an "atomic wedgie" (defined in *The Entertainment Weekly Seinfeld Companion* as "Underwear torture in which the waistband is stretched up over the victim's head—George suffered it in high-school gym class").[c] But would such a joke resonate with those who live in countries where there may be no gym class, and perhaps not even a public school? Could the idea of a "wedgie" be offensive in certain cultures?

[a]Richard Linnett, "Host of TV Superstars Boost Bullish Syndication Market," *Advertising Age,* March 8, 2004, p. S-4.
[b]Dottie Enrico, "Humorous Touch Resonates with Consumers," *USA Today,* May 13, 1996, p. B3.
[c]Bruce Fretts, *The Entertainment Weekly Seinfeld Companion,* New York: Time Warner Books, 1993.

Typography

Typography is the art of selecting and setting type. Because almost every advertisement has some reading matter, type has tremendous importance. Typefaces affect an advertisement's appearance, design, and readability. As illustrated by the opening vignette, art directors rely on stark, eye-catching typefaces to help break through the clutter of competing advertisements.

Type Families

All typefaces (or type fonts) come in families, just as human faces do. Many of them have proud family names, usually inherited from the original designer of the typeface, such as Bodoni, Gothic, Goudy. Certain families offer all kinds of variations. To present his client's product well, Steve Ohler, creative executive of McCann-Erickson, tapped graphic designer David Carson's talents to invent a new typeface for AT&T Lucent Technologies. The type font he used is a member of the Bell Gothic family with angular wings on the edges of its Ns and diagonal tops on its Ts.[3] Most traditional types have small cross strokes, called serifs, that appear on the arms of certain letters. Some of the more modern type designs do not have these tiny extensions on the ends of letters. Such typefaces are called sans serif. Each family offers capital letters and small letters, referred to by typographers as "uppercase and lowercase," and may usually be italicized.

Typefaces

Families of type fall into one of several "faces." These include roman (Bookman, New Century Schoolbook, and Times), sans serif (Franklin Gothic, Futura 2, and Helvetica), square serif or Egyptian (Aachen Bold), script (Calligrapher and Nuptial), and Pi faces (Woodtype Ornaments and Zapf Dingbats). Typographic noise is said to occur when type families of the same face are mixed in an advertisement. Sans-serif types are best used for headlines and serifs for body copy as the serif enhances readability. According to Tom Lichty in *Design Principles for Desktop Publishers,* the serif makes reading easier because "it cuts down the reflection of light from around the letter into the reader's eye (halation); it links the letters in a word and provides a horizontal guideline; and it helps distinguish one letter from another."4 The word Illinois provides a classic example. Figure 10.1 demonstrates this. Because of their superior readability, serif types are also preferred for copy that will be faxed as individual letters lose clarity in faxing. Most of the type you see in textbooks, novels, newspaper stories, and magazine articles is roman type (see Illustration 10.1).

Points

Type is measured in points. There are 72 points to 1 inch vertically. Most families of type offer sizes from tiny 6 point to giant 72 point and larger. When fairly long text is being set in type, 10-point, 12-point, or 14-point size makes for good reading. Beyond 14 point are the display or headline sizes. The ad layout includes the amount of space between the headline, any subheads, and the text, as well as the actual length and width of the advertisement itself.

Pica Measurements

In typography the unit of area measurement is called a pica. There are 12 points in a pica, 6 picas to an inch. A copy block might be termed 16 picas wide by 36 picas deep.

Desktop Publishing

Enormous technological progress has taken place in graphic arts due to the revolutionary application of computers and electronics. Today's graphic artist or designer can do much of the work previously performed by hand retouchers and pasteup artists on the computer. In fact, small IBM PC and Macintosh-based systems are ideal for desktop publishing—the process that enables individuals with desktop

Illinois   Illinois   *Illinois*

FIGURE 10.1. Three examples of typefaces. On the left is the familiar roman typeface, New Century Schoolbook. In the center is the sans-serif typeface Helvetica. On the right is a script typeface, Amazone. All are 18 point size. Notice the improved legibility and character recognition of the roman type. (*Source:* Adapted from Tom Lichty, *Design Principles for Desktop Publishers,* Second Edition, Belmont, CA: Wadsworth, 1994, p. 34.)

computers to "publish" print materials. In fact, most large circulation newspaper editors now scan photographs directly into computers, eliminating the time-consuming process of halftoning photos. Also, writers type their stories directly onto computer layouts, eliminating the need to typeset and paste up newspaper pages.

Desktop publishing software enables the user to word process text, to create or import and manipulate graphics and other art, and to bring these elements together in sophisticated layouts with a variety of page dimensions (for example, legal, tabloid, and magazine size), formats (including compact disc), and orientations (using the page Wide or Tall). A brochure that previously took days or even weeks to be typeset, halftoned, pasted-up, and printed via an outside vendor, can now be produced in just a few hours with a desktop publishing program.

The two leading desktop publishing programs are Adobe Page-Maker and QuarkXPress. PageMaker enjoys popularity with book and magazine publishers as well as public relations professionals because the program is geared toward the desktop publication of brochures, newsletters, and the double-page spreads often required for books and magazines. QuarkXPress is used by many newspaper publishers and advertising agencies because its text boxes allow for a wide range of layout possibilities and for easy layering of text and graphics. Adobe Photoshop and Adobe Illustrator are also used in advertising production. While Photoshop is commonly used to manipulate photographs and other art, Adobe Illustrator allows artists to draw their own pictures and graphics. Adobe Illustrator's tools enable artists to draw, paint, and "mix" exactly the desired color from a full-spectrum color wheel.

BROADCAST ADVERTISING PRODUCTION

Broadcast media production (both television and radio commercials) is, indeed, a different world from print media production. Both print and broadcast production require skilled talent, of course. However, the production process is very different. The television or radio production team requires specialized training and technical skills. The advertising team, from the account executive to the copywriter, must understand the broadcast production process and how television and radio communicate advertising messages. They also must have command of basic broadcasting terminology.

Television Advertising Production

The purpose of television production is to translate the narrative of the written script into an audio-visual medium. Concepts for commercial television spots must employ the medium's predominantly visual storytelling vocabulary. It is important to think in terms of how the Big Idea can be communicated with an emphasis on visual image, with as few spoken words as possible. Television's distinctive feature is that it provides moving pictures. It is not a good choice for relaying instructions or informational listings. For instance, retailers who wish to detail sale items and prices most often choose print advertising as the appropriate medium. Since the advent of MTV and the music video in the early 1980s, many television commercials have been conceived in this fast-paced style, which combines lightning-fast, rhythmic editing with a strong musical integration. The visual image and the sound and words of the music work together to tell a story or to create a mood or feeling that viewers come to associate with a certain brand or product. For instance, the Levi's 501 commercial described in Chapter 9 used a series of meaningful images to tell a story, but the lyrics of the background music contributed to the story as well with the singer's plaintive plea, "Be My Baby."

Advertisers use computers to digitally manipulate music and to animate TV commercials. The United "Interview" ad described in the chapter's opening vignette was animated via computer. Its rotoscope style was achieved by tracing live action frame by frame.[5] Bob Garfield's ad review described the effect: "Here the animators opted mainly for the less literal, more stylized image, with but a few moments of more intense photo-reality." He points out that the animators chose, as the most lifelike image, a close-up of the young man's shoes, showing that, despite all his efforts dressing that morning, he was wearing mismatched shoes, one black and one brown. This is the ad's most "poignant . . . sweet, human" moment, said Garfield.

Special effects entertain viewers and win advertising awards. However, no technique should so enthrall viewers that they pay more attention to it than to the product or the message. The Big Idea for the United ad came from its category benefit, the role the airline played in getting the young man to his moment of success. It worked. But the most talented production team cannot salvage an unworkable concept or a muddled script. Commercial television scripts must be written so that the production team recognizes the format and understands the creative team's vision of how the concept or story will unfold. To do this, copywriters must be familiar with broadcast format and the ter-

ETHICS TRACK:
THE WAR ON ADVERTISING

Is there no place on earth still safe from advertising, a sacred place that product placements have not yet reached? Today we can find advertisements in schools and tattooed on people's bodies, two of society's most sanctified spaces. The question becomes, when is enough enough? Groups such as The Billboard Liberation Front, Powershift, and *Adbusters* have had enough; they are dedicated to fighting back against advertising.

Culture Jamming refers to rearranged and irreverent ads created by a sophisticated group determined to undermine the power of advertising messages and icons. These groups change ads by subverting (producing anti-ads), slashing (also known as word poaching), and hacking into public spheres in order to change or parody mass media messages. One of the battles in this war against advertising was waged against Apple Computers. In an advertising billboard campaign, Apple pictured famous leaders throughout history—Amelia Earhart, the Dali Lama, and Ghandi —next to an Apple logo with the phrase underneath, "Think Apple." However, The Billboard Liberation Front took exception to these ads and decided to "improve" upon them. Soon Amelia Earhart was paired with the phrase, "Think Doomed" and the Dali Lama's slogan became, "Think Disillusioned."[a] Although the changes The Billboard Liberation Front made to Apple Computers' campaign were illegal, the popularity of their message continues to grow.

Adbusters, a Canadian quarterly also dedicated to fighting back against advertising, has reached 30,000 subscribers, mostly in the United States. It has published parodies of well-known ads with visuals and messages rearranged.[b]

Sometimes the Big Idea can come back to haunt you. At least, the international consumer movement known as Culture Jam hopes it will.

Arianna Stella

[a]The Billboard Liberation Front <www.billboardliberation.com>, April 4, 2004.
[b]Mary Kuntz, "Is Nothing Sacred?" *Business Week,* May 18, 1998, p. 130.

minology. To keep the scripts as brief as possible, many terms are abbreviated.

Camera Shots

What do you want the viewer to see on the screen? It depends on the product and concept, or Big Idea. The shot that will best fulfill the need of the product and story should be specified. The following are some basic camera shots.

Extreme close-up (ECU). In this shot, the camera gets as close as possible to show part of a person's face or body or a close-up detail of a product. The ECU may be used for dramatic effect (for instance, an ECU of someone's wide-open eyes and raised eyebrows may convey the person's surprise), for persuasive appeal (an ECU of a model's lips may show the dewy, moist quality of a lipstick), or for demonstration purposes (an ECU might show a close-up of a blemish before and after the application of a concealing medication).

Close-up (CU). Here a face or product dominates the screen (or, as in the United ad, a pair of shoes). The CU is often used to draw viewer attention to food products. For instance, the only image on the screen may be the advertiser's new fast-food sandwich. Cosmetic and hair products also use close-up shots. For example, a head shot of a model might show what the advertiser's shampoo has done for her hair. A close-up communicates the importance of an image or creates a sense of intimacy.

Medium shot (MS). In this shot, the camera shows a person from the waist up. In a two-shot, two people appear. Often the MS is used to feature spokespersons so that their facial expressions are visible yet the viewer can discern their appropriate roles by their attire. For example, Karl Malden appeared in American Express commercials for over twenty years wearing a businesslike suit and hat that suggested he had credibility to discuss financial matters. A Toyota ad created by Machado Garcia-Serra Publicidad, Miami, used a medium two-shot of two male parking valets buckled into the front seat of a Toyota, smiling adoringly at each other, to set up the humorous final shot of the commercial—the back of the car with a "Just Married" sign, cans dragging behind it.

Long shot (LS). Because this shot may give the viewer a frame of reference as to location, it is often called an establishing shot. Although a person or persons may appear in an LS, it is the setting that fills the screen. Although long shots are used in commercials to establish place, such a shot is less effective on the small television screen than on theater screens where panoramic shots have great impact. Therefore, establishing shots in commercials are used sparingly. However, a long shot was used in a 1998 Taco Bell spot to spoof the famous balcony scene from the musical *Evita*. Taco Bell's famous Chihuahua appeared on a balcony to address the crowd below. Aflac's "film noir" commercial, described in Chapter 9, used a long shot of a rain-swept, neon-lit street to create the visual characteristics of film noir style—the image of alienation in the foreboding big city. The long shot suggests an impersonal physical or emotional distance.

Pan. In this shot, the camera moves from a fixed point to follow a moving object or to give a panoramic effect. Sometimes a pan can be used to invoke a "searching" camera which takes in meaningful objects that shorthand the story. For instance, in the film *Dances with Wolves,* a pan of an uninhabited landscape contrasts the gruesome beginning footage that depicts the carnage of war. The natural beauty of the panned scenery provides what the film's hero, Lieutenant John Dunbar (Kevin Costner) has been seeking—a respite from the brutality of the "civilized" world.

Zoom. In a zoom-in, the camera moves in so that the image gets larger and appears to be closer; a zoom-out has the opposite effect.

In most cases, a television commercial will employ a variety of camera shots. For example, the storyboard for the "Stop Hate" public service announcement in Illustration 10.2 shows the variety of camera shots envisioned by the creative team and also shows how these visuals will correspond to specific parts of the script. "Stop Hate" begins with a medium shot (MS) of Jason Alexander, followed by a cutaway to a medium shot of a crowd of people. After the initial medium shots, the camera is to show a close-up of Alexander's face, followed by a long shot of a burning cross, an image dramatized by its contrast with the black night sky. Medium shots, such as those of Alexander, are typical of testimonial spots. However, the close-ups of his face allow viewers to get "inside" his thoughts and feelings. Every camera shot is chosen for meaningful communication of the television spot's message.

ANTI-DEFAMATION LEAGUE
"STOP HATE" :30 PSA

JASON ALEXANDER: My wife and I have a son. Perfect little boy.

And suddenly I looked at the world in which he'd live,

and was terrified.

Hate crimes

don't just devastate their victims.

They reach past individuals

to strike at the very heart of communities.

The best response is to fight.

Unite under the banner of decency, equality, respect.

I want to give my son a better, wiser, more loving world than this one.

STOP HATE

ADL

(Localized for your area)

ILLUSTRATION 10.2. Screening the television spot. The storyboard allows the client and/or the production team to preview a television commercial. This storyboard shows the shots that will make up "Stop Hate," a public service announcement for the Anti-Defamation League (ADL). The spot's final "screen" may be used by a television station to localize for its viewing area. The station might add its own call letters or record a voice-over that identifies the station as the commercial's sponsor.

The Storyboard

Just as a print ad concept is conveyed to the art director by a rough sketch, the concept of a television commercial is conveyed to the production team through the storyboard. Inside a frame shaped like a TV screen, the storyboard displays a picture of each individual camera shot. The appropriate portions of the script appear beside or below these "screens" so that producers can see how the visuals correspond to the script. As it is difficult for people to visualize the concept from just a script, an agency may also use the storyboard to sell the commercial to a client. The agency identifies the storyboard in the upper-left corner with the name of the company or product, the running time, and the commercial's title. The ADL public service announcement (see Illustration 10.2) might have been identified with these three lines:

Client: ADL
Time: 30 TV (film)
Title: "Stop Hate"

Notice that, after the time designation, the storyboard identifies the medium on which the spot will air (TV, radio, or film). For instance, film is the medium for a movie trailer, an advertisement shown in the movie theater that previews an upcoming film. In parentheses, the medium in which the commercial will be produced is identified. These are the three basic types of production in television—live, film, and videotape.

1. *Live production.* Live TV production is action as it takes place. Such a proposition is risky—anything can go wrong, and you only have one take. Most advertisers, local as well as national, prefer the assurance of videotape.
2. *Film production.* Since the first television commercial was made, film has been the most popular form for TV production. The majority of America's commercial film production for national advertisers is done in Hollywood and New York City. Film has long enjoyed superiority over videotape in several areas, including resolution (clarity and distinction of the components of a picture) and depth of field. Especially in long shots,

depth of field adds dimension to filmed images. Whereas the movie camera can capture distinctions between backgrounds, midgrounds, and foregrounds, the video camera produces a flat image. Also, prior to the introduction of the computer as an editing option, film could be more precisely edited. Film strips can be spliced on the exact frame intended, whereas video editing, which involves the copying of one tape onto another, is less precise. Picture quality is lost each time a tape is copied.

3. *Videotape production.* The most wondrous development in television production has been videotape because the tape does not have to be processed, as film does, and—after editing—is immediately ready to air. The majority of local television commercials are recorded on videotape because it is less expensive than film. However, increasing numbers of television commercials for national advertisers are being videotaped. The reason for this is the computer. As already noted, the computer has made animation in commercials much easier and more sophisticated. Furthermore, computer editing of videotape is faster and more precise than with previous editing equipment.

The Final Process

The client generally has to approve the commercial before production begins. The visuals and camera shots depicted on the storyboard submitted at this point in the production process are either drawn by hand or created with computer programs such as Adobe Illustrator. For the big national advertiser with a big agency and a big budget, the television production process begins the moment the storyboard is okayed by its management. At the same time that the idea is okayed, a tentative budget is approved. Once the advertiser approves a storyboard and budget, the production process begins. At the advertising agency, a producer is assigned. The producer (either in-house or freelance) is responsible for completing the job on schedule and within budget. The commercial is not produced in the agency. Instead, copies of the storyboard are first sent to several independent production companies selected by the agency producer.

Video production is always a team effort. Once an independent production company is hired, the next major step is the preproduction meeting. Here, the producer, director, set designer, talent director, and various other key people meet with the agency producer and copywriter to iron out details that must be settled before going into the studio to shoot the film. The cast is selected, the set is built, and all other details are arranged. Only then can a television commercial be produced. The producer, a person especially skilled in that medium, may make changes in the script based on experience of what will and will not work in communicating messages on television.

The need for multinational advertisers to create multicountry ads has meant that corporations such as General Motors have had to produce separate commercials for various world regions. Multiple productions can be expensive. GM saved $4 million in production costs with "a collaborative ad development system for its Latin American, Middle Eastern, and African region."[6] One agency coordinated strategy and creative development with each local office, creative ideas were pretested in several countries prior to production, and different actors for separate shoots were brought together at one location. In a multicultural global community, this production process was a breakthrough in efficient and essential individualization.

A "rough cut," the first edited version of the spot, is usually shown to the advertiser and/or the agency. Further changes can then be made so that the produced commercial meets everyone's satisfaction. Rough cuts may also be aired for focus group responses. In an interesting twist on rough cuts and focus groups, HBO showed three versions of the final episode of its hit series *Sex and the City* to focus groups to determine which of three produced endings would actually be aired.

Editors are responsible for much of the art in film and television production. Basic editing terms include the following:

- *Cut.* A film editing term referring to the actual cutting of a strip of film between frames to change quickly and cleanly from one shot to another. Since video actually involves the dubbing of a master tape onto another tape, video editing equipment allows the editor to select a precise image on a videotape to make a "cut"—or to copy that image—within a frame or two of another shot.
- *Dissolve.* Instead of abruptly cutting from one shot to another, a dissolve allows one image to fade out before being replaced with another, which fades in. The two images may also be superimposed—appear simultaneously on the screen.

- *Super.* Instead of superimposing one picture on top of another, this term refers to placing graphics or text over a shot. For instance, the advertiser's name and logo may be supered (appear) over the final footage of a commercial shot.
- *Voice-over.* Off-screen narration creates a situation in which the viewer can't see the person speaking but can hear a voice. Aflac's "film noir" used the voice-over to intensify the spot's ominous tone. The voice-over was made famous when Sir Laurence Olivier used the technique in his production of Shakespeare's *Hamlet* to suggest that Hamlet's "To be or not to be" soliloquy reflected his innermost, unspoken thoughts, eliminating the modern conception that a soliloquy is just talking out loud. In many commercials, an authoritative announcer's voice reads the tagline as the advertiser's name and/or logo appear at the end of the spot. Sometimes the text of the tagline may also be supered on the screen so that the viewer both hears and reads the words.

The Role of the Computer in Production

The personal computer (PC) created a revolution in video production. Desktop video production employs a variety of computer-driven equipment. In addition to animation, which has already been discussed, the benefits of this type of equipment include image manipulation accomplished by digital video effects (DVE) systems. DVEs can rotate, flip, shrink, or expand an image. A flipped picture can give the impression that someone has just turned a page. Picture shrinkage allows for a smaller picture to be layered over another image that fills the screen; for instance, a graphic of a gun may appear in the corner of the screen, above a news anchor's shoulder, while the anchor talks about a local shooting. The digital image is actually a series of stored numbers, so the computer changes the image through numerical recalculation.

Perhaps the most-often used equipment in television commercial production is the character generator. Today's sophisticated character generator (CG) is used primarily to put text on the screen. Text is often placed on the lower third of the screen if it is to be juxtaposed with a picture. Many commercials conclude with the tagline and/or company or product name and logo generated in the center of the screen.

The background on which the text appears may be just color or it may be a continuation of the commercial's final shot. It is not unusual for the last frames—with the tagline and identification of the company or product—to be voiced-over. For instance, an announcer might read the tagline aloud as it appears on the screen. Sometimes, for dramatic effect, the last frames appear with text only and no sound.

Radio Advertising Production

Once the concept (Big Idea) for a radio commercial has been decided and the spot has been scripted, the creative team must be certain that the commercial's producers will understand what they want. The more specific the script is regarding SFX (sound effects), music, and distinctions between voices as well as tones of voice, the more likely the commercial will be produced as it was conceived. However, as with television production, flexibility can be a virtue—sometimes changes made in production work better than the original script would have and create a more effective or aesthetic commercial. Also, as is customary with television production, the production team works with the company's or agency's creative team. Script changes usually must be approved and the final product reviewed by the advertiser and/or its agency.

Radio commercials are produced in one of two ways. They are either taped and duplicated for distribution, or they are recorded live. The more common form is the taped radio commercial. National radio commercials are produced by an advertising agency, and duplicate copies of the tape are distributed to local stations around the country. Commercials for local advertisers might be produced by local stations, with the station's staff providing the creative and production expertise. The recording is done in-house using the radio station's studio. Those involved in radio production should be familiar with some basic terminology.

- *Music in, music out, and fade under.* Some radio spots begin with music (in) that ends (out) when an actor begins to speak. The volume of the music may also be gradually decreased (fade) so that the music can be heard faintly (under) the speaker's voice.
- *Up, down.* Volume may be increased (up) or decreased (down).

- *SFX.* The use of sound effects (abbreviated SFX) is common in radio commercial spots; for instance, a spot which begins with children coming home from school may be enhanced by the sound of hurried feet hitting the pavement and a door slam.
- *Segue.* This term refers to a musical or verbal transition to bridge sections of a commercial.

In live radio advertising, a typewritten script is read by whichever regular station announcer is on duty. The inclusion of sound effects, music, or additional speaking parts would require studio production. The live script is advantageous to the local retailer who must get a message on the air in a matter of hours. However, like live television, the live radio spot is risky due to the possibility of human error. Occasionally the copywriter leaves five seconds open at the end of the script so that the announcer can add a live tagline to the taped commercial. Copy points such as sale prices and dates can be easily updated without having to produce a completely new audiotape.

Radio production depends upon the talent of the performers as well as effective sound effects and music that grabs attention, enhances the mood or story, or otherwise contributes to conveying the Big Idea. Since generally only national advertisers have sufficient budget to pay royalty fees for the use of popular music and artists, local radio stations buy rights to generic music tracks in order to provide inexpensive alternatives. Also, local radio announcers often perform in commercial spots, which eliminates the need to pay for outside professional talent and helps local advertisers cut costs. Some radio station personnel are adept at doing voice impersonations of celebrities and politicians. Their spots can gain attention and appeal to the listener's sense of humor.

Some local advertisers like to perform in their own spots. Because the voice of a "real" person at the company or organization can personalize the spot for a local audience, this technique can work—but only when the person has a background in acting or some natural talent. The difficulty for the production team arises when the company's representative lacks this talent and still insists on doing the spot. Telling a client that he or she can't act can be a treacherous situation.

INTERNET ADVERTISING PRODUCTION

The newest medium experiencing advertising clutter is the Internet. In November 2002 Coca-Cola, American Express, Unilever, and Delta Airlines began to run animated rich-media ads that combined the visual appeal of television with the interactive possibilities of the Internet. These ads cut through the clutter with two to eight times the effectiveness of "static banner ads in generating brand awareness."[7] Banner ads allow Internet users to surf without paying site subscription fees (advertisers provide the financial support). Nevertheless, these ads are often viewed by site visitors as a "necessary evil."[8] The rich-media ads have drawn more traditional advertisers who "previously believed online ads could never approach" the storytelling capacity of television.[9] A rich-media Gateway ad, in which a computer hopped across the screen, had twice the number of clicks as a non-rich ad. Table 10.1 shows which industries most often produce rich-media ads.

Multimedia companies such as Narrative Communications developed software to "jazz up" banner ads with animation and audio. Eddie Bauer, Godiva Chocolate, and 1-800-FLOWERS use Narrative Communications' Enliven/Impulse software that allows secure sales transactions within the banner ad. For instance, buyers merely click on an "Order" icon on an Eddie Bauer banner ad to begin a sales transaction. One of a series of screens even depicted swatches of stonewashed fabric in various colors. Banner technology companies have expanded the production possibilities for banner advertising, allowing sites such as Eddie Bauer's to stand out from the clutter.

TABLE 10.1. Who's using them? Animated ads by industry.

Industry	Share of impressions (percent)
Hardware, electronics	33.1
Entertainment	26.4
Telecommunications	20.9
Software	19.2
Business to business	17.2

Source: Adapted from Robert W. Ahrens and Quin Tian, "Who's Using Rich-Media," *USA Today,* November 29, 2003, p. B8.

Internet advertising resembles print and broadcast advertising in its purpose (to market goods, services, and images with persuasive messages) but differs in key respects. It has the ability to reach a narrowly defined niche audience, to enable immediate interaction between the consumer and the advertiser, and to link the consumer to other product or company information. Copywriters work with graphic designers to come up with concepts. Ads may be of any length, from banner ads, the primary advertising format, to deep, multiple-page ads that usually span a page width and are an inch or so deep. Typically, Internet ads feature bold or decorative headlines, a graphic image, and a link to further information with the click of a button.

The demands of Internet users—browsers expect current information—make it a medium in a class of its own. Fortunately, the nature of the Internet makes frequent updates possible. Products, prices, and promotional messages can be changed as often as circumstances dictate. A growing number of Web design services meet the needs of this new advertising medium. The services provide monthly activity reports to give the advertiser an accurate account of site traffic and make regular updates after the site has "gone live." For example, Shamrock Net Design is a full-service interactive communications consulting firm that specializes in interactive marketing and Web site design. Omnicom, U S Web, and iXL in Atlanta are among the growing list of interactive agencies.

In cyberspace, a Web site must compete with hundreds of thousands of other sites, many of which link visitors to still more channels (see Illustrations 10.3 and 10.4 for one company's interrelated Web site pages). Therefore, the Internet designer and producer face immense challenges. Those creating Internet Web sites and advertisements should keep in mind the guidelines detailed in Exhibit 10.1.

Advertising production on the Internet follows the same process as print and broadcast advertising, e.g., the advertising concept results from research, planning, and creative collaboration. It has been said that interactive advertising is one part creativity, one part technology, and one part business.[10] Graphic designers, programmers, and copywriters work together to produce the online ad. Web producers and creative teams must have technical skills and a knowledge of Internet applications. Most production is done in HTML (hypertext markup language) that enables the embedding of hypertext links in the docu-

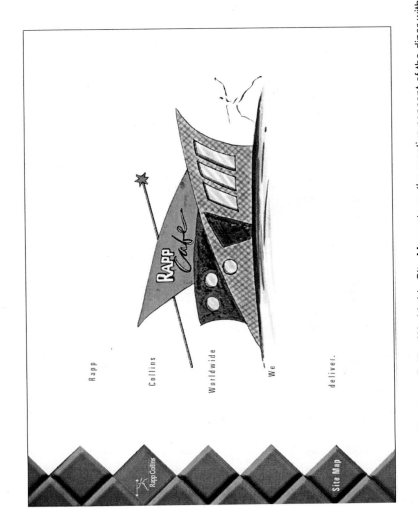

ILLUSTRATION 10.3. The Rapp Collins Worldwide Site Map sets up the creative concept of the diner with the Rapp Cafe image and the tagline, "We Deliver."

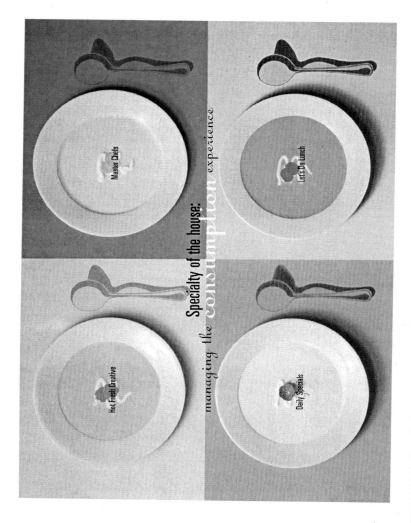

ILLUSTRATION 10.4. Following up on the café idea, this Rapp Collins Worldwide Web site page offers visually exciting, colorful click options.

EXHIBIT 10.1. Guidelines for Web site creation.

1. A Web site should serve as a forum for the exchange of ideas, rather than as a corporate brochure.
2. Content should be organized in a thoughtful, accessible manner with creative visual design and navigational clarity.
3. Encourage interaction, offering the customer an outlet for comment, question, or complaint as well as a way to immediately receive additional information.
4. The Web site should function in the same role as a trade show exhibit, enhancing corporate image, generating leads, and enabling direct sales through online ordering.
5. Register the Web site on all major search engines (such as Yahoo and Alta Vista). Work to have your site recognized with a "What's Cool" or "What's Hot" rating by one of the major search engines. These ratings will guarantee that the engines pull your site up first and increase traffic to your site dramatically.
6. Draw attention to your site by holding contests and giveaways.
7. Encourage the advertiser to promote the URL (Web address) of the site as part of the company's existing corporate communications strategy, placing the URL on letterhead, business cards, press releases, print and broadcast advertising, envelopes, and mailing labels. This increases public awareness of the site and its advertising messages.
8. Engage in cooperative advertising with another company. The Internet is built on cooperation, and it rewards companies that leverage off each other's efforts.

Source: Adapted from Shamrock Net Design's Web site <http://www.ShamrockNetDesign.com>.

ment. FTP (file transfer protocol) uploads files from a computer to the Internet (Fetch is a common FTP application).

SUMMARY

Production is what happens between the time an idea is approved and the time it finally appears in its proper medium. Print, broadcast, and Internet production all have some common characteristics—they rely on the creative team's prior research, planning, and scripting of the advertising concept. It is important for the creative team to convey the concept envisioned to the production team in the expected format and as descriptively as possible. In all cases, the production team generally works with members of the creative team to ensure that the advertisement, as it was conceived, has actually been produced. This is where similarities end. Print, broadcast, and Internet production involve very different channels of communication and employ distinctly different processes. Each has its own specific terminology and format. Because advertisers today often employ multiple media channels to communicate advertising messages, those responsible for the strategic or creative side of advertising need to have a basic understanding of the terminology and processes used in the ever-changing arena of print, broadcast, and Internet production.

:60 Spot

:60 "Vicki's Choice: Healthy Challenges"

7:55 a.m. Monday—I arrive at LeSEA Broadcasting and check my e-mail. I find a message from the production manager saying that I have a :30 spot that needs to be shot and edited by 5 p.m. today for the Making Healthy Choices Angle Pack. Quite an unrealistic goal, but that's the way it mostly happens around here.

8:10 a.m.—I walk down the hallway to see if Terri or Krista is available to talk about what the most important copy points are so that I can write the script. After that, I sit at my desk and quickly try to write so that I can have the copy approved before the production coordinator leaves for the day.

8:57 a.m.—The copy for the spot is approved. I have decided on a spot featuring children eating unhealthy food given to them by their mom. It's a great script. There is only one problem: I have to come up with a location, children, and a mom so I can start shooting by 11 a.m.

9:32 a.m.—I am on the phone with the engineer's wife asking if she can pick up some lunch and meet me at her mother-in-law's with her kids so we can shoot the spot. She agrees.

9:35-11 a.m.—I build the graphic in Adobe Photoshop that will be used to tag the spot at the end. It has the name of the pack, the contents, and price. I have developed a graphic for Making Healthy Choices already, so I stay with the same format, knock out the graphic, and save it to disk to be transferred into the Avid. I also drop the script off to radio so that I can have the voice-over done when I get back.

10:45 a.m.—I pack up a camera, tripod, lights, microphones (just in case), batteries for the camera, a beta tape, and a card for the white balance.

11:10 a.m.—After laying bars and tone and doing a white balance, I begin shooting. I start with product shots. I always want to have more footage than I actually need, so I shoot a minimum of thirty minutes for a :30 spot.

12:45 p.m.—I head back to the station to start editing.

1:00 p.m.—I take my lunch into the Avid suite and begin to digitize the material. If the shot is fifteen seconds long, it takes fifteen seconds to enter into the computer. The nonlinear editing system allows me to go back and make corrections in the middle of a shot without having to re-create the beginning or end again. While all this is going on, I pick up the script from audio, dub the voice-over from the reel to a beta tape, and pick out background music.

2:08 p.m.—I have digitized enough footage, the music, and the script. I am now ready to put the sequence together. Most people think that a :30 spot takes :30 to edit. That's a misconception! From my experience, a :30 spot takes about two hours to put together, providing there are no major changes.

3:54 p.m.—I have completed the spot with enough time to get it to Master Control so they can log it and get it on air. I call Terri down to see if she can give me the final approval so I can dub it to tape.

4:29 p.m.—Terri finally comes down and says that the graphic is wrong. I run to the computer, rebuild the price, retransfer the graphic, and have the spot reapproved.

4:59 p.m.—Terri is satisfied with the spot. I dump it to a recycled beta tape and drop it off at Master Control.

5:02 p.m.—I head upstairs to my desk to check my voice mail, and then start to fill out the paperwork on the spot that I've just completed.

5:24 p.m.—It's too late for me to start working on another spot which needs to be done Wednesday, so I decide to call it a day and begin the whole process tomorrow. However, I remind myself why I went into television in the first place: the excitement, and the challenge of being creative on the fly.

Learn the Term

Avid System—A nonlinear, computer-based editing system

Bars and tone—Set machine recording and playback levels. Bars set video levels at the proper hue, brightness, and black levels. Tone helps the machine calibrate audio levels at zero.

Beta tape—Beta cameras and beta tapes are used in television production in preference to VHS, which is the prevailing type used by home video producers. Beta utilizes half-inch oxide tapes to record audio and video.

Digitize—The term refers to the transformation of analog video into digital. Tape is shot in analog in order to edit the video, then converted to digital.

Master Control—This department at a television station plays videotaped programs and commercials for on-air viewing.

White balance—The act of telling the camera what is white by placing a white card in front of the lens. This allows all the other colors to be true since all colors make white.

Vicki Palk
Associate Producer/Editor
LeSEA Broadcasting
South Bend, Indiana

Chapter 11

Advertising Media Planning and Selection

In Poland, presentation matters. Magazine glossies for even moderately priced restaurants make full use of four-color printing possibilities with photographs of restaurant settings in picture-frame layouts. Typically, these pictures show dining rooms with starkly white lace cloths on tables laid out with gorgeously hued fresh flowers, fine china, and elegantly presented entrees. Dark wood paneling, glowing sconces, and green plants seem to be commonplace, and it all looks, well, carefully planned.

On May 1, 2004, Poland became a full member of the European Union, abandoning its national currency, the zloty, in favor of the euro. Optimistic about its multinational future, Poland's advertisers plan their advertising campaigns as carefully as they arrange their publicity photos. For example, Obory Dairy in Kozienice, Poland, hired CB4 advertising agency and laid out specific goals—to create awareness of the Jogi yogurt brand "as an exclusive product, to increase sales, and to build a positive image."[1] In the campaign's print ad, two young women sit in the lotus position and meditate as a new day dawns. The tagline that spans the print ad, "zaczyna się od Jogi" (Start Your Day with Jogi), ends with the product name, the Polish word for "Yoga," a double entendre meaning both the Eastern meditation technique and the product.

Obory's plan was to reach a fifteen- to thirty-nine-year-old audience of educated consumers with average to high income. The campaign targeted Warsaw and the Mazovia Province via billboards in the Metro, radio ads, and advertisements on buses, Web sites (Gadu-Gadu and <www.jogi.pl>), and point-of-sale materials. The campaign's time frame was divided between two products: April to July,

If this is your idea of geographic exploration...

It's time to call **TravelZone**®

We travel to cities across the world for less
than you thought possible.

Call us at **1-800-TRAVELZ** or visit our website at **www.travelzone.org**

ILLUSTRATION 11.1. Global image. Paula Winicur's design uses a picture window format, one of the basic print ad layouts, for a travel advertisement. Her generous use of white space frames the globe, which dominates the page. The ad also refers the consumer to an 800 number and Web site address, increasing the number of media choices.

2004, for Jogi Sport Active promotion, and August to November for Jogi Slim Line. In addition, CB4 was responsible for generating public relations and media buys.

Advertisers spend tremendous amounts of money on advertising media. Since 9/11 the lagging world economy resulted in cutbacks in these expenditures; thus, advertisers have sought more bang for their buck. To derive maximum results from media expenditures, marketers must develop effective media plans. Some marketers believe that traditional media such as television, newspapers, magazines, and radio are not as effective in producing sales as they were in the past as markets rapidly change and advertisers must much more selectively reach the product's best prospects (see Illustration 11.1). Thus, CB4 employed a combination of traditional and nontraditional media for the Jogi campaign.

Initiative Futures conducted research of thirty-six worldwide markets over a period of four years to determine which media had the most profitable cost per thousand (CPT) rate, e.g., the cost to reach 1,000 people.[2] Surprisingly, perhaps, "movies obtained the highest and best rate in the media ranking," followed by the Internet. The study found that television's CPT rate varied depending upon "the gross domestic income of the country investigated." The United States, Japan, and Switzerland showed the highest CPT rates, but the highest growth took place in Central Europe where the CPT for radio advertisements grew 70 percent during the four-year period. CPT rates, also designated CPM, will be discussed more fully in this chapter.

To use media effectively, it is important to understand not only the media but also how best to plan for and buy media space or time. Media planners are challenged now, more than ever, to choose the best media placements to reach increasingly segmented consumers. As Integrated Marketing Communication theory has entered the corporate world, marketers realize how crucial it is to use all available channels of communication, both traditional and nontraditional, to reach both mass markets and individual consumers.

MEDIA PLANNING

Media planning is the process of directing the advertising message to the target audience at the appropriate time and place, using the appropriate channel. Media planners must consider the following:

- What audiences do we want to reach?
- When and where do we want to reach them?
- How many people should we reach?
- How often do we need to reach them?
- What will it cost to reach them?

When all questions have been asked, answered, and decisions made, the recommendations and rationales are organized into a written document called a media plan. When approved by the advertiser, the plan becomes a blueprint for the selection and use of media. Once the advertiser has approved the plan, it also serves as a guide for actually purchasing the media.

Media planning involves the coordination of three levels of strategy formulations: marketing strategy, advertising strategy, and media strategy. The overall marketing strategy provides the impetus and direction for the choice of both advertising and media strategies. The media strategy consists of four sets of interrelated activities: (1) selecting the target audience, (2) specifying media objectives, (3) selecting media and vehicles, and (4) buying media.

Selecting the Target Audience

Successful media strategy requires that the target audience be clearly pinpointed. Because people who have common characteristics tend to act in similar ways, advertisers like to break down the population into consumer segments, that is, groups of potential buyers with key similarities. This process of segmentation allows advertisers to design messages specifically for the people who are most likely to buy their product. The consumer segments considered the best prospects for a product or service are called target groups. Advertising messages are directed to these potential buyers.

THE GLOBAL PERSPECTIVE:
THE OPTIMIZER AND THE BRITISH INVASION

Producers of original American plays have complained for decades about the British invasion of Broadway. Andrew Lloyd Webber's *Cats* slinked onto the scene in the early 1980s, and the parade of British imports hasn't stopped. However, a British import in the business world, the "optimizer," received red-carpet treatment from U.S. media buyers and planners when it arrived in 1997.

European users had found the optimizer helpful, and representatives of Super Midas and X*pert were "quite modest" about their software's advantages and disadvantages.[a] But that didn't repress America's "optimizermania." "Optimizer" became an industry buzzword. Procter & Gamble has even required "agencies competing for its billion-dollar media buying assignment to include optimizing systems in their proposals."[b]

Europeans have used optimizers, "computer programs that use algorithms to evaluate schedules" and compare alternatives, for a number of years. The programs assist media buyers and planners in identifying the best media and the schedule that "maximizes efficient reach" to better meet clients' objectives at the best price.

Of course, as *Advertising Age* writer Neil Braun cautioned, an optimizer program can help implement strategies, "but it cannot design a strategy for you." Still needed is a media planner with "a Midas touch."

[a]Neil Braun, "There's No Magic in TV's Optimizers," *Advertising Age*, May 11, 1998, p. 36.
[b]"Optimizers and Syndication," *Advertising Age*, April 27, 1998, p. A22.

Specifying Media Objectives

A firm usually has certain organizational objectives that shape the marketing objectives. The advertising objectives must then work with the higher-level marketing objectives. Media objectives must contribute to the advertising objectives. Five objectives are fundamental to media planning: reach, frequency, weight, continuity, and cost.

1. *Reach.* What proportion of the target audience must see, read, or hear the advertising message during a specified period—for example, one month? Reach is a measure of how many different members (or what percentage) of the target audience is exposed at least once in a given period (usually four weeks) to the advertiser's message.

2. *Frequency.* How often should the target audience be exposed to the advertisement during this period—for example, at least two times a week? Frequency measures the average number of times the target audience is exposed to—sees, reads, or hears—the advertiser's message during a given period.

3. *Weight.* How much total advertising is necessary during a particular period to accomplish the reach and frequency objectives? Message weight is the size of combined target audiences reached by the advertiser's message in a single media plan. Message weight is calculated by adding all the reach numbers for each ad in the plan, ignoring any overlap or duplication. Message weight can be expressed in terms of gross impressions or gross rating points (GRPs). Impression represents one person's opportunity to be exposed to a program, newspaper, magazine, or outdoor location. Impressions measure the size of the audience either for one media vehicle (one insertion in *Time* magazine) or for a combination of vehicles (*Time* and *Business Week,* for example) as estimated by media research. In practice, media planners discuss gross impressions—the sum of the audiences of all the media vehicles used in a certain time spot when dealing with multiple vehicles in a schedule. The summary figure is called "gross" because the media planner has made no attempt to calculate how many different people have viewed each show. Gross values simply refer to the number of people viewing, regardless of whether each viewer saw one, two, or all of the TV shows. The numbers for gross impressions for mass media such as network television, can become very large. For convenience, media planners sometimes express message weight in terms of GRPs, which are the sum of the ratings of all programs in the television schedule; in the context of one media plan (TV, for example), GRPs measure the total target audience exposed to all the vehicles in that plan. One percent of the target audience is equivalent to one rating point. To calculate GRPs for the entire media plan, multiply the proportion of the target audience reached by the frequency ($GRP = R \times F$).

4. *Continuity.* How should the advertising budget be allocated over time? Continuity involves the matter of how advertising is allocated during the course of an advertising campaign. Advertisers have three general alternatives related to allocating the budget

over the course of the campaign: continuous, pulsing, and flighting schedules. In a continuous advertising schedule, a relatively equal amount of advertisement dollars is invested throughout the campaign. In a pulsing advertising schedule, some advertising is used during every period of the campaign, but the amount of advertising varies considerably from period to period. In a flighting advertising schedule, the advertiser varies expenditures throughout the campaign and allocates zero expenditures in some months.

5. *Cost.* What is the least expensive way to accomplish the other objectives? Media planners must resolve cost issues as they attempt to allocate the advertising budget in a cost-efficient manner while still satisfying other objectives. One of the most important and universally used indicators of media efficiency is the cost-per-thousand criterion (abbreviated CPM, with the M representing the Roman number for 1,000). The basic formula for CPM is

$$\text{Cost per thousand} = \frac{\text{Cost of media unit} \times 1000}{\text{Number of total contacts}}$$

The term *contacts* is used here in a general sense to include any type of advertising audience (television viewers, radio listeners, magazine or newspaper readers, etc.). To illustrate how CPM is calculated, consider the following situation: According to A.C. Nielsen TV ratings in a week in October 2003, NBC's top-rated *Friends* commanded a rating of 14.0 (note that a rating point is equal to 1,084,000 U.S. TV households; the total U.S. TV households numbered 108.4 million at the time). The broadcast prime-time thirty-second spot TV ad rate for *Friends* was $473,500.[3] Therefore,

$$\text{CPM} = \frac{\$473,500 \times 1000}{108,400,000 \times 14 \text{ percent}} = \$31.20$$

The CPM statistics are useful for comparing the cost efficiency of reaching your target audience through various media. They must be used cautiously, however. These cost comparisons do not take into account variations in media audience, comparability across different media, and creative execution. CPM can be a handy yardstick to support media selection and a good way to measure cost, but it does not measure the effectiveness of an advertisement in certain media.[4]

Selecting Media and Vehicles

As an element of media strategy, media channels of communication carry messages from the advertiser to the audience. Media organizations sell space (in print media) and time (in broadcast media). The most frequently used advertising media are television, newspapers, magazines, radio, outdoor and transit, direct response, and digital, including the Internet.

Vehicles are the specific broadcast programs (for example, the television program *Survivor*) or print choices (for example, *Time* magazine) in which advertisements are placed. Each medium and each vehicle has a set of unique characteristics and virtues. Advertisers attempt to select those media and vehicles whose characteristics are most compatible with the advertised brand in reaching its target audience and conveying its intended message.

People respond to or react to advertisements in different ways. For example, "networkers," about 23 percent of the population, are the heaviest users of print media. They do their own research, rather than buying products simply out of brand loyalty. Diet colas and 100 percent fruit juices are the beverages of choice of networkers. "Interfacers," 15 percent of consumers, prefer face-to-face contact when it comes to shopping. They are the most ethnically diverse segment, with four in ten non-Caucasian. Interfacers are heavy users of television, and they like to be first with the latest trend. Their preferred beverage is regular cola.[5]

Carat House Media's survey of 1,000 British television viewers revealed another way people respond to advertisements. The research sought to determine the respondents' abilities "to remember advertising spots 30 minutes after their broadcast." Carat learned that many "changed the channel during ads and those who did watch them remembered only a little if the block [of commercials] contained nine spots." When commercials were presented in blocks of seven, 55 to 75 percent had increased recall. The study concluded that "ad blocks which are too long diminish the effectiveness of advertising."[6]

An advertiser might use only one medium (e.g., television) to reach the target audience when it is believed that this concentration will give special impact. On the other hand, an advertiser might reach the target audience by building a media mix of two or more media (e.g., television and magazine). A media mix makes sense when a single medium will not reach the target audience in sufficient numbers or with sufficient impact to achieve media objectives (e.g., product awareness).

Unilever's health and beauty division has used a creative media mix to reach its growing Hispanic market. The corporation partnered with *Glamour en Espanol* to create "a digest-size 32-page booklet sent three times a year as a direct marketing to Hispanic households in the top 10 Hispanic markets." The booklet contains coupons for a variety of Unilever health and beauty products, such as Dove, Suave, Caress, and Pond's. Using a large tent pitched at Hispanic events, Unilever also "offers an almost spa-like experience" to introduce Hispanic women to its health and beauty lines. Unilever's foods' campaigns have combined Spanish-language television commercials, corporate sponsorships, and "grass-roots sampling of food and fun at Hispanic events and retailers' store fronts." Unilever's innovative media mix circumvents overreliance on commercial time on network television, which has become amazingly expensive.[7]

The CBS network sold thirty-second spots during the 2004 Super Bowl for a record $2.3 million to generate a $140 million windfall for CBS parent Viacom.[8] Approximate costs for a thirty-second spot on prime-time shows in fall 2004 are shown in Table 11.1.

TABLE 11.1. Costs for :30 spots on prime-time shows, fall 2004.

Show	Network	Approximate cost (in U.S. dollars)
ER	NBC	479,250
Survivor: Vanuatu	CBS	412,833
The Apprentice	NBC	409,877
Monday Night Football	ABC	323,000
Everybody Loves Raymond	CBS	315,850

Source: Adapted from "Ad Age's Fall 2003 Prime Time Pricing Survey," *Advertising Age FactPack,* February 28, 2005, p. 21.

MEDIA BUYING

The eventual selection of a medium and specific media vehicles depends on the availability of media research and information supplied to media planners and buyers on the size and profile of the audience and the media costs for space or time. Buying and selling media is not the straightforward process it once was. There are many more media and vehicles to choose from these days. Moreover, to get a bigger share of the advertiser's budget, larger print and broadcast media companies now bundle the various stations, publications, or properties they own and offer them together as a packaged incentive.

Media buying can be a lucrative part of an advertising agency's business. Nevertheless, many media planners and buyers are hired right out of college and given entry-level salaries for work that requires a great deal of responsibility and long hours. Media departments at agencies constitute starting points for advertising careers. Because these twenty-somethings control millions of ad dollars in placements, their power is often disproportionate to their salaries. Some media executives complain that young planners and buyers have no understanding of older targets and no interest in media channels that specifically target affluent baby boomers—they are uninterested in publications they see as targeting their parents. Agencies do make an effort to educate young planners and buyers about the "different targets and demographics so that they'll be aware of media for older audiences."[9] Nevertheless, clients who hope to target an aging population may prefer to work with media department personnel who have industry experience and an understanding of that market's needs—and it's the client who pays the bill.

If media buying ever was predictable, it certainly isn't any more. NBC decided to charge all advertisers the same amount for the coveted ad spots on the *Seinfeld* series finale in May 1998.[10] In addition, cable TV viewer numbers have been catching up to the networks'. Hispanic viewers watch 7 percent more television, on average, than other groups.[11] Hispanic viewers, who tend to be younger than the national average as a whole, flock "to Univision, the dominant Spanish-language broadcast network" as well as to the smaller networks, Telemundo, Galavision, and Telefutura.[12]

Internet ad buys have added to the confusion. Two different techniques are currently used to measure Internet reach and frequency:

- *Consumer-centric approach.* This measurement uses a PC meter to determine the length of time a user has spent on various activities. The measure of interactivity is referred to as the "click-through."[13]
- *Site-centric measurement.* This approach involves analysis of server activity log files. Since the vehicle is the unit of measurement in traditional media, with the advertising cost based on potential audience delivery capabilities of the vehicle, John D. Leckenby and Jongpil Hong believe that "the site would seem to be a compatible object of measurement."[14] A disadvantage of this method is that measurements taken at the Web site track "hits" but do not record movement back to pages previously viewed.

Media buyers remain frustrated with online-measurement data produced by the two main providers, comScore Networks' comScore Media Metrix and Nielsen/Net Ratings. Nielsen panel recruitment uses random digit dialing while ComCast uses that method combined with "online banner ads designed to entice potential panelists with virus-protection software and speedier broadband connections." Media buyers feel the samples are skewed, thus they lack the information needed to make buying decisions.

Nevertheless, computers have made the media planner's job easier. Yet even with computer technology, it is still up to the media planner to know the product, the market, the media, and to make the call. Computers help in the planning process, but—with subjective judgment now such a crucial part of the process—they cannot take the place of people.

SUMMARY

The tenets of Integrated Marketing Communication have affected media planning: the marketer must now, more than ever, choose the right media to reach increasingly segmented consumers. That challenge is compounded by the proliferation of media from which to choose today. To develop an effective media strategy, media planners must select and understand the target audience, establish media objectives, choose the right medium (or media) and vehicle(s), and buy media and construct media schedules. The final step is to prepare and implement the media plan.

ETHICS TRACK:
PLACING THE BLAME FOR OBESITY

When a rainy day kept Sally and her brother from going outside to play in Dr. Seuss' *The Cat in the Hat*, these old-fashioned kids didn't know what to do. They were creatures of another time. Today kids don't go out to play much anymore. They have video games and an infinite number of television programs to occupy their Saturday mornings. In fact, research released by the Henry J. Kaiser Family Foundation in late 2003 showed that 80 percent of children up to age six are as likely to spend their time with a screen media as to play outside on an average day. Males aged seven and under are the most ardent watchers of cartoons. Interspersed with the cartoons, they see advertisements for everything from sugar-based soft drinks to sugar-covered cereals. No wonder the epidemic of childhood obesity has become a concern for U.S. parents. The 2003 Roper Youth Report showed that 80 percent of youths ages eight to twelve said it was their parents who most influenced their food choices. Under 5 percent attributed their choices to advertising.[a]

Nevertheless, the Kaiser study and another released by the American Psychological Association concluded that advertising is, indeed, making children fat.[b] By 2005 the American Psychological Association's Task Force on Advertising to Children pressed "for federal restrictions on all advertising to kids under age 8, citing research that shows these youngsters cannot 'recognize persuasive intent.' "[c] Licensers of cartoon spokescharacters have authorized such characters as Time Warner's Warner Bros. Bugs Bunny to advertise healthy foods such as "milk, water, juices, and veggies."

When the reports came out, marketers for the Kellogg Company in Battle Creek, Michigan, had already responded to long-time criticisms that sugar-coated packaged cereals were the culprits. Watch any Saturday morning cartoon program, and you're sure to see commercials for sugar-coated cereals. In the spring of 2003, Kellogg hired Leo Burnett USA, Chicago, to launch a $50 million advertising campaign for its new breakfast brands, Eggo Froot Loops Waffles and Pop-Tart Yogurt Blasts.[d] Sensitive to the obesity issue and stung by category advances made by competitors General Mills and Kraft, Kellogg shared new global guidelines on childhood obesity with its agency. A TV commercial targeted to children ages six to twelve featured Froot Loops spokescharacter Toucan Sam. In early 2005 McDonald's Corp. "unveiled an agressively positive global marketing campaign to promote eating right, and staying active, especially in messages geared to children."[e]

Do you think that Kellogg's response should alleviate criticism? How do you feel about the use of spokescharacters to reach children? Is your opinion based on whether the messages promote foods believed to be nutritious? Who determines which products will be healthy for children?

Is diet the whole story regarding childhood obesity? What role do you think advertising plays in childhood obesity?

[a]Pat Dando, "Healthier Fast-Food a Reality," *Advertising Age,* March 29, 2004, p. S-7.

[b]Mercedes M. Cardona, "Marketers Bite Back as Fat Fight Flares Up," *Advertising Age,* March 1, 2004, p. 3.

[c]Tiffany Meyers, "Marketing to Kids Comes Under Fresh Attack," *Advertising Age,* February 21, 2005, p. s-2.

[d]Stephanie Thompson, "Kellogg to Spend $50 Million," *Advertising Age,* March 10, 2004, p. 3.

[e]"McDonald's Unveils Global Ad Campaign Aimed at Children," <adage.daily@adage.com>.

Chapter 12

Print Media

The principal Greek god, Zeus just could not stay away from mortal women. He disguised himself as a swan to seduce Leda, a queen of Sparta. He took on the shape of a bull to seduce Europa, a Phoenician princess. The story of Europa and the bull resonated so deeply with a continent that it took its name from the princess in the Greek myth. For as long as bulls have roamed the earth, Europeans "have feared, been intrigued by, and exalted their graceful strength."[1] Ancient representations of the bull survive on cave paintings in France and Spain, and the animal continues to fascinate the continent that bears Europa's name.

A 1954 campaign to advertise the brandy Veterano featured black bull cutouts designed and erected as billboards in Spain. The bull, El Toro de Osborne, became a national icon when, in 1994, Osborne removed its bull-boards. A public outcry erupted in all levels of society, bringing the bull-boards back, sans the company name. The Osborne bull will be discussed further in Chapter 15, "Alternative Advertising Media."

The bull was a frequent theme in the work of Spanish artist Picasso; it also became the theme of a series of billboard and print advertisements created by Havas' Euro RSCG 27, Paris. The agency appropriated the bull's mythic appeal and Picasso's powerful images to bring a sense of artistry to the campaigns for the Citroen Xsara, a midpriced French car. Havas art director Volker Gehr turned the car's engine into the head of a powerful black bull.[2] This transformation recalls Zeus's old disguise tricks.

The image of the bull represents strength, valor, and grace to Americans as well as Europeans. In a print ad designed for Steak and Ale restaurants, graphic artist Eric Remington placed the image of a bull imposingly atop the ad's headline and copy (see Illustration 12.1).

ILLUSTRATION 12.1. Strength and valor. Eric Remington's print ad for Steak and Ale restaurants draws on centuries of human fascination with the power and grace of the bull.

Just as the best commercials allude to legendary, mythic stories, the best print advertising displays meaningful, memorable images that turn heads. Such ads keep interest through a complex of cultural connections, especially allusions to shared experiences and stories. Another animal that has long fascinated humans is the owl. An Armando Testa, Milan, print ad for Emporio Armani sunglasses became a collector's item, landed on postcards, and made an appearance in *The New York Times*.[3] The ad employed black-and-white photographs of an owl wearing sunglasses. In one of the ads in the campaign, the owl hooted just one line of copy: "Daywear for night owls." In another version, the text read, "That's what the girls like: a real head turner."

Each advertising medium and vehicle has a set of unique characteristics and virtues. Advertisers attempt to select those media and vehicles whose characteristics are most compatible with the advertised product and which will enhance the product's image (e.g., see Illustration 12.2). In addition to the potential for artistry, print has the capacity for fine color reproduction. Although the Citroen Xsara and Armani ads ran in black and white for aesthetic reasons, color is a necessity for certain kinds of product advertising, such as food and makeup. Many magazines are able to reproduce ads with excellent color fidelity and other attributes such as pullouts and inserts. Remington's Steak and Ale ad was created for newspaper, so color was not a concern. Most newspaper ads run in black and white, but these ads are able to give the advertiser something that magazines cannot— quick turnaround time to let readers know about current price cuts, grand openings, or sales. This chapter explains how magazine and newspaper advertising differ, and how print advertising enhances the advertiser's media mix.

MAGAZINE ADVERTISING

Throughout the 1980s and 1990s, the magazine industry experienced rapid growth with increases in advertising revenues, the lifeblood of print media. This growth was fostered by magazines' ability to serve the educational, informational, and entertainment needs and interests of a wide range of readers in both the consumer and business markets. The wide variety of magazines appeals to advertisers inter-

ILLUSTRATION 12.2. The wave of the future. Graphic artist Paula Winicur chose a font for this dramatic ad that would appeal to a youthful target. The wave crashes diagonally in a dynamic visual to match the excitement and energy associated with the jeans-wearing generation.

ested in the diversity of magazine types, which allows them to target more specific groups than media such as television or newspaper (see Illustration 12.3). However, the tragedy of 9/11 and the economic recession rocked the magazine industry.[4]

Newsstand sales had been in a decline throughout the last quarter of the twentieth century, and circulation revenues suddenly plummeted between 1992 and 2002, a period that showed a 53 percent circulation drop.[5] Media buyers have to justify magazine advertising expenditures through circulation figures, so these buys became difficult to justify in the belt-tightening years after 9/11. As circulations fell, so did advertising revenues. The recovery has been slow. In 2003, magazines experienced a modest 6.3 percent increase in ad spending, while local newspapers, cable and syndicated TV, and the Internet reported twice that figure.[6] Business-to-business magazines came in at a dismal .7 percent increase.

A magazine tends to be read at leisure, kept for long periods of time, and passed along to others. The four-color printing process and glossy paper as well as issue-specific themes make magazines attractive to advertisers. Some magazines have had sufficient cultural power to catalyze social movements, e.g., Hugh Hefner's *Playboy* helped launch the sexual revolution, *OUT* helped gays move mainstream, and *New York Magazine* changed national perspectives on the importance of individual cities. A magazine may set a national tone, e.g., a publisher in Poland targeted a magazine, *Twoja Nadzieja,* to women in the twenty to forty-five age range. To encourage positive thinking, the magazine featured "real-life stories with happy endings."[7] Magazine editor Tina Brown believes that, despite magazines' problems, the desire "for depth, imagination, scope, for time and length [has] never been more pressing," and only magazines fully address these needs.[8]

Media buyers remain interested in magazines' "constellation of niched titles" and the "ability to pinpoint specific audiences" such as homemakers, brides, new parents, sports enthusiasts, computer geeks, and geographically defined groups (for example, Hoosiers read the category's ad revenue leader, *Indianapolis Monthly*).

Classifications of Magazines

Thousands of different magazines are published in the United States. They are so diverse that it is helpful to classify the main types.

ILLUSTRATION 12.3. Strategic placement. Although the practice has become controversial in the magazine industry, advertisers have long been able to request complementary placements of their ads alongside related editorial copy. On this page from *The Northern Indiana Source*, the publisher enhanced the credibility of an ad purchased by massage therapist Dale Huston by placing it next to a guest column he contributed.

THE GLOBAL PERSPECTIVE:
DEFINED BY THE WORLD AND TIMES

A meta-narrative is said to drive global news. According to the chair of *The New York Times,* "The war on terror is clearly the prism through which international affairs are viewed. Big events change the way people see life." During a visit to Northwestern University's Medill School of Journalism on February 27, 2004, Arthur Sulzberger Jr., chair of *The New York Times,* reclined comfortably, his legs crossed, as he talked about the number two U.S. newspaper (see Table 12.4). With 1,200 at work in its newsroom, *The Times* is one of the world's most profitable, fastest-growing brands.

"For a democracy to survive, you need an educated populace and different voices," Sulzberger said. The fourth member of his family to chair the *Times,* he described the psychographic profile of its readers. A knowledge audience, their interests are defined by the world around them and its culture—they step outside themselves to engage with the world. The average reader's age is forty-two, and that has not changed in a decade, so he assumes *The Times* is picking up new and younger readers. The paper goes after this demographic "in all media and countries," he said, stressing that *The Times* is a "24/7 operation that feeds the Web," although a print story cannot go directly onto TV or the Internet.

The New York Times owns eight U.S. TV stations, a regional newspaper group, the cable channel *Discovery Times,* and the *International Herald Tribune.* From his poise under pressure to his matching tie and socks, Sulzberger's "together" persona exemplifies the way he envisions the newspaper's future. "That's where things are headed," he said, "combining all methods of news distribution. Each medium has its own abilities, and all—print, digital, television—are needed for success."

Times competitor *The Wall Street Journal* took diversification a step further in March 2004 with the launch of its Spanish-language edition. *The Wall Street Journal Americas,* circulated to 1.7 million Latin American readers, was the prototype for the eight-page tabloid designed to reach a knowledge audience of U.S. Hispanic readers.[a]

Lauren Siegel

[a]"'WSJ' to Produce Tabloid in Spanish," *Advertising Age,* February 9, 2004, p. 10.

Magazines are commonly categorized by the broad audiences they service: (1) consumer magazines, (2) business magazines, (3) farm magazines, (4) computer/Internet magazines, and (5) online magazines.

Custom publishing (a billion-dollar category of publications tailored to their sponsoring marketer) had grown quickly in the 1990s, but the in-flight category saw only a .6 percent increase in paid ad pages in 2003.[9] In addition to in-flight, major consumer magazine categories include automotive, computers, home, men's, music/entertainment, parenthood, travel, women's/fashion, youth, business/national, business/regional, and newspaper Sunday magazines.

Consumer Magazines

Advertisers do not choose magazines as a medium as often as they once did for general mass-appeal products. Yet magazines are very good at reaching certain kinds of consumer segments—target groups. *Better Homes and Gardens* is oriented toward homemakers and family service. *Sports Illustrated* is oriented toward sports enthusiasts. Even for the same general target market, for example, women, niche magazines appeal to specific consumer interests and lifestyles. For instance, there are publications for women who decorate, garden, cook, and sew. There are also magazines about weddings, travel, fitness, fashion, careers, and health. Still others (general-interest magazines) try to cover a little bit of it all. Although the general interest magazine has survived for over a century, magazines targeted to niche markets have become increasingly popular and successful (see Table 12.1).

Magazines also reach target markets within geographic areas. Many U.S. magazines publish regional editions that are distributed only in certain parts of the country (e.g., North, South, East, and West). Advertisers use these regional editions to advertise only in certain areas or to change their advertising messages from one region to another. Some magazines, such as *Midwest Living,* target only a specific geographic area.

Business Magazines

Whereas consumer magazines are directed at those who buy products for their own consumption, business magazines are directed at business readers. There are several types of business magazines: industrial magazines directed toward manufacturers (e.g., *Chemical Week*), trade magazines directed toward middlemen (e.g., *Progressive Grocer*), and professional magazines directed toward a specific

TABLE 12.1. Top ten consumer magazines by circulation.

Magazine	Circulation January-June 2004
1. *AARP The Magazine*	22,720,073
2. *Reader's Digest*	10,228,531
3. *TV Guide*	9,016,188
4. *Better Homes and Gardens*	7,628,424
5. *National Geographic*	5,468,471
6. *Good Housekeeping*	4,623,113
7. *Family Circle*	4,372,813
8. *Ladies' Home Journal*	4,108,619
9. *Woman's Day*	4,060,619
10. *Time*	4,034,491

Source: Adapted from "Paid Circulation in Consumer Magazines," *Advertising Age,* August 23, 2004, p. 30.

profession (e.g., *National Law Review*). In North America, *Canadian Business,* Canada's only business magazine with 100 percent paid circulation, provides stories that are not covered in the newspapers and a Canadian perspective on international business. It reaches one million readers. Since 1946 the *Far Eastern Economic Review,* published weekly in Hong Kong, has been one of Asia's top business magazines. Its more than 100,000 readers are concentrated in Hong Kong, Malaysia, Singapore, and other parts of Southeast Asia, although it sells 13,000 copies in North America and Europe.

Farm Magazines

The third category of magazines is farm publications, directed toward farmers and their families or to companies that manufacture or sell agricultural equipment, supplies, and services. The top titles are *Successful Farming* and *Progressive Farmer.* Some advertisers overlook the farm publication marketplace or may not use it effectively.

Computer/Internet Magazines

Magazines targeted to computer and Internet users experienced a growth spurt in the mid- to late 1990s. However, the category had only a 1.9 percent advertising linage increase in 2003. *PC Magazine* was the decided leader in ad page revenues, followed by *PC World* and *Wired*.[10]

Online Magazines

Print publishers were initially hesitant to launch online versions of their magazines, afraid that they would "cannibalize their print properties."[11] Nevertheless, the field of online magazines has been pioneered by such publishers as Time Warner, which expanded from a Web site supported by only five advertisers in 1994, to the current Time Warner's "Pathfinder" network that houses the online editions of *Time, People, Money, Fortune,* and *Entertainment Weekly,* among other titles. The main advantage of online magazines is said to be reader loyalty and niche targeting.

Controlled or Paid Circulation

Magazines may be distributed on either a controlled-circulation or paid-circulation basis. The top nonpaid circulation (controlled-circulation) magazine in 2003 was *AARP The Magazine*. A paid circulation magazine requires the recipient to pay a subscription price to receive it. The top paid circulation magazines in 2003 were *Reader's Digest, TV Guide,* and *Better Homes and Gardens* while *People* was the top consumer magazine by ad revenue (see Table 12.2).

Advantages and Disadvantages of Magazine Advertising

Three pages of simulated auto upholstery materials, a keepsake motoring game, and a pullout poster of a Colorado pickup were created as a result of U.S. automakers' determination to push the creative limits of magazine advertising. Automakers turned to magazines to make a big "creative splash" when TV seemed too expensive and it became clear that readers "spend more time with print ads" than television commercials.[12] Infiniti alone spent $56 million in 2003. According to David Carey, the publisher of *The New Yorker* magazine, his staff did "more different kinds of insert configurations [in 2003] than in its entire history."

Furthermore, "newsstands are as segmented as a high school lunchroom," making magazines appeal to that hard-to-reach audience

TABLE 12.2. Top ten consumer magazines by ad revenue.

Magazine	Total gross revenue 2004
1. *People*	1,235.1
2. *Sports Illustrated*	936.2
3. *Time*	920.8
4. *TV Guide*	916.6
5. *Better Homes and Gardens*	836.3
6. *Parade*	617.2
7. *Newsweek*	597.9
8. *Reader's Digest*	563.7
9. *Good Housekeeping*	520.0
10. *Woman's Day*	440.1

Source: Adapted from *Advertising Age FactPack,* February 28, 2005, p. 37.

of eighteen- to thirty-four-year-old men.[13] Popular categories with this age group include laddies, metrosexuals, sports enthusiasts, and alternative newsweeklies such as *The Stranger.* Young men find these publications more relevant to their lives than TV shows, and they are making longer-term commitments to them.

Magazines have general characteristics and qualities that make them particularly attractive as an advertising medium.

- The ability to pinpoint specific audiences distinguishes magazine advertising from other media.
- Magazines are noted for their long lives and high reader involvement.
- Magazines have good color quality.
- Magazines offer flexible formats that permit different sizes of ads as well as inserts and scent strips, often used by perfume companies to allow readers to sample new scents. A "bleed" page is one in which the dark or colored background of the ad extends to the edge of the page. Magazine publishers usually charge a 10 to 15 percent premium on them, although the top paid circulation magazine, *Reader's Digest,* offers bleed at no additional cost. The advantages of bleeds include greater flexi-

bility in expressing the advertising idea, a slightly larger printing area, and a more dramatic impact. A junior unit is a large ad (60 percent of the page) in the middle of a page surrounded by editorial matter. Similar to junior units are island halves, except that more editorial matter surrounds them. Advertisers may also choose multipage spreads.

- Sometimes an advertiser chooses a magazine insert rather than a standard page. The advertiser prints the ad on special, high-quality paper stock and ships the finished ad to the publisher for insertion into the magazine at a special price.

Although the advantages offered by magazines are considerable, they are limited by certain factors.

- Advertising in mass circulation magazines can be very expensive. However, the costs of ad space in more specialized publications (e.g., *fitness*) with smaller circulation is less.
- Magazine ads must be submitted well in advance of the publication date, usually thirty to ninety days.
- Magazines generally gauge their success in terms of the number of advertising pages they attract. Thus, clutter becomes a very big problem for the advertisers.

Buying Magazine Advertising Space

Magazines provide rate cards offered by Standard Rate and Data Service that show how much they charge for their advertising. SRDS contains more than just advertising rates. It also contains an estimate of the circulation, closing dates, mechanical requirements, readership profiles, and additional information (see Exhibit 12.1). Advertising space is generally sold on the basis of space units such as full page, half page, and quarter page, although some publications quote rates on the basis of column inches. Ads can be produced or run using black and white, black and white plus one color, or four colors. The more colors used in the ad, the greater the expense because of the increased printing costs. The rates for magazine advertising space can also vary according to the number of insertions during a specific period. Cumulative quantity discounts offered by magazines are based on the total space purchased within a contract year and provide clear incentives for advertisers to maintain continuity with a particular

EXHIBIT 12.1. *Reader's Digest* rate card.

Rate base:	10,000,000
MRI audience:	42,605,000
Median age:	49.732
Median HHI:	$49,210
Frequency:	12×

Full page four-color:	$221,600	Full page black-and-white:	$193,790
Half page four-color:	133,000	Half page black-and-white:	116,310
3/4 page:	199,500	3/4 page:	174,470

Source: MRI, Spring 2003.

magazine. Advertisers can also save money by advertising in magazine combinations (e.g., two different magazines).

The CPM (cost-per-thousand) measure is used by advertisers to compare different magazine buys. The magazine with the lower cost per thousand will be the more economical.

$$\text{Cost per thousand} = \frac{\text{Page rate}}{\text{Circulation}} \times 1000$$

Cost-per-thousand information for each magazine is available from two syndicated magazine services: Mediamark Research, Inc. (MRI) and Simmons Market Research Bureau (SMRB). Cost-per-thousand data are useful in making magazine-vehicle selection decisions, but many other factors (e.g., readership profile) must also be taken into account.

NEWSPAPER ADVERTISING

Newspapers have historically been the leading advertising medium in the United States, edging out network television as the medium that receives the greatest amount of advertising expenditures (see Table 12.3). People continue to turn to the daily newspaper for in-depth news coverage and other current information. Readership is especially high in cities with colleges and more than one daily newspaper.

Newspapers are an especially important advertising medium to local advertisers and particularly to retailers, who account for a large amount of newspaper advertising. Because newspapers allow for immediate communication, retailers use this medium to announce sales and offer discount coupons. Many people buy the newspaper specifically for the coupons and sale information.

Classifications of Newspapers

Like magazines, there are different classifications or types of newspapers: daily newspapers, weekly newspapers, national newspapers (e.g., *The Wall Street Journal* and *USA Today*), special-audience newspapers (e.g., *Advertising Age* for those in the advertising and marketing fields), and Pennysavers (local publications with newspaper format and minimal nonadvertising content, primarily funded by advertising and delivered free of charge to all addresses in a geographic area). The top ten U.S. newspapers appear in Table 12.4.

Newspaper magazines are a hybrid of the two print media. In this case, the newspaper has a separate magazine editor and staff, and the format resembles that of a magazine with longer feature stories illustrated by large color photos. Newspapers easily target geographic areas through special editions. *The Chicago Tribune Magazine,* e.g., targets prosperous Chicago areas through a special VIP edition. This allows advertisers more precise targeting as it reaches households in selected areas where median income exceeds $55,000, and 60 percent of its readers will be professional women and/or college-educated adults. Like other magazines, the newspaper magazine may

TABLE 12.3. Ad spending by media.

Media	Ad spending January-December 2003 (in billions of dollars)
1. Direct Mail	48.37
2. Newspaper	44.84
3. Broadcast TV	41.93
4. Radio	19.10
5. Cable TV	18.81
6. Yellow Pages	13.90

Source: Advertising Age FactPack, February 22, 2005, p. 14.

ETHICS TRACK:
MAGAZINES ON TRIAL

Rosie O'Donnell made a career as a funny lady, but it wasn't so funny when she went to court with Gruner & Jahr USA Publishing to settle conflicts over *Rosie,* a magazine launched in April 2001. By December 2002 the Broadway and TV star and her *Rosie* editors had come to an impasse, and the magazine folded. If that wasn't enough bad news for the publisher, the trial rocked the magazine industry.

O'Donnell's brother, Ed, a senior vice president of marketing at NBC, took the stand and testified that the "publisher had provided false circulation numbers to the Audit Bureau of Circulations" (ABC).[a] Newsstand sales were "much lower than the 407,500" the publisher claimed for summer 2002.[b] In 2002, the publisher overestimated *Rosie* newsstand sales by 20 percent. Worse yet, Ed O'Donnell testified that he was told at *Rosie* that this was common practice in the magazine industry.

Media buyers had long worried about the credibility of circulation and sales figures provided to them by magazine publishers. What did publishers consider to be paid circulation, and how did they report the figures? Everyone knows that figures can be used to support almost any case if they are manipulated.

Because circulation figures form the rate bases for magazine advertising space, cuts in rate bases became a contentious issue. Advertisers and their buyers believed that the large advertising budgets of the 1990s led publishers to fatten their rate bases. Furthermore, buyers have not been "shy about expressing displeasure over paying freight they feel should be borne by consumers," e.g., they want rate bases cut and consumers to pay more for the magazines instead of "relying on advertisers to support them."[c] *The Atlantic Monthly* received praise from the advertising industry when it cut its rate base 27.8 percent and raised its subscription price to $30.

The counterargument regards the singling out of magazines with pressure to charge more to the consumer. What if viewers had to pay per view for such popular television shows as *Survivor* and *Friends*? Would viewers pay the price? Should consumers be expected to pick up more of the tab for their information and entertainment? Would the problem of advertorials, the ad copy published in magazines that looks deceptively like editorial copy, be eliminated?

Stage a debate about the issue. Divide the class, and allow half to argue for the advertising industry and the other half to argue for magazines. Consider adding a third group to the debate—the consumer.

[a]Jon Fine, "Mags Go on Trial Along with Rosie," *Advertising Age,* November 10, 2003, p. 1.

[b]Ann Oldenburg, "Finger-Pointing Court Battle," *USA Today,* October 27, 2003, p. D3.

[c]Jon Fine, "Circ Model Cries for Hard Choices," *Advertising Age,* March 15, 2004, p. S-13.

TABLE 12.4. The top ten U.S. newspapers by ad revenue.

Newspaper	Ad revenue (in millions of dollars)
1. *Los Angeles Times*	1,500
2. *The New York Times*	1,354
3. *Chicago Tribune*	1,070
4. *Wall Street Journal*	1,003
5. *The Washington Post*	705
6. *USA Today*	667
7. *Dallas Morning News*	663
8. *Boston Globe*	564
9. *Newsday*	537
10. *San Francisco Chronicle*	530

Source: Adapted from *Advertising Age FactPack,* February 28, 2005, p. 38.

Note: Weekday averages for March 2004 through September 2004.

offer special-themed issues such as "Weddings" and "Summer Activities."

The years 2004 to 2005 saw the building of national Spanish-language brands, such as the Tribune Company's newspaper, *Hoy,* consolidating individual newspapers in the same way Spanish-language TV stations had already consolidated to lure national advertising revenue.[14] *La Opinion,* another newspaper, and *Hoy* boasted circulations around 100,000 in early 2004, evidence of a growing market for Spanish-language publications (see Table 12.5). Census 2000 revealed that 28 million U.S. residents over the age of five speak Spanish at home.

Newspapers are typically available in two sizes. The first, referred to as the tabloid size, is about fourteen inches deep and eleven inches wide. The standard size, or broadsheet, is about twenty-two inches deep and thirteen inches wide and is divided into six columns. The newspaper industry in the United States uses a standard advertising unit (SAU) system that uses column inches as the main unit of measure for advertisers to place ads. There are fifty-six standard ad sizes for standard papers and thirty-two for tabloids.

TABLE 12.5. Top Hispanic print publications, 2003.

Publication	Type of publication	Ad revenue January to November 2003 (in thousands of dollars)
1. *El Nuevo Herald*	Newspaper	55,369.57
2. *La Opinion*	Newspaper	36,497.24
3. *El Diario La Prensa*	Newspaper	26,770.20
4. *Vanidades*	Magazine	23,279.73
5. *People en Espanol*	Magazine	22,269.45
6. *Hoy*	Newspaper	19,368.13
7. *Latina*	Magazine	12,987.34
8. *La Raza*	Newspaper	10,292.40
9. *Hoy/Exito/Chicago*	Newspaper	9,876.80
10. *Glamour en Espanol*	Magazine	8,348.26

Source: Adapted from "Fit to Print" and "Titles en Espanol," *Advertising Age,* January 5, 2004, p. 16.

Advantages and Disadvantages of Newspaper Advertising

Advantages of Newspapers

- Newspapers provide complete coverage and are not restricted to specific socioeconomic or demographic groups—almost everybody reads newspapers.
- Newspaper advertising is timely. Short lead times (the time between placing an ad and running it) permit advertisers to tie in advertising copy with local market developments or newsworthy events. The results of newspaper advertising are also quick (see Illustration 12.4).
- Ads can be quickly and easily changed.
- Newspapers appeal to those already interested in reading, so newspapers provide both the audience and space for long, detailed copy, including lists and prices.
- Special editions allow for precise targeting, e.g., those who read food sections are looking for ads with recipes and coupons, etc.
- Most newspapers are geographically targeted—even big city newspapers have special editions for the various neighborhoods and suburbs.

SIGNAL
TRAVEL & TOURS, INC.

Your Honeymoon Specialists

Making Honeymoons Memorable Since 1968

Ask About Our Bridal Registry

FOUR CONVENIENT LOCATIONS

Niles	South Bend	Dowagiac	St. Joseph
219 E. Main St.	North Village Mall	146 S. Front St.	223 State St.
(616) 684-2880	(219) 271-8700	(616) 782-9825	(616) 983-7323
1-800-535-1070	1-800-327-1032	1-800-535-1025	1-800-535-1035

Being The Best Doesn't Mean Being More Expensive!
Voted Best Travel Agency In Michiana

Travel Services
Representative

ILLUSTRATION 12.4. Timely and targeted. Retail and service ads often have a "creative handle." This Signal Travel & Tours, Inc., ad ran in June newspapers, tying into the proliferation of June weddings and the subsequent proliferation of honeymoon bookings.

Disadvantages of Newspapers

Newspapers do not have the long life of a magazine—most are recycled or thrown away.

- The national advertiser must deal separately with each newspaper publisher. Another problem for national advertisers is that the rates charged to them may be higher than those charged to local advertisers.
- There are also great variations in newspaper printing and color quality. Newspapers have traditionally been printed by the rotogravure process. If color work is desired, the advertiser provides halftoned color separations for the separate color plates used in the rotogravure four-color printing process. Most newspaper presses are geared toward speed, not quality. Generally, don't expect the printing and color quality of magazine publishing.

Paper quality is also inferior—you usually won't get the slick magazine paper surface.

- Like magazine advertising, many newspaper ads appear amidst the clutter of other ads.

Types of Newspaper Advertising

Classified Advertising

Classified ads usually appear under subheads (e.g., Help Wanted, Cars for Sale) that describe the class of goods or the need the ads seek to satisfy. Classified rates are typically based on the number of lines the ad occupies and the number of times the ad runs.

Display Advertising

Display advertising is found throughout the newspaper and generally uses illustrations, headlines, white space, and other visual devices in addition to the copy text. Display advertising is further divided into two subcategories—local (e.g., local retail stores) and national (e.g., national advertisers) display advertising.

Preprinted Inserts

Preprinted inserts are ads that do not appear in the paper itself but are printed by the advertiser and then taken to the newspaper to be inserted before delivery. A retail advertiser who wants to reach only those shoppers in its immediate trading area can place an insert in the local-zone editions.

Public Notices

Public notices include a variety of governmental and financial reports and notices and public notices of changes in business and personal relationships (such as marriage announcements provided by a government agency).

Buying Newspaper Space

Buying newspaper space follows the same basic procedure as buying magazine space. The advertising rate is the amount the newspaper charges for advertising space. As noted, newspapers may charge local and national advertisers different rates, with the national rate generally higher. Newspapers attribute the higher national rates to the added costs they incur serving national advertisers (e.g., they may have to pay an ad agency a 15 percent commission).

There are two ways to measure newspaper advertising space—by the column inch and by the agate line. However, in recent years, national advertising rates in U.S. newspapers have been based solely on the column-inch measurement. The column inch is a space one inch high and one newspaper column wide. Usually, there are about 126 or 129 column inches for a one-page newspaper ad. Some newspapers charge the same advertising rate (flat rate) no matter how much space a single advertiser buys. Most newspapers, however, offer a lower rate (discount or volume rate) for advertisers who buy space regularly or in large amounts. An open rate is the highest advertising rate. It is used for advertisers who do not earn a discount. An advertiser who contracts to buy a specific amount of space during a one-year period at a discount rate and then fails to do so is charged a short rate.

Combination rates are often available for placing a given ad in (1) two or more newspapers owned by the same publisher; (2) morning and evening editions of the same newspaper; and (3) in some cases, two or more newspapers affiliated in a syndicate or newspaper group. Run of paper (ROP) advertising rates entitle a newspaper to place a given ad on any newspaper page or in any position it desires. An advertiser can ensure a choice position for an ad by paying a higher preferred position rate. When advertisers want to experiment with two different creative approaches, some large newspapers will print an ad using one approach in half its papers, then stop the printing presses to substitute an ad using the other approach for the second half. This is called a split run. This way, the advertiser tests the pulling power of each ad.

As with other media, advertisers are interested in comparing different newspaper buys. Since most newspapers have switched from the agate line- to the column inch-based rate method, the cost-per-thousand method (abbreviated CPM, with the M being the Roman numeral for 1,000) is now used to make cost comparisons among newspapers.

$$CPM = \frac{\text{Cost of one-page ad}}{\text{Newspaper circulation}} \times 1000$$

Circulation figures provide the media planner with the basic data for assessing the value of newspapers and their ability to cover various market areas. Data on newspaper audience size and characteristics are available from commercial research services and from studies conducted by the papers. Statements regarding newspaper circulation are verified by the Audit Bureau of Circulation (ABC), an independent auditing group that represents advertisers, agencies, and publishers. Members of the ABC include only paid-circulation newspapers and magazines. Commercial studies providing readership information for the top 100 or so major markets are supplied by the Simmons-Scarborough Syndicated Research Associates. The audience information available from these studies is valuable to the media planner for comparing newspapers with other media vehicles that generally have similar data available. Many newspapers commission and publish their own audience studies so as to provide current and potential advertisers with information on readership and characteristics (e.g., demographics and shopping habits) of readers.

Magazines and newspapers play an important role in the media plans and strategies of many advertisers. However, rising costs and declining readerships continue to present problems for print publications. In addition, advertisers suspect that magazines may inflate circulation figures (see this chapter's Ethics Track). Print publications also face increasing competition from other media such as TV, direct mail, and the Web. In the 1990s, newspaper publishers themselves flocked to the World Wide Web like gold miners to the hills, chasing the advertising revenue (Internet ad spending increased by over 15 percent in 2003). The number of U.S. newspapers on the Web doubled from 1995 to April 1996.[15] By 1998 creative Web sites and interactive advertisements were included in the print category at the 45th International Advertising Awards in Cannes, France. The online publication continues to be viewed by U.S. journalists and advertisers alike as the wave of the future.

SUMMARY

Each advertising medium has its own set of unique characteristics and virtues. Advertisers attempt to select those media and vehicles whose characteristics are compatible with the advertised product and which will enhance the product's image. Many magazines are able to reproduce ads with excellent color fidelity and to specifically target niche markets, although online magazines have become a venue for the same color fidelity and specific targeting. Newspapers remain a force in the marketplace and have become increasingly adept at targeting more specific audiences in the same short production time. Print advertisements reflect the culture and interests of the segments they target; print ads frequently appear on billboards and online simultaneously with paper publications.

:30 Spot:
First Day Print Ad

:30

Starting a new job is always a little unnerving—sometimes even a little scary. No one really knows what to expect the first day. It is usually the endless paperwork for the personnel files, the tax information, and all those other little documents you must fill out before officially becoming an employee. So, just imagine my surprise when my first job after graduating from college turned out to be not quite what I expected.

I was very nervous and more than a little scared of this new career I was embarking upon. I remember thinking, "I survived college, so I can handle anything." I just reminded myself over and over how prepared I was to do this job. However, my first day in my new career proved to be very interesting, to say the least.

I drove to work, excited, nervous, and praying that I was ready to handle all the marketing duties for Signal Travel & Tours, Inc., a travel agency nationally affiliated with American Express. I knew I would have a lot of responsibility since I would be the only marketing person in the department. The president/owner decided that she could no longer handle all the marketing responsibilities for all four offices branched in different cities—so, the new marketing director would do it all. That was me.

As I was praying I would be successful, I was speeding through the small town where the Signal headquarters is located. I was pulled over by the local police. Not only was I embarrassed—I was going to be late. What a great first impression! I walked into the office to find that everyone already knew I was pulled over. To this day, I don't know how the news spread so fast, but when I walked in the door, everyone—including the president—knew about it. That was only the beginning.

I was sent to the personnel department for the paperwork. That was easy. Then I came downstairs, preparing myself for some on-the-job training. Instead, I was informed that we had a half-page advertisement due for a Bridal Extra in the local newspaper that was due yesterday, and I had a one-day extension—the end of the day. I had completed ads in college, but even then, I had direction and time. I had to complete an ad that would be viewed by at least 35,000 people, and it had to be done in two hours. Talk about pressure. I also had to utilize suppliers who had cooperative funds to defray the cost of the advertisement. I quickly learned that day what cooperative funding was and how to obtain it.

Needless to say, since I am still the marketing director at Signal, I completed the ad and the president liked it. I will have to admit I learned a lot that day. I realized I had what it took to succeed in the marketing field. Plus, my first day reaffirmed that all those late-night study sessions, all those exams, and all those papers actually did pay off.

I guess the one thing I learned from my whole experience was that you should never assume what your days will be like in marketing and advertising. Something different, surprising, and scary always pops up day to day. Some people may call these things "problems," but I call them "opportunities." Yes, really great opportunities.

Judeanne Wilson
Director of Marketing
Signal Travel & Tours, Inc.
Niles, Michigan

Chapter 13

Broadcast Media

When Beulah Annan, a Chicago garage mechanic's wife, shot her boyfriend in 1924, she left him to die while she played "Hula Lou" on her Victrola. Eighty years later, she would probably click on a Comcast cable televison channel and watch "zoned" commercials.

Chicago Tribune reporter Maurine Dallas Watkins covered the murder trial of Beulah Annan and turned the real-life murderess into the fictional Roxie Hart for her 1926 Broadway hit, *Chicago.* Watkins' play was adapted numerous times before it found its way to a movie musical version that swept the Academy Awards in 2003, winning Best Picture of that year. The media also changed and adapted in the years between 1924 and 2004, when the TV advertising market became a $28 billion pie, and Comcast wanted as big a piece as possible.

Comcast, the largest U.S. cable company, purchased AT&T Broadband in 2002, acquiring twenty-two of the top twenty-five markets and a line into 22 million businesses and homes. In the Chicago area alone, Comcast upgraded 7,000 miles of "cable lines from analog to digital, enabling it to target viewers in specific towns or even neighborhoods—something its broadcast competitors can't do," and created thirty-eight specific zones. "Zoned" advertising allows "an auto dealer to pitch pickup trucks in one town while selling SUVs in another" (see Table 13.1).[1] The upgrade also makes video on demand and high-definition TV possible. In addition, Comcast centralized its advertising staff in New York. Advertisers can place ads nationwide with just one phone call (see Illustration 13.1).

In the 1920s, Beulah Annan loved her Victrola. No one then could have imagined the broadcast systems we have today. Broadcast media include both television and radio. Advertisers have been spending more and more on them in recent years mainly because of broadcast

ILLUSTRATION 13.1 From Chicago to the Caribbean, Richard Gere to Johnny Depp. The largest U.S. cable company upgraded to digital cable lines to offer popular movies and zoned advertising in twenty-five top markets.

TABLE 13.1. Comcast zoned advertising rates in the Chicago area.

Area	Households viewing	Cost of spot
Entire Comcast area	2.2 million	$1,200
Elgin, Illinois	24,432	40
Mt. Prospect, Illinois	61,308	75
Chicago City North	92,689	65

Source: Comcast. Adapted from "Hitting the Spot: Examples of Zoned Advertising," *Chicago Tribune,* March 20, 2004, Sec. 2, p. 1.

Note: Table shows cost of a :30 spot during ESPN's 10 p.m. *Sportscenter* broadcast.

media growth, primarily from television. In this chapter, we will explore broadcast media and its place in advertising.

TELEVISION ADVERTISING

Television remains America's primary form of entertainment. TV has virtually saturated households throughout the United States, and many other countries as well, and has become a mainstay in the lives of most people. For over half a century, television has been the world's most powerful medium, although network TV has struggled to recover from audience declines in the 1990s and spot-TV ad spending post-9/11. Ad spending for network TV increased an unimpressive 1.8 percent during 2003, while cable and syndicated TV rose over 15 percent during that year.[2] Nevertheless, television remains the advertising medium with the broadest reach. In countries with developing markets, such as Poland, network television has experienced growth (see Table 13.2).

Two major categories of television broadcasting important in advertising are network and cable. In network television, an independent business called a network (e.g., ABC, CBS, NBC, and Fox) joins individual television stations (affiliates) that broadcast its programs and advertising. Usually, only one station per market carries each network's programs. Rather than go through the networks, advertisers may also deal directly with the local television station, individual sta-

TABLE 13.2. Television broadcasting in Poland, 2003.

	Broadcast type	Rating (in percentages)	Advertising revenue (in percentages)
TVP 1	Government-owned	25.6	26.6
TVP 2	Government-owned	20.5	14.6
Polstat	Cable/Satellite	16.5	26.3
TVN	Cable/Satellite	14.0	25.1
TVP 3	Local Station	5.1	1.8

Source: Adapted from "Polish TV Market in 2003," *The Warsaw Voice,* February 22, 2004, p. 6, and <www.TVRadioWorld.com>, March 25, 2004.

tions broadcasting within a small geographic area. In fact, few advertisers are large enough to afford expensive network advertising time, so most of them deal with local stations.

The networks typically begin their annual up-front ad sales for fall prime-time schedules in May. In 2004, the Olympics and the presidential election ad campaigns boosted local TV sales as much as network sales. Whereas some major corporations continue to focus on network TV to advertise their brands (see Table 13.3), TV price increases have led others to focus on alternative advertising media.

Perhaps the most significant development in the broadcast media has been the growth and expansion of cable television. Cable subscribers pay a monthly fee for which they receive on average thirty or more channels, including the local network affiliates and independent stations, various cable networks (e.g., CNN, MTV, and ESPN), superstations (e.g., WTBS-Atlanta and WGN-Chicago), and local cable system channels. As with network television, cable television advertising can be purchased on a national, regional, and local level. Cable has created significant competition for network TV. For example, while the average American home receives only six networks, it "receives nearly a hundred cable channels." The network prime-time audience share showed a 56 percent decrease in 2001 and cable showed a 50 percent increase.[3] Furthermore, cable has been able to offer "edgier fare" with its original series. Witness the popularity of HBO's *Sex and the City* and *The Sopranos.* Nonetheless, cable faces its own competition—satellite television. For example, satellite took 10 percent of the Chicago area television market in 2004.

TABLE 13.3. Network TV's top five brand spenders, 2003.

Brand	Ad spending (in millions of dollars)
1. Procter & Gamble Co.	833.6
2. General Motors Corp.	641.4
3. Johnson & Johnson	527.5
4. Ford Motor Co.	449.6
5. Pfizer	442.4

Source: Adapted from *Advertising Age FactPack,* February 28, 2005, p. 16, based on TNS Media Intelligence.

Advantages and Disadvantages of Television

Advertisers would not invest large sums of money in television commercials unless these advertisements were effective. The major strengths of television that make it appealing as an advertising medium include the following:

- The cost-per-thousand method can be efficient: for an advertiser attempting to reach an undifferentiated market, a thirty-second spot on a top-rated show may cost a penny or less for each person reached.
- Television allows for the demonstration of products or services.
- Television is versatile, allowing for the combination of sounds, color, and motion. As a primarily visual medium, TV employs pictorial storytelling, a strong point in a world where the amount of time spent reading has declined. Research also shows that visual images bypass the logical brain processes and are directly conveyed to the brain's emotional center, creating the strong emotional impact characteristic of television and film.
- It is hard for viewers to tune out a commercial: television advertisements engage the senses and attract attention even when one would prefer not to be exposed to an advertisement.
- Since the early days of television in the 1950s when U.S. families gathered "around the set on Sunday nights to watch *Ed Sullivan,*" the average number of hours a household watches TV has grown from less than five to eight, with 76 percent of households owning more than one TV set.[4]

THE GLOBAL PERSPECTIVE:
TELEVISION GLOBALIZES AND SPECIALIZES

A late-night Italian television show, in which viewers watched a woman prepare for bed each night, seemed amusingly primitive compared to U.S. programming in the 1970s. However, always the innovator, Italy "was one of the first European countries to 'loosen the grip' on broadcasting by governments, resulting in a race to build stations" that certainly improved the television industry.[a] Today, television networks and stations all over the world have expanded from governmentally controlled broadcasting to national, regional, and local stations as well as cable/satellite broadcasters (see Table 13.2).

For example, several countries recognized among the top in media revenues outside the United States offer a variety of broadcasting to their citizens. In Brazil the Nacional Televisao Redes broadcasts nationally while Regiao Televisao Redes serves regional viewers. The Nacionais Cable Canais broadcasts via cable and satellite.[b]

Another top world market, Germany, offers seven national television networks (DSF, ARD, Pro-7, RTL Deutschland, Sat 1, Vox, and ZDF) as well as a long list of regional networks and cable/satellite television broadcasters that include names familiar to North Americans such as *Discovery Channel, Disney Channel,* and *Fox Kids,* but adapted for Deutschland viewers. To further target specific markets, AFN Europe is a regional television network for U.S. military stationed in Germany while SSVC-TV uses low-power transmitters to reach British troops. Regional stations include BR in Bavaria, HR in Hesse, MDR in Saxony, and NDR in northern Germany. Local station SFB serves Berlin, and tv.nrw and WDR3 serve the Rhine area.

French broadcasting targets national and regional viewers as well as viewers in other countries. In August 2001 TV5 USA began broadcasts to U.S. viewers with five programming blocks: news, movies and drama series, weekend programming, children's shows, and soccer.

Countries not among the top ten in media revenues also have diverse yet targeted broadcasting. Israel's government controls Arutz Echad (Channel 1) and cable/satellite station Artuz Shalosh (Channel 3), which broadcasts in Arabic. Three franchised stations share air time on national network Channel 2 (Reshet Network, Keshet Broadcasting, and Telad Studios). E! Israel and Fox Sports Israel adapt U.S. programs for Israeli viewers. India offers four national networks and a long list of regional ones. National offerings include Metro (DD-2) for an urban audience of younger people in 42 cities, broadcast via satellite.

Clearly, international broadcasting is more than amusement—it's serious business, market savvy, and viewer responsive.

[a]<http://www.oldradio.com/archives/international/italy.html>, March 25, 2004.
[b]Information about Brazil, Germany, Israel, and India derive from <http://www.tvradioworld.com>, March 25, 2004. Information about TV5 USA derives from Cultural Services of the French Embassy in the United States, <www.frenchculture.org>, March 25, 2004.

On the other hand, males eighteen to thirty-four, that hard-to-reach marketing group, watch less TV than other demographic segments. As an advertising medium, television suffers from several other distinct problems:

- The absolute cost of producing and running commercials has become extremely high.
- With the invention of the remote control, the VCR, DVD players, and TiVo, much of a viewer's time is spent switching from station to station, zipping commercials (skipping through commercials in programming recorded on a home system) or zapping commercials (changing channels at the beginning of a commercial break using a remote control).
- Clutter has been created by the networks' increased use of promotional announcements to stimulate audience viewing of heavily promoted programs and by the increase in shorter, ten- and fifteen-second commercials. Chapter 11 cited research showing that viewers do not retain information about spots included in large commercial blocks. Jean Pool of J. Walter Thompson, New York, viewed this clutter as industry desperation to offset its declining audiences and to pay for high-budget shows that cost millions of dollars per episode.[5] Commercial time represents as much as a quarter of total broadcast time.

Buying Television Advertising

The purchase of television advertising time is a highly specialized phase of the advertising business, particularly for large companies spending huge sums of money. Large television advertisers generally utilize agency media specialists or specialized media buying services to arrange the media schedule and purchase television time (see Table 13.4).

Methods of Buying Advertising Time

A number of options are available to advertisers that choose television as part of their media mix. Some of these options include sponsoring an entire program, participating in a program, purchasing spot announcements between programs, and purchasing spots from syndi-

TABLE 13.4. Top media specialist companies, 2003.

Company (location)	Billings (in billions of dollars)
Global	
1. OMD Worldwide (New York)	19.34
2. MindShare Worldwide (London)	19.16
3. Starcom MediaVest Worldwide (Chicago)	18.87
4. Carat	17.77
5. ZenithOptimedia (London)	15.53
United States	
1. MindShare Worldwide (New York)	9.4
2. OMD Worldwide (New York)	8.33
3. Starcom MediaVest (Chicago)	7.51
4. Universal McCann Worldwide (New York)	7.40
5. Mediaedge:cia Worldwide (London/New York)	5.27

Source: Adapted from "Top Media Specialist Cos," *Advertising Age,* April 26, 2004, p. S-14.

cators. An advertiser can also sponsor an entire program. For example, Hallmark Cards has sponsored the critically acclaimed *Hallmark Hall of Fame* since the 1950s. Under a sponsorship arrangement, an advertiser assumes responsibility for the production of the program and, usually, the content of the program as well as the advertising that appears. However, the cost to produce and sponsor a thirty- and sixty-minute program make this option too expensive for most advertisers today.

Under a participation option, advertisers pay for ten, fifteen, thirty, or sixty seconds of commercial time during a particular program. Although this is less expensive, participations do not create the same high impact as full sponsorship, and the advertiser has no control over program content. Whereas Olympic sponsorship was popular with major advertisers throughout the 1990s, IBM declined to renew its sponsorship for the Sydney Games in 2000 because of skyrocketing costs. In addition to worldwide sponsorship fees of $40 million, the price tag can triple—to over $100 million—with other expenses, including network ad costs.

Spot announcements refer to the breaks between programs that local affiliates sell to advertisers who want to show their advertisements locally. Note that the word "spot" is also used in conjunction with a time frame, such as a "fifteen-second spot," and that this usage should not be confused with spot announcements.

Syndicated programs are an increasingly popular alternative to network advertising. In the early days of television, stations purchased shows on a cash basis and sold all the commercial time on these shows to local advertisers. Today, syndication comes in three forms: off network, first run, and barter. Off-network syndication refers to reruns of network shows that are bought by individual stations. First-run syndication includes original shows produced specifically for the syndication market, such as HBO's original shows. Under barter syndication, both off-network and first-run syndicated programs, such as the popular TV shows *Wheel of Fortune* and *Oprah,* are offered free or for a reduced rate to local stations, but with some advertising time sold to national advertisers.

Local businesses and retailers, often in cooperation with nationally known manufacturers, may buy time from local network affiliates or independent stations. Most local stations sell spot announcements. However, some local advertisers do develop and sponsor local programs or buy the rights to a syndicated series.

Categories of Television Time

Television time is divided into day parts (see Table 13.5). There are different levels of viewing during each day part, the highest being prime time (8 to 11 p.m. eastern standard time or 7 to 10 p.m. Pacific time). The network advertising time just before and just after prime time is called fringe time because it is on the fringes of the highest audience viewing times. Daytime and late night time tend to have smaller audiences and lower advertising rates.

Costs of Buying Television Advertising

Network television advertising rates are negotiable. Larger advertisers may be able to get more economical, discounted rates than

TABLE 13.5. Television and radio day parts.

Day part label	Specific time period
Television day parts	
Early fringe daytime	9:00 a.m.-4:00 p.m.
Early fringe	4:00-5:30 p.m.
Early news	5:00 or 5:30-7:30 p.m.
Prime access	7:30-8:00 p.m.
Prime	8:00-11:00 p.m.
Late fringe late news	11:00-11:30 p.m.
Late fringe	11:30 p.m.-1:00 a.m.
Radio day parts	
Morning drive	6:00 a.m.-10:00 a.m.
Daytime	10:00 a.m.-3:00 p.m.
Afternoon or evening drive	3:00 p.m.-7:00 p.m.
Nighttime	7:00 p.m.-12:00 a.m.
All night	12:00 a.m.-6:00 a.m.

Note: All times are eastern standard time (EST).

smaller, occasional advertisers. An advertiser must contact the networks to begin buying advertising time and negotiating the prices. As much as 98 percent of TV time is purchased by advertising agencies and media specialist companies that have the experience and expertise to negotiate the best rates and programs.

The Standard Rate and Data Service (SRDS) can help advertisers find local advertising rates for individual television stations. Each station bases its rates on the demand for its advertising time and the size of its audience. Chapter 11, Advertising Media Planning and Selection, illustrated the way media buyers calculate the CPM (cost per thousand) for a :30 television spot. Although media buyers use CPM to compare the efficiency of different television programs, CPM-TM (target market) is a more appropriate cost-per-thousand statistic due to its use of target market instead of total market in the calculation. The CPM-TM formula for assessing cost efficiency of television advertising is as follows:

$$CPM - TM = \frac{\text{Cost of a commercial} \times 1000}{\text{Number of TM contacts}}$$

Ratings and shares are calculated with the following formulae:

$$\text{Rating} = \frac{\begin{array}{c}\text{40 million households watching} \\ \text{the Super Bowl}\end{array}}{\begin{array}{c}\text{108 households with a TV set,} \\ \text{whether the set is on or not}\end{array}} = \text{a 37 rating}$$

$$\text{Share} = \frac{\begin{array}{c}\text{40 million households watching} \\ \text{the Super Bowl}\end{array}}{\text{80 million households with a TV set on}} = \text{a 50 share}$$

Cooperative Advertising

Because of the high cost of television advertising, two companies—often a manufacturer and a retailer—may arrange to share the cost. Not all cooperative advertising involves buying television time, of course. Manufacturers of brand-name products encourage retailers to carry and promote their products through cooperative print advertising, such as free-standing inserts placed inside newspapers. Cooperative advertising gives both partners more exposure at a reasonable price, effectively doubling both advertising budgets. For example, a travel agent that serves a local market area might share the cost of a television spot with an international cruise line. The final screen will typically show the name of the travel agent and its logo next to the name and logo of the cruise line. In addition to cost benefits, cooperative advertising may also result in a higher commercial quality. The cruise line may be able to provide professionally filmed footage so that the local spot will look like a national commercial.

RADIO ADVERTISING

Radio advertising is available on national networks (e.g., ABC, CBS, NBC) as well as local markets (spot radio). Many local or regional stations belong to more than one network, with each network providing specialized programming to complete a station's schedule. Advertisers may use one of the national radio networks to carry their messages to the entire national market simultaneously via stations that subscribe to the networks' programs. In spot radio advertising, an advertiser places an advertisement with an individual station rather than with a network.

Advantages and Disadvantages of Radio

According to Arbitron's *Radio Today 2003 Edition,* radio's popularity has not diminished over time. In many areas, radio stations are considered an integral part of the community and their on-air personalities—local, regional, or national—are like extended family members (see Illustration 13.2). In 2002, 13,685 radio stations broadcast across the United States, 80 percent of them commercial stations.[6] Radio is popular in local retail advertising because of its relatively low cost and its localized coverage. However, it is not for every advertiser. If retailers use radio properly to promote their products, the store will benefit from advertising. Retailers are the largest radio ad spenders. Radio ad sales exceeded $20 billion by 2004.

In particular, radio allows advertisers to reach specific audiences (such as African Americans, Hispanics, women, and youths) and regions. For example, African-American stations account for 800 of the 13,685 in the United States, and the medium maintains popularity among over 20 million African Americans. In the hard-to-reach youth demographic (ages twelve and up), black stations showed a dramatic share increase, from 8.6 in 1999 to 15.1 in 2002.[7] Shares also increased in the critical eighteen to thirty-four and twenty-five to fifty-four age groups. Because most "radio listening is done by women, but most programming is done by men," Arbitron and Joint Communications conducted a groundbreaking study, "What Women Want: Five Secrets to Better Ratings," published at <http:/www.arbitron.com/study/www_5_secrets.asp>. The findings show that, as with television commercial clutter, too many commercial radio spots cause people to tune out. The study found that too many commercials was the leading cause of tune out for women listening to the radio.

Arbitron's study also shows that "Spanish-radio-format fans are 68 percent more likely than the norm to buy or lease a new van or

ILLUSTRATION 13.2. Helping. Community service helps radio stations establish visibility as a positive part of the community. When The Local Radio Stations of Southwest Michigan sponsored a Thanksgiving food drive, Glenna Revis created this emotionally appealing print ad encouraging community participation and emphasizing the stations' down-home ("where we belong, in our home . . . and yours . . ."), local ties ("other companies may come and go").

minivan" and are more likely than the general population to buy furniture, spend $200 or more on groceries per week, see a new movie within the first two weeks of its opening, and eat at fast-food restaurants.[8]

In a Canadian study, radio advertising cost less than television advertising, yet sales of Imperial Margarine were higher in the radio-only market.[9] A German study showed that radio "had a much higher return on investment than TV" for the Imperial Margarine brand.

To make smart media-buying decisions it is important, then, to understand the relative strengths and weaknesses of this medium. The advantages of radio include the following:

- Radio is flexible. Advertisements can run almost any time and on short advance notice.
- Radio commercials are also inexpensive to produce. Live commercials read by an announcer are least expensive because they eliminate production costs. The cost of radio time is also relatively low. The low cost of radio time also means that, given a fixed budget, advertisers can build more reach and frequency into their media schedules.
- Radio can reach specific (niche) audiences.

Like any medium, radio has its disadvantages:

- Although radio stations offer diverse audiences, in addition to the smaller operators, large companies own station groups (see Table 13.6). This makes billing complicated for media buyers.
- Radio is strictly a listening medium, and listeners cannot see the product. Therefore, radio would not be appropriate for advertising that requires demonstration. Listeners need to hear the commercial more than once for it to be effective. A good radio script will repeat the company and/or product name at least three times to be certain that the listener has heard it. Such repetition may not be aesthetic, but it is necessary.

Buying Radio Time

The following are major considerations that influence where and how to buy radio time.

TABLE 13.6. Top radio companies, 2003.

Media company	Net radio ad revenue (in millions of dollars)
1. Clear Channel Communications	$3,695
2. Viacom	2,098
3. Walt Disney Company	612
4. Westwood One	539
5. Cox Enterprises	426

Source: Adapted from "Top 10 Radio Companies," *Advertising Age FactPack 2005 edition*, p. 35.

- Radio advertisers are interested in reaching target customers at a reasonable cost while ensuring that the station format (classical, country, etc.) is compatible with the advertised brand's image.
- Radio advertising is offered both on a national network (with complete market coverage) and on an individual local market spot basis (with air time purchased from individual stations in various markets).
- An advertiser has to decide on a schedule of radio advertisements. Most stations offer anywhere from two to five day parts (see Table 13.5). These include morning drive time (6:00 a.m.-10:00 a.m.), daytime (10:00 a.m.-3:00 p.m.), afternoon/evening drive time (3:00 p.m.-7:00 p.m.), nighttime (7:00 p.m.-12:00 a.m.), and all night (12:00 a.m.-6:00 a.m.). Rate structures vary, depending on the attractiveness of the day part. Information about rates and station formats is available in Spot Radio Rates and Data, published by the Standard Rate and Data Services.
- Radio commercial time is usually sold in ten-, thirty-, or sixty-second time slots.

Advertisers continue to discover ways to make effective use of radio in their media plans, often using radio to supplement other media. Some feel radio just doesn't get the recognition in the media marketing mix that it deserves. Although 40 percent of the average person's media time is spent with radio, "radio attracts only 8 percent of media ad spending."[10] Particularly troubling, "80 percent of all radio reve-

ETHICS TRACK:
THE CONTROVERSIAL CAMPAIGN COMMERCIAL

When President Franklin D. Roosevelt ran for reelection in 1944, he visited Pearl Harbor to launch his campaign and used images of the Harbor's WWII devastation in his advertising. So what prompted widespread criticism of President George W. Bush's first broadcast commercial in his 2004 reelection campaign?

The International Association of Fire Fighters expressed "outrage that the Bush campaign used the image of firemen carrying a flag-draped stretcher out of the World Trade Center rubble," and families of 9/11 victims also expressed public outrage at the use of images of Ground Zero destruction.[a]

Bob Garfield refused to give the commercial campaign even one star in his Political AdReview, characterizing "the first broadcast attack from the Bush/Cheney campaign" as "nasty."[b] Furthermore, its allegation that presidential candidate John Kerry opposed funding to U.S. soldiers in Iraq was, Garfield said, "a fundamental lie. . . . It smears. It undermines the dignity of the presidency. . . . Get used to those zero stars."

In Charles Krauthammer's essay in *Time,* he raised questions about the controversy over the Bush/Cheney campaign: Was its use of 9/11 images "off-limits? Beyond the bounds of decency?" Should a sitting president exploit images of a national tragedy in a quest for reelection? Krauthammer argues that 9/11 differed from a "house fire," a situation in which the feelings of victims' families should preclude showing images of the tragedy; 9/11 was, he said, an act of war. Advertisers were highly sensitive to these images in the months and years following the 9/11 tragedy (see Preface). Does the presidency have a right to use national icons that would be inappropriate for use in the public sector? Negative advertising did not impede the president's reelection goal, but would consumer goods advertisers have success with the sort of negative campaigns launched by politicians? Why is consumer advertising more sensitive to viewer reaction?

Debate these questions and related issues regarding governmental control of national broadcasting systems. How much power, whether direct or indirect, should public officials possess over the media of their nations?

[a]Charles Krauthammer, "Why 9/11 Belongs in the Campaign," *Time,* March 15, 2004, p. 100.
[b]Bob Garfield, "Bush Ad Built on Technicality," *Advertising Age,* March 22, 2004, p. 4.

nue is local," and local radio has not responded to improving economic conditions as quickly as other media.

A BIGresearch survey in October 2003 showed that, in terms of the ways men eighteen to thirty-four years of age preferred to spend their leisure time, watching television, surfing the Internet, and listening to music were neck and neck at the top, all in the 70+ percentile. Going to the movies came close, in the high 60s. Radio figured into the "listening to music" category, but the Internet and CDs also meet young men's listening needs. For women age eighteen and up, only watching TV made it to the 70th percentile; surfing the Internet and listening to music were rated in the low 60s, with reading just a breath behind.

Nevertheless, broadcast media are here to stay. Radio and television, whether network or cable or satellite, remain ad campaign staples. If Beulah Annan were around today, and not in jail for murder, she would surely be enjoying one or all of these media.

SUMMARY

Broadcast media include both television and radio. Advertisers have spent more and more on broadcast media in recent years, mainly because of the growth of the broadcast industry. Most of this growth came from television, especially cable. Comcast has developed "zoned" advertising to improve audience targeting in the top markets. Both radio and television offer advantages and disadvantages to advertisers. It is important to understand these advantages and disadvantages in planning advertising campaigns.

:60

:60 Spot:
The Two Sides of Radio

Everybody knows about their favorite DJ on their favorite radio station. (I hope it's Classic Rock 97.7 WZOW.) But most never realize that in order to provide *free* music and entertainment on the radio, a team of salespeople have to sell several radio advertising campaigns to local, regional, and national businesses. You see, these commercials pay the DJs and all the bills at a radio station.

I am one of the strange ones in our business—I actually wanted to be in radio advertising sales. I chose this profession twenty years ago because most college students don't even know the career exists. So, when I graduated I had less professional competition and was offered a faster career track (it's still that way today). But don't get me wrong, it's not an easy job. In fact, 70 percent of people who try the career won't succeed.

Radio advertising salespeople need a variety of different skills. The one skill or talent I find to be most important is to be "whole brained," to be able to use both the logical and the creative hemispheres of the brain.

Let's first talk about the *creative* side (that's always more fun!). Advertising salespeople need to be creative in the search for new businesses to advertise on the radio station. They need to find categories of businesses that will appeal to their listeners (consumers of products and services). They need to be creative in their approach to stand out from all the other advertising people coming through the door. They need to be creative in how they present or sell, through commercials, the products or services of the business. They may even need to come up with creative promotions or events to help that business accomplish its marketing goals.

Then the radio advertising salespeople need to use the *logical* side of the brain (of course!) to execute a time management system to juggle multiple prospects and customers who are at different points in the marketing process. They need to meet deadlines. They also need to present their ideas and strategies in a logical manner so the business owner can justify the investment in the marketing campaign. Then, if a creative promotion or event is involved, they make sure all the preparation details of that event are accomplished to the satisfaction of all involved.

So, as you can tell, radio advertising sales isn't just selling radio time or "spots." It is everything you've ever learned about marketing and advertising. That's why we call our people marketing consultants. They consult with clients on every aspect of the *marketing bridge* of their business.

Do you wish you had a job that offered a new challenge every day? Where no day is ever the same? Well, be careful what you wish for because a career in radio ad sales is just that . . . a *new challenge every day*.

Dave Wisniewski C.R.M.C.
Station Manager
WZOW & WHLY Radio
South Bend, Indiana

Chapter 14

Internet Advertising

In the background Jerry Seinfeld and Superman (yes, Superman) lean on a fence to have a chat in New York City's Central Park. In the foreground a white dog wearing a Superman cape takes a stroll with a "civilian" black dog. In another frame, the headline of the Daily Planet proclaims, "THE ADVENTURES BEGIN AT AMERICAN-EXPRESS.COM."

Broadband allows the user to view large-file content, including audio, video, and in three-dimensional format, across the Internet. American Express took advantage of broadband technology to create: "a supersized TV spot that doesn't feel like a commercial at all," breathe new life into comedian Seinfeld's career, and "leverage its brand advertising investment in ways that were not possible just a few years ago."[1] The Seinfeld spot utilizes the user-initiated audio and animation capacities of rich-media advertising.

When America Online opened the last uncommercialized window in cyberspace by making its public "chat rooms" available to advertisers in 1996, ads rotated every minute, appearing at the top right-hand corner of the screen.[2] Consumer Internet advertising grew to $7.2 billion, 5 percent of total ad spending by 2002. U.S. and Japanese automotive advertisers alone increased online ad budgets 21 percent in 2002, heading toward $1.7 billion by 2008 in just the automotive category.[3] Advertisers who seek those hard-to-reach eighteen- to thirty-four-year-olds may also bump into senior citizens, who "constitute the fastest-growing category of online users" (see Exhibit 14.1).

Internet pioneer General Motors scored more than 300,000 hits in its first twenty-four hours online, paving the way for customers to choose option packages and price a new car. In 1997 Bell Atlantic Eletronic introduced its Interactive Yellow Pages to enable companies to reach Internet-savvy consumers who are ready to buy; today

ILLUSTRATION 14.1. The Information Superhighway. The view from the highway of the future is nothing but Net, literally, as a highway billboard proclaims, *OPEN YOUR EYES TO THE WORLD.* Photo © Dana Hanefeld.

EXHIBIT 14.1. Senior citizens with home Internet access.

By year

In 1998: 14.5 percent
In 2001: 43.0 percent
In 2002: 47.1 percent

By Income

Median Family Income 1992: $32,000
Median Family Income 2002: 35,800
Median Financial Assets 1992: 25,117
Median Financial Assets 2002: 38,598

Source: Adapted from "The State of 50+ America," AARP, *AARP Bulletin,* March 2004, p. 34.

Yellow Pages "have digitalized ads and listings and now offer local pay-per-click advertising."[4]

What was called the "new marketspace" just a few years ago now may be considered a traditional marketplace (see Table 14.1). A survey conducted by the Association of National Advertisers showed that 69 percent of marketers "planning to reallocate dollars from TV would shift those dollars to the Internet. . . . For a medium whose entire future was called to question [in 2002], this is quite a turnaround."[5]

Although the Internet has been edging out television with its capabilities and superresiliency in its economic recovery (Internet ad spending increased 24.49 percent compared to network TV's –4.67 percent and cable's +21.79 percent during the month of January 2004), it is unlikely to "replace its predecessors."[6] In fact, the Internet has become a complementary venue to bolster the effects of broadcast commercials. 1-800 Mattress offered online coupons, ran the latest TV commercials, and presented alternative shopping methods using the PointRoll FatBoy, recording a 15 percent business transaction increase during the course of the multimedia campaign. Integrating the TV and radio advertising, the FatBoys "ran across major portals" from September 2002 to May 2003.[7]

Welcome to the world of cyberspace marketing and communication.

TABLE 14.1. Ad spending by media, 2003.

Medium	January to December 2003 revenues (in billions of dollars)	Percent change from 2002
Direct mail	48.37	5.0
Newspaper	44.84	1.8
Broadcast TV	41.93	−0.3
Radio	19.10	1.2
Cable TV	18.81	15.4
Yellow Pages	13.90	0.9
Consumer magazines	11.44	4.0
Internet	5.65	15.7
All media total	245.48	3.6

Source: Adapted from *Advertising Age FactPack,* February 28, 2005, p. 14.

THE INTERNET

The Internet, also referred to as cyberspace or the information superhighway, permits the electronic transfer of information (see Illustration 14.1). It is a global network of interconnected computers where an individual connected to one network can speak to any of thousands of other computers if the network is linked to other networks. Geographical boundaries are irrelevant. Regardless of the operating system of the network or PC (personal computer), the Internet offers several modes of information exchange:

- E-mail—still the dominant source of traffic and a versatile delivery vehicle
- World Wide Web (WWW)—the first multimedia platform
- Gopher—first menu-driven browsing tool
- Usenet groups—groups who use Internet "chat rooms" to discuss areas of mutual interest
- IRC (Internet relay chat)—real-time, text-based, chat talk
- Finger—a way to share public information about oneself
- Telnet (remote login)—allows use of remote PC and its programs regardless of distance

The Internet began as a U.S. Department of Defense project in the 1960s as a tool to guarantee communications during nuclear attack. It grew into an information-sharing vehicle for universities in the 1970s and 1980s for research projects. Key tools for using the Internet, such as Gopher, Usenet, and Mosaic, all developed as freeware. The Internet opened to commercial vendors in 1991, with growth soaring at a rate of 300 percent by 1994. It took only three years after the introduction of commercial activity on the Internet for commercial hosts to pass the once-dominant educational hosts.[8]

The 1990s saw the birth of the World Wide Web (WWW), hypertext markup language (html), and graphical browsers such as Netscape. The Web, hypertext, and graphical browsers made cyberspace a very friendly place and spawned a rush to get connected. The term Internet refers to the physical infrastructure of an interconnected global computer network. The Web refers to just one of many modes of data storage and transfer commonly used on the Internet, for example, e-mail. Every Internet connection goes through an Internet Service Provider (ISP).

In early 2004, advertising and paid subscriptions netted tech firm Yahoo nearly $550 million in first-quarter revenue, exclusive of online advertising profits.[9] America Online (AOL) remains the dominant Internet Service Provider with as many as 35 million worldwide online subscribers. AOL offers a wide variety of informational, entertainment, commercial, and other resources, only one of which is access to the wider, global system we call the Internet (including the Web). Twenty years after its launch, this unit of Time Warner considered breaking from subscribers-only services to make its "news, sports, music and other content" available to all online users.[10] Although it was still the number one service provider, AOL's ad revenues had plummeted by half, perhaps prompting this decision.

Internet Regulation

Today, a marketer can set up "a virtual storefront on the Web and instantly gain access to the global market," according to *Newsweek's* Steven Levy.[11] The U.S. government, the initiator of the computer communication system known as the Internet, has typically taken a hands-off position on Internet regulation. The Clinton administration's position was to act aggressively and globally to nurture digital

THE GLOBAL PERSPECTIVE:
INTERACTIVE IN CANADA

If you can chew gum, talk on the phone, and watch television at the same time, you're probably simultaneously online. Watching TV, reading a magazine, and surfing the Internet have become so commonplace that the Interactive Advertising Bureau of Canada devoted a multiyear study to cross-media learning. Its second participant, RBC Insurance, and its media agency, M2 Universal, were interested in discovering the most effective creative practices to reach "defined key targets."[a]

U.S.-based Dynamic Logic, a media research company, conducted the study of 1,100 respondents who were either exposed or not exposed to an online campaign that promoted multiple insurance products. Both groups were surveyed at the same time regarding their attitudes toward the brand featured in the online creative.

Findings revealed that brand favorability increased 37 percent among the online-exposed group versus the unexposed. The study also segmented respondents in terms of whether they were primary decision makers regarding insurance products, whether they shared this responsibility, or whether someone else made the decision for them. "Significantly, it was determined that 54 percent of the audience were key insurance decision makers," a fact that reinforced the "unparalleled strength" of the Internet to accurately target key groups.

[a]"Internet Advertising Is Noticed, Effective and Complimentary," Interactive Advertising Bureau of Canada, <www.iabcanada.com>, April 7, 2004.

commerce through improving security and protection of free speech in a tax- and tariff-free zone. The administration used its influence to encourage China and Singapore not to censor the Internet. However, setting online standards and discouraging regulation or censorship has primarily been left to the U.S. private sector.

Early public concerns centered on the availability of pornographic content to children. Federally funded schools and libraries now protect children from "indecent" material on the Internet through the installation of filtering software, thanks to Senator John McCain's filtering bill (S. 1619).[12] In January 2004 President George W. Bush signed into effect antispam legislation to regulate commercial e-mail. "Spam," the name given to computer junk mail, has been a contentious issue for many online users (see the discussion of the "Disadvantages of Web Advertising" in this chapter). Pop-up ads may be "the most contentious online advertising format," although the availability of ad blockers makes regulation a moot possibility.[13]

WEB ADVERTISING

Thousands of marketers have turned to the Internet as a prospective medium to promote their brands and transact sales. Marketers have become increasingly reliant on direct-marketing online advertising; in fact, Nielsen/Net Ratings showed an industry-wide increase in online ads from 66 percent in 2002 to 77 percent in 2003 (see Table 14.2). In fact, marketers surveyed by GartnerG2 in 2004 said that about 10 percent of their marketing pie would go to interactive media spending. For the consumer category, ad spending increased from 32 percent in 2002 to 37 percent in 2003, according to the Interactive Advertising Bureau.

Procter & Gamble, a $3-billion-a-year ad spender, invested $12 million in Internet marketing in 1998; by 2004 the automotive industry, with $16 billion in annual media spending, spent nearly $196 million for online advertising.[14] Hyundai Motors ran a month-long online campaign estimated at $24,000 on MSN.com in spring 2003 with excellent results: the ads generated over a million hits on <hyundaiusa.com>, generated nearly 10,000 requests for dealer price quotes, brought 685,000 new visitors to the site, increased online brand awareness by 113 percent, and increased brand favorability overall by

TABLE 14.2. Top ad spenders online.

Industry (ranked by 2003 share)	Q4 2002 share (in percent)	Q4 2003 share (in percent)
1. Telecommunications	78	91
2. Financial services	69	86
3. Software	66	85
4. Travel	60	82
5. Public services	67	81
6. Hardware and electronics	78	79
7. Retail goods and services	63	73
8. Business-to-business	77	72
9. Web media	62	72
10. Consumer goods	63	65

Source: Adapted from "Nielsen/Net Ratings: Direct Marketing vs. Branding in Online Advertising, 2003," *i.Intelligence,* Spring 2004, p. 25.

13 percent among entrants in a sweepstakes promotion.[15] Those in the market for a new car aren't the only consumers flocking to the Web; car rental companies have found the Internet to be a thriving marketspace (see Table 14.3).

Hundreds of thousands of companies have launched Web sites, also known as home pages. Most of these offer advertisements for the company's products or services. Home pages are also used to disseminate promotional materials such as press releases, backgrounders (company histories), newsletters, and consumer education materials.[16] To facilitate online traffic, software agents called "shopbots" allow consumers to compare products and prices from a virtual database of available products on a variety of Web sites.

In addition, companies now use the Internet for product promotions and other incentives. BonusMail and ClickRewards provide incentive-points programs to encourage orders from such participating sites as 1-800-FLOWERS. A variety of formats generate Internet ad revenues (see Table 14.4).

Advantages of Web Advertising

In 1994 the Internet as a whole doubled in size, as it had done every year since 1988. According to *The Economist,* "The growth of the Net is not a fluke or a fad, but the consequence of unleashing the power of individual creativity," fostering "openness and interactivity, making it a combination of community and marketplace."[17] As prices came down, the home became the hottest computer market. Internet popularity continues to grow, and given its popularity with young demographics, that growth should continue well into the future. Grunwald Associates research showed that young people ages nine to seventeen years old typically "multitask," with almost 80 percent listening to radio while they're online, and nearly 70 percent watching television while on the Internet.[18] A third combination, at over 50 percent, is Internet/telephone. More importantly, over 40 percent of children in the nine- to twelve-year-old age range reported visiting a Web site they had just seen on TV. Fully 40 percent of children ages six to eight reported the same action.

According to Simba Information Inc., "Perhaps the most promising demographic statistic for all marketers and advertisers entering the electronic marketplace is the affluence of new media users. Con-

TABLE 14.3. Online ad spending–rental car companies (first quarter 2003).

Company	Online ad spending	Overall ad spending
Avis	$800,000	$10 million
Budget	545,000	14 million
Enterprise	291,000	28.5 million
Hertz	1.6 million	19 million
Thrifty	1.0 million	2.9 million

Source: Adapted from "Wheels on the Web" and "The Bigger Picture," *Advertising Age,* October 27, 2003, p. 44.

TABLE 14.4. 2003 ad revenues by format.

Format	Percentage
1. Keyword search	35
2. Display ads (banners)	21
3. Classified	17
4. Sponsorship	10
5. Rich media	8
6. Slotting fees	3
7. E-mail	3
8. Interstitial	2

Source: Adapted from "Annual Industry Revenues Grow Nearly 21% As Year Totals Nearly $7.3 Billion," a report of the Interactive Advertising Bureau, April 21, 2004.

sumers with more discretionary income tend to make more purchases that are not necessities." Ogilvy & Mather Direct has dubbed this person the "technology savvy consumer." Fifty-four percent of the company's clients have a household income of at least $100,000. Prodigy subscribers have tended to surpass the national average in measures of affluence, activity, and influence, with 75 percent having attended or graduated from college, compared to the average U.S. household, which has only 33 percent college graduates.

The Internet allows advertisers to "reach a narrowly defined audience with unique demographic characteristics or special interests."[19]

ETHICS TRACK:
THE AMBULANCE CHASERS

When ninety-six people died in two U.S. nightclub tragedies within five days, memorials were constructed, family members mourned, and law firms began their hunt for clients. Doesn't sound quite right? Yet that was the case following the stampede at Chicago's Epitome nightclub, also known as E2, on February 17, 2003.

Internet users who typed "E2 nightclub" or similar key phrases into Yahoo's search engine generated an ad for Chicago law firm Kenneth B. Moll & Associates Ltd. The same phenomenon occurred following the tragic fire at The Station nightclub in Rhode Island three days later. Illegal use of pyrotechnics during a live concert sparked the fire. In the Chicago tragedy, patrons were crushed attempting to vacate a nightclub after a fight prompted security guards to use pepper spray.

Direct solicitation is prohibited in such cases, so the question emerges: Did Moll's Web site unethically solicit victims? Or was this simply a clever marketing ploy? Regardless, Kenneth Moll pulled the online ads on March 5 after being questioned about their propriety.

Moll claimed that the tactic was not a means to lure clients and, since he had not asked for money, the activity could not be called "ambulance chasing." His stated purpose was to see whether he could locate any witnesses to the tragedy. The Internet is a convenient way for consumers to locate and research law firms, and Web marketing is nothing new for lawyers. However, the American Bar Association admitted that Moll and his boys were the first to use a search engine advertisement to seek clients. The ethics of this form of marketing were still ambiguous. James J. Grogan, chief counsel of the Attorney Registration and Disciplinary Commission, seemed to think the incident was comparable to direct mail or purchasing newspaper ads soliciting clients who have suffered some tragedy and may be in need of representation. If Moll's technique fell under the same category, it would be constitutionally protected.

A more clear ethical violation of professional conduct was evident when the Illinois State Bar Association reprimanded lawyers for allegedly camping out near the medical examiner's office following the Chicago accident. And a bit of irony to add to the whole thing: At the time, Moll was facing disciplinary action for not taking down his Web site during a three-month suspension from practicing law in 2000.

Katie-Nell Scanlan

Source: Ameet Sadachev, "Lawyer's Web Links to Club Tragedies Raise Questions," *Chicago Tribune,* March 5, 2003, Sec. 3, pp. 1,4.

In this respect, the medium resembles direct mail; however, the Internet serves "not only as a communications channel but also a transaction and distribution channel" through which consumers, "without resorting to other means," instantly receive "information and make purchases and payments." No other medium can duplicate the Internet's potential for customized content, two-way communications, and interactivity. Finally, as the Jerry Seinfeld example shows, the Internet has the capacity for multimedia content including text, graphics, audio, and/or video. No other medium can offer the same "high-impact advertising"—animated banner ads, sponsor logos, and interstitials (see Illustration 14.2). For obvious reasons, online advertising has also come to be viewed as a superior vehicle for building customer relationships and brand awareness.

Interactive Web sites have become particularly effective in reaching consumers. Some packaged-goods companies have also found success with online publications, such as Procter & Gamble Co.'s Home Made Simple with its 4 million subscribers. Of 152,056 Internet users in February 2004, 6,950 visited Kraft/Nabisco sites; 6,645 visited Procter & Gamble sites, including Home Made Simple; and 1,899 visited Unilever's sites, including <mymealssweepstakes. com> and <benjerry.com>.[20] Web sites can be advantageous for business-to-business commerce as well. Toshiba America Business Solutions reported that over 80 percent of its sales revenues came from the Internet, with 95 percent of its customers' orders placed on its Web site.[21] The site includes a Dealer Lead Referral System so that customers may locate their nearest Toshiba dealer. In a unique checks-and-balances system, if the dealer does not respond to the customer within two hours, one of the Toshiba sales managers will respond.

In addition to American Express, such major advertisers as Coca-Cola, Unilever, and Delta Air Lines have run rich-media ads that "marry TV's visual appeal with the Internet's interactivity . . . drawing traditional advertisers who previously believed online ads could never approach television's storytelling prowess."[22]

Digital media technology now provides advertisers with the possibility of *streaming,* "the simultaneous transfer of digial media (video, voice, and data) so that it is received as a continuous real-time stream" by users, according to <www.streamingmedia.com>. *Webcasts* are live events produced in-house or outsourced to a service provider. In addition to its applications for online advertisements,

ILLUSTRATION 14.2. Twinkle, twinkle. Blinking banner ads for Children's Memorial Hospital urge Internet users to "Brighten the life of a child," a message that transforms into a specific call to action in the blink of an eye: *Buy our corporate holiday cards*. Banner ads remain the predominant advertising vehicle on the World Wide Web.

streaming media may deliver "tighter and more frequent cross-company communication [and] more personal and effective customer communication," according to streamingmedia. Electronic communication has been "a blessing" for business managers.[23] More than 45 percent of 400 managers polled by the American Management Association and Ernst & Young reported using e-mail more than any other communication tool.

Electronic communication is especially beneficial for global marketing. It is a powerful tool for overcoming time-zone problems. Some U.S. companies communicate almost entirely with foreign markets via the Internet or fax.[24] Stephan H. Haeckel, director of strategic studies at IBM's Advanced Business Institute, believes that "low-cost global digital networks give us the potential to collaborate with one another in a new medium, on a scale unprecedented in human history."[25] He also cautions that "learning to exploit these potentials might require the development of substantially different cognitive processes." This brings us to the area of the medium's disadvantages.

Disadvantages of Web Advertising

Although Hormel Foods Corporation officials have objected to the generic use of its trademark name for a canned meat product, "Spam," the word has become part of the vocabulary of Internet users. "Spam" is "slang for the practice of sending commercial e-mail in bulk."[26] America Online has reported junk e-mail as the number one complaint of its subscribers. Unsolicited electronic messages hawking a wide range of products are sent to millions of Americans each day. For some small businesses with a limited advertising budget, "spam mail" is considered a "free" way to get a message out.

The purpose of e-commerce is not to irritate the prospective customer, of course. E-mail marketing campaigns can be categorized by broad marketing objectives, e.g., customer retention and customer acquisition. Customer retention campaigns target a company's in-house list while acquisition campaigns "seek to convert strangers into permission or sales relationships."[27] At an average six cents per message, an in-house list is considerably more cost effective than the 20 cents per address typically charged for a rented list.

Spam's evil cousin, "spim," otherwise known as "instant-messenger spam," was up to 4 billion messages in 2004, according to Ferris Research.[28] Although spam messages number up to 2 billion *each day,* unsolicited spims pitch porn sites and concerts, "unwelcome intrusions" for those who enjoy their time sending instant messages. Automated programs facilitate the sending of spims, and antispam filters do not remove them.

Pop-up ads seem to be as unpopular as spam and spim, although the jury is still out. A Dynamic Logic study found that "users are actually more tolerant of pop-ups than previously thought."[29] According to the survey, "72 percent of U.S. Web users accept limited use of pop-ups, and 47 percent agree as many as two to six ads per hour are appropriate to support free content." However, a contemporary study conducted by PlanetFeedback showed that 64 percent of consumers polled were "furious" over pop-ups, with 58 percent "furious" about spam (see Table 14.5). It appears that those furious about spam simply choose to erase it: in 2003 Bigfoot interactive surveyed over a thousand adult users and found that 70.4 percent of them simply hit the delete button when they receive unsolicited bulk e-mail.

Another challenge to Internet advertisers has been the possibility of Internet intrusions. Credit card buying and selling via the Internet has been slowed by the challenge of protecting customers from cyber thieves who steal credit card numbers. A company's home page may be vandalized, with information and graphics changed to embarrass the company or to impede the flow of business. Some companies are now protected from Internet intrusions by fire walls. A fire wall or bastion is a system that protects one network from another. A proliferation of viruses has caused havoc for corporations and other organi-

TABLE 14.5. Negatively perceived ad formats.

Format	Percentage polled
1. Pop-up ads	Slightly more than 80
2. Spam	80
3. Telemarketing	Just under 80
4. Infomercials	40
5. TV and print ads	Under 20

Source: Figures based on "Negative Feedback," *Advertising Age,* August 25, 2003, p. 21.

zations in recent years, making virus protectors standard equipment for business and personal computers as hackers infiltrate the Information Age.

Another issue regards disparities between the two Internet measurement services, Nielsen NetRatings and comScore Media Matrix. In January 2004 the disparity was especially dramatic in the two services' measurements of online activity by males and females ages eighteen to thirty-four years old. NetRatings reported that 56 percent of men in that age group actively used the Internet during that month, while comScore placed the number at 77 percent, intensifying "frustration over inexact measurement by Internet companies who rely on the research to sell advertising."[30]

Whether it is a "perfect" marketspace or not, the Internet must be recognized as a major player among advertising media.

INTERNET DIRECTORY ADVERTISING

The Yellow Pages has taken a relatively smooth journey from an exclusively print publication to electronic publishing. The scope of electronic Yellow Pages is broad, ranging from community to international (see, e.g., Illustration 14.3). Local electronic directories, such as the Banana Pages in Seattle, include traditional Yellow Pages content in select special-interest categories, information on communities in the regional territory served, yet link the user to national Yellow Pages listings. Regional directories are constantly being expanded and enhanced. Yellow Pages offers consumers a number of electronic platform choices:

- CD-ROM is an integral part of home computing. Half of computers shipped today have CD-ROM players. Some electronic directories, such as BellSouth Raleigh, offer multimedia CD-ROM, with audio tips and maps, free to consumers.
- Audio text allows consumers to call a telephone number to access free information. Yellow Pages takes this service beyond the standard time and weather—consumers are prompted to push buttons to access general Yellow Pages information, consumer tips (ranging from tips on etiquette to theater reviews),

and talking ads. Audio text advertising is packaged with print Yellow Pages purchases.

- In addition to business listings and advertisements, electronic Yellow Pages offer hyperlinks to other Web pages and search engines, and enable consumers to conduct business transactions, such as orders for merchandise, restaurant reservations, or service requests.

ILLUSTRATION 14.3. Looking for liner. Kathy Michael-Wise reaches customers looking for permanent makeup services through her Yellow Pages ad for A Younique Image. She even adds an incentive—a spring special coupon worth $100 toward a service.

SUMMARY

The Internet has become an established marketspace. Advertising on the World Wide Web has its advantages and disadvantages. Advertisers no longer ignore this medium. Electronic publishing, including Internet directory advertising, has been growing at dramatic rates. Finally, electronic communication allows those in the business world to more easily exchange ideas and general knowledge with colleagues, customers, consumers, and vendors all over the world.

:60 Spot:
STARGAZING

As I dodge through the foot traffic at Union Station, I give my watch a quick glance: 8:22 a.m. Picking up an already speedy pace, I make my way to the Canal Street exit, running through a mental checklist of things I will have to do upon reaching the "Mart," as we Burnetters like to call it. It is the beginning of my second week with iLeo, and I'd like to make sure it's just the second week of many more to come.

8:34 a.m. I push through the revolving door at the Merchandise Mart, squeeze into the crowded elevator and push the button for the twenty-first floor. I streamlined my routine after the first couple of days on the job and am eager to prepare the office before my co-workers arrive. I drop my jacket and bag off at the front desk and quickly get started. First, I make my way through the winding hallway that is the bull pen, a group of open-air cubicles reserved for temps and freelancers. As I walk into the kitchen, there's coffee to be made. While the regular is brewing, I make a quick run-through of the four conference rooms to make sure that any traces of brainstorm sessions have been cleared away so that they look presentable for the day's meetings. Since that brings me back up to reception, I make sure to restock our bowl of apples. Leo Burnett himself started that tradition in 1935, and I am not about to change that now.

In August of that year, during the Depression, Burnett opened up his advertising agency with only eight associates and a bowl of shiny red apples to give to visitors. One naysayer said Burnett would soon be selling those apples instead of giving them away. This was not to be the case, and to just think about how far Leo Burnett has come since that first bowl of apples makes me feel like I'm a part of history every day.

8:46 a.m. Just enough time to brew the decaf, unlock the security gates, grab some water for myself, and turn on the DVD player. Whew! I've made it. It's 8:58 a.m., and I'm sitting at reception with a smile on my face and the switchboard turned on.

This is my routine each morning and I relish every minute of it.

My love affair with Leo Burnett began when I was about ten years old. My father took me to visit a family friend at the company, and I was given the grand tour. I have always been a creative person, and to be among the people who actually create for a living piqued my interest in such a way that it grew to be a passion over the years. I felt a sort of kinship with the company, a creative connection.

While in college, I ran the gauntlet of advertising courses: Campaigns, Writing for Advertising, Persuasion, Two Dimensional Art, and even Advertising in Society. All the while, I still had one goal in mind. To be accepted into Leo Burnett as a fellow team member and creator of ideas and concepts that millions of consumers across the globe would see. This was my dream.

My first opportunity arose as a junior in college when I worked as an intern for Lápiz, the Hispanic Marketing Division of Leo Burnett. I spent three months out of my summer absorbing, learning, and participating as much as I could. I had the chance to work on presentations for Ball Park, conduct competitive tracking for Sears, and edit case studies for Luvs and Kellogg. This made my desire to work in advertising even more concrete, and I promised myself that I would become a part of this bustling company in the very near future.

My second opportunity came in March 2003. I was looking at career opportunities on the Leo Burnett Corporate Web site, as I regularly did, and saw a position that played to my abilities and previous experience. Believe it or not, I balked at the idea originally, and thought it over for a couple of days before doing anything about it. I ultimately applied because I could not let that opportunity pass me by. After a month or so of persistent follow-up and interviews, I was offered the position. I was in. I had done it. I had finally made my dream a reality.

Looking back, it is amazing to see the road I have traveled since childhood to become part of the powerhouse I am involved with today. I was persistent and tackled the roadblocks that barred my path with determination and an optimistic attitude. As Leo Burnett once said, "Reaching for the stars may sound a little naive, but it is a thought in which I passionately believe; and maybe the world could use a little more naivety of that kind."

I am now a part of iLeo, a newly formed, independently operating global network that unifies Leo Burnett's direct, digital, and database marketing resources. Our mission revolves around creating customers and customer values with great focus on insights, ideas, and interactions. I am surrounded by a great creative space, inspiring people, a company rich with a history of groundbreaking advertising, and blue chip clients including Starbucks, Gateway, Hallmark, and Disney. Although I'm still learning the business, I feel positive that good things will happen for me here. I will advance, I will grow, and I will keep all those apples in mind.

María Pilar Paulick
Guest Relations Associate
iLeo
Chicago, Illinois

Chapter 15

Alternative Advertising Media

A bright orange tennis ball's thoughts are encapsulated in a bubble, the cartoonist's technique to convey what is in or on a character's mind (see Illustration 15.1). But this is not a cartoon, it's a billboard just outside the train station in Florence, Italy. The ad's text paraphrases Martin Luther King's famous words, "I have a dream," to express the "dream" of the tennis ball: "I have a drink," e.g., the new Gatorade flavor. This billboard message might be acceptable in Florence, but it would most likely cause a protest in a U.S. city (where Americans could perceive disrespect for Dr. King) and might be viewed as lacking verbal sophistication in the United Kingdom.

Billboards are a part of the communities in which they are placed, and community occurs in a *place,* shaped by both a shared experience and an identity. As a component of place, alternative advertising both reflects and shapes experience and identity. For example, billboards frequently employ double entendre, sexual innuendo, and puns to catch attention with deftly equivocal sexual appeals in the staid British Isles. In the heavily Catholic countries of southern Europe, such as Italy, where the audience is adept at visual encoding due to the long tradition of iconography in the Catholic Church, the use of cultural icons, including those translated from American culture, seems to abound (see this chapter's Global Perspective).

The black "bullboard" cutouts that dotted hilltops across the Andalucian region of Spain in 1954, discussed in the opening to Chapter 12, occupied the plains of La Mancha to the seacoast of Spain's Costa del Sol, until September 1994 when the Ministry of Public Works, Environment and Tourism, in conjunction with a 1988 law prohibiting public advertisements near main roads, brought the billboards down.[1] Osborne, makers of the advertised brandy, removed its bullboards, but the nation's love for them brought the bull-boards back without the advertising text. Today, the black bulls remain on Anda-

ILLUSTRATION 15.1. A drink or a dream? A tennis ball dreams of a new Gatorade flavor in this billboard placed near the train station in Florence, Italy.

lucian hilltops and in public squares (see Illustration 15.2) and, additionally, they appear on postcards, coffee cups, and T-shirts. Such was the power of the bull's meaning to the community in which it was placed; the Osborne bull, whose initial purpose was to sell brandy, became a national icon, rooted in southern Spain's identity.

In addition to the traditional media (television, radio, magazines, newspapers), marketers find themselves looking at unique, new, and sometimes odd, media: police cars, street furniture, and even a cow. Under an Adopt-A-Car program in Crown Point, Indiana, police cars carried signs acknowledging local businesses that paid $1,500 each for the publicity. New York City spent $1 billion on a twenty-year contract to design, build, and install bus shelters and other street furniture that would carry lucrative advertising space.[2] Viennese advertisers could literally have a cow if they forked over $375 to the Cow Placard Company. A Swiss cow's flank carried painted messages, although animal rights groups criticized the cow's owner, Cow Placard founder Frank Baumann.

Alternative advertising ranges from perfume ads printed on the back of subway passes to corporate logos (and promotions for movies, most notably *The Passion of the Christ*) on race cars. This chapter will cover out-of-home advertising, including outdoor (billboards and signs) and transit (both inside and outside the vehicle) that, as noted, have their own significant place in advertising lore. Specialty

ILLUSTRATION 15.2. No bull: Spaniards took to the streets to protest the removal of the Osborne brandy bullboards, an effort that restored the bulls to Spanish hillsides and public squares, including this roundabout in Seville.

advertising, Yellow Pages advertising, infomercials, and cross-promotions will also be discussed.

OUT-OF-HOME ADVERTISING

Media that reach prospects outside their homes are called out-of-home media. These include outdoor advertising (e.g., billboards and signs) and transit advertising (e.g., bus and taxicab advertising, subway posters, and terminal advertising). Out-of-home advertising or outdoor advertising is regarded as a supplementary advertising medium. In 1997, Greyhound buses accepted exterior and interior advertising for the first time. In 2003, outdoor advertising revenues rose 8 percent over the previous year, bringing the annual revenue to $2.67 billion, in less than a decade, increasing well above 1995's $1.83 billion.[3]

As evidenced in the example of the bullboard cutouts, outdoor advertising has the ability to be innovative. To promote its release of *The Frighteners,* Universal Pictures used new special-effects posters with three-dimensional images. The studio was the first marketer to use Extreme Vision in the United States. In the poster for the Universal movie, a skull seemed to move closer to the viewer as the words

"Dead yet?" appeared. The advertisement appeared on bus shelters, vending machines, and the sides of delivery trucks.[4]

Outdoor Advertising

Billboard advertising is the major outdoor medium due to its cost efficiency—the ability to reach more people at less cost than other media. Billboards are highly visible—in fact, unavoidable—and the audience can neither turn them off (as with television) nor turn the page (as with print) to avoid seeing them.[5] Whereas readers and viewers must choose to direct their attention to print publications and electronic programming, outdoor advertising is part of the landscape. Although billboard advertising has high visibility, viewing time is brief—about ten seconds.

The major forms of billboards are poster panels and painted bulletins. Posters are lithographed or silkscreened by a printer and shipped to an outdoor advertising company. They are then prepasted and applied in sections to the poster panels that face oncoming traffic. The standard sizes of poster boards are the thirty-sheet poster, with a printed area of 9 feet 7 inches by 21 feet 7 inches, surrounded by margins of blank paper; and the bleed poster, with a printed area of 10 feet 5 inches by 22 feet 8 inches that extends all the way to the frame. Smaller eight-sheet posters are 5 feet high and 11 feet wide. These "junior posters" are used by grocers and local advertisers and are generally placed for exposure to pedestrian traffic as well as vehicular traffic. The design for an outdoor board is supplied by the advertiser or agency. Copy should be limited and emphasis given to art (pictures), headlines, and the product or company name.

For poster panels, art is printed on a set of large sheets of paper. Thousands of copies can be printed and distributed around the country. The sheets are then pasted like wallpaper onto existing boards by local outdoor advertising companies that own the boards. Painted bulletins are hand painted directly onto the billboard by artists hired by the billboard owner. The standard size of painted bulletins is fourteen feet by forty-eight feet. Some use a rotary plan and are moved to different places every thirty, sixty, or ninety days for greater exposure. The time commitment the advertiser makes can be a disadvantage of the medium. Some billboards remain permanently at one location.

Outdoor advertising is purchased through companies that own billboards, called plants. Plants are located in all major markets throughout the nation. Companies such as Gannett Outdoor (which was acquired by Outdoor Systems in August 1996) have the larger plants with operations in multiple metropolitan areas. To simplify the national advertiser's task of buying outdoor space in multiple markets, buying organizations—or agents—facilitate the purchase of outdoor space at locations throughout the country.

When an advertiser needs to saturate a market with a new product introduction or to announce a change in package design, outdoor advertising makes broad coverage possible overnight. The basic unit of sale for billboards, or posters, is 100 gross rating points daily or a 100 showing. One rating point is equal to 1 percent of a particular market's population. Buying 100 gross rating points does not mean that the message will appear on 100 posters; rather, it means that the message will appear on as many panels as needed to provide a daily exposure theoretically equal to the total size of the market's population. Actually, a showing of 100 gross rating points achieves a daily reach of about 88.1 percent of the adults in a market over a thirty-day period.[6]

By far, the largest outdoor advertiser is the entertainment industry. Although cigarette and liquor advertising once occupied as much as 50 percent of U.S. poster panel and painted bulletin space, social pressures, lifestyle changes, and governmental regulations decreased these categories to less than 20 percent. Although the rugged cowboy of the mythic Old West can no longer ride boards on his own range, cigarettes are still advertised on billboards abroad, e.g., the Marlboro Man rides at a bus stop in the sleepy whitewashed town of Mijas, Spain (see Illustration 15.3).

The outdoor advertising business has picked up new clients these days as advertisers hunt for cheaper alternatives to media such as TV, where it is becoming tougher and tougher to stand out.

Transit Advertising

A second form of out-of-home advertising is transit advertising. Transit advertising includes the posters seen in bus shelters and train, airport, and subway stations. Occasionally, we also see trucks that carry billboards on the highway.

ILLUSTRATION 15.3. Ride 'em. The Marlboro man rides again at a bus stop in Mijas, Spain.

There are three basic types of transit advertising: inside cards, outside posters, and terminal posters. Inside cards are placed above the seats and luggage area, usually eleven inches high by either twenty-eight, forty-two, or fifty-six inches wide. Outside posters may appear on the sides, back, and/or roofs of trains and taxis. External panels or posters are designed like small billboards—simple, bold, catchy, and legible. Terminal posters are located at railroad, subway, bus, and air terminals. In cities with major mass-transit systems, advertisers can also buy space on bus shelters and on the backs of bus stop seats.

Outdoor and transit advertising may be combined, as they were for the highly visible Galeries Lafayette department store campaign in Paris. The Galeries boasts the world's largest perfumery and a Yves Taralon-designed emporium. In these ads, an exuberant woman wearing outdoor boots with a neon yellow negligee and a fur coat declares, *"J'ai toujours envie d'aller aux Galeries"* (I always want to go to the Galeries). Ads appeared on the sides of buses, in signage on the Champs Elysées, Paris' grand promenade, and on the Metro's underground walls (see Illustration 15.4).

As with outdoor advertising, the cost basis for transit advertising is the number of showings. A full showing (called a No. 100 showing) means that one card will appear in each vehicle in the system (e.g., bus system in one city). A showing of 50 would mean that half the vehicles would carry the advertisement.

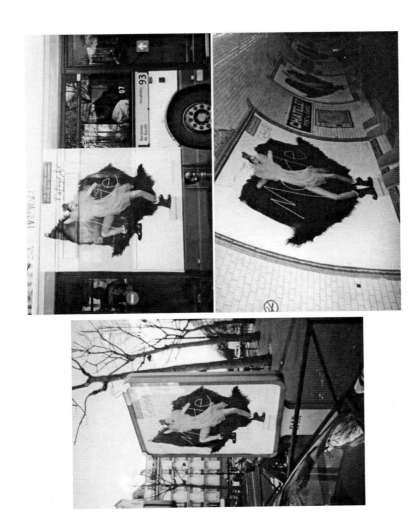

ILLUSTRATION 15.4. Stompin' everywhere. Whether you walked around Paris, took the Metro, or jumped on a bus, it was impossible to miss the image of the Lafayette lady who donned her boots to stomp all over Paris.

OTHER ALTERNATIVE ADVERTISING MEDIA

Specialty Advertising

Specialty advertising has been defined as "an advertising, sales promotion, and motivational communications medium which employs useful articles of merchandise imprinted with an advertiser's name, message, or logo."[7] Specialty advertising is often considered both an advertising medium as well as a sales promotion medium. There are more than 15,000 different advertising specialty items used by businesses with the advertiser's name printed on them. Specialty items can be sent to consumers and business customers. These specialty items can serve as continuous, friendly reminders of the advertiser's business.

Yellow Pages Advertising

Although one of the "least glamorous" of the media businesses, Yellow Pages remains "one of the most profitable."[8] Over half of adult Americans make weekly use of the Yellow Pages. Classified advertising and Yellow Pages advertising constitute a special category, directional advertising, which directs consumers to a vendor at the time they are ready to buy. Yellow Pages directories are distributed annually to hundreds of millions of consumers, with over $14 billion a year spent on Yellow Pages advertising. Local businesses place the majority of Yellow Pages advertisements, but national advertisers are also frequent users.

A new category of Yellow Pages-type advertising is emerging on the Internet in the form of "shopbots," Web sites that offer software "agents" to assist consumers in sorting through the proliferation of online stores. Online shoppers search for specific information. Web sites such as Buy.com and Travelzoo provide a virtual database of available products and services. Featured businesses pay to be listed at shopbots, which allow the consumer to select by the desired price, brand, or company.

Although Yellow Pages use is less frequent in the twenty-first century, the decline attributed to the Internet "has leveled off in recent years," and YP revenues rival those of local television and the magazine industry.[9]

THE GLOBAL PERSPECTIVE:
INTERNATIONAL BILLBOARD

In Rome's Pza. della Repubblica, a billboard displays a famous portrait of Abraham Lincoln (see Illustration 15.5). The copy reads: "Lincoln ha liberto gli uomini dalla schiavitu. Banca 121 anche (Lincoln has freed man from slavery. So, too, Bank 121)." The advertisement's tagline, "Banca 121. Liberta di Banca (Bank 121. Banking Freedom)," seems especially interesting in the context of its placement: the Pza. della Repubblica is the gateway to the Baths of Diocletian, a vast complex built by 40,000 Christian slaves between A.D. 295-305. The use of the slavery premise to promote a banking product would not have the same impact were the billboard placed in another location. In a country such as the United States, where the issue of slavery remains contentious, the billboard might have an unintended impact.

With outdoor advertising, the advertising message (image and text) and its chosen placement carry the same importance as the placement of a print ad in the right niche magazine or a television commercial on a show watched by the targeted demographic. However, the Banca 121 placement actually added textual dimension to the advertisement's message.

In other cases, billboards and signage placed in one location might not even be suitable for placement in another. Many U.S. cities and towns have ordinances prohibiting certain images and messages from appearing on billboards in close proximity to schools and playgrounds. A Cornetto ice cream ad placed on a busy street in Madrid and an Avon ad in Warsaw might be viewed as too sexually suggestive for public consumption in another city or country (see Illustration 15.6 and 15.7). The Phytomer CelluliMask sign was set out on a side street near a store selling children's books in the provincial French town of Amboise in the Loire Valley (see Illustration 15.8).

Whereas the sensuality of advertising in southern Europe might not resonate with communities in England, the famous British wit gives language a free rein. A Lambrini billboard in the London tube played on the resemblance of the name of an astrology sign, Virgo, to the sign's root word, *virgin,* in its text: "So he said are you a virgin? And I said no, a Scorpio" (see Illustration 15.9). A petrol billboard carried a sexual innuendo with its "Pump up your points" tagline and, to U.S. sensitivities, might seem surprisingly located beneath a church window and overlooking a landmark castle in Dover, home of the famous white cliffs (see Illustration 15.10).

ILLUSTRATION 15.5. Freedom. The image of Abraham Lincoln captured the subtext of slavery in the Roman piazza in which this banca 121 billboard was placed.

ILLUSTRATION 15.6. Sharing a bite. This signage for Cornetto ice cream might have drawn attention on a U.S. street, but it raised no eyebrows in Madrid.

ILLUSTRATION 15.7. Avon calling. This Avon lady appeared nude on a busy street in Warsaw, Poland. Photo courtesy of Regina Stefancic.

ILLUSTRATION 15.8. Dump the plump. This sign for Phytomer cellulite cream was propped up against a wall in a provincial French town.

ILLUSTRATION 15.9. Birth sign. A billboard placed in the London Underground played on the idea of horoscopes.

Infomercials and Home-Shopping Networks

Infomercials were introduced to television in the early 1980s. Most are thirty minutes long—a substantial time increase from the usual :30 to :60 television spot. Infomercials are produced by advertisers yet are designed to be perceived as regular television programming. They typically offer consumers a toll-free 800 number to place an order or to obtain further information. Many advertisers have found the infomercial to be an extremely effective promotional tool for moving merchandise.

ILLUSTRATION 15.10. Nothing sacred. Signage for a petrol brand appeared in the shadow of an ancient church overlooking a medieval castle in the sleepy seaport of Dover, England.

Although often associated with products that sell for such small-ticket prices as $19.95, the infomercial also hawks big-ticket items. For instance, in July 1998 Chrysler Corporation aired a thirty-minute infomercial on national cable TV and United Airlines Sky TV that advertised the Chrysler 300M and two redesigned sedans, all of which sold for considerably more than $19.95.[10]

Much of the criticism of informercials regards the medium's resemblance to regular programming, which some view as deceptive. Many informercials use a talk show-type format with celebrity hosts. Furthermore, the 800 number makes ordering so easy that some

ETHICS TRACK:
COMING SOON TO A THEATER NEAR YOU

Outkast's popular song "Hey Ya" features Polaroid's music debut. Its lyrics, "Shake it like a Polaroid picture," became so popular that Polaroid released a statement to the public warning them not to shake their Polaroid camera or the images would not come out right. America's favorite pastime is not immune. There have been proposals to increase product placements within America's signature sport, baseball. However, the newest proposal is not to place the product advertisement in the stadium but on individual player's uniforms. Most controversial is the pressure advertisers have placed on magazine publishers to increase product placement in their texts at a time that the magazine industry feels strongly that "church and state," i.e., editorial content and advertising, need to be separate.

Sure, Debra Winger eats Ben & Jerry's ice cream out of the carton in the movie *Forget Paris*. Malcolm and Reese drive to a party in a Mustang convertible in Fox's *Malcolm in the Middle*. Alex needs a security guard for her Van Cleef & Arpels jewels in ABC's sitcom *I'm with Her*. Product placements have become props and players in everything from sports programming to *The Sopranos*, from dog shows to big budget films. Guess what's next.

Commercials and celebrity endorsements, step aside for the new star of advertising.

No one expected to see product placements starring on Broadway. Theater seemed to be safe from big advertisers because it is, after all, viewed as an art form rather than a media outlet. But no place is too far out of reach for advertisers. Product placements have debuted on Broadway. Skechers adorned the foot of every cast member in *Footloose,* and Visa USA found itself *Movin' Out* with Billy Joel.

Marketers say that the union between Broadway and advertising has many benefits. Mainly, theaters can get more money while advertisers get the attention of a lucrative captive audience. Advertisers hope to reach the typical theatergoer's demographic—affluent and female.[a] Critics disagree that this is harmless marketing; they fear product placements will transform theatrical fare into corporate billboards and threaten the credibility of the theater.

Of course, not all advertisers are running to get their tickets for Broadway. Many say that product placement is not effective on stage because the audience cannot see the small details. Also, the curtain rises on as many as thirty Broadway plays each night, so competition is fierce, and clutter is what most advertisers seek to avoid. For these reasons, many would-be product placers believe the time and effort are better spent on television.

Either way, product placements have made their stage debut.

Arianna Stella

[a]Atkinson, Claire, "Big Marketers Take to the Broadway Stage," *Advertising Age,* February 23, 2004.

viewers lose perspective and "max" their credit cards with gadgets they do not need. Despite criticism, substantial numbers of consumers order from infomercials.

Beyond the thirty-minute infomercials, entire networks devote their time exclusively to home shopping programs. These include the Home Shopping Network (HSN), QVC, ShopAtHome, and America's Store (AS). According to its Web site, HSN began in 1977 as Suncoast Bargaineers, a radio show in Clearwater, Florida. On December 6, 2003, HSN hit a record one-day take of $30 million. QVC, Inc., founded in 1986 by Joseph Segel, founder of The Franklin Mint, is one of the world's leading electronics retailers. In 2002, more than 107 million units were shipped to customers worldwide as a result of more than 150 million phone calls and $4.4 billion in sales, according to the QVC official site. In addition to the television network, QVC owns QVC International and QVC Retail Stores.

To encourage home shoppers to order, an 800 number appears on the screen throughout the programming while hosts of such exotic fare as *Brazilian Amethyst* chat with callers. On-screen information boxes give the product's item number, a brief description, and price (often "special introductory" or "one-time only"). Like infomercials, home shopping programs frequently employ product demonstrations and hyperbolic rhetoric such as, "Isn't this just absolutely gorgeous!"

New Media

Conventional advertising media have served advertisers' needs for many years, but advertisers and their agencies have been increasingly interested in new media that might be less costly, potentially more effective, and less cluttered than the established media. At one time the Internet was considered among the new media. Today the new media tends to include any advertising medium that doesn't fall into any other category. For example, a grocery store chain paid for poster space in a Colorado elementary school to urge students to read. Floor tiles imprinted with advertising have been installed in grocery stores coast to coast. Avis equipped rental cars with cassette-tape ads that pitch local restaurants, hotels, and other vendors. Advertisers may pay as much as $1,500 a month for single-city ad spots.[11] To drive readers to its Web site, PointRoll, creators of a variety of pop-up ads, placed stickers on the front page of *Advertising Age*. A new technology made it possible for promotional messages to be printed right on Pringles potato chips.[12] Partnered with Hasbro's relaunch of Trivial Pursuit Junior, Pringles repackaged its canisters and printed game questions and answers on the chips themselves in an attempt to differentiate the Pringles snack food from competitor Frito-Lay.

Product Packaging

Ever since motivational research in the 1950s revealed that a product's package color or shape may affect consumer purchasing decisions, manufacturers have realized the power of packaging to move products on the shelf. When Unilever Bestfoods launched a new product, Skippy SnackBars, it gave its peanut butter brand a new look with a repackaging from Smith Design.[13]

In 2004 McDonald's changed its Happy Meals packaging as part of a global marketing campaign. The new packaging reflected key menu changes for specific markets: the addition of 1 percent milk and Apple Dippers to the U.S. Happy Meal, fruit cups for Italy, and Dannon lowfat yogurt for Spain. Along with the new packaging and menu changes, McDonald's added incentives such as a United Kingdom product-centered magazine and special parking places for moms in New Zealand and Canada.[14]

Although advertising using famous athletes is hardly a new idea, the advent of relationship marketing changed the faces displayed on cereal boxes. Some cereal boxes now feature the faces of local heroes instead of national ones. Carlisle Cereal in Bismarck, North Dakota, prepackages cereal for a major manufacturer with hometown heroes for limited, specific geographic markets. General Mills has featured amateur athletic teams on its cereal boxes.

If amateur athletes on cereal boxes sounds like an innovative idea, consider Miller Brewing Company's scratch 'n' sniff package labels for novelty. A summer 1998 promotion featured scented labels on Miller Lite multipacks. Those who sniffed a coconut-scented label won a trip to Barbados, one of the promotion's 3.5 million prizes.[15]

Product Placements

Product placement in Hollywood movies gained momentum in 1982 when E. T. ate Reese's Pieces and increased candy sales for Reese's. As the cost of producing a movie has escalated to $100 million and more, product placements supplement studio production and promotions budgets while they also help generate product sales for manufacturers in what is called the "halo effect." Since *E.T.,* Hollywood has provided moving billboards for advertisers' products. What began as a matter of mutual back-scratching—advertisers supplying edibles and drinkables for the movie crew, cars, computer equipment, helicopters, clothing, hotel scenery and lodgings, phones, electronics—has resulted in business alliances between movie studios and media services representing diverse clients.

One of the classic product placement success stories is the James Bond film, *Tomorrow Never Dies.* The 1997 release provided alternative advertising for Visa, Heineken, Smirnoff, BMW, and Ericsson in what has been called "an unprecedented cross-promotional partnership."[16] In addition to featuring products in the film (James Bond rides a BMW, Agent Q carries a Visa CheckCard), eight promotional partners also spent $98 million on a worldwide advertising blitz tied to the film. BMW reported 10,000 preorders for the Cruiser motorcycle that Bond rode in the movie and its numerous televised trailers (commercial spots that preview movies).[17]

Product placements have entered the realm of televised programming, music recordings, and even Broadway productions (see this chapter's Ethics Track). For example, the Discovery network's hit show *Trading Spaces* formed a mutually beneficial alliance with the show's exclusive sponsor, Home Depot. In addition to building an advertising campaign "around the series, the store also provides products and materials for the design projects on the shows."[18]

Product placements work best with sixteen- to forty-nine-year-olds, a generation fascinated with celebrities and movies (see Table 15.1), according to a WPP Group study based on 11,300 interviews conducted in 20 countries.[19] Asian youths, in particular, said they would be inclined to try a product they had viewed in a movie. Clearly, the impact of a product placement depends upon the age and culture of the person who views it (see Table 15.2) as well as the viewer's ability to recall it (see Table 15.1.). The desired end result is that the viewer will not only recall the placement but act on it by buying the product.

TABLE 15.1. Most memorable product placements based on U.S. network sit-coms, February 16 to March 14, 2004.

Brand	Program
G.I. Joe	*The King of Queens,* Feb. 11
Mustang	*Malcolm in the Middle,* Feb. 22
Disney Cruise Line	*According to Jim,* Feb. 24, March 2
Van Cleef & Arpels	*I'm with Her,* Feb. 24
Cadillac	*The Bernie Mac Show,* March 7

Source: Adapted from "Fast Facts," *Advertising Age,* March 29, 2004, p. 8; Suzanne Vranica, "Advertising Spotlight," *The Wall Street Journal,* March 24, 2004, p. B5.

TABLE 15.2. Percentage of global viewers influenced by product placements.

Country	Percent
Mexico	53
Singapore	49
Hong Kong	33
United States	26
France	8

Cross-Promotions

Various media, both traditional and alternative, may be employed in an advertising or marketing campaign. Cross-promotions involve the use of one product to promote another product and may be reciprocal. Although cross-promotion is nothing new (Bob Hope used his radio show during World War II to promote his movies), with the advent of new media, the possibilities for cross-promotion now seem endless.

- In addition to promoting via electronic press kits (trailers and features intended to air on television or in movie theaters), print advertising, outdoor advertising (posters and billboards), MGM promoted *Tomorrow Never Dies* on its own Web site. The home page featured a dramatic picture of Pierce Brosnan as James

Bond, wearing a tuxedo and brandishing his handgun. The site provided a menu with subject categories similar to those of the electronic press kit—Cast, Characters, Story, Production, Media, and Soundtrack. But the Web site provided options that no other media could: a TND Shockwave game, access to sweepstakes entry information, and interactive contacts.

- MGM partnered with Revlon to introduce the 007 Color Collection along with the 2002 Bond release, *Die Another Day.* The film's female lead and long-time Revlon spokesmodel Halle Berry touted the Revlon products in advertising that declared, "Inspired by Bond. Created by Revlon," with lipstick colors named after such Bond films as *From Russia with Love.* The cooperative marketing deal was good for Revlon while it reminded Bond fans to get out and see the film.[20]
- For its video release of *Liar, Liar* in late 1997, Fox chose to place advertisements on 12 million apples in supermarkets at a cost of only $6.50 per thousand apples, compared to $450,000 or more for a thirty-second commercial.[21]
- Grey Worldwide New Zealand and Mediacom China came up with a strategy employing television commercials, print ads, and billboard advertising to selectively reach key markets in a nationwide Chinese campaign for Grand River Group, a leading Chinese motorcycle manufacturer.[22]
- During the 2003 holiday season, fans of Fox's *American Idol* spent almost $45 million on *Idol*-themed books, music, karaoke machines, perfume and body spray, sunglasses, clothing, and ties. The show's sponsors also strengthened their ties to the *Idol* brand. AT&T Wireless offered *Idol* fans "the chance to text-message judges and singers, and even a ring tone of the program's theme."[23]
- DKNY used stills in its print ads from its own film shorts, the premiere film series *New York Stories* and its Spring 2004 follow-up, *Road Stories,* to drive customers to DKNY stores to see the movies. Visitors to the DKNY Web site <http://dkny.com> could also download and watch the movies. Featuring Scarlett Chorvat, Waylon Payne, and DKNY jeans, the "stylish romps" were directed by Steven Sebring.
- MSNBC, the mother of online cross-promotions, pioneered cross-media promotions in the late twentieth century. Launched

July 15, 1996, MSNBC is a twenty-four-hour news, information, and talk network available in 30 million U.S. cable households and on the Internet. NBC joined with Microsoft in anticipation of an Internet-driven future.[24] The concept was to target network and cable television viewers and PC users with promotional messages designed to drive NBC's viewers to its cable station CNBC and to the MSNBC Web site. PC users receive frequent updates on network news stories, and the cable station sends viewers to both the network and the Web site. Programs for MSNBC are developed simultaneously for cable and the Internet using crossover staff, including network personality Katie Couric.

• Web users search for news, weather, and entertainment using service providers as "jumping-off" points, and advertisers pay top rates to appear on these pages. For example, NBC partnered with CNET and Microsoft, owners of the Web directory service Start and NBC's partner in MSNBC.

SUMMARY

This chapter offered just a sample of the increasingly extensive and diverse use of alternative advertising and new media. Outdoor advertisements reflect the shared experiences, norms, and identities of the people in their host communities. A race car spewing flames urges fans to see a movie about Christ's crucifixion. Buses and subway walls carry life-sized posters with advertisers' images and messages. People ready to buy a specific product turn to classified advertising to find the right retailer. Online shopbots and manufacturers' Web sites not only encourage purchases but also make immediate sales possible. Today, any space is a potential medium for a marketer's message. From the *American Idol* T-shirts to the sophisticated cross-promotional expertise of NBC, alternative advertising provides a way to make products and services stand out from traditional media clutter.

Chapter 16

Direct Marketing/
Direct Response Advertising

Each fall, close to 3 million U.S. shoppers await the arrival of the Neiman Marcus Christmas catalog with almost as much excitement as the holiday season itself. This retailer/direct marketer decided to find out whether brand-conscious Japanese consumers could get into the same spirit. When Neiman Marcus Company launched its first-ever overseas marketing effort, it mailed Christmas catalogs to 100,000 Japanese buyers.

Many Japanese, especially young people, celebrate Christmas by exchanging gifts, even though Buddhism remains the predominant religion. Neiman Marcus did not veer from its U.S. roots; the Japanese version of the catalog was almost identical to the original, with a few exceptions such as food items that might spoil during overseas shipment. Instead of buying mailing lists for direct marketing of the catalog, Neiman Marcus placed Japanese-language advertisements in upscale magazines, large circulation newspapers, and mail-order publications. The campaign also included promotional inserts in credit card mailings. Handled by the Tokyo office of J. Walter Thompson, advertisements offered subscriptions to the Japanese catalog for $13.50, more than double the $6.50 U.S. price tag, for the Christmas catalog. The response was encouraging, with 100,000 catalog subscriptions.[1]

Whereas mail order catalogs represent "classic" direct marketing, the Information Age has ushered in the era of multichannel direct marketing. Neiman Marcus combined traditional advertising with invoice inserts to market its Christmas catalog in Japan. Other companies employ electronic channels to provide immediate, convenient, personalized service. Electronic commerce may also be supported by print and television advertising.

ILLUSTRATION 16.1. A dimensional mailer. To cut through mailbox clutter, Rapp Collins Worldwide created this "Year 2000" direct mail package for PLATINUM technology, Incorporated. The mailing included a pound of coffee, two glass mugs, and a letter on stationery with a bagel graphic on top. Such innovation ensures that the direct mailing will be effective. The recipient will not only open the mailing but will also, most likely, keep the mailing's contents which serve as a reminder of the company or product.

As early as 1995, 68.7 percent of the U.S. adult population had ordered merchandise or services by phone or mail, according to the Direct Marketing Educational Foundation, Inc. Although the direct marketing industry fell off sharply following the 9/11 attacks and the subsequent anthrax scare, its recovery was surprisingly fast even though the way to recovery was fraught with a weak economy and an "ailing U.S. Postal Service, which was hit particularly hard by September 11 and anthrax and was struggling financially even before those events."[2] Of a worldwide projected advertising total of $498.28 billion for 2004, direct mail looked to enjoy $51.51 billion in revenues, up 5 percent over the previous year.[3]

Although we include examples of direct-response advertising in other chapters of this book, e.g., infomercials, home shopping channels, and Internet advertising, much of which employ a mechanism for two-way communication, this chapter explores direct marketing/direct response advertising in greater depth (see Illustration 16.1 for an example of direct marketing mailing).

DIRECT MARKETING:
DEFINITION AND HISTORY

What is direct marketing?

The Direct Marketing Association, a trade group whose members practice various forms of direct marketing, defines direct marketing as an interactive system of marketing that uses one or more advertising media to effect a measurable response and/or transaction at any location.[4] Embedded in this definition are four components:

1. Direct marketing is an interactive system in that it entails personalized communications between marketer and customer. With the advent of computers and the development of extensive databases, it has become possible for an advertiser to develop one-on-one, two-way communication with those most likely to be in the market for a certain product at the time the customer is ready to buy. Some industry leaders believe that all Internet advertising should be categorized as direct marketing.
2. Direct marketing involves one or more media (e.g., mail and telephone).

3. Direct marketing is measurable. That is, direct marketing allows the marketer to calculate precisely the costs of producing the communication effort and the resulting outcome.

4. Location is not an issue in direct marketing. Direct marketing takes place at a variety of locations—by phone, mail, or Internet—and the order can be made at any time of the day or night. Product delivery can also be made to the consumer's home or to the business client's workplace.

Direct marketing dominated the marketing services industry in 2003, with revenues of $2.87 billion making up 48.2 percent of the marketing services pie, followed by sales promotion at $1.71 billion (28.8 percent of the pie), and interactive at $1.37 billion (23 percent), according to data compiled by *Advertising Age*.[5] Direct mail (other than catalogs) remained the preferred direct marketing method. Other direct marketing methods commonly utilized appear in Table 16.1.

Direct marketing terminology can cause some confusion. For example, direct response advertising is a term used synonymously with direct marketing although, strictly speaking, direct marketing could include direct selling (such as Avon) and direct response advertising. Direct response channels include direct mail, catalogs, telephone,

THE GLOBAL PERSPECTIVE: A DIAMOND IN THE TRASH?

Should you throw away direct mail or keep it? Consumers are infamous for tossing away direct mail without reading it. Some consumers in The Netherlands might rethink their position on this practice.

To celebrate its tenth anniversary, a Netherlands jeweler sent out a direct mailing to 3,800 customers. The direct mail piece included 200 authentic diamonds; the rest were fakes. Recipients of the mailings were supposed to take the "diamond" to the jeweler's store to verify its authenticity. However, only thirty of the diamonds taken to the store tested authentic. The rest must have ended up in the trash.

What happened to the other 170 diamonds? The marketer wasn't the only one to waste his money in this direct mail fiasco. Some consumers may have later regretted putting their diamonds in the rough.

Source: "There Is a Diamond in the Mail," *The World Journal,* January 7, 2004, p. D8.

TABLE 16.1. Primary direct marketing methods used by marketers, 2003.

Method	Percentage of total direct marketing methods
Direct mail to customers	77
Direct mail to prospects	76
E-mail to customers	55
Web site	45
E-mail to prospects	43
Catalogs	34
Online ads.	33
Direct response promotions	27
Telemarketing (outbound and inbound)	27
Direct response space ads	26
Co-op mailings	18
Statement stuffers	16
Package inserts	16
Search engine	16

Source: Adapted from a Primedia, Inc., research report, 2003.

print, television and electronic shopping, interactive media, and many more. Lists and databases assist direct response advertisers in identifying customers and demographic trends. Direct response advertising is not limited to consumer marketing but includes business-to-business and financial services as well. Nonprofit organizations use direct response advertising extensively for fund-raising and membership retention. Direct response advertising differs from other forms of advertising in a number of ways, but most distinctly in its concern with the sales transaction process, which includes back-end activities such as order fulfillment and customer service.

Direct response advertising has become a fast-growing segment of the advertising industry. The industry's growth has been attributed to both social and technological factors. The rise in the number of single-parent homes and the influx of women into the workforce in recent decades are two societal factors. Furthermore, with both men and women spending long hours working in or out of the home, out-of-home shopping can sometimes be a nuisance or a waste of time. The credit card has also made direct marketing more attractive to the consumer. The previous payment system—cash on delivery (c.o.d.)— was less convenient (the shopper has to be at home when the delivery is made) and less reliable (customers not having the cash on hand, etc.). Now people can just sit at home, make purchases with their credit cards via telephone or computer, and find the prepaid packages on their doorsteps when they come home from work.

Technological advances have made direct marketing more efficient for marketers and more beneficial for shoppers. Advances in computer technology in the 1960s accelerated the industry's growth. Initially, the database allowed marketers to identify customers and prospects by name, and to determine the best possible purchasers and prospects for a given offer at a given time through the availability of quantifiable information. The automotive industry has found the Internet particularly helpful in identifying "hand raisers," those who log onto Web sites looking for quotes and product information. Of course, the advent of cybershopping has motivated retailers to maintain online storefronts. Some potential online shoppers still fear credit card fraud or loss of privacy, such as being placed on unsolicited mailing lists.

Direct Marketing History

Direct marketing is an industry that spans seven centuries, developing from the rural distribution of seed catalogs to database marketing. According to Susan Jones in *Creative Strategy in Direct Marketing,* the history of direct marketing begins around 1450 with Johann Gutenberg's invention of the printing press.[6] The new invention allowed European merchants to publish product catalogs, such as those in which English nurserymen advertised seeds and plants to farmers. In the United States, Benjamin Franklin began the first "continuity-style book club" with members selecting from almost 600 book titles by 1744.

Early direct marketers learned their trade from an abundance of door-to-door peddlers who traveled with such wares as soaps and medicines. Aaron Montgomery Ward was one such peddler who decided to advertise and sell by catalog. This catalog grew to 240 pages by 1884. Richard Warren Sears was a peddler of watches before he teamed with Alvah Curtis Roebuck and started Sears, Roebuck &

Company. The two created a catalog that reached 75,000,000 through the mail by 1927. The catalog business was catalyzed by Rural Free Delivery in the 1890s and Parcel Post in 1913, allowing direct marketers to ship to the most remote areas of the United States.

The Direct Marketing Association (DMA) was established as the Direct Mail Advertising Association in 1917. After World War II the baby boom created a demand for goods that were in short supply in neighborhood stores, and consumers turned to catalog shopping in greater numbers than ever. Advances in computer technology and the widespread availability of credit cards in the 1960s and 1970s further accelerated direct marketing growth.

Computer technology allowed for the storage and retrieval of information about customers, paving the way for more effective marketing and the creation and management of relationships between the buyer and seller. For this reason, some industry leaders argue that direct marketing is synonymous with "relationship marketing." Others use the term "database marketing." Database marketing has led to more efficient new customer acquisition, value maximization (i.e., development of product bundles or cross-sell opportunities), customer status change identification, identification of customer problems, participation of customers in contact management, and winback opportunities to target good customers who have defected.[7]

What information about customers do direct marketers most often add to a database? Over half of marketers maintain information about customer loyalty, e.g., the length of time an individual or company has been a customer. Other frequently databased information is detailed in Table 16.2. Marketers build models to cast diverse information into predictive patterns. These are called "predictive models."

TABLE 16.2. Types of customer data most marketers maintain.

Type of data	Percentage who maintain it
Length of time individual/company has been a customer	68.0
Dollar value of purchases	67.0
Number of annual purchases	63.2
Source of original lead or contact	56.8

Source: Adapted from the Direct Marketing Association's *1996 Statistical Fact Book*, p. 24.

Hundreds of direct marketing agencies work to meet clients' needs from research through creative services. These agencies may be specialized, full-service, advertising organizations, or independents (see Table 16.3).

DIRECT MARKETING MEDIA

Major direct marketing media include direct mail, catalog marketing, telemarketing, nonprofit direct marketing, business-to-business direct marketing, and "marketing without borders," e.g., marketing to U.S. ethnic and international audiences. The characteristics and special issues of each of these will be individually discussed; however, the issue of privacy affects them all and will thus be discussed first.

Privacy Issues

It may sound like a James Bond gizmo, but spyware actually refers to "programs surreptitiously buried in your computer that monitor your activities."[8] Adware, a common type of spyware, tracks Web surfing, feeds the data to an advertiser, then hits the user with pop-up ads. Wells Fargo and Hertz sued spyware firms that showed rival companies' ads to consumers visiting their Web sites. Google also created controversy with its Gmail, that can "automatically scan the body of messages for keywords used to tailor ads and match other information in its vast database."[9]

"Privacy is a central element of the FTC's consumer protection mission" in a time when advances in computer technology "have

TABLE 16.3. Top five direct marketing agencies, January 2005.

Company	U.S. revenue (in millions of dollars)
1. WPP Group	(92)
2. Omnicom Group	33
3. Interpublic Group of Companies	93
4. Publicis Groupe	366
5. Havas	62

Source: Adapted from Mercedes Cardona, "Adwatch," February 28, 2005, p. 8.

made it possible for detailed information about people to be shared more easily and cheaply than ever."[10] As part of its mission, the FTC seeks to educate consumers and businesses regarding the importance of personal information security; the FTC Act, the Fair Credit Reporting Act, the Children's Online Privacy Protection Act, and the Gramm-Leach-Bliley Act outline specific rules and strengthen the Commission.

The direct marketing industry has also sought to self-regulate. Requests to be on the no-call list of the Telephone Preference Service of the DMA may have reduced telemarketing calls by 70 percent. This is one way the Direct Marketing Association has responded to rising consumer concerns about privacy. Despite the industry's attempts to self-regulate, the public must be aware of name removal procedures and take action.

Direct Mail

Direct mail advertising refers to any advertising matter sent directly to the person the marketer wishes to influence. These advertisements take the form of letters, catalogs, and so on. This direct-marketing medium constitutes what has been commonly referred to as "junk mail"—the unsolicited mail you find in your mailbox. Direct mail can be anything and look like anything, but most pieces follow a fairly conventional format. A direct mail package usually includes a letter, a brochure, supplemental flyers, and a reply card with a return envelope inside an outer envelope. Mailing lists drawn up from databased consumer and/or customer information are key to the success of a direct mail campaign. Databased information allows for market segmentation. Lists have become increasingly more current and more selective, eliminating waste coverage. The most commonly employed lists are of those individuals who have been past purchasers of direct mail products.

List brokers have thousands of lists tied to demographic, psychographic, and geographic breakdowns. Most major firms can put together a list for a buyer by combining (merging) lists and deleting (purging) repeat names.

Although direct mailings are less constrained by the time and space considerations of print, broadcast, and other media, they do need to adhere to postal rules and regulations. The creative possibili-

ETHICS TRACK:
BEHAVIORAL TARGETING
OR ONLINE STALKING?

Big Brother may not just be watching you—Big Brother may be following you around on the Internet.

In what might be described as online stalking, users labeled as "travel seekers" were segmented within a database and "'followed around" on a Web site, no matter what section of the site they engaged.[a]

A 2003 integrated advertising campaign delivered online ads "through a database-driven behavioral targeting system," achieving "higher results than any other ad format used" and at a 25 percent cheaper price tag. American Airlines got a 26 percent "rise" in its ability to reach a specific target—the one-flight-a-year visitor to the travel columns and features of *The Wall Street Journal* online, <wsj.com>.

American Airlines has not been the only corporation to take off on the new application, called "promising" by some and "killer" by others.[b] The advantage for online advertisers is the ability to reach "actual, identifiable customer groups rather than buying mere packages of page views." Early results were impressive: in a Dynamic Logic study of a Snapple campaign on iVillage, behavioral targeting resulted in "73 percent greater brand favorability" in comparison to ads placed in content areas.[c] Behavioral targeting—defined as "the practice of delivering ads to individuals based on their previous surfing behavior"—makes online advertising more targeted and relevant, but the power of this application has made it controversial. In fact, those familiar with George Orwell's *1984* or Anthony Burgess' *A Clockwork Orange* may wonder if this isn't science fiction; the application's "true power" is that, "once an audience member is identified, a targeted ad can be delivered to that person at any time and in any way—no matter where they go on a Web site or even other sites as well."[d] In other words, there's no escaping the so-called "search on steroids."

Software provider Claria boasts a massive reach of 43 million-plus users, but critics wonder whether the approach isn't too intrusive and the ad delivery excessively "in-your-face."[e] While behavioral targeting can be "brand-lifting," marketers are challenged to deploy it "while respecting consumer choice."

[a]Kris Oser, "Targeting Web Behavior Pays, American Airlines Study Finds," *Advertising Age,* May 17, 2004, p. 8.
[b]Richard Karpinski, "Behavioral Targeting," *i.Intelligence*, Spring 2004, p. 14.
[c]Pamela Parker, "Study: Behavioral Targeting Works," *Search Engine Strategies,* <http://adres.internet.com/stories/article/0,1401,7561_3348431,00.html>, May 17, 2004.
[d]Karpinski, p. 16.
[e]Karpinski, pp. 16-17.

ties of direct mail materials are almost endless. Mailings may involve any combination of pieces, including outer envelopes, letters, brochures, response cards, reply envelopes, inserts, postcards, and product samples, informational computer disks, and/or videotapes (see Illustrations 16.2 and 16.3). Of these, the letter has been the single most important piece as it can stand alone, personalize the mailing, and enhance the mailing's credibility through its length—a factor which, research has shown, adds to the receiver's perception of the marketer's credibility. Typically, direct mail letters

- employ attention-getting openings;
- communicate product benefits;
- establish a personal relationship by using the receiver's name in the salutation, a real person's signature, a friendly tone, and you-oriented language; and
- close with a final pitch.

A postscript (PS) is recommended since it is one of the parts of the letter that receivers tend to read first. The PS may "restate the prime product benefit; highlight the urgency of the offer; refer the reader to the brochure, order form, testimonials or other component of the package; remind the prospect about the premium; offer a toll-free number for ease in ordering; or emphasize the risk-free nature of the offer."[11]

Recipients are most likely to read direct mail received from the government, followed by mail from charitable or political organizations. The average consumer receives 27.29 direct mail pieces a week, with January the peak mailing month, followed by September and October.[12]

Catalog Marketing

Now an industry over 500 years old, catalog marketing is a form of direct mail. With more high-income families shopping at home, specialized "niche" catalogs are becoming big business. Name a product, and at least one company is probably marketing that item via catalog—clothing, health and beauty products, sporting goods, gardening supplies, office supplies, and other types of products (see Illustration 16.4). For example, One Hanes Place markets Bali and Playtex prod-

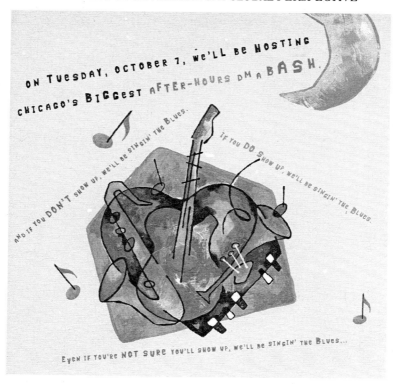

ILLUSTRATION 16.2. Postcards. The postcard provides a cost-effective mailer. Rapp Collins Worldwide/Chicago mailed this card as an invitation to Direct Marketing Association conferees to "Make a little room on your calendar" to attend a party at Chicago's House of Blues for "the biggest baddest blues club in the world's best blues town."

ucts via catalog. For decades, some retailers, such as JCPenney, had their own full-line merchandise catalogs. Business-to-business marketers send catalogs to their customers to supplement their sales force's time and effort.

Although catalog marketing is pervasive, this industry has reached the mature life-cycle stage. Although book, music, and video catalog purchases had a 37 percent growth rate, and customer orders averaged $135, mail catalog volume decreased overall from 2001 to 2002.[13] As a result, some companies, notably historic catalog pio-

ILLUSTRATION 16.3. Outer envelopes. Direct mailings can look like anything and be enclosed in envelopes of any shape or size as long as they adhere to postal regulations. The message on the back of the 9-by-9-inch outer envelope in this Hallmark Gold Crown Card Program mailing to preferred members directs the recipient to look inside for a bonus point statement and newsletter. The unusual shape and size of the envelope attracts attention, and revealing the contents encourages the recipient to open it. A window on the envelope's front makes the mailing look more official and important.

neers Sears and Montgomery Ward, pulled out of the mail-order business. At the same time, some mail-order-only firms such as Banana Republic opened retail stores.

The U.S. catalog business in Japan has grown rapidly. Before its Christmas catalog was sent to 100,000 Japanese customers, Neiman Marcus had conducted year-long Japanese tests of two other Neiman Marcus-owned catalogs, Horchow and Trifles. Lands' End, a U.S. catalog retailer comparable to L.L. Bean, thrust into Hong Kong and Singapore, countries that were small enough to be manageable yet

Brighten the life of a child.

1998 Holiday Card Collection
CHILDREN'S MEMORIAL HOSPITAL

ILLUSTRATION 16.4. Unlimited creativity. The cover reveals the catalog's theme. The child's drawing of a personified star, the splash of stars, and the words "Brighten the life of a child" suggest that buying cards from the Children's Memorial Hospital's 1998 Holiday Card Collection catalog will do more than the purchase of other cards might. The theme is reinforced with the words "You have a hand in the future when you're taking care of children" written in star-colored gold across the sky-blue inside cover paper. Courtesy of Rapp Collins Worldwide/Chicago.

had efficient postal and express delivery systems and highly educated consumers, including a sizable number of Americans. Also a factor, these countries had large professional classes proficient in English.[14] These areas are of interest to catalog marketers as they expand globally.

The catalog offers room for almost unlimited creativity. The catalog cover is a major consideration in catalog design. The cover often reveals the catalog's "theme"; for instance, a department store's Christmas catalog might feature a snowy, winter scene with an old-fashioned, decorated pine tree in a city square. Cover art also defines the company's image, i.e., the tree might reflect the store's long tradition while the city square would suggest its sophistication. The back cover customarily features the products most likely to generate customer interest. Inside, key pages where top-selling or new products are often pictured include the inside pages of the front and back covers, and the center spread.

Other creative decisions include the catalog size (both dimensional and number of pages), paper quality, art and graphics (products may be photographed or illustrated), and layout style. Some catalogs are now quite distinctive in style—for instance, the SelfCare catalog has featured customer testimonials in shaded boxes next to pictures and descriptions of the products being praised; Victoria's Secret often features full-page photographs of glamorous models posed against deep-hued Victorian backdrops; The Tog Shop shows its clothing lines in stylized illustrations.

The catalog message has become crucial in an industry that must come to terms with saturated markets. The most important part of the catalog message is the graphics. Products are displayed in attractive settings showing as many details and features as possible. People scan through a catalog, looking at the pictures. When a visual appeals to the customer, the person stops scanning and decides to read the copy blocks. Magazine-style pages may have headlines and sub-heads. Both copy style, and the size and style of the type in which the copy is set, should complement the layout and, overall, reflect the "personality" or image of the issuing store or company. Copy may be long and detailed or very short. Typically, copy describes the product, notes distinctive features, and provides such additional information as fabric and color choices, sizes, and price.

Catalogs may encourage purchases by offering sale merchandise, free gifts with purchase of certain products or an order in a set dollar amount, discounts for volume orders, gift wrapping and cards, and gift certificates. Blank space on the reverse side of the order form may be used to prominently display these encouragements. Many order forms also include a section for referrals so that customers can have catalogs sent to others who might be interested in the products.

Telemarketing

With the escalation of the cost of the personal sales call, many companies now use the telephone to support or even replace their conventional sales forces. To compound the cost, it can take as many as four to six personal calls to close a sale.

Personal sales calls are very expensive but very persuasive (see Table 16.4). Telemarketing is almost as persuasive, but a lot less expensive. However, telemarketing is not appropriate for all organizations and has to be efficient to be justifiable. Business-to-business marketers reported that telemarketing produced the highest sales value by medium, according to the DMA's *2003 Statistical Fact Book.*

Two forms of telephone marketing are practiced. One involves inbound calls for orders, inquiries, and complaints. The other involves outbound calls from telephone salespersons. The company may handle its telemarketing in-house, employing and overseeing its own telemarketers, or may contract a telemarketing company to provide the service. Despite the cost, in-house telemarketing is generally preferable, as company employees may know the product line better and may have a greater sense of company loyalty.

Most companies that use telemarketing hire a specialized company to handle the solicitations and order taking. Companies usually do not have the facilities to handle a mass response, and that response, known as back-end marketing, is crucial to the process. For example, a company may advertise a product on television and be flooded by calls into the company's switchboard. Respondents have come to expect immediate information and/or order taking as well as prompt product delivery. If that company cannot quickly gratify the respondent, another company will be available to do that in today's competi-

TABLE 16.4. Cost of a personal sales call.

Year	Average cost per call (in dollars)
1980	128
1984	196
1988	240
1992	292
2001	329

Source: Adapted from Direct Marketing Association's *2003 Statistical Fact Books,* p. 163.

Note: Cost includes salary, benefits, commissions, travel and other expenses, promotional materials, and samples.

tive direct marketplace. "World class" call centers are able to deliver high levels of service at 17 percent lower costs per contact, e.g., $4.28 at a call center versus "average" call centers' $5.16 per contact cost.[15]

In addition to the use of telemarketing calls in business-to-business activities, telemarketing calls are also made to consumers. According to a national survey reported in the DMA's *1997 Statistical Fact Book,* 63 percent of consumers surveyed said they had received telemarketing calls from long-distance telephone companies. Other types of calls consumers frequently received included local charities (62 percent), household product companies (49 percent), magazine subscription services (46 percent), and credit card offers (45 percent). Consumer responses to the calls ranged from highly favorable ratings for calls from charities to the greatest dissatisfaction with calls offering free vacations, household services, and sweepstakes.

Reputable telemarketers, aware of their industry's negative image, have abandoned practices that annoy and anger consumers. A better-designed message can reduce complaints and sell products more effectively. The outbound message needs to be simple, compelling, and short since most people will not stay on the telephone longer than two to three minutes for a sales call. Nevertheless, many consumers are disgusted with all forms of telephone marketing. They are besieged by calls from telemarketers at undesirable times, particularly during dinner hours. Telemarketing scams are everywhere.

In response to consumer complaints, government regulators have taken action to try to prevent further abuses. The Telephone Consumer Protection Act (TCPA), enacted by Congress in 1991, regulated autodialing. The Federal Communication Commission (FCC) and Federal Trade Commission (FTC) established a national do-not-call registry in 2003. "Consumers need only make one phone call or access the FCC's DNC Registry Web site to have their phone added to the registry."[16] In 2004 President George W. Bush signed into law a bill giving the FTC the authority to administer a do-not-call registry; the FTC acted immediately to begin enforcement.

Nonprofit Direct Marketing

Total donations brought in a historic $240.92 billion to nonprofit organizations in 2002, according to *The Direct Marketing Association's Statistical Fact Book 2003.* Religious organizations received

35 percent of total contributions, followed by human service organizations, educational institutions, and health-related groups (see Table 16.5). As much as 94 percent of the bulk of charitable giving comes from individuals with the remainder derived from corporate giving and foundations.

Direct mail and person-to-person communication have been the most common fund-raising techniques for decades. Direct mail has provided a cost-effective, measurable way to target prospective donors, providing the organization's "story" in such written formats as letters and brochures.[17] Database marketing has increased the efficiency of direct mail solicitations, and computers have allowed for personalization of appeals through individualized salutations. Some organizations follow up direct mail appeals with phone calls.

Direct mail pieces for fund-raisers generally utilize the same methods as profit marketers, i.e., human interest, personalization, and celebrity endorsements.[18] Many organizations send membership cards, merchandise and insurance offers, organization newsletters, and notices of conventions or social events to fulfill the donor's need for a sense of affiliation. Nonprofit organizations such as AARP offer special insurance rates, a motor club program, and discounts at participating hotels, among other member benefits. Animal rights organizations such as the National Wildlife Federation, People for the Ethical Treatment of Animals (PETA), and the United States Humane Society all send attractive, sophisticated newsletters to contributors. Once an initial contribution has been made, organizations may send unsolicited gifts, especially greeting and note cards, along with appeals for additional contributions. These appeals frequently work because they make the recipient feel guilty or obligated to pay for the gift.

TABLE 16.5. Nonprofit rankings by recipient organizations, 2003.

Type of organization	Percent of contributions
1. Religion	35.0
2. Education	13.1
3. Unallocated giving	12.6
4. Health	7.8
5. Human services	7.7

Source: Adapted from AAFRC Trust for Philanthropy/Giving USA 2003; *The Direct Marketing Association's Statistical Fact Book 2003.*

Nonprofits have reached beyond direct mail solicitations to utilize other direct response strategies in their fund-raising campaigns. The trend toward the use of merchandising to raise dollars for charities has troubled some. For instance, the Paralyzed Veterans of America, a U.S. nonprofit charitable organization over a half century old, continues to use merchandising "to obtain some discretionary dollars that were not earmarked for philanthropy."[19]

WGBH, a public television station in Boston, raises additional dollars by selling merchandise through its *Signals* mail-order catalog. PBS, a private, nonprofit corporation owned by the nation's public service television stations, raises money through the sale of merchandise advertised in its slick, four-color catalog, *PBS Home Video*. Public television stations routinely offer merchandise premiums during their pledge drives. When the nation's number one PBS station, Chicago's WTTW, offered those who pledged $250 a videotape of *Les Miserables* as an exclusive on-air promotion in a 1996 pledge drive, the station had 2,500 takers. However, the station discovered a problem with merchandise-for-pledge offers. Since the technique focuses as much on merchandising as philanthropy, it has proven difficult to get first-time pledgers to renew during the next drive unless the station can come up with comparable merchandise.

As federal dollars for nonprofit organizations have declined and the number of nonprofit organizations has continued to grow, competition for fund-raising dollars has become intense. In 1999 there were over 1.25 million exempt organizations that had formally obtained recognition of their tax-exempt status from the IRS, according to the National Center for Charitable Statistics (NCCS). Individual and corporate donors expect more for their money than purely philanthropic givers of the past. WTTW hired an outside fulfillment house to ensure that its pledgers would receive their premium merchandise as quickly as they would receive goods ordered from a mail-order company. Tax deductions, mentions in programs, newsletters and brochures, and on-air acknowledgments of program sponsors are a few of the "perks" expected today in return for a donation. Fund-raising is no longer as simple as it once was—just sending out a solicitation letter or asking volunteers to make door-to-door calls.

Business-to-Business Marketing

In 1995 U.S. businesses spent $51.7 billion on marketing and communications, 37.4 percent of the total U.S. marketing dollars, to sell their products and services to other businesses, according to an OutFront Marketing Research Study.[20] In addition to the growth of direct response consumer marketing, business-to-business direct marketing has also experienced tremendous expansion, with this category's advertising expenditures expected to grow by 6.3 percent to $1.4 trillion from 2002 to 2007, according to the Direct Marketing Association (see Table 16.6). DMA statistics for 2003 showed that the cost of reaching a potential customer in an ad in a niche business publication (24 cents per contact) cost significantly less than a personal sales call with a price tag of $329.

Direct mail selling, newspaper, telemarketing, and other forms of direct marketing provide attractive options for firms who either prefer to avoid the huge expense of a traveling sales force or desire to supplement sales-force efforts with supportive marketing communications. In the 1990s the business-to-business area experienced a trend away from mass market communication to direct marketing that allowed for relationship-building two-way communication. According to a report of the Patrick Marketing Group 2002, direct marketing came to be "perceived as the top tool to generate leads."[21] Business-to-business marketers have been ahead of consumer marketers in advertising and selling goods using online networks, the Internet, CD-ROMs, floppy disks, and kiosks.

Marketing Without Borders

Reliable, a $175 million office supplies company, decided to go into international direct marketing when its U.S. growth rates began

TABLE 16.6. Direct marketing expenditures by market (in billions of dollars).

Year	Consumer	Business to business
1997	$75.8	$76.9
2002	$93.2	$99.9
2007	$120.2	$135.4

Source: Adapted from "The DMA Report: Economic Impact—U.S. Direct Marketing Today," 2003.

to decline and the global information superhighway created customer awareness abroad. The strategy included a 1988-1990 venture with a United Kingdom contract stationer. Industry background looked favorable. A major competitor, Viking, was already successful in Western Europe, and superstores were not expanding aggressively overseas. Reliable implemented its plan by defining catalog offerings and product sources, then cloning its U.S. operational system. Reliable called this "marketing without borders."[22]

The future of direct marketing depends upon its ability to cross cultures and other borders, whether at home or abroad.

Direct Marketing and Ethnic Communities

Direct marketing is increasingly becoming an effective way to reach the lucrative U.S. Hispanic market. Hispanic households receive less than the national average of 27.29 pieces of direct mail per week, and less volume in the mailbox can translate into better response rates. In addition, Hispanics are now turning to direct marketing, thanks in part to unpleasant shopping experiences, according to a study conducted by DraftWorldwide, Chicago. A survey of 750 Hispanics found that about 49 percent of respondents said that they are not treated with respect in stores, and 41 percent said that they buy direct because it is less threatening than in-person shopping. The survey also found that about 94 percent of the respondents said that they receive direct mail, and 66 percent said that they always open and read it. Marketers are increasing their usage of direct mail to the Hispanic market because of improvements in mailing lists and better executions (e.g., the usage of a bilingual package—English and Spanish). Marketers can also convey respect in direct mail pieces by featuring Hispanic talent and models and culturally relevant visuals that emphasize family and use "traditional" bright, tropical colors like reds, yellows, and greens.[23]

African Americans surveyed also showed a positive attitude toward receiving direct mail, especially subscription magazines, personal letters, and catalogs from familiar companies.[24] Younger African Americans reported that receiving such mail reflects their independence and their own perceptions of "where they are in their lives." This younger subset's need to be acknowledged as important in society makes this target receptive to direct mail. Furthermore, urban dwellers are more likely to respond to direct mail offerings than suburbanites because city dwellers are more price sensitive and appreciate the opportunity to fulfill needs quickly in a hectic environment where control is limited. Since "the little things in life" were most important to African Americans surveyed, direct marketers should pay attention to details in mailings, for instance, accuracy in spelling the target's name.

International Direct Marketing

Taiwan had the highest projected growth rate (18.96 percent) in international direct marketing advertising expenditures among non-U.S. countries and ranked number 8 in a 2002 Direct Marketing Association forecast.[25] Ranked by millions of U.S. dollars in international direct marketing ad spending, the top countries were Japan, Germany, the United Kingdom, France, and Italy, based on the years 1997, 2001, 2002, and forecasts for 2006 and 2007. The report also disclosed that Japan and Germany had the highest direct marketing sales among non-U.S. countries.

The euro has enabled marketers to "offer the same goods at the same price everywhere, eliminating the need to make complex calculations about inter-country exchange rates."[26] Direct marketers who typically prepare mailings in the customers' native language and tailor offers to specific consumer profiles now also tailor payment options. Still, many issues remain unresolved, such as proposed bans on telemarketing and advertisements in English in countries where English is not the native language.

Interactive marketing abroad has been accelerated by international Internet use, which has grown at a faster rate than in the United States. Those setting up international electronic direct response advertising should use the consumer's native language, recognize cultural differences, post relevant content, form strategic alliances with international organizations, segment audiences by language, country, or currency, and use both print media and all electronic delivery platforms (telephone, cable, satellite, and digital TV).[27] Spam messages have become problematic in Europe, with the majority originating in the United States and most senders not even bothering to convert their prices to the euro.[28] U.S. antispam laws do not extend abroad, and European enforcement of its own statutes varies. In Germany alone a study showed that 35 percent of all spam messages originated in the United States followed by 7 percent from China.

The Internet has also become a channel to reach the Latin American market. Web sites sold $17 million in goods and services in Latin America in 1996, with most customers coming from the upper-middle and upper socioeconomic classes.[29] The number of Internet sites has grown dramatically in some Latin American countries. The North American Free Trade Agreement (NAFTA) and the spread of democracy have also made Latin America an attractive target market for interactive commerce.

SUMMARY

Whether you call it "direct marketing," "direct response advertising," "interactive marketing," "relationship marketing," or "database marketing," this industry has reached individual customers directly and personally for centuries—from its beginning in catalog advertising and sales to its roots in door-to-door peddling to its current international, technological thrust. Direct response mechanisms allow for the two-way communication that is requisite for today's relationship marketing and company-consumer dialogue. The direct marketing industry has been proactive in crossing cultural and geographic borders, all the while pioneering the use of electronic media.

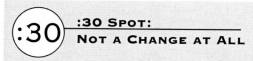

:30 SPOT:

NOT A CHANGE AT ALL

There comes a time in everyone's life when a career change is needed. The true challenge is whether to continue with your original career of choice or to move in another direction. Career changes can be scary but may end up one of the better decisions of your life.

My first job consisted of managing the marketing and advertising department for an American Express-affiliated travel agency. This was truly a great first out-of-college position. I was responsible for all aspects of marketing the travel agency externally and internally. I was on top of the world, doing what I had only dreamed of doing throughout college. In five years at the agency, I created television, radio, and print campaigns, and planned and implemented special events. Everything and anything marketing related I did and did it well. I was gaining so much knowledge and experience, I thought I would stay forever. Little did I know.

I never thought I'd end up back at my alma mater in the development office. How did I get from marketing a travel agency to fund-raising for a private college? Although I was uncertain how my marketing experience would figure into my new career, I soon learned that fund-raising, marketing, and advertising go hand in hand.

It was quickly apparent that a marketing approach to fund-raising would achieve maximum benefits. My responsibilities are to conduct extensive direct mail campaigns to alumnae, parents of current and former students, and friends of the college (see Illustration 16.5). I also supervise the annual phone-a-thon and student leadership campaigns, which ask students to take a leadership role and make a gift back to the college in honor of their graduating class.

It has been critical to develop relationships with donors and students through direct mail, personal contact, and special events. I had to step into this role and design programs that would create a profitable annual fund, and the only way I knew was through marketing.

Marketing was not fully utilized when I arrived; there were signs of marketing, but no real marketing plan. So I began to implement a marketing strategy. I began with market research, developed a segmented marketing strategy for each of our audiences, then further segmented by generation, giving behaviors, and other factors. This segmentation ensures that each appeal matches its audience. I wanted each group to feel that I was talking directly to them. There would be no mass mailings to one large audience and no general appeals. Segmented marketing is the key to success.

It has been four years since I changed careers, and I am happy to say that marketing is now fully utilized within the annual fund. Revenue and relationships have increased with every attempt to segment and directly address each audience.

My career change was not a career change at all. It was just a new opportunity in marketing.

Judeanne Wilson
Director, Annual Fund
Saint Mary's College
Notre Dame, Indiana

ILLUSTRATION 16.5. Market a latté. Judeanne Wilson created specifically targeted direct mailings, such as this campaign, "Give a latté," designed to reach recent graduates who have not yet amassed a lot of disposable income.

Chapter 17

Sales Promotion

Georgia-Pacific spent $20 million on "sampling, TV, print, radio and online" promotions of its Brawny paper towels in 2004 when the original Brawny muscleman was replaced with a younger, citified "metrosexual."[1] Like other marketers and suppliers, Georgia-Pacific tailored the sales promotion to stand out from the crowd. A massive sales promotion effort distributed samples in 1,800 Wal-Mart stores and in bags hooked to half a million U. S. doors.

MilkPEP spent about $30 million on its "24 Ounces in 24 Hours: Milk Your Diet. Lose Weight!" campaign, with $10 million of the tag spent on sales promotions.[2] The campaign also included public relations and "extensive advertising tied to the long-running Milk Mustache campaign." The promotion also tied into *Shape* magazine's milk-purchase giveaway of 13 million copies of *The Shape You Want to Be In,* a weight-loss guide published by *Shape.* A "Show Off with the Top Down" sweepstakes gave away a VW Beetle convertible each of twenty-four days. Consumers entered by logging in milk carton UPC codes at <www.2424milk.com> from mid-July through mid-August in 2004. The Milk Mustache Mobile took weight-loss info on a 100-city tour, visiting high-traffic areas such as retail stores and malls. The mobile featured a milk smoothie sampling bar staffed by dieticians. Year-long TV and print ads carried the weight-loss theme. The campaign also incorporated a rebate offer that netted diligent dairy consumers a series of $5 checks. Visitors to the "Snackulator" Web site were eligible to win dairy coupons and subscribe to an e-newsletter.

Whereas the MilkPEP campaign ran no risk of depleting available dairy products, the McDonald's initial Teenie Beanie Babies giveaway in 1997 turned sour when the restaurant chain depleted its supply of 80 million babies offered free with children's Happy Meals in a special promotion. McDonald's heard distressing stories of disgrun-

ILLUSTRATION 17.1. Creating relationships. A continuity program encourages continued purchases by offering the consumer a benefit or reward. The Hallmark Gold Crown Card Program rewards its members with cash certificates, newsletters, special gifts, and special offers. Cash certificate rewards are based on points earned for every dollar spent at Hallmark Gold Crown Card Stores. Hallmark Cards, Inc. sent this holiday postcard to its Gold Crown Card Program members to encourage holiday shopping. The offer was a 100-point bonus on purchases made the weekend after Thanksgiving.

tled customers "throwing away Happy Meals they had bought just for the toys."[3] When McDonald's repeated the Teenie Beanie premium offer in spring 1998, it began with 160 million babies this time. The company also modified the offer so that, in addition to coming free with a Happy Meal, the Teenie Beanies could be purchased outright with any food item. Results were impressive. Some franchises reported sales increases of more than 30 percent over the previous year. McDonald's Teenie Beanie success speaks to the power of sales promotion.

Sales promotions can effectively appeal to consumers. What exactly is sales promotion? The objective of this chapter is to provide an introduction to the role of sales promotion in marketing and to introduce its types.

THE ROLE OF SALES PROMOTION IN MARKETING

As mentioned in an earlier chapter, the marketing mix consists of four major components: product, place, promotion, and price. A primary goal of a marketing manager is to create and maintain a marketing mix that satisfies consumers' needs. As a part of this mix, promotion involves informing individuals, groups, or organizations about an organization's products or services, and persuading them to accept these products or services. The promotional mix refers to the communication aspects of marketing: advertising, personal selling, sales promotion, and public relations. Marketers strive for the right promotional mix to make sure that a product is well received. Sales promotion is an activity or material (or both) that acts as a direct inducement, offering added value or incentive for the product to resellers, salespersons, or consumers (see Illustrations 17.1 and 17.2).[4]

The purpose of all marketing communications is to help the company achieve its marketing objectives. Typical marketing objectives include

- introducing new products;
- inducing present customers to buy more;
- maintaining sales in off-seasons;
- obtaining greater shelf space; and
- combatting competition.

ILLUSTRATION 17.2. Added incentive. Arline Thoms designed this newspaper advertisement to promote Lafayette Interior Fashions' holiday sale. In addition to the 25 percent discount, the store offers free in-home consultation and free installation.

THE GLOBAL PERSPECTIVE:
THE CELLULITE DILEMMA

American women and French women are "equally preoccupied with body image and appearance," but Americans turn to diet and exercise to resolve problems with their figures, while the French "are confident that all problems can be solved by lotions."[a] In Adam Gopnik's memoir of his years in Paris, *Paris to the Moon,* he reveals that cellulite creams and electrical stimulators supersede counting carbs and aerobics in the world's fashion capital.

Le Club des Createurs de Beaute offered price incentives and a gift to stimulate sales of the Paris-based retailer's 2004 anticellulite spring line. The Au Lip-Activ hydro-gel was offered with an incentive, the acti-massager at half price; customers would receive a spa robe and a free product with the purchase of any three cellulite-fighting products. With summer approaching, the sales promotion was timed to capitalize on women's concerns about the coming bathing-suit season.

Le Club des Createurs de Beaute competes with other French cosmetic companies, such as Yves Rocher and Dr. Pierre Ricaud, for a market of U.S. women interested in sweat-free solutions to cellulite and other beauty problems. While French retailer Yves Rocher sells beauty products in stores located all over Paris and in other parts of France, it makes the same products available globally through a Web site and a direct-mail catalog; special online and catalog promotions change monthly. Dr. Pierre Ricaud has offered attractive sales incentives, such as a Majorca pearl bracelet free with any purchase during its initial U.S. catalog launch.

In a smart sales promotion, Le Club des Createurs gave away hot pink mouse pads to put its Web address, <www.ccb-paris.com>, in the right place at the right time.

[a]Adam Gopnik, *Paris to the Moon,* New York: Random House, 2001, p. 65.

The marketing strategy the company uses to achieve these objectives may include the marketing mix—product, place, promotion, and price. Some consider sales promotion supplementary to advertising and personal selling because it binds the two together, making both more effective by increasing sales. In reality, however, sales promotion is far more than supplementary. For example, many companies (e.g., Ralph Lauren) distribute more than 500,000 free samples in Daytona Beach each spring break to get college students to try a new product.

Product publicity, an important hybrid of sales promotion and public relations, is similar to public relations in that both seek to create and maintain relationships between prospective buyers, and the publicity is nonpaid. Yet it publicizes a product using sales promotion techniques such as sampling and incentive programs. Although product publicity may relay new information about products through the media, it is not considered traditional advertising because it does not use paid time or space. Product publicity can generate high levels of introductory sales by making consumers aware of the product. Many of the techniques of product publicity will be detailed in the section on Consumer-Oriented Sales Promotion in this chapter.

Ben Cohen and Jerry Greenfield, cofounders of Ben & Jerry's Homemade, Incorporated, have become famous as innovators of product publicity techniques. They personally distributed samples of their superpremium ice cream as they drove a converted motor home, dubbed the "Cowmobile," across the country in 1986. As a company that did not purchase traditional advertising until the mid-1990s, Ben & Jerry's employed a variety of product publicity techniques throughout the 1980s, such as tours of the factory in Waterbury, Vermont, where they also staged festivals and other special events. In 1998 Ben & Jerry's teamed up with United Airlines to promote a new flavor, "Dilbert's World—Totally Nuts." On April Fool's Day, Ben & Jerry's awarded business commuters checks for the average ticket price of their United Airlines flights and dished out free samples of the new flavor at the gate.

Starbucks Coffee Company has also made innovative use of such sales promotions. Before opening a new store, Starbucks engages "local ambassadors," families and friends of local employees, to spread the word of the opening throughout the community and to share free-drink coupons with friends. Starbucks also employs a continuity program with *passports,* punch cards entitling customers to a free half-pound of coffee once a *world tour* has been taken by buying Starbucks coffee beans from a variety of countries.[5] Product publicity may also involve the company in environmental preservation or other causes. Starbucks' CARE promotion mug benefitted both this worldwide relief and development foundation and the customers, who received a discount on coffee refills when the mug was presented.

Effective sales promotion maximizes sales volume. Advertising helps develop and reinforce quality, differentiate brand reputation, and build market volume. Sales promotion helps build market volume, and its subset, product publicity, helps build long-term company-consumer relationships.

TYPES OF SALES PROMOTION

Sales promotion refers to the use of any incentive by a manufacturer or service provider to induce the trade (wholesalers and retailers) and/or consumers to buy a brand and to encourage the sales force to aggressively sell it. Most sales promotion methods can be grouped into trade sales promotion and consumer sales promotion. Manufacturers who market through normal channels must secure the cooperation of wholesalers and retailers. So, their push strategies include trade promotion tactics, such as advertising allowances and slotting allowances. Consumer sales promotion methods encourage or stimulate consumers to patronize specific retail stores or to try particular products. Major manufacturers use a pull strategy to reach their consumers, such as coupons, sweepstakes, and in-store advertising.

Trade-Oriented Sales Promotion

To encourage resellers, especially retailers, to carry their products and promote them effectively, producers use trade-oriented sales promotion methods. There are various types of trade-oriented sales promotion techniques.

Trade Allowances

Off-invoice allowances. The most frequently used allowance is an off-invoice allowance, deals offered periodically to the trade (wholesalers and retailers) that permit them to deduct a fixed amount from the invoice.

Buy-back allowances. When introducing a new product, manufacturers sometimes offer retailers a buy-back allowance for the old product that has not been sold.

Bill-back allowances. Retailers receive allowances for featuring the manufacturer's brand in advertisements (bill-back advertisement allowances) or for providing special displays (bill-back display allowances).

Slotting allowances. In response to the glut of new products, some retailers charge manufacturers slotting allowances for the privilege of obtaining shelf or floor space for a new product. Some retailers have even begun charging an exit fee to remove unsuccessful new products from their distribution centers. These exit fees could just as well be called deslotting allowances.

Advertising allowances. An advertising allowance is a common technique employed primarily in the consumer-products area in which the manufacturer pays the wholesaler or retailer a certain amount of money for advertising the manufacturer's product. Cooperative advertising (co-op advertising) involves a contractual arrangement between manufacturer and reseller whereby the manufacturer agrees to pay a part or all of the advertising expenses incurred by the resellers. Special co-op deals are used to introduce new products, advertise certain lines, or combat competitors. Unlike advertising allowances, co-op programs typically require the resellers to submit proof of the advertising (tearsheets from the newspaper or affidavits of performance from radio or TV stations) along with invoices from the media.

Display allowances. More stores now charge manufacturers display allowances—fees to make room for and set up displays. In-store displays include counter stands, shelf signs, and special racks.

Push Money or Spiffs

This is additional compensation provided to retail salespeople by the manufacturer to push a line of goods. This method often helps manufacturers obtain commitment from the sales force, but it can be very expensive.

Point-of-Purchase Displays

A point-of-purchase (POP) display is designed by the manufacturer and distributed to retailers to promote a particular brand or group of products. Marketers use a variety of items in point-of-purchase communications. These include various types of signs, mobiles, plaques, banners, shelf talkers, full-line merchandisers, wall posters, and numerous other materials (see Illustration 17.3). POP advertising is a multibillion-dollar industry.

ILLUSTRATION 17.3. Related. The point-of-purchase display may promote one brand or a group of related products. Here a POP display for a brand-name film is flanked by cameras. Photo © Dana Hanefeld.

Trade Incentives and Contests

To get retail dealers and salespeople to reach specific sales goals or to stock a certain product, manufacturers may offer special prizes and gifts. A trade contest typically is directed at store-level or department managers. Whereas contests are typically related to meeting sales goals, trade incentives are given to retail managers and salespeople for performing certain tasks. As an incentive to encourage retailer participation in their special promotional programs aimed at the final consumers, the manufacturer gives the special promotional items to the store manager when the sales promotion is completed. Bigger prizes in the form of vacations and other high-ticket items are sometimes used as incentives.

Count and Recount

The count-and-recount promotion method is based on payment of a specific amount of money for each product unit moved from a reseller's warehouse in a given time period. Units of a product are

ETHICS TRACK:
THE CARBO CRAZE

Dr. Atkins didn't live long enough to see the craze he created. Carbohydrates replaced fats as the villains when his low-carb diet swept the nation.

The Atkins diet is basically a call to change lifestyle and lose weight. The diet's major premise is to decrease carbohydrates based on Atkins' assertion that low-fat/low-calorie diets are not effective. According to his book *Dr. Atkins' New Diet Revolution,* 90 percent of his patients were overweight because of a disturbed carbohydrate metabolism. This diet attempts to correct that problem. In doing so, dieters supposedly feel better physically and emotionally.[a]

Many Americans have taken Atkins seriously and now limit their carb intake. The number of people watching carb intake increased from 11 to 40 percent from 2003 to 2004.[b] The increased awareness and participation in the low-carb way of life led manufacturers and advertisers to reposition, invent, and reinvent a number of product lines. Unilever announced the release of a new product line, Carb Options; Hershey created low-carb chocolate; General Mills released a cereal called Total Protein, and even ice cream kings Ben & Jerry introduced Carb Karma, a low-carb ice cream. Following the trend, Anheuser-Busch, Adolph Coors, and SAB-Miller came out with low-carb beer to attract consumers.

Although each year the number of people participating in the low-carb lifestyle has increased, it does raise a number of questions. First, with manufacturers adding low-carb items into their product mixes, what happens to those consumers who do not adhere to the lifestyle prescribed by Atkins? Are they lost in the mix? According to Burt P. Flickinger of the Strategic Research Group, a New York firm that works with consumer packaged-goods companies, "The consumer demand hasn't dictated the level of product development and new-product initiatives that the market has seen so far."[c] Second, the verdict is still out as to how safe the low-carb diet is over the long term. Is it entirely ethical for advertisers to exploit this diet in order to sell products to consumers when the long-term effects are still unknown?

Arianna Stella

[a]Robert C. Atkins, *Dr. Atkins' New Diet Revolution,* New York: M. Evans & Company, 1992, p. 15.
[b]Stephanie Thompson, "Low-Carb Craze Blitzes Food Biz," *Advertising Age,* January 5, 2004, p. 1.
[c]Brian Steinberg, "Food Makers Playing Up Nutrition," *The Wall Street Journal,* March 26, 2004, p. B3.

counted at the start of the promotion and again at the end to determine how many units have moved through the warehouse.

Consumer-Oriented Sales Promotion

Consumer-oriented sales promotions are directed at the ultimate user of the good or service. The primary strengths of consumer-oriented sales promotions are their variety and flexibility. They include floor ads "that talk, messages that swoop down from the ceiling and motion sensors that trigger on-shelf light shows"—a variety of new technologies have broadened the scope of in-store marketing.[6] Because retailers today "know more about the manufacturer's product and its performance in their stores than ever before," sales promotions at the retail level are particularly powerful.[7] The advent of the Universal Product Code (UPC) and the use of information technology, such as the scanner and the computer, allow the retailer to more efficiently determine which items should be ordered and stocked.

Coupons

A coupon is a certificate with a stated value which is presented to the retail store for a price reduction on a specified item during a specified time period. Marketers use coupons to attract new users to their products, to encourage repeat purchases, and to maintain user loyalty. There are five main vehicles for distributing coupons: mass media (newspapers and magazines), direct mail, package (in- and on-pack), online, and in-store. Typically, consumers have clipped coupons from colorful, preprinted advertisements called freestanding inserts (FSIs) that are inserted into newspapers at the time of delivery. FSI coupons accounted for 86 percent of the 248 billion manufacturers' coupons in 2002, according to the *Direct Marketing Association Statistical Fact Book 2003,* although overall coupon redemption dropped 5 percent.

Today, coupons are also accessed and printed out at shopbot and manufacturers' Web sites. Coupons are clipped and saved by nearly 90 percent of American adults, according to Decision Analyst Inc., Arlington, Texas.

Except for in-store coupons, coupon clipping depends on customer forethought. The point of purchase, e.g., the store itself, may be considered "a media channel," and it is also the place where 70 percent of buying decisions are actually made.[8] As reported in "What Beguiles in the Aisle," a Knowledge Networks survey revealed that 24 percent of consumers choose a particular product or brand on the spur of the moment during almost every shopping trip (see Table 17.1). Also a downside for the coupon, as many as 25 percent of coupons are misredeemed. U.S. manufacturers lose millions of dollars annually on fraudulent coupon submission, including expired coupons, coupons for items not purchased, or coupons for a smaller-sized product than that specified by the coupon.[9]

Refunds and Rebates

The terms *refund* and *rebate* both refer to the practice in which manufacturers give cash discounts or reimbursements to consumers who submit proofs of purchase. Though often used interchangeably, a refund typically refers to cash reimbursement for packaged goods (such as vitamins or a camera) whereas a rebate more often refers to reimbursements for durable goods (cars or household appliances). Rebates have enjoyed on-and-off popularity since they originated in the 1960s, but by the late 1990s rebate offers popped up everywhere, on everything from dishwashers to paper shredders. Rebate fraud, which plagued the 1980s and early 1990s, has been controlled by the Postal Service, and even though they stimulate sales, only about two out of five consumers bother to redeem them resulting in a low payoff risk for the manufacturer.[10]

In some cases, successful rebate programs have even enabled manufacturers to cut consumer prices. When Sharp Electronics offered a $500 rebate on a $4,695 TV, sales increased dramatically and unex-

TABLE 17.1. Influencers of in-store purchases.

Tactic	Percentage of shoppers affected
Product tasting/sampling	63
Brand-specific stand-alone displays	42
Brand-specific shelf displays	29
Product giveaways	28
In-store TV ads	6
Interactive kiosks	4
Floor ads	3

pectedly. As a result, Sharp permanently lowered the TV's price to $3,995. Rebate checks sent out by companies such as PepsiCo Inc. and OfficeMax have been estimated at 30 million a year.[11] In spite of the frustrating amount of paperwork required for mail-in rebates, psychologists say that customers still perceive that they're saving money, even if they don't follow through. Also, "the larger the savings, the more consumers tend to follow through" and claim the rebate.[12]

Although rebate offers increased 30 percent from 2003 to 2004, the Federal Trade Commission recorded twice as many complaints about rebate offers during that time. The use of rebate-processing centers, or fulfillment houses, may be partially responsible for this problem; however, the fault sometimes rests with companies that "deliberately make it difficult to redeem rebates by imposing complex qualifying terms and conditions."[13]

Sweepstakes

On Memorial Day 1998 Philip Morris launched a sweepstakes for those who would like to visit mythic "Marlboro country"—the top prize was a five-day stay at an Arizona or Montana ranch. The prize was appropriate for the tobacco company's most macho brand. The $40 million campaign also included outdoor, magazine, and direct-mail advertising as well as retail promotions—cents-off coupons and a merchandise incentive program.[14]

Sweepstakes offer prizes based on a chance drawing of entrants' names and cannot require a proof of purchase as a condition for entry. If an advertiser requires a proof of purchase, it becomes a lottery, which is illegal in some states of the United States. Therefore, sweepstakes require only that the entrant submit his or her name for consideration in the drawing or selection of the prize or prizes.

Two of the titans of magazine sweepstakes—American Family Enterprises and Publishers Clearing House—became enmeshed in legal difficulties in 1998. Both American Family and Publishers Clearing House sell magazines at discount prices, although only 10 to 25 percent of the money actually goes to the magazine publishers who profit, primarily, from renewals.

The Florida attorney general investigated an American Family mailing in February 1998 when about twenty contestants, many senior citizens, flew to Tampa to claim what they believed was their $11 million jackpot. None of them had won, although the wording of the mailing—declaring, "We have reserved an $11,000,000.00 sum in your name"—suggested that they had.[15] In March the company agreed to voluntary compliance in modifying its promotional messages, but it still had forty lawsuits pending, one of which paid 12,000 New Yorkers $60 each for magazine subscriptions they purchased from American Family. By July American Family was looking for an agency to help overhaul its damaged image.[16]

A game is a type of sweepstake but is conducted over a longer time. It requires customers to make repeat visits to the retailers to continue playing. After a decade of independent game offerings, McDonald's partnered with Best Buy in October 2003 to launch "a new Monopoly game promotion" in which customers could "win from $50 to $1 million in cash," an SUV, or a food prize.[17] Prizes also included a variety of Best Buy electronics products.

Contests

A contest offers prizes based on the skill or ability of the entrants, e.g., solving a puzzle, although entrants may be required to submit proofs of purchase. Contests have been popular in the competitive, sports-oriented culture of the United States. Since state lotteries are now offering extremely large cash prizes, companies have been challenged to come up with more substantial or innovative prizes. For example, Faygo awarded $2,500 to Jeannie Traviss in a competition to name and help develop a new soft drink flavor. Traviss came up with Candy Apple flavor and, as a reward, has her name and image on every can and bottle of the product, manufactured by Faygo Beverages, Inc.[18]

Contests may also tie into corporate sponsorships. For example, Capitol One financial services, a top ad spender, launched a beauty pageant to select team mascots, a promotion linked with its ESPN college football sponsorship.[19]

Companies sponsoring big-prize contests must consider the probability that someone will be able to perform the feat. Once the risk has been assessed, companies ask underwriters to insure them in order to defray the actual cost to the company in awarding the prize. For instance, by paying a 2 percent premium to an underwriter, a company might pay only $20,000 to award a $1 million prize. SCA Promotions Inc. insured only nine contest-type events with million-dollar prizes in 1990, but insured more than 100 in 1997. National Hole-in-One Association, another contest underwriter, insured only 80 promotions with million-dollar prizes in 1990, but insured 500 such promotions by 1997.[20]

Insurance coverage isn't a cure-all for contest woes, however. Sometimes the fine print in contest rules leads to problems with consumers who litigate to claim their prizes. For example, Randy Giunto shot a puck into a target at a Florida Panthers hockey game to win a $1 million prize but was disqualified when the puck bounced out. A civil-court jury awarded Giunto the prize, but the sponsors—the Florida Panthers and Coca-Cola—have appealed. Publicity about such disputes defeats the manufacturers' intended purpose—product awareness and goodwill.

Premiums

A premium is an item offered free or at a bargain price to encourage the consumer to buy an advertised product. A good premium should have strong appeal and value and should be useful or unusual. There are two premium categories—direct and delayed. Direct premiums offer a free product or reduced price at the time and place of purchase. In- and on-pack premiums offer a premium item inside or attached to a package or make the package itself the premium item. Near-pack premiums provide the retail trade with specially displayed premium pieces that retailers then give to consumers who purchase the promoted product.

Delayed premiums include free-in-the-mail premiums, a type of sales promotion in which consumers receive a premium item from the sponsoring manufacturer in return for submitting a required number of proofs of purchase with or without postage costs. A self-liquidating premium is one in which the consumer mails in a number of proofs of purchase along with sufficient money to cover the manufacturer's purchasing, shipping, and handling costs of the premium item.[21]

Sampling

Allowing the consumer to experience the product or service free of charge or for a small fee is called sampling. It is one of the most effective ways to introduce a new product. However, it is also the most costly of all sales promotions. Samples can be distributed to consumers by mail, door to door, on- or in-pack, or personally through a representative in the retail store. Samples are often distributed to target markets, such as baby diapers to mothers of newborn infants. Several firms provide specialized sample distribution services, including GiftPax.

Ben Cohen and Jerry Greenfield, cofounders of Ben & Jerry's Homemade, Incorporated, could not afford traditional advertising when they started their superpremium ice cream business, so they took to the road in an old van they dubbed the Cowmobile to personally scoop ice cream samples across the country. Ben & Jerry's continues to use product sampling with good results, although not all companies have been as lucky. Problems with the use of sampling do exist, including mishandling by the Postal Service, misuse by consumers, and sample distribution that misses the target market.

Continuity Program (Frequent-User Incentives)

A continuity program requires the consumer to continue purchasing the product/service in order to receive the benefit or reward. For example, most major airlines offer frequent-flyer programs through which customers who have flown a specified number of miles are awarded free tickets for additional travel or ticket class upgrades. Other service providers have joined the airlines in these programs by offering frequent-flyer miles for their purchase of products or services. For instance, American Airlines AAdvantage miles may be earned by ordering flowers from FTD, staying at participating hotel chains, or using MCI phone service. AAdvantage Marketing's Web site claims that 8,000 join the American Airlines incentive program daily, representing 5 percent of U.S. discretionary spenders. The incentive program can be tailored to a one-time or long-term promotion.

Hallmark Cards' Gold Crown Card loyalty program rewards consumers for purchases in its Gold Crown stores with coupons for dollars-off retail merchandise. The value of the coupons is based on accumulated purchase points. The program keeps in touch with its members via direct mailings. In one year Hallmark traced $1.5 billion in sales to purchases of the program's 16 million members.[22]

In general, the automotive industry has come to rely more heavily on price incentives and lease and interest deals than on the more expensive alternatives such as television advertising. Whether the manufacturer wishes to build market volume for a potato chip or a new SUV, sales promotion has become a valuable component of the marketing mix.

SUMMARY

Marketers have shifted more marketing dollars from advertising to sales promotion in recent years. A variety of factors (e.g., reduced brand loyalty, costs of network advertising, and emphasis on product price) account for this shift in budgetary allocations. In-store promotions have become increasingly important with the rise of the retailer through such superstores as Wal-Mart. Sales promotion complements advertising and personal selling by stimulating or accelerating sales, introducing new products or businesses, and fostering long-term customer relationships. Of course, while it has become an innovative and cost-effective tool, sales promotion cannot do the job alone.

Chapter 18

Public Relations, Publicity, and Corporate Advertising

The people of the Brittany region, a peninsula on the northwest edges of Europe, have historically considered themselves a separate nation from the rest of France. Into this picturesque place of fishing boats and harbors came an unexpected act of violence. In 2000, Breton separatists bombed a McDonald's restaurant, killing a young French worker and sending thousands to protest her death to the Breton regional parliament.

Terrorism has become the public relations tool of the twenty-first century. Many associate bombings and bloodshed with fundamentalist fanatics; however, McDonald's experienced terrorism at the hands of French separatists and nationalists determined to rid France of the Big Mac. However, even "bloodshed failed" to stop the spread of McDonald's France, with its 1,030 French locations bringing in $3 billion in 2003.[1] In another incident, demonstrators destroyed a McDonald's in Millau, "a busy little southern city in the heart of Roquefort cheese country," causing $150,000 in damage but failing to prevent the restaurant's opening.

Aware that one of the tenets of public relations is that a positive image takes decades to build and only seconds to lose, the Chicago-based corporation responded with its own public relations campaign. It ran "newspaper ads listing how many French cows, potatoes and heads of lettuce it used each year," and continues to remind the French public that McDonald's "supports French farmers and employs 42,000 French workers."[2] Although its detractors decry it as "the end of civilization," the international chain adjusts its menu for the local clientele, serving "France's beloved croque-monsieur of cheese and ham on toast, along with high-carb pastries and fresh fruit." French nutritionists have since declared the Big Mac to be

Sara Lee Corporation
Three First National Plaza
Chicago, IL 60602-4260

News

Media: Julie Ketay, 312.558.8727
Media: Marie José Weber, Sara Lee Apparel Europe, +33.14.149.5004
Analyst: Aaron Hoffman, 312.558.8739

SARA LEE CORPORATION SELLS ITALIAN HOSIERY BUSINESS

CHICAGO (Dec. 11, 2003) – Sara Lee Corporation today announced the divestiture of its Italian hosiery business, Filodoro Calze S.p.A., to Gilfin S.p.A., the parent company of Golden Lady S.p.A., which is headquartered in Castiglione Stiviere, Italy. The sale also includes Filodoro's Spanish and Portuguese hosiery operations.

The divestiture was completed today and will have no material impact on Sara Lee's second quarter results. Terms of the transaction were not disclosed.

Filodoro, which generated approximately US$83 million in annual sales in fiscal 2003, is headquartered in Casalmoro, Italy. Filodoro markets sheer hosiery products under the *Filodoro, Filodoro Club, Filodoro Classic, Philippe Matignon* and *Filoverde* brands and its products are primarily sold in Italy, Spain and France. During the last several years, the sheer hosiery category in Europe has suffered from volume declines, driven largely by casual dress trends.

"We are pleased to have completed this transaction, which will allow us to focus our resources on areas that have the greatest potential for long-term growth," said C. Steven McMillan, chairman, president and chief executive officer of Sara Lee Corporation.

Sara Lee Corporation (www.saralee.com) is one of the world's leading branded consumer packaged goods companies, selling its products in nearly 200 countries. The company has three global businesses – Food and Beverage, Intimates and Underwear, and Household Products – through which it manufactures and markets products of exceptional quality and value under leading, well-known brand names such as *Sara Lee, Earth Grains, Jimmy Dean, Douwe Egberts, Chock full o' Nuts, Hanes, Playtex, Bali, DIM, Kiwi, Ambi Pur* and *Sanex.*

#   #   #

ILLUSTRATION 18.1. Taking off the hosiery. This announcement release conveys the news of Sara Lee's sale of its Italian hosiery business. Corporations also use press releases to announce appointments, special events, and new product lines.

healthier than a quiche lorraine. Since McDonald's set up in Paris in the mid-1970s, it has allowed French patrons to "walk in off the street and use the bathroom" and to "hang out for hours without buying anything. Try that in a French café."

Across the English Channel, the British monarchy had its own public relations war. A 1997 *Daily Mail* poll showed that 70 percent of the British public felt that the Queen should consider abdication in favor of her grandson, Prince William. The Royal Family, including the Queen herself, was perceived as culpable for the death of William's mother, the popular "people's princess" Diana. What insiders refer to as the "Family Firm" was in deep trouble for—like any "firm"—it depends upon public goodwill and financial support for its existence.

Although Queen Elizabeth, like her father George VI, initially enjoyed the cooperation of the media in depicting the Royal Family in "touching, homey little stories" which showed an ideal family "waving to the crowds, taking tea in a garden, feeding the ducks in St. James's Park, taking a picnic lunch at Windsor,"[3] the relationship between the "Family Firm" and the media turned sour in the 1990s. Increasing media exposure of the private lives of its members conspired to bring an end to the Royal Family's hard-won positive public image.

The thirst for information drives the news cycle today. As Queen Elizabeth struggled to re-create a positive public image, on the other side of the Atlantic, President William Jefferson Clinton entered into his own public relations crisis as his relationship with a White House intern created a media frenzy fed by almost daily information leaks and rampant rumors.

For people—and corporations—in the public eye, "image isn't everything. It's the only thing."[4] Facing child molestation charges, Michael Jackson met with members of Congress and received praise "for his work fighting AIDS in Africa." Photos of Jackson with young African AIDS victims appeared everywhere and visually challenged the idea that he was a man who would molest a child. Manhattan publicist Dan Klores handled an image makeover for Jennifer Lopez following her "overexposed relationship" with Ben Affleck through a series of "anti-diva" bookings (the *Kids' Choice Awards,* an episode of NBC's *Will & Grace,* and Bravo's *Inside the Actors Studio*). Klores has also represented the image-embattled Sean "P. Diddy" Combs.

Although numerous and various definitions for public relations exist, simply defined, public relations practitioners act as mediators between an organization and its various publics. These various publics include customers, company employees, suppliers, stockholders, governments, labor groups, citizen action groups, the general population of consumers, and the media. Every business and public figure must develop and maintain goodwill with most, if not all, of these publics. Failure to do so may result in loss of customers and revenues, filing of lawsuits, and damage to reputations. This chapter examines the field of public relations and its subset, publicity, and the related topic of corporate advertising.

PUBLIC RELATIONS

Whereas advertising involves controlled communication in paid-for media time and space, public relations involves nonpaid publicity that is often difficult to attain and, once attained, extremely difficult to control. Nevertheless, public relations represents a crucial part of the promotional mix. The most extravagant advertising blitz cannot substitute for a positive public image and goodwill. Crisis management, public relations writing, mediating relations with an organization's various publics, and public relations campaign management are among the most important public relations activities.

Crisis Management

The classic crisis management case occurred in 1982 when seven people in the Chicago area died after taking Johnson & Johnson's pain reliever, Tylenol. A criminal had mixed bottles of Tylenol with cyanide and put them back onto retail shelves. Johnson & Johnson's handling of this tragedy was brilliant. The company removed Tylenol from retail shelves quickly. Spokespersons appeared on television and cautioned consumers not to take Tylenol capsules. Tylenol designed and produced a new tamper-proof package, prompting other pharmaceutical companies to follow suit. The company also offered consumers free replacements for products they had purchased before this tragedy happened. Many analysts were surprised at how quickly Tylenol regained its market share and the public's confidence since lost reputations are generally difficult to recover.[5]

THE GLOBAL PERSPECTIVE: WORTH A THOUSAND WORDS

Certainly the old cliché—a picture's worth a thousand words—proved to be true during the Vietnam War. "The defining image of the Vietnam War was the naked little girl running down the road crying, her clothes burned off by napalm," wrote columnist Gwynne Dyer.[a] He also argued that the "defining image of the Iraq war" would be shameful photos of U.S. soldiers abusing Iraqi prisoners at Abu Ghraib prison. Indeed, an image can turn the tide of public opinion overnight.

Knowing that, President George W. Bush took advantage of a White House briefing to issue a public apology for U.S. troops' mistreatment of Iraqi prisoners of war at Abu Ghraib prison. Photographs provided horrific images of the abuse, including the picture of a twenty-one-year-old American servicewoman giving a thumbs-up as she stood behind a pile of naked Iraqi male prisoners. In another photo, the same woman appeared with a leash in her hand, a naked Iraqi at the end of it, prone on the ground. The word *humiliation* was plastered across newspaper pages.

Compounding the public relations scandal was the fact that Bush was in the midst of a run for reelection. Democratic presidential candidate John Kerry issued harsh criticism of Bush's handling of the atrocities, the House of Representatives passed a resolution to deplore and condemn the abuses, and *The Washington Post* released another photo showing "a naked prisoner handcuffed to a bed with women's underwear over his head."[b] A photo gallery of the abuses was available at <www.usatoday.com>.

Although the president "scolded" Secretary of Defense Donald Rumsfeld, he refused to eject him from the Cabinet.[c] As a result of the scandal, a Gallup poll showed an immediate drop in public approval of the war in Iraq from 52 percent on April 18, 2004, to 44 percent following publication of the prison photos in early May. U.S. desire to withdraw troops from Iraq increased from 21 percent on April 18 to 29 percent after the abuses were revealed.[d]

Fraser P. Seitel has argued that political shifts toward democracy, new technology, and regional trading alliances will make public relations increasingly important in the twenty-first century.[e] Public relations activity is an everyday part of a U.S. president's life. Following his second inauguration in 2005, President Bush toured Europe to try to recover the support of major U.S. allies and launched a major nationwide campaign to promote his proposed overhaul of Social Security.

Of course, public relations isn't just for presidents. Martha Stewart's release from federal prison in March 2005 "generated a whirlwind of positive publicity," but attention to public relations was required to try to bring back *Martha Stewart Living* advertisers who were "still resisting a renewed association with a magazine whose figurehead" was also "a convict."[f]

[a]"Prisoner Abuse Was Part of a System," *South Bend Tribune,* May 12, 2004, p. A7.

[b]Bill Nichols, "Bush Apologizes for 'Stain on Our Country's Honor,'" *USA Today,* May 7, 2004, p. 6A.

[c]Jim Drinkard, Dave Moniz, and John Diamond, "Rumsfeld Faces Lawmakers," *USA Today,* May 7, 2004, p. 1A.

[d]USA Today CNN Gallup Poll, *USA Today,* May 11, 2004, pp. A1-A2.

[e]*The Practice of Public Relations,* Upper Saddle River, NJ: Prentice-Hall, 1998, pp. 478-479.

[f]"Assessing Martha Stewart Company's Ad Inventory," <adage_alerts@adage.com>.

Public relations specialists sometimes call the media together for a press conference to issue breaking news or new information on a crisis, or simply to consolidate reporters' questions and give all media representatives the opportunity to gain information and get photographs and video footage of key officials. The questions are generally fielded by a public relations professional or by key officials with the affected organization. Although a press conference may be necessitated by a far-ranging crisis, it can also be risky. For example, President George W. Bush called a rare press conference on April 13, 2004, to respond to criticisms of the administration's handling of the war in Iraq. His statement to the press took slightly more than fifteen minutes; the press spent an hour posing its questions. Although its purpose was to quiet opposition, the press conference brought the issues to the front pages of national newspapers the next day and gave those who opposed the policies a forum to voice their own concerns and views.

Advertising is sometimes used to respond to a public relations crisis. To address concerns of its publics when Cingular Wireless acquired AT&T Wireless in March 2004, Cingular bought a full-page advertisement in national newspapers to explain the acquisition's benefits to customers and shareholders, promising "a new level of world-class wireless service." The ad was headlined: "A Letter from Cingular Wireless" and was signed by its president and CEO. In the past, other companies used advertising to reassure their publics. For example:

- When one of its planes crashed, USAir ran full-page ads in national newspapers to accept responsibility and to assure the public that safety procedures were being reviewed.

- In the aftermath of the cyanide poisonings, Tylenol ran full-page ads explaining in their own words what had happened, what they would do to prevent further criminal tampering, and how customers could replace their Tylenol capsules with Tylenol caplets at the company's expense.
- In 1993, Pepsi published a full-page advertisement in national newspapers to inform the public that a claim that a syringe had been found in a Diet Pepsi can was a hoax. The ad's headline stated, "Pepsi is pleased to announce . . . nothing." The ad also announced price-saving special offers for the July 4th weekend.
- In July 1998 the University of Virginia Medical Center publicly apologized in newspaper ads for the accidental switching of two baby girls shortly after their births at the Charlottesville, Virginia, facility. These ads, referring to the families involved, said, "We share their grief."

Sensitivity to the public mood is crucial in handling a crisis. Whereas USAir communicated with the public through advertisements following the crash of one of its airplanes, advertisers pulled their ads in the days following the 9/11 tragedy. Most advertisers now have guidelines in place to handle a crisis before an emergency situation arises. To control rumors, organizations and corporations have turned to the Internet to respond quickly and to deliver direct, unfiltered messages to a number of publics, including the media, employees, and shareholders.

When advertising resumed after 9/11, most were image ads in which organizations and corporations expressed their patriotism, their pride about the U.S. response to the tragedy, and concern for the victims' families. Similarly, following its Flight 800 disaster, TWA had rolled out a national advertising campaign it had been planning for months but changed a television commercial. It had showed airline employees unloading cargo bound for a football celebration.[6] When Swissair Flight 111 crashed in the waters near Halifax, Nova Scotia, in early September 1998, the airline responded swiftly and sensitively to the needs of victims' families, providing transportation to the crash site, cash payments, and even police protection to facilitate grieving families' privacy.

One of the complaints of crisis management professionals has been that lawyers often get in the way or take over communications with various publics. Rarely does this help the client. For example, in the early months of her criminal case, Martha Stewart's longtime handlers at the Susan Magrino Agency "failed to put out any kind of message."[7]

Stewart's lawyers had usurped the communications function, and that's not a good thing. Stewart eventually hired Citigate Sard Verbinnen, a crisis management firm that started to get Stewart's message out "with careful prime-time interviews and the Internet." The firm created a Web site, <marthatalks.com>, to post "notes from well-wishers and upbeat messages from Stewart." The 16 million hits and 81,000 e-mails sent to the site justify this strategy. It's only speculative to wonder whether the outcome of the case might have been different had Stewart engaged a crisis management team from the beginning.

Public Relations Writing

Since Edward L. Bernays taught the first public relations course in 1923 at New York University, over 200 schools of journalism and departments of communication have offered programs in concentrated public relations study. Although the practice of public relations takes place largely in the business or corporate world, the public relations practitioner must thoroughly understand the media and be able "to interview, gather and synthesize large amounts of information, write in a journalistic style," and produce copy on deadline.[8] Writing remains the primary entry-level skill for the profession. A main goal of public relations is to secure third-party endorsement through the dissemination of press releases, fact sheets, backgrounders, feature stories, pitch letters, and press kits that consolidate key documents regarding the organization. For instance, a press release that presents factual, positive information about a company may appear in a respected media outlet. Unlike an advertising message, which the public understands to be biased information from the company who has paid for it, information that appears in an objective news story tends to be viewed as credible.

The news release (or press release) is the single most important public relations document (see Illustrations 18.1 through 18.3). Information about the organization is released to the media ready to publish as is. Releases must be newsworthy, i.e., significant, timely, and

NEWS RELEASE

FOR FURTHER INFORMATION CONTACT:
Aaron H. Hoffman
GATX Corporation
312-621-6493

FOR RELEASE: IMMEDIATELY

GATX CENTENNIAL WEB CONTEST TEACHES KIDS TO HELP THOSE IN NEED

CHICAGO, October 13--GATX has been celebrating its Centennial with a lot of kids' play this year. Employees have built two playgrounds in neglected neighborhoods near GATX facilities in Buffalo and Chicago, and will soon build another near GATX's facility in Hearne, Texas. Now the company is focusing its celebration on another arena where kids love to play: the world wide web. GATX is sponsoring a unique web-based contest in which the winners receive, well, nothing. Or, to be more accurate, what they win they have to give away to families in need of assistance. But GATX hopes that what they get to keep for life is the experience of helping out the less fortunate.

The idea for GATX's web contest grew out of another Centennial program, "Tanksgiving," a year-long nationwide food drive conducted in partnership with Second Harvest, a national food bank network, and held at two dozen GATX facilities across the country. To publicize the drive, the financial services and supply chain management company ran a brightly painted GATX tank car around the country, including an appearance on September 10 on Wall Street in front of the New York Stock Exchange, tracks and all. The web contest centers on a "virtual" tank car as it travels to and from major GATX sites over a six-week period. Each week, a new question is introduced, related to the area of the country that the tank car crosses. Three winners are selected each week; one for each eligible grade level, third through fifth. And as frosting on the GATX birthday cake, the grand prize winning class will receive a computer for its classroom.

Each winning class receives $200, but they don't get to keep it. Instead, guided by their teachers and a local food bank, the class must spend the money buying food for the hungry. Therefore, playing and winning the contest begins with learning about history, geography, and math, and ends with economics, nutrition, and helping others.

The contest begins October 19 and ends Thanksgiving week. The colorful contest web page may be accessed through GATX's home page: www.gatx.com.

ILLUSTRATION 18.2. The single most important document. This GATX news release represents the qualities of effective copy; the contest the company sponsors is timely and of interest to the public as it informs the community about GATX's good citizenship. The contest also represents an integrated public relations campaign including a publicity event featuring the appearance of a brightly painted GATX tank car on Wall Street, the building of playgrounds in neglected neighborhoods, the dissemination of the press release to the traditional media, and the colorful contest Web page on the Internet.

MEDIA RELEASE

PLAYS ABOUT THE
BEGINNING OF THE
MODERN WORLD

SHAW FESTIVAL

10 QUEEN'S PARADE
POST OFFICE BOX 774
NIAGARA-ON-THE-LAKE
ONTARIO, CANADA L0S 1J0
(905) 468-2153
DIRECT FROM TORONTO
(416) 690-7301
FAX (905) 468-5438

Shaw Festival Tops $11 Million in 1998 as it Announces 1999 Season
presented by Royal Bank Financial Group

Press Release #1

Niagara-on-the-Lake, Ontario, November 4, 1998 . . .The Shaw Festival once again produced record breaking box office results, topping the $11 million dollar mark ($11.75) for the second consecutive season. Paid attendance reached 321,000 or 81.2% of capacity for The Shaw's 765 performances.

The Shaw Festival's Artistic Director, **Christopher Newton** today announced the 1999 season. A total of 12 productions will be running in repertory from April 9th to October 31st in The Shaw's three theatres. The 1999 mystery, **Rebecca**, will run until November 28th. In making the announcement Mr. Newton commented, "wit, ideas, love and a number of explosions - what more could one ask of a season that connects an imaginary past with present-day realities."

The flagship play for the 1999 season will be Bernard Shaw's profound classic **Heartbreak House** directed by Polish actor and director *Tadeusz Bradecki*. Due to its overwhelming success in 1998, Kaufman and Hart's hilarious comedy **You Can't Take It With You**, directed by Shaw resident director *Neil Munro*, returns to the Festival Theatre in 1999 for a limited engagement. Also presented in the Festival Theatre in recognition of his centenary, is Noel Coward's humorous attack on social pretensions, **Easy Virtue**, directed by *Christopher Newton*. Arthur Miller's **All My Sons**, also directed by *Mr. Munro*, is a gripping drama about guilt and responsibility that establishes one code of ethics for private life and another for business.

The Court House Theatre will feature four plays including Bernard Shaw's **Getting Married**, a witty exposé on love and marriage, directed by *Jim Mezon*. **S.S. Tenacity**, a wistful French comedy by Charles Vildrac, will be directed by *Dennis Garnhum*. Sharing the Court House stage is one of Anton Chekhov's great plays, **Uncle Vanya**, directed by *Ian Prinsloo*. The Shaw will stage the sixth production in its Granville Barker series, **The Madras House**, directed by *Neil Munro*.

-more-

ILLUSTRATION 18.3. A credible format. This Shaw Festival release illustrates the expected format—a headline with a present-tense verb; a dateline with city, state, or province, and date; double-spacing within paragraphs and quad-spacing between; -more- at the bottom of the page to indicate another page follows. Many companies, as does the Shaw Festival, use letterhead printed with *News release, Press release, Media release*, or simply *News*, to label the purpose of the communication. Shaw also numbers its releases, this being the first release for the 1999 season.

of interest to the public. For example, announcement releases inform about new products, acquisitions and mergers, or key personnel changes and appointments. Since the goal is to have the release printed exactly as it is written, the release should be in inverted pyramid style, with the five Ws (who, what, when, where, and why) addressed in the first paragraph (lead). The release should also be concisely written according to the guidelines of the Associated Press or United Press International stylebooks. Release headlines are written to gain the interest of the media editor and let the editor know what the release is about.

News releases are typed with one-inch margins on the organization's letterhead (some companies have special letterhead for releases with the words "NEWS" or "NEWS RELEASE" printed prominently near the company name and logo). A contact name and phone number prominently appear on the release so that the right person might easily be reached to answer questions, verify details, or offer further information. Releases may be mailed or disseminated electronically via fax or computer. Overnight delivery services may be used when other materials, such as press kits or photographs, are to accompany the release. Increasingly, though, publicity photographs are scanned into the computer and electronically delivered. Organizations and businesses now customarily post their news releases on their Web sites.

Public service announcements (PSAs) are news releases intended for the broadcast media. These documents are released in a ready-to-air format for radio and in a combination of script and storyboard form for television. The PSA announces an event, gives information about an organization, or provides other information of benefit to the public.

Sometimes agencies provide produced television spots that stations and networks air for free as a public service. For example, the International Dyslexia Association's PSA "Naigiem" used an elegant, simple technique to allow viewers to visually experience the "reality of dyslexia and contemplate its quiet but devastating impact on daily life."[9] The spot was created by a Canadian agency in Vancouver.

Fact sheets, usually just a page in length, allow reporters to quickly reference key details about an organization, product, or event (see Illustration 18.4). *Backgrounders* also provide key details about an

Clifton Gunderson L.L.C.

Firm Profile

◆ Clifton Gunderson provides close personal attention to our clients, backed by unlimited firmwide resources and expertise. This level of service is available to our clients through our unique structure and size —

   ◆ The individual local office structure of the firm allows our members and staff to work closely with each individual client to develop an awareness of their specific business needs;

   ◆ Yet our overall size allows us to offer our clients unlimited service opportunities backed by the expertise of our nationwide network.

◆ Since 1960 we have experienced rapid growth. Currently employing more than 400 CPAs with a total staff exceeding 1,000, we are ranked by the AICPA as the 13th largest CPA firm in the United States. Our staff-to-member ratio of less than 5 to 1 assures our clients significant member attention and personnel continuity.

◆ Being an independent, objective party, we often make observations that those close to the situation do not see. Also, we bring along ideas and experience from similar engagements that can be useful to the organization.

◆ From an original Midwest base, we have expanded across the country and now have

47 offices in 11 states — Arizona, Colorado, Illinois, Indiana, Iowa, Maryland, Missouri, Ohio, Texas, Virginia, and Wisconsin.

◆ As members of NEXIA International, a worldwide association of independent accounting firms, we serve an ever-expanding list of clients and have extended our service capabilities to more than 70 nations on six continents.

◆ In order to assure that we meet our commitment to clients in providing quality service, Clifton Gunderson has specific procedures with respect to the quality of our work. These procedures are designed to provide reasonable assurance that, in performing services, our personnel will be competent, objective, and will exercise due professional care.

Exploring a unique partnership

©1996 Clifton Gunderson L.L.C.
988-CPA FIRM TOLL FREE 888-272-3470
www.cliftoncpa.com

ILLUSTRATION 18.4. Quick reference. Clifton Gunderson L.L.C.'s fact sheet features factual information which constitutes the Firm Profile. As this one does, many fact sheets use bullets to set off paragraphs that cover specific aspects of the featured information. In the interest of integration—one sight, one sound—this fact sheet also employs the distinctive font, used in the firm's other promotional materials as well as its advertising, for the headline Firm Profile and the tagline, "Exploring a unique partnership." Visuals are also used to enhance reader interest.

organization, product, or event, but do so more extensively, in greater length and depth (see Illustration 18.5). Although backgrounders are strictly factual, they resemble feature stories in style, often written with anecdotes (short human-interest stories) and quotes. A *feature release* is a longer manuscript prepared for a specific publication, usually a magazine, news magazine, or special section of a newspaper. Features generally profile people—for example, a company employee with an unusual or significant accomplishment—or detail the history of a company or product. For example, Florida orange growers might send a feature about the history of the cultivation and use of the orange to newspaper food section editors. *Pitch letters* propose, or pitch, story ideas to newspaper editors with the hope that a reporter will be assigned to write an article. Essential facts and details about the story must be conveyed in such an attention-getting, interesting way that editors will see the attraction such a story might have for their readers. *Press (or media) kits* bring together a variety of documents useful to reporters writing about an organization. Usually placed in a pocketed folder, material may include news releases, fact sheets, backgrounders, company brochures and/or annual reports, and publicity photos. Kits may also be distributed to prospective employees and shareholders.

Other public relations documents target nonmedia audiences, especially employees and investors. *Newsletters* became a popular public relations tool during World War II to enhance employee morale and company loyalty, thus increasing production efficiency. Newsletters continue to inform employees about company policies and events and to improve and maintain relationships between the employer and its employees.

All publicly traded companies are required by the Securities and Exchange Commission to issue an *annual report* to stockholders. Since the required financial information may not be particularly good reading, annual reports typically engage readers with human-interest stories, the president or CEO's letter, usually a sort of "pep talk," four-color graphics and photographs, glossy pages, and attractive covers. The public relations value of the annual report may extend beyond the stockholder with dissemination to potential investors and employees. Annual reports may also be released to the media or included in press kits.

SMUCKER'S

FOR IMMEDIATE RELEASE

CONTACT: Nicole Oppolo
219-277-3114
oppo3456@saintmarys.edu

THE SMUCKER STORY

In the early 19th century, John Chapman, or "Johnny Appleseed," wandered the Ohio countryside, sowing apple seeds and securing a place in American legend.

It was from the fruit of Johnny Appleseed's trees that Orrville, Ohio resident Jerome M. Smucker first pressed cider at a mill he opened in 1897. Later, he prepared apple butter too, which he offered in crocks that bore a hand-signed seal—his personal guarantee. Before long, J.M. Smucker's name became well-known in its own right, as residents throughout the region— and eventually the nation—came to associate it with wholesome, flavorful fruit products.

HISTORY

The J.M. Smucker Co., the leading manufacturer of jams, jellies and preserves, celebrated its 100th anniversary in Dec. 1997. What began with Jerome M. Smucker selling his apple butter door-to-door from the back of his horse-drawn wagon, has grown into a $5.42 million organization employing approximately 2,000 people with products available in more than 60 countries.

The foodservice division of Smucker's was created in the 1950s in response to an ever increasing demand for high quality, convenient products for use outside the home. As America began to eat out regularly, Smucker's wished to follow its consumers to the restaurants. Today the list of restaurants, hotels, and other foodservice institutions that serve their customers Smucker's products is in the tens of thousands nationwide.

- more -

ILLUSTRATION 18.5. A factual feature. The backgrounder often provides information about a company and its history in storytelling style. As a student in a public relations writing course, Nicole Oppolo was assigned to write a backgrounder for an established company. Oppolo researched the history of Smucker's and wrote this creative copy. Notice that a feature-type lead generally precedes subsectioned body copy. Nicole's subsections include History, Growth, Independence, and Today.

Public relations professionals also write public addresses for their clients and employers. *Speechwriting* requires special attention to the speaker's public address skills, personality, objectives, and time constraints. Some public relations writers are employed exclusively to write speeches.

Relations with Various Publics

Public relations professionals deal with various publics in matters involving company decisions, policies, or actions. The company has to maintain a level of goodwill with its suppliers as well as its customers. It also has to demonstrate to community members that the organization is a good citizen. It has to provide stockholders and investors with financial information regarding the firm and to deal with governments in matters of public policy. Media relations occupies a great deal of many practitioners' time. In the course of mediating between the organization and its publics, the public relations professional has frequent occasions to speak with these publics, from daily telephone contacts to hosting special events. This requires interpersonal and public communication skills.

Economic woes since 9/11 have, more than ever, created a time of "huge opportunity for PR shops."[10] When General Motors vice chair Bob Lutz spoke to his brand managers about the introduction of thirteen vehicles in 2004, he made it clear that they should focus on the public relations techniques of "buzz-building," media relations, and special events rather than the more expensive option of television advertising. Public relations takes marketers away from "zappable commercial space" to meet consumers and their influencers "face-to-face." Procter & Gamble, the world's leading advertiser, told its marketing managers to "focus on messages via influential consumers" at the corporation's "Buzzpoint" convention in 2003.

Public Relations Campaigns

Before the public relations professional decides how and what to communicate to a specific public, the situation and the audience must be researched and analyzed. A public relations campaign is usually conducted using the R-A-C-E formula (research, analyze, create, and evaluate). At the research stage, a public relations team might conduct polls and surveys to determine the audience's existing attitude toward a company, product, or problem. Once that attitude is understood, a campaign will be planned to carry out the organization's objectives.

For example, marketers for PepsiCo's Frito-Lay unit hoped "to land on the right side of the obesity debate."[11] In the research phase, Frito-Lay consulted with Dr. Kenneth Cooper of the Cooper Institute. The objective of the public relations campaign was to create awareness of new, more healthful products such as the American Heart Association-certified Rold Gold Heartzels, "a vitamin-fortified Munchies Kids Mix and a new low-carb line dubbed Edge." At the creation stage of the campaign, Frito-Lay chose to build awareness of the new products by influencing the influencers—the medical profession. Frito-Lay established a presence at medical conventions, created brochures, sponsored the American Dietetic Association and Physicians Assistants conferences, and launched a Web site, <SnackSense.com>, for health care professionals. Print ads bolstered the public relations campaign.

Evaluation of success has become one of the thorniest areas in public relations. As a flagging economy has pressured corporations to demand measurable results for their advertising expenditures, they are also looking for quantifiable results from their public relations programs, agencies, and campaigns. Traditionally, public relations activity has been evaluated in terms of gross impressions, percentage of favorable content, media placement, press clippings produced, message fidelity (the printed message corresponds to the intended message), and cost per impression.[12] Problems with these evaluation methods sometimes arise. For instance, Frito-Lay may not have had numerous clippings to show extensive and positive press coverage, and the cost of launching the new products hit $37 million.[13] How can a list of appearances at medical conventions justify the costs? In this case, nine Frito-Lay products had met "Class 1" standards for fat and sodium content, and sales increased 18 percent. A campaign evaluation could include goals met, e.g., creation of a healthier product line and its recognition by key publics, and improved sales (Illustration 18.6).

Public relations professionals must deal with increasing demands for accountability. In public relations it is not enough to have the requisite communication skills. As the Frito-Lay case suggests, the public relations practitioner must also understand and speak the language

Applications of THERAPEUTIC MASSAGE

ILLUSTRATION 18.6. Relations with various publics. Massage therapist Dale Huston disseminates his brochure to clients and to massage therapists who enroll in his educational seminars.

of finance, sales, and business operations and objectives. Integrated Communication theory confirms what public relations professionals have always known—they need to be involved in every facet of an organization or corporation's structure, from product and service conception and packaging to the messages conveyed by all contacts and communications, including advertising, sales, and distribution.

Public Relations—Challenges of Change

Public relations is not a new profession. Public relations tactics were central in the founding of the United States, from Thomas Jefferson's position paper (the Declaration of Independence) to a special event known as the Boston Tea Party. As a profession, public relations has suffered its own public relations problems. Hucksters such as P. T. Barnum were early contributors to negative public perceptions of public relations as the practice of publicity stunts and the purveyor of propagandistic messages. The attachment of the words "spin" and "spin doctors" to the profession has been a recent setback. The Public Relations Society of America (PRSA) has worked diligently to maintain respect for the profession.

Changes in technology greatly impacted the field in the 1990s. The computer has made some aspects of public relations practice easier. For example, desktop publishing has dramatically cut the production time and cost of creating brochures and other public relations documents. Options for delivery of releases and other documents have increased the speed of message dissemination. However, the speed with which information is delivered today has created unprecedented challenges for public relations professionals and the organizations they represent.

The pitfalls of lightning-fast message dissemination were made clear during the 1992 presidential campaign. Faxes literally flew from the desks of the media directors of both the Bush and Clinton campaigns to the press, many of them disseminating charges of the opponent's incompetence or corruption. President Clinton's handlers assembled their "war room" to monitor print and broadcast coverage by the minute so that responses and corrections could be fired out instantaneously. The longer negative information is out there undisputed in the public forum, the more damage to a person's or organization's image is likely to occur.

The speed of information flow has also impacted the media—and, thus, public relations, since the relationship between the two fields is so intimate. The mainstream press, now in competition with the tabloids, has been accused of losing journalistic integrity by printing—or broadcasting—unconfirmed rumors or improperly, sometimes even fraudulently, investigated stories. According to *USA Today* columnist DeWayne Wickham, "the line between hard news and the voyeurism of supermarket tabloids has been trampled."[14] For instance, the *Cincinnati Enquirer* ran a story accusing Chiquita Brands International Inc. of exposing people to dangerous pesticides. When Chiquita denied charges based on stolen information, the newspaper agreed to a $10 million out-of-court settlement and issued an apology.

The ability of Web site publishers to get stories out instantaneously has created unprecedented pressure for print and broadcast journalists. Exposure of numerous prominent reporters' fabricated quotes and stories has raised questions about the difficulty of maintaining accuracy and ethical standards when stories must see print in unrealistically short amounts of time. Cases of faulty reporting have created public cynicism about journalism. This is an uncomfortable situation for public relations practitioners who depend upon the media for fair and accurate coverage. The organizations who receive negative press coverage—whether fairly or unfairly—increasingly require public relations assistance with image recovery.

Investor relations has become a crucial area as global corporations begin to understand that public relations involves more than "filing financial details" and "placing advertisements in local financial journals."[15] Just weeks after a Chinese company, China Life Insurance Co., "completed the largest initial public offering of stock in Hong Kong and New York in late 2003, Chinese government auditors accused its parent company of widespread accounting irregularities"; subsequently, investors "punished their stocks." Even though many Chinese companies "want only short-term [public relations] help ahead of a stock listing," the plummet of China Life's shares taught the "hard way that bad publicity can be costly."

Today, the importance of public relations to those who must create and maintain positive relationships with various publics remains unquestioned. When a sample of the top 1,000 U.S. advertisers was asked to rank thirteen advertising and marketing subjects in terms of time and attention given these areas, public relations was viewed as one of the most important areas by both consumer and business marketers.[16] If effectively integrated with advertising, personal selling, and sales promotions (the other components of the promotional mix), public relations is capable of accomplishing objectives beyond goodwill. It can create or re-create a positive image, increase brand awareness, build favorable attitudes toward a company and its products, and encourage purchase behavior.

PUBLICITY

Imagine walking through Times Square only to be confronted by a swarm of young adults wearing Toyota tattoos on their foreheads. On "the latest twist on a traditional sandwich board," Toyota recruited forty youth, mostly college students, to "spread the word about Toyota's Scion and its latest model, the tC coupe."[17] The one-day publicity gig, "the brainchild of guerilla marketing firm," London-based Cunning, brought the Scion into national headlines on April 7, 2004. It coincided with Toyota's unveiling of its tC sports coupe at the New York Auto Show that day, a fact conveniently mentioned in news coverage of the Cunning publicity stunt. Best of all, the event appealed to the brand's target market—"consumers in their 30s and 40s."

Because publicity frequently results from various public relations efforts, it is often viewed as part of public relations. On another history-making spring day in New York City, two publicity stunts occurred simultaneously. To introduce Virgin Cola, intended to be a new contender in the cola wars in 1998, the British billionaire Richard Branson, founder of the Virgin Group, perched atop a tank as it crashed through a wall of Virgin Cola cans in Times Square.[18] An hour later, at a restaurant just blocks away, figure skating champion Tara Lipinski was introduced as the new spokesperson for Snapple Refreshers. In all these cases, publicity was intentionally generated to increase brand awareness.

International retailer IKEA, headquartered in Sweden, employed publicity gimmicks in its quest for a nontraditional way to edge the competition. It transformed the interior of elevators in twenty Beijing apartment buildings and brightened the Berlin train station with colored fabrics for the walls and lampshades for the ceiling lights to demonstrate the power of home decorating.[19] In Spain, the IKEA tagline "Redecorate your life" has become a catch phrase as IKEA's "guerilla" marketing permeates everyday life.

However, sometimes publicity arises unintentionally, and sometimes this publicity is bad rather than good. The Johnson & Johnson's Tylenol case demonstrates the impact of unwanted publicity. News of unintended acceleration in its cars started a sales slide in 1986 for Audi of America, but three years later, U.S. federal officials cleared Audi, blaming the consumer complaints on driver error. The recovery from bad publicity took Audi a decade.[20]

General Motors Acceptance Corporation suffered an image setback when it became the defendant in a class-action lawsuit that alleged "the company discriminated against black car buyers by charging them higher interest rates for car loans."[21] At the same time, Chrysler was reeling from allegations that its Midwest financial arm "often used slurs that maligned African-American employees and customers."[22]

Publicity can also intentionally or unintentionally contribute to product scarcity. When Oprah Winfrey listed UGG boots "among her favorite things" and celebrities such as Kate Hudson, Cameron Diaz, and Kate Winslet strutted around in the funky, chunky fleece-lined footwear, the popularity of the boot completely sold out available stock from fall 2003 until spring 2004.[23] The only UGGs left were auctioned on eBay for as much as four times their usual upscale selling price. Sarah Jessica Parker plodded around in the boots in a final-season episode of *Sex and the City,* and UGG Australia placed ads in Oprah's *O* magazine, pushing the product to unprecedented scarcity. Fashion editors and retailers swore they had never seen anything like it.

Those who were around during the 1996 holiday season in the United States might remember the Tickle Me Elmo doll shortage. Publicity about the shortage sent consumers running to stores, consequently ensuring a depleted supply of the dolls. Although shortages frustrate consumers and retailers, the perception of scarcity benefits the manufacturer. A similar situation occurred again in 1998 when publicity about the scarcity of Beanie Babies pushed consumers to spend as much as $100 for Beanie Babies intended to retail for about $5.

Several major differences between public relations and publicity exist. First, public relations is a program extending over a period of time. Publicity is typically a short-term strategy (see Illustration 18.7). Second, public relations is designed to provide positive infor-

ETHICS TRACK:
EVEN HEROES MAKE MISTAKES

During an interview at a Detroit radio station on March 30, 2004, former Notre Dame Heisman Trophy winner Paul Hornung made controversial comments about how Notre Dame could help its football team to victory. Hornung said, "We [Notre Dame] can't stay as strict as we are as far as academic structure is concerned because we've got to get the black athletes."[a] This comment sent Notre Dame into action immediately. Soon after the release of Hornung's comments, Notre Dame issued a statement saying, "Paul Hornung in no way speaks for the University, and we strongly disagree with the thesis of his remarks. They are generally insensitive and specifically insulting to our past and current African-American student athletes."[b] Although Hornung initially defended his statement, days later, after he apparently received an overwhelming number of calls and e-mails, Hornung apologized for his comments.

The storm surrounding Hornung's comments quickly calmed because of the apology and in large part because of the quick response of the Notre Dame Sports Information office. Over the years, the office has handled communications for the university's high-profile football program and become recognized for its effectiveness in the area of crisis management.

It is difficult enough to deal with questions about safety procedures (as airlines have had to do following crashes) or about product flaws (as, for example, some toy companies have had to do when children choked on toy parts). But when an organization's basic values are called to question, the public relations damage can take much longer to repair. Coors Brewing learned this when racial slurs were attributed to its chair in *The Rocky Mountain News* in 1984. Even though the newspaper subsequently ran a retraction, it still took Coors years of effort, at a price tag in the millions, to recover its damaged image.

Despite the theory that a quick response is best, legal issues sometimes impede an organization from immediately responding. For example, R.J. Reynolds refused comment when it was named in a lawsuit brought by plaintiffs in Niger and Gambia against companies alleged to have "profited from slavery."[c] Likewise, Texaco faced a legal crisis when 1,500 black employees filed a discrimination lawsuit against the corporation. Nevertheless, Texaco responded quickly, forming a special diversity panel to overhaul company programs and launching an advertising campaign headlined "Where we go from here . . ." Some felt the company acted too quickly, assuming responsibility before all the facts were in. Furthermore, damage done to Texaco's credibility with its publics, including its employees, is among the most difficult to repair.[d]

Perhaps that is the reason Cracker Barrel Old Country Store, the Tennessee-based restaurant/gift shop chain, decided to agree to a settlement in the suit brought against it by the Justice Department, but admitted no wrongdoing. Although Cracker Barrel argued that it had "policies banning discrimination," it "agreed to adopt 42 pages of Justice requirements to improve, enforce and monitor its compliance with anti-discrimination policies."[e] Facing a public relations crisis similar to the one that faced the Denny's restaurant chain several years earlier, a spokesperson for Cracker Barrel stated publicly that employees do make mistakes.

Consider other cases in which organizations have had to respond to accusations of racism. What is the best crisis management procedure to follow? Should the organization assume responsibility for the accusations quickly and apologize? What other considerations must be taken into account?

Arianna Stella

[a]Kelly Whiteside, "Hornung 'Black Athlete' Comment Irks Notre Dame," *USA Today,* <www.usatoday.com>, April 1, 2004.

[b]Pat Leonard, "Hornung Apologizes for Comments," *The Observer,* April 1, 2004, p. 1.

[c]James Cox, "Descendants of Slaves Accuse Companies of Genocide," *USA Today,* <www.usatoday.com>, March 30, 2004.

[d]Fraser P. Seitel, *The Practice of Public Relations,* Upper Saddle River, NJ: Prentice-Hall, 1998, pp. 15-18.

[e]Julie Schmit and Larry Copeland, "Cracker Barrel Customer Says Bias Was Flagrant," *USA Today,* May 7, 2004, pp. B1-B2.

mation about the organization and usually is controlled by the company or its agent. Publicity, on the other hand, is not always positive and is not always solicited by the firm. Typically, publicity—both positive and negative—originates from sources other than the company.

CORPORATE ADVERTISING

Corporate advertising is an extension of the public relations function designed to promote the firm overall—by either enhancing its image (through image advertising or sponsorships) or by communicating the firm's position on a social issue or cause (issue or advocacy advertising). Whereas the goal of corporate advertising is improved relations with its publics, corporate advertising differs from public relations in that, except for sponsorships, it involves the purchase of media time or space.

ILLUSTRATION 18.7. Special event. Kristina Jonusas, left, and Carla Johnson chat with a customer, far left, during a book signing at a Borders store in Mishawaka, Indiana. The event publicized the release of Johnson's book, *21st Century Feature Writing;* Jonusas was a contributor. Photo courtesy Tod Moorhead.

Image Advertising

Corporate image advertising attempts to increase a firm's name recognition and establish goodwill between the company and its publics. According to Wilcox and colleagues, in *Public Relations Strategies and Tactics,* "Image-building advertising is intended primarily to strengthen a company's identity in the eyes of the public and/or financial community."[24] For example, Sears bought a full-page newspaper ad to honor its "Partners in Progress," a short list of suppliers selected for their outstanding performance from the 10,000 associated with Sears. The ad does not directly sell a specific product or service; instead, it seeks to create the image of Sears as a corporation that places high value on "providing quality products and services" to its customers through these exemplary suppliers and on its role as a good community member, e.g., one that builds "lasting relationships" with its various publics. Image ads designed to depict corporations as sensitive community citizens following 9/11 are detailed in the Preface.

Sponsorships

Sponsorship marketing is a form of corporate image advertising accomplished by corporate support of special programs or events. Hallmark Cards' longtime sponsorship of the *Hallmark Hall of Fame* promoted the company as a good citizen. By associating itself with high-quality, educational programming, the firm helped shape its own image as a company that creates high-quality greeting cards. Noting the opportunity to reach an enormous and influential group of upscale decision makers, many companies choose to sponsor such special programming as coverage of the Olympic games (see Ethics Track in Chapter 8). Sponsors for the 2002 Winter Olympic Games in Salt Lake City shelled out $1.6 billion.[25] Sports events have long attracted sponsors willing to reach deeply into their big pockets for the positive public exposure. For example, multiple sponsors paid as much as $30 million each "to be associated with the six-week long quadrennial World Cup Cricket tournament," a fourteen-nation event held in South Africa, Zimbabwe, and Kenya in spring 2003.

Corporations now also sponsor Broadway shows to reach an upscale market (a third of the audience earns over $150,000 a year), in particular, women, who make up over half of the audience. In return for the financial sponsorships, the corporations receive theater "naming rights, in-theater advertising, product placement and product integration" in the shows.[26] Some theaters already bear the names of their sponsors such as: The American Airlines Theater, The Cadillac Winter Garden, and the Kennedy Center for the Performing Arts.

Toyota bolstered its image as a world-class citizen when it teamed with eBay to host an auction in support of The Fight Against Women's Cancers in spring 2004. Toyota auctioned a Solara convertible, packed with a trunk full of cosponsor Revlon's products. The winning bid went toward cancer research funding and national outreach programs. Toyota, a double platinum sponsor, has been associated with the Revlon Run/Walk For Women since 1999 and a national sponsor of the American Lung Association's Asthma Walk, the International Motorcycle Shows, the Kraft Nabisco golf championships, the 2004 NASCAR season, and the *Sports Illustrated* fiftieth anniversary tour. Nextel Communications cut a ten-year, $700 million deal for a NASCAR sponsorship at the Daytona 500 a year after R.J. Reynolds dropped its sponsorship. RJR left its thirty-three-year relationship with the event after "restrictions on tobacco advertising" made the sponsorship impractical and unaffordable.[27]

Advocacy or Issue Advertising

According to Jonah Bloom in an *Advertising Age* Viewpoint, a "smart PR operator" will embed its brand in the editorial content of mainstream media channels by adopting a position on a particular issue rather than promoting the organization itself.[28] A company uses advocacy or issue advertising to communicate its views on social issues to make a political or social statement. Although seeking to portray a "good citizen" image for the company or organization, advocacy or issue advertising builds image in an indirect manner, by adopting a position on a particular issue rather than promoting the organization itself. For example, Allstate Insurance Company ran an advertisement that communicated its commitment to enacting tougher drunk driving laws through organizations such as MADD (Mothers Against Drunk Driving) and the National Commission Against Drunk Driving. This advertisement performed a community service with its "Don't drink and drive" message. Although such advertisements consume only a small part of a corporation's advertising budget, they may "touch sensibilities" and, therefore, receive much positive attention.[29]

Grand Marnier, a French cognac, gave image advertising a whole new spin with a campaign created by Omnicom for a $15 million "Conversations that Matter" campaign in 2004. Ads placed in the *New York Times Magazine* and *Atlantic Monthly* were "the first mainstream pitches to directly address the controversy over gay marriage."[30] The campaign's tagline, "The conversation is waiting. Go there," was meant to remind people that some things may be most easily discussed over drinks.

SUMMARY

What are the differences between public relations and advertising? Both use the media to create awareness or to influence attitudes and/or behaviors of targeted audiences. But, they are not the same. Advertising reaches its market through media for which the advertiser pays. Also, advertisers control the messages they deliver to their audiences. Hence, the public views advertisements with some skepticism. The media receive public relations communications in such forms as news releases, feature articles, press kits, or press conferences. Since the public thinks such messages are coming from the medium rather than a company, it accepts and trusts them more readily. Certain communications about individuals and organizations (e.g., bad publicity) are neither solicited nor paid for. Such publicity, especially when negative, must be dealt with through crisis management strategies.

:60 Spot:
Defining Public Relations—
What's Your Function?

Most people do not know that public relations has been a communication function since the time of ancient Greece; in America, the function dates back to the seventeenth century. Public relations has been instrumental in shaping America throughout its history as a means to mediate effective communication between a person(s) or company and the consuming public. In fact, examples of PR are found in our country's most important documents and events—the Declaration of Independence, the midnight ride of Paul Revere, and the Constitutional Convention. Our founders employed such PR tools as writing, public speaking, special events, and strategic planning to inform citizens and shape public opinion. Despite these historical examples of good public relations, it was not Thomas Jefferson, Paul Revere, or George Washington who put PR on the map.

George Creel, Ivy Ledbetter Lee, and Richard Nixon are three public figures who negatively impacted PR's reputation. Creel, a former journalist, headed U.S. propaganda efforts during World War I, using "all aspects of the U.S. media, including film, posters, music, paintings and cartoons" to ensure "full public backing" of the war.[a] After the war, many Americans felt U.S. involvement had been unnecessary. Prior to the eruption of World War II, Lee, a journalist who had become a publicity agent, served as adviser to the German Dye Trust, a cartel that supported Adolf Hitler's restrictions on religion and freedom of the press. Lee's relationship with Hitler prior to the dictator's rise to power resulted in Lee "being branded a traitor and dubbed 'Poison Ivy.'"[b]

The largest detriment to PR's reputation did not originate from sources within the industry itself but was a result of one of the worst political scandals of the twentieth century. Fraser Seitel, senior counselor for Burson-Marsteller, has said that the Watergate scandal gave public relations a "black eye." President Richard M. Nixon and his aides used what the public identified as public relations tactics to cover up the break-in at Watergate. According to Seitel, "what Nixon and his henchmen wrought was the exact opposite of public relations."[c] Unfortunately, Nixon reaffirmed the public view when he used the term "to PR a situation" in talking about the cover-up tactics.

The core of public relations is public opinion. The founders of the United States used public relations slogans, staged events, and published pamphlets and essays to influence public opinion in colonial-era America. They realized that informing the public through the available means of the day would enhance their fight for freedom from tyranny and their vision of self-government.

More than 200 years later, public relations is still used for the same purpose. Although some critics remain convinced that PR is a means to "spin" the truth, modern America understands the value of good, credible communication. This does not mean creating a facade but rather informing the public, allowing people to create their own opinions.

Note: The opinions expressed herein are my own, and do not reflect those of The American Academy of Periodontology, or the Academy's officers, members, or employees.

Catherine A. Justak
Program Manager—Education
The American Academy of Periodontology

[a]"Who's Who: George Creel," <FirstWorldWar.com>.
[b]Fraser Seitel, *The Practice of Public Relations,* Seventh Edition, London: Prentice-Hall, 1998, p. 31.
[c] Seitel, p. 35.

Notes

Preface

1. Hillary Chura, "Sept. 11, a Year Later: Consumers Still Wary," *Advertising Age,* September 9, 2002, p. 1.
2. Ibid.
3. Cara B. DiPascquale, "Direct Hit After Anthrax Threat," *Advertising Age,* October 22, 2001, p. 1.
4. Bob Garfield, "2002 Year in Review," *Advertising Age,* December 11, 2002, p. 12.

Chapter 1

1. Claire Atkinson, Hillary Chura, and Lisa Sanders, "What's Eating Burger King?," *Advertising Age,* January 26, 2004, pp. 1, 30.
2. Don E. Schultz, "The Evolving Nature of Integrated Communications," *Journal of Integrated Communications,* 1997-1998, p. 15.
3. Don E. Schultz, "Integration Helps You Plan Communication from Outside-in," *The Marketing News,* March 15, 1993, p. 12.
4. Don E. Schultz, "The IMC Process," in Ron Kaatz (Ed.), *Integrated Marketing Symposium,* Lincolnwood, Illinois: NTC Business Books, 1995, pp. 6-13.
5. Mercedes M. Cardona and Bradley Johnson, "The Ad Market," *Advertising Age,* January 12, 2004, p. 8.
6. "Magazines and TV Spar over Drug Ads," *The Wall Street Journal,* October 16, 1997, p. B8; Melanie Wells, "First Prozac TV Ads Air on Cable," *USA Today,* September 15, 1998, p. 2B.
7. "Direct-to-Consumer Drugs by Sales," *Advertising Age,* December 22, 2003, p. 29.
8. "10 Most Successful Product Launches," *Advertising Age,* December 22, 2003, p. 26.
9. Bruce Horovitz, "Viewers' Favorite Ads Crude, Rude and Furry," *USA Today,* February 2, 2004, p. 7B.
10. Miriam Jordan, "In Rural India, Video Vans Sell Toothpaste and Shampoo," *The Wall Street Journal,* January 10, 1996, p. B1.
11. "AMA Board Approves New Marketing Definition," *Marketing News,* March 1, 1985, p. 1.
12. Stephen Fox, *The Mirror Makers,* New York: William Morrow, 1984; James Playsted Wood, *The Story of Advertising,* New York: Ronald Press, 1958; William Leiss, Stephen Kline, and Sut Jhally, *Social Communication in Advertising: Persons, Products, and Images of Well-Being,* New York: Routledge, 1990; Frank

Presbrey, *The History and Development of Advertising,* Garden City, NY: Doubleday, Doran, 1929.

13. Bob Schulber, *Radio Advertising: The Authoritative Handbook,* Lincolnwood, IL: NTC Business Books, 1989.

14. Sherilyn K. Zeigler and Herbert H. Howard, *Broadcast Advertising,* Third Edition, Ames: Iowa State University Press, 1991.

15. Roland Marchand, "The Parable of the Democracy of Goods," in Sonia Maasik and Jack Solomon (Eds.), *Signs of Life in the USA,* Boston: Bedford Books, 1994, pp. 110, 115.

16. Gary C. Woodward and Robert E. Denton, Jr., *Persuasion & Influence in American Life,* Prospect Heights, IL: Waveland Press, 1996, pp. 228-291.

17. Jack Solomon, "Masters of Desire: The Culture of American Advertising," in Gary Colombo, Robert Cullen, and Bonnie Lisle (Eds.), *Rereading America,* Boston: Bedford Books, 1995, p. 490.

18. Ibid, p. 493.

19. Ibid, p. 499.

20. Ibid, p. 495.

21. Sonia Maasik and Jack Solomon, "Brought to You B(u)y," in Sonia Maasik and Jack Solomon (Eds.), *Signs of Life in the USA,* Boston: Bedford Books, 1994, p.107.

22. Schultz, "The Evolving Nature of Integrated Communications," pp. 11-18. All the direct quotes in this section are from this article.

23. Michael Krauss, "New Tech Still Suffers Old Marketing Woes," *Marketing News,* March 3, 2003, p. 12.

24. Al Ries, "The Disintegration of Integrated Marketing," <www.adage.com>.

Chapter 2

1. Laurel Wentz, "Hollywood Embraces Latin Culture," *Advertising Age,* February 2, 2004, p. 27.

2. Ibid, p. 27.

3. Laurel Wentz, "Unilever Ramps up Latin Effort," *Advertising Age,* March 1, 2004, p. 32.

4. Armas C. Genaro, "Latino Population Expected to Reach 60 Million by 2020," *Chicago Tribune,* October 15, 2003, p. 18.

5. Courtney Crandall, "It Pays to Advertise," *New England Business,* May 1991, p. 35; Horst Stipp, "Crisis in Advertising?" *Marketing Research,* March 1992, pp. 39-45.

6. Robert J. Samuelson, "The End of Advertising?" *Newsweek,* August 19, 1991, p. 40; Neil H. Borden, *The Economic Effects of Advertising,* Chicago: Richard D. Irwin, 1942, pp. 734-735; Mark Landler, "Fear of Flying in Ad Land," *Business Week,* November 19, 1990, pp. 100-105.

7. David Rynecki, "Latin America Crisis Could Tame U. S. Bull," *USA Today,* August 25, 1998, p. B1.

8. Courtland L. Bovee, John Thill, George P. Dovel, and Marian Burk Wood, *Advertising Excellence,* New York: McGraw-Hill, Inc. 1995, pp. 56-58; George E.

Belch and Michael A. Belch, *Introduction to Advertising & Promotion,* Homewood, IL: Irwin, 1993, pp. 828-830.

9. Kirk Davidson, "Look for Abundance of Opposition to Television Liquor Advertisements," *Marketing News,* January 6, 1997, pp. 4, 30.

10. Bob Garfield, "Bud's 'Tune Out' Is Pick of an Otherwise Predictable Ad Pack," *Advertising Age,* February 2, 2004, p. 32.

11. Yumiko Ono, "Sometimes Ad Agencies Mangle English Deliberately," *The Wall Street Journal,* reprinted in *The South Bend Tribune,* November 9, 1997, p. B5.

12. Kathleen Hall Jamieson and Karlyn Kohrs Campbell, *The Interplay of Influence: News, Advertising, Politics, and the Mass Media,* Third Edition, Belmont, CA: Wadsworth, 1992, pp. 173-174.

13. Martha T. Moore, "Study: Ads Improve Little in Diversity," *USA Today,* August 29, 1992, p. B1.

14. Ernest F. Cooke and Monle Lee, "Advertising Follows, Not Leads the Culture: The Example of Women in Liquor Advertisements," *Marketing: Moving Toward the 21st Century,* edited by Elnora W. Stuart, David J. Ortinau, and Ellen M. Moore, Proceedings of the Annual Meeting of the Southern Marketing Association, New Orleans, LA: Southern Marketing Association, 1996, pp. 327-331.

15. Jim Kirk, "Deal with It: Women Are Sick of Stereotypical Advertising," *The Chicago Tribune,* February 22, 1998, p. C1.

16. David Goodman, "For New Kellogg Ads, Thin no Longer Is 'in,'" *The South Bend Tribune,* February 9, 1998, p. C7.

17. Cheryl Berman, "The Cause of Women in Advertising," "How Is Advertising Shaping the Image of Women?," a symposium sponsored by the Advertising Educational Foundation, Northwestern University, October 18, 2003.

18. Gloria Steinem, keynote speaker, "How Is Advertising Shaping the Image of Women?" Advertising Educational Foundation. Northwestern University, Evanston, IL, October 18, 2003.

19. Ellen McCracken, *Decoding Women's Magazines,* New York: St. Martin's Press, 1993, p. 279.

20. "Kmart Introduces High-Tech Changes to Make Sales Come Back," *Marketing News,* October 28, 1991, p. 7.

21. Debra Aho Williamson, "Web Ads Mark 2nd Birthday with Decisive Issues Ahead," *Advertising Age,* October 21, 1996, pp. 1, 43.

22. Elizabeth Weise, "Net Use Doubling Every 100 Days," *USA Today,* April 16, 1998, p. A1.

23. Jon Swartz, "Web Shopping Gains Popularity," *USA Today,* November 26, 2003, p. B3; Byron Acohido, "Rich Media Enriching PC Ads," *USA Today,* February 25, 2004, p. B3.

24. Robert Risse, "Is the Price Right?" *Silicon Alley Reporter,* March 1998, p. 6.

25. Debra Aho Williamson, "Outlook '97: Will Web Ads Go Mainstream?" *Advertising Age,* October 26, 1996, p. 38.

26. Skip Wollenberg, "KFC Ads to Use Animated Colonel," *The South Bend Tribune,* September 8, 1998, p. C8.

27. Jolie Solomon and Arlyn Tobias Gajilan, "A Tale of a Tail," *Newsweek,* November 11, 1996, pp. 58-59.

28. Jonathan Karp, "Medium and Message," *Far Eastern Economic Review,* February 25, 1993, pp. 50-52.

Chapter 3

1. Arundhati Parmar, "Objections to Indian Ad Not Taken Lightly," *Marketing News,* June 9, 2003, pp. 4, 9.

2. Ibid.

3. Catherine Arnold, "Cinematic Ads Viewed Darkly," *Marketing News,* March 17, 2003, p. 3.

4. George Rodman, *Making Sense of Media,* Boston: Allyn & Bacon, 2001, p. 327.

5. Ira Teinowitz, "Appeals Court Rules Against Pork Council," *Advertising Age,* October 27, 2003, p. 4; "Beef Program Ruled Unconstitutional," *Advertising Age,* July 14, 2003, p. 10; <www.AdAge.com>.

6. Todd Pruzan and Chuck Ross, "Absolut Considers Breaking TV Ad Ban," *Advertising Age,* March 11, 1966, pp. 1, 33.

7. Kate MacArthur, "Coors Slammed for Targeting Kids," *Advertising Age,* November 3, 2003, pp. 1, 59.

8. Rich Thomaselli, "Industry Wrestles with Comparative Ads," *Advertising Age,* October 27, 2003, p. 10.

9. Sally Goll Beatty and Richard Gibson, "Taste-Test Wars Heat up Among Rivals," *The Wall Street Journal,* March 30, 1998, p. B8; Louise Kramer, "Papa John's Blasts Rival Pizza Hut's Ad Imagery," *Advertising Age,* January 25, 1999, p. 4.

10. Federal Trade Commission Act, section 5(a)(1).

11. Deborah L. Vence, "Marketing to Minors Still Under Careful Watch," *Marketing News,* March 31, 2003, pp. 5-6.

12. "FDA Orders Halt to Allegra Spots," *Advertising Age,* January 19, 2004, p. 16.

13. "Firm Pleads Guilty in Zoladex Marketing," *The South Bend Tribune,* June 21, 2003, p. B10.

14. "10 Ads We'll Never See in the U.S.," *Advertising Age,* December 22, 2003, p. 30.

15. Barbara Martinez, "Gap Is Named in Infringement Suit over Eyewear Included in an Ad," *The Wall Street Journal,* January 6, 1998, p. B4.

16. Antoaneta Bezlova, "China Subjects U.S. Direct Marketers to Party Line," *USA Today,* April 29, 1998, p. B2.

17. "Main Chinese Channel Bars Spirits Spots from Prime Time," *Advertising Age International,* November 1997, p. 23.

18. Louisa Ha, "Concerns About Advertising Practices in a Developing Country: An Examination of China's New Advertising Regulations," *International Journal of Advertising,* 1996, 15: 91-102.

19. "Bates Asia Gets Another Chance," *Advertising Age,* December 15, 2003, p. 16.

20. "Shantel Wong," AdAge Special Report, *Advertising Age,* January 26, 2004, p. s-2.

21. "Japanese Clear Smoke out of Some Media," *Advertising Age International,* November 1997, p. 23.

22. Rochelle Burbury, "International Special Report," *Advertising Age International,* October 1996, p. 113.

23. Fair Trade Law. Taiwan, Republic of China: Preparatory Office of the Fair Trade Commission, 1991, p. 9.

24. "New Payment Plan Aimed at Reducing Fraud on Internet," *Taiwan Headlines,* <http://publish.gio.gov.tw>.

25. *Selling Dreams: How Advertising Misleads Us,* Penang, Malaysia: Consumers' Association of Penang, 1986.

26. Michael H. Anderson, *Madison Avenue in Asia: Politics and Transnational Advertising,* Cranbury, NJ: Associated University Presses, 1983.

27. Burbury, "International Special Report," p. 113.

28. Ibid.

29. "New Decree Clarifies Advertising Regulations," *The Vietnam Investment Review,* March 17, 2003.

30. Ellen Hale, "Junk Food Super-Sizing Europeans," *USA Today,* November 18, 2003, pp. 13A-14A.

31. "Review," *Campaign (UK),* Issue 3, January 17, 2003, p. 5.

32. Catherine Arnold, "Do Not Call Has Foreign Origins," *Marketing News,* November 24, 2003, pp. 6-7.

33. Barbara Sundberg Baudot, *International Advertising Handbook,* Lexington, MA: Lexington Books, 1989.

34. Burbury, "International Special Report," p. 113.

35. "FYI," *Advertising Age,* September 30, 2002, p. 14.

36. Jeffery D. Zbar, "Latin America Cracking Down," *Advertising Age International,* October 1996, p. 116.

37. Deborah L. Vence, "Free Trade Pact Looks Promising for Marketers, Advertisers," *Marketing News,* August 18, 2003, pp. 6-7.

38. "Argentina Bans Ads on Pay TV," *Advertising Age,* January 5, 2004, p. 11.

39. "U.S. Reaches Trade Deal with Morocco," *USA Today,* March 3, 2004, B1.

40. Portions of this chapter were derived from the following book and booklets: Adnan Hashim, *Advertising in Malaysia,* Malaysia: Pelanduk Publications (M) Sdn. Bhd, 1994; The Indonesian Association of Advertising Agencies, *Media Scene Indonesia,* Indonesian, 1989/1990; Consumers' Association of Penang, *Selling Dreams: How Advertising Misleads Us,* Malaysia, 1986; Ramesh Shrestha, editor and publisher, *The Advertising Book: A Guide to the Advertising Industry in Thailand,* Thailand: AB Publication, 1984; Antonio V. Concepcio and Nimia G. Yumol, *Profile of the Philippine Advertising Industry,* Philippines: Advertising Board of the Philippines, 1989; and other materials collected by the Institute of Southeast Asian Studies, Republic of Singapore.

Chapter 4

1. "'94 Advertising Agencies Report," *Advertising Age,* Chinese Edition, May 1995, p. 62.

2. R. Craig Endicott, "Industry Revenue Increased Only 0.6 Percent Last Year," <www.adage.com>.

3. Ibid.

4. Frederick R. Gamble, *What Advertising Agencies Are—What They Do and How They Do It,* Seventh Edition, New York: American Association of Advertising Agencies, 1970, p. 4.

5. Judann Pollack, "McDonald's to Aim Its Arch at Grown-ups," *Advertising Age,* April 8, 1996, p. 3; Judann Pollack and Pat Sloan, "McDonald's Looking Beyond Core Agencies," *Advertising Age,* May 13, 1996, p. 52.

6. "Adweek's Marketing," March 12, 1990, RC27; Mark Gleason, "McCann to Buy Health Agency," *Advertising Age,* June 3, 1996, pp. 1, 53.

7. Keith J. Kelly and Jeffery D. Zbar, "Spanish Magazines Capture Attention with 3 New Entries," *Advertising Age,* June 3, 1996, p. 44.

8. Jeffery D. Zbar, "Honda U.S. Hispanic Shop Widens Reach," *Advertising Age,* January 29, 1996, p. 3.

9. Melanie Wells, "Procter & Gamble Tells Ad Agencies to Diversify," *USA Today,* April 26, 1996, p. 2B.

10. Sally Beatty, "'Integration Fees' of TV Networks Draw Ire of Ad-Group President," *The Wall Street Journal,* April 3, 1998, p. B7.

11. Gregory White, "Ford's Better Idea: Incentives for Agencies," *The Wall Street Journal,* September 10, 1998, p. B11.

12. Sally Beatty, "BankAmerica Invites 6 Agencies to Pitch," *The Wall Street Journal,* December 6, 1996, p. B5.

13. Melanie Wells, "Ad Agency, Nabisco End Long Relationship," *USA Today,* June 18, 1997, p. 2B.

14. Beatty, "'Integration Fees' of TV Networks Draw Ire of Ad-Group President."

15. Stuart Elliott, "A Group Is Making a Multiyear Effort to Show the Importance of Ads to Marketers and Consumers," *The New York Times,* June 18, 1998, p. C6.

16. Kate Fitzgerald, "Beyond Advertising," *Advertising Age,* August 3, 1998, p. 1.

17. Dottie Enrico, "Leadership Problems, Bad Decisions Devastate Ad Agency," *USA Today,* March 6, 1998, p. B1.

18. Sally Beatty, "Merger Boom Expected in Ad Industry," *The Wall Street Journal,* May 21, 1998, p. B10.

19. Sally Beatty, "Citigroup May Need to Trim Brand Names," *The Wall Street Journal,* April 7, 1998, p. B10.

20. Sally Beatty, "Agencies Get Creative with Shops to Dodge Conflict Issue for Clients," *The Wall Street Journal,* November 14, 1997, p. B6.

21. "Minishops at Leo Burnett," *The Wall Street Journal,* November 14, 1997, p. B6.

Chapter 5

1. Kate Fitzgerald, "Entertainment Missing a Punch Line," *Advertising Age,* July 8, 2002, p. s-10.

2. "Meet the Grandparents," *AARP The Magazine,* July/August 2003, p. 13.

3. Robert Frank, "Potato Chips to Go Global—or So Pepsi Bets," *The Wall Street Journal,* November 30, 1995, pp. B3, B10.

4. William M. Pride and O.C. Ferrel, *Marketing,* Twelfth Edition, Boston: Houghton Mifflin, 2003.

5. "Coke Consolidates Media at Starcom," *Advertising Age,* January 12, 2004, p. 14.

6. Rebecca Piirto, *Beyond Mind Games: The Marketing Power of Psychographics,* Ithaca, NY: American Demographic Books, 1991; Warren J. Keegan and Mark C. Green, *Global Marketing,* Third Edition, Upper Saddle River, NJ: Prentice-Hall, 2003.

7. U.S. Census Bureau, "North American Classification System," <http://www. census.gov> and <http://www.naics.com>.

8. Wendy Bounds, "Meredith Introduces 'More' for Women," *The Wall Street Journal,* June 19, 1998, p. B4.

9. Barbara Martinez, "Dog Food, Toothpaste and Oreos Star on Popular Hispanic Television Program," *The Wall Street Journal,* March 25, 1997, pp. B1, B7.

10. Sally Beatty, "Some Great Ads You'll Probably Never See," *The Wall Street Journal,* June 2, 1998, p. B12.

11. Scott Boeck and Elys A. McLean, "A Look at Statistics That Shape the Nation—Baby Boomlet," *USA Today,* September 4, 1997, p. B1; Terence A. Shimp, *Advertising, Promotion, and Supplemental Aspects of Integrated Marketing Communications,* Sixth Edition, Mason, OH: Thomson/Western, 2003.

12. Joshua Wolf Shenk, "The New Anti-Ad," *U. S. News and World Report,* October 20, 1997, p. 80.

13. Daren Fonda, "Baby, You Can Drive My Car," *Time,* June 30, 2003, p. 46.

14. Ibid, p. 47.

15. Dottie Enrico, "Admakers Narrow Focus to Zero in on Income Groups," *USA Today,* June 29, 1998, p. 5B.

16. Dottie Enrico, "Popular Ad Campaigns Can Bridge Generation Gap," *USA Today,* June 2, 1998, p. 6B.

17. *Ayer's Dictionary of Advertising Terms,* Philadelphia: Ayer Press, 1976.

18. Jeff Jensen, "Chief Auto Steers for Quality Positioning," *Advertising Age,* April 1, 1996, p. 8.

19. Nikhil Deogun, "'The Exorcist' Meets 'Goodfellas' in New Pepsi Ad Challenging Coke," *The Wall Street Journal,* July 9, 1998, p. B12.

20. A. Jerome Jewler, *Creative Strategy in Advertising,* Fourth Edition, Belmont, CA: Wadsworth, 1992, p. 69.

Chapter 6

1. Norihiko Shirouzu, "Flouting 'Rules' Sells GE Fridges in Japan," *The Wall Street Journal,* October 31, 1995, p. B1.

2. Paul Sherlock, *Rethinking Business to Business Marketing,* New York: Free Press, 1991, pp. 19-22.

3. Courtland L. Bovee, John V. Thill, George P. Dovel, and Marian Burk Wood, *Advertising Excellence,* New York: McGraw-Hill, 1995, pp. 108-109.

4. L. W. Turley and Scott W. Kelley, "A Comparison of Advertising Content: Business to Business versus Consumer Services," *Journal of Advertising,* Vol. XXVI, No. 4, Winter 1997, p. 40.

5. Turley and Kelley, "A Comparison of Advertising Content," p. 47.

6. Kevin Goldman, "Women Endorsers More Credible Than Men, a Survey Suggests," *The Wall Street Journal,* October 12, 1997, p. B1.

7. Gary C. Woodward and Robert E. Denton Jr., *Persuasion & Influence in American Life,* Prospect Heights, IL: Waveland Press, 1992, pp. 227-228.

8. Bill McDowell, "New DDB Needham Report: Consumers Want It All," *Advertising Age,* November 18, 1996, p. P32.

9. Melanie Wells, "Marketers Can't Get Old Tunes Out of Their Heads," *USA Today,* June 2, 1997, p. B1.

10. Kate MacArthur, "Burger King's Big Idea: Have It Your Way, Again," *Advertising Age,* February 16, 2004, p. 1.

11. Rebecca Piirto, "Beyond Mind Games," *American Demographics,* December 1991, pp. 52-57.

12. Wayne Weiten, *Psychology Applied to Modern Life,* Second Edition, Belmont, CA: Brooks/Cole, 1986, p. 19.

13. Marco R. della Cava, "Luxury-Car Makers Happily Cater to Any Whim," *USA Today,* February 16, 1998, p. 3B.

14. Peter Francese, "America at Mid-Decade," Market Report, *American Demographics,* 1995, p. 1.

15. Editorial, *Journal of Direct Marketing,* Summer 1994, p. 3.

16. Lisa-Fortini Campbell, *Hitting the Sweet Spot: How Consumer Insights Can Inspire Better Marketing and Advertising,* Chicago: The Copy Workshop, 1992, p. 176.

Chapter 7

1. Gary Levin, "CBS, NBC Own the Sweeps," *USA Today,* March 3, 2004, p. 4D.

2. Emily Nelson and Sarah Ellison, "Nielsen's Feud with TV Networks Shows Scarcity of Marketing Data," *World Street Journal,* October 28, 2003, pp. Al, A6.

3. Brian Lowry, "Researchers Can Track Our Every Media Move," *Chicago Tribune,* June 7, 2003, Sec. 5, p. 3.

4. Jack Honomichl, "Research Revenues Rise 9 Percent for Industry's Top 50 Firms," *Marketing News,* June 8, 1998, pp. H1-32.

5. Jack Honomichl, "Top 25 Global Firms Earn $5.6 Billion in Revenue," *Marketing News,* H2, 30(20), September 23, 1996.

6. Jack Honomichl, "Research Revenues Rise 9 Percent for Industry's Top 50 Firms."

7. Fara Warner, "France's Sofres Overtakes Nielsen for China's Television Ratings Service," *The Wall Street Journal,* February 21, 1996, p. B6.

8. Jack Honomichl, "Revenues up, but Little Real Growth," *Marketing News,* June 9, 2003, p. H13.

9. Ibid.

10. Terence A. Shimp, *Advertising, Promotion, and Supplemental Aspects of Integrated Marketing Communications,* Fourth Edition, Fort Worth, TX: The Dryden Press, 1997.

11. Jack Honomichl, "Revenues up, but Little Real Growth."

12. Ibid.

13. Joe Schwartz, "Back to the Source," *American Demographics,* January 1989, pp. 22-26.

14. Jack Honomichl, "Revenues up, but Little Growth."

15. Leslie Kaufman, "Enough Talk," *Newsweek,* August 18, 1997, p. 48.

16. Kaufman, "Enough Talk," p. 49.

Chapter 8

1. Elizabeth Cornell, *Hoover's Online,* <www.hoovers.com>.

2. Bill Richards, "Nike Had $67.7 Million 4th-Period Loss, First in over 10 Years, Amid Asia Woes," *The Wall Street Journal,* July 1, 1998, p. B12.

3. Dottie Enrico and Melanie Wells, "Lee, Levi's Design New Ad Approach," *USA Today,* May 5, 1998, p. 2B.

4. Nikhil Deogun, "Pepsi Has Had Its Fill of Pizza, Tacos, Chicken," *The Wall Street Journal,* January 24, 1997, p. B1.

5. Kate Fitzgerald, "Bank's Magazines Target Customers," *Advertising Age,* Nov. 18, 1996, p. 30.

6. Mercedes M. Cardona, "Differentiation Works for Banana Republic," *Advertising Age,* February 9, 2004, p. 6.

7. "Advertising & Marketing," *The Advertising Age FactPack 2004 Edition,* pp. 8, 12.

8. Don E. Schultz and Beth E. Barnes, *Strategic Advertising Campaigns,* Fourth Edition, Lincolnwood, IL: NTC Business Books, 1995, pp. 54-57.

9. Charles H. Patti and Vincent J. Blasko, "Budgeting Practices of Big Advertisers," *Journal of Advertising Research* 21, December 1981: 23-29.

10. Denis Higgins, *The Art of Advertising: Conversations with Masters of the Craft,* Lincolnwood, IL: NTC Business Books, 1989, p. 92.

Chapter 9

1. "Film Noir," <http://greatfilms.org/filmnoir.html>.

2. "No. 1: AFLAC," *Advertising Age,* March 8, 2004, p. 13.

3. Bob Lamons, "Research Won't Yield the Big Idea," *Advertising Age,* November 18, 1996, p. 18.

4. Don E. Schultz and Beth E. Barnes, *Strategic Advertising Campaigns,* Fourth Edition, Lincolnwood, IL: NTC Business Books, 1995, pp. 172, 174.

5. Jolie Solomon and Arlyn Tobias Gajilan, *Newsweek,* November 11, 1996, pp. 58-59.

6. James Webb Young, *A Technique for Producing Ideas,* Lincolnwood, IL: NTC Business Books, 1975, pp. 53-54, cited in Schultz and Barnes, *Strategic Advertising Campaigns,* pp. 177-178.

7. Arthur Miller, "Introduction to the *Collected Plays,*" in Robert A. Martin (Ed.), *The Theatre Essays of Arthur Miller,* New York: Penguin, 1978, pp. 141-143.

8. Edward deBono, *Lateral Thinking for Management,* New York: American Management Association, 1971, cited in Schultz and Barnes, *Strategic Advertising Campaigns,* pp. 179-182.

9. Dottie Enrico, "Kellogg's Generic Ads: Thinking Outside the Box," *USA Today,* February 9, 1998, p. B1.

10. Dagmar Mussey, "German Audi Spot Features Hoffman," *Advertising Age,* March 15, 2004, p. 22.

11. Anthony Vagnoni, "They Might Be Giants," *Advertising Age,* April 27, 1998, p. 24.

12. Bradley Johnson, "Levi's Boos 'Box' Thinking," *Advertising Age,* May 11, 1998, p. 8.

13. Dottie Enrico, "Automakers Switch Gears on Ads," *USA Today,* October 1, 1997, p. B3.

14. David A. Aaker and John G. Myers, *Advertising Management,* Third Edition, Englewood Cliffs, NJ: Prentice-Hall, 1987, p. 350.

15. Rich Thomaselli, "Las Vegas Ad Slogan Takes on Life of Its Own," *Advertising Age,* March 8, 2004, p. 6.

16. Charles F. Frazer, "Creative Strategy: A Management Perspective," *Journal of Advertising,* Vol. 12, No. 4, 1983, pp. 36-41, cited in A. Jerome Jewler, *Creative Strategy in Advertising,* Fourth Edition, Belmont, CA: Wadsworth, 1992, p. 69.

17. "Ad Meter XVI," *USA Today,* February 2, 2004, p. 7B.

18. Dottie Enrico, "Soft-Drink Maker Pours on Humor in Super Ads," *USA Today,* January 27, 1998, p. B1.

19. Bruce Horovitz, "Viewers' Favorite Ads Crude, Rude and Furry," *USA Today,* February 2, 2004, p. 7B.

20. Melanie Wells and Dottie Enrico, "Humor Pays Off When Toying with Emotions," *USA Today,* December 9, 1996, pp. 1A, 2A, 3B; Dottie Enrico, "Humorous Touch Resonates with Consumers," *USA Today,* May 13, 1996, p. 3B; "Snickers Ad Wins Award," *USA Today,* June 4, 1998, p. B1.

21. David Ogilvy, *Ogilvy on Advertising,* New York: Random House, 1985, pp. 103-113.

22. Ogilvy, *Ogilvy on Advertising,* pp. 113-116; Bob Weinstein, "Radio Is a Riot," *Madison Avenue,* June 1985, pp. 70-74.

23. William F. Arens and Courtland L. Bovee, *Contemporary Advertising,* Fifth Edition, Burr Ridge, IL: Irwin, 1994.

Chapter 10

1. Bob Garfield, "Beleaguered United May Find Relief with Simple, Artful Ads," *Advertising Age,* March 8, 2004, p. 53.

2. Sally Goll Beatty, "Latest Ads Star a Clean, Modern Face," *The Wall Street Journal,* October 3, 1996, pp. B1, B11.

3. Ibid.

4. Tom Lichty, *Design Principles for Desktop Publishers,* Second Edition, Belmont, CA: Wadsworth, 1994, p. 34.

5. Garfield, "Beleaguered United May Find Relief with Simple, Artful Ads."

6. "GM Saves $4M with Ad System," *Advertising Age,* March 1, 2004, p. 12.

7. Paul Davidson, "AOL Aims to Make Mark in Rich-Media," *USA Today,* November 29, 2003, p. B8.

8. "Online Shopping Gets Even Easier," *Newsweek,* May 11, 1998, p. 90.

9. Davidson, "AOL Aims to Make Mark in Rich-Media."

10. N. Y. Times News Service, in *Simon & Schuster College Newslink,* August 3, 1998, <www.penhall.com>.

Chapter 11

1. *Marketing Communications Magazine* staff, "Hey Jogi!," *The Warsaw Voice,* February 22, 2004, No. 8, p. 12.

2. Adam Rafalski and Mariusz Piaseczny, "Marketing Mix," *The Warsaw Voice,* February 22, 2004, No. 8, p. 12.

3. "Nielsen Ratings," *USA Today,* October 15, 2003, p. D3; *Advertising Age FactPack 2004 Edition,* pp. 30-31.

4. Ed Papazian, "CPM: Friend or Foe?" *Marketing & Media Decisions,* June 1990, pp. 53-54; Karen Ritchie, "Media Accountability: An Innovative Idea," *Marketing & Media Decisions,* March 1990, pp. 81-82.

5. Kevin Goldman, "Study Finds Ads Induce Few People to Buy," *The Wall Street Journal,* October 17, 1996, p. B10.

6. Adam Rafalski and Mariusz Piaseczny, "Marketing Mix," p. 12.

7. Laurel Wentz, "Unilever Ramps up Latin Effort," *Advertising Age,* March 1, 2004, p. 32.

8. Michael McCarthy, "To Ad Buyers, Super Bowl = Young Men," *USA Today,* January 14, 2004, p. B1.

9. Melanie Wells, "Media Firms Lure Young Ad Buyers' Business with Pleasure," *USA Today,* August 10, 1998, p. 6B.

10. Skip Wollenberg, "Seinfeld Ads Aren't About Nothing," *South Bend Tribune* (AP Business Writer, New York), May 6, 1998, p. D3; Sally Goll Beatty, "NBC Looks to Cash in on 'Seinfeld' Finale," *The Wall Street Journal,* March 4, 1998, p. B11; Dottie Enrico, "Advertisers Pick Spots for 'Seinfeld' Finale," *USA Today,* May 11, 1998, p. 4B.

11. Julie Snider, "TV Households," *USA Today,* September 10, 2003, p. 2A.

12. Gary Levin, "Hispanics Finally Break the TV Barrier," *USA Today,* September 1, 2003, pp. 1A-2A.

13. John D. Leckenby and Jongpil Hong, "Reach/Frequency and the Web," *Journal of Advertising Research,* January/February 1998, p. 11.

14. Ibid, p. 10.

Chapter 12

1. Carla Johnson and Alyson Leatherman, "El Toro de Osborne: Advertising, Community, and Myth," *The Social Science Journal,* Vol. 42, No. 1, 2005, p. 135.

2. Laurel Wentz, "Work/Citroen," *Advertising Age,* March 15, 2004, p. 22.

3. Laurel Wentz, "Armani Makes Owls Stars of Campaign," *Advertising Age,* February 9, 2004, p. 12.

4. Carla Johnson, "The Magazine Industry," *21st Century Feature Writing,* Boston: Allyn & Bacon, 2005, p. 120.

5. Jon Fine, "Circ Model Cries for Hard Choices: How Magazines Got in a Jam, and a Bevy of Hard Choices for Getting Out," *Advertising Age,* March 15, 2004, p. S-2.

6. Mercedes M. Cardona, "Ad Watch," *Advertising Age,* March 15, 2004, p. 8.

7. Adam Rafalski and Mariusz Piaseczny, "Marketing Mix," *The Warsaw Voice,* February 22, 2004, p. 12.

8. Johnson, "The Magazine Industry," p. 120.

9. Brooke Capps, "Consumer Magazine Advertising Linage for Third Quarter 2003," *Advertising Age,* January 19, 2004, p. 12.

10. Ibid.

11. Andrew Zipern, "After Year of Floundering, a Magazine Monolith Finds Its Market," *Silicon Alley Reporter,* Vol. 2, No. 11, November 1998, p. 57.

12. Jean Halliday, "Auto Industry Pushes Print's Creative Limits," *Advertising Age,* March 8, 2004, p. 4.

13. Jenna Schnuer, "Mags Help Men Make a Statement," *Advertising Age,* January 19, 2004, p. S-10.

14. Laurel Wentz, "Newspapers Turn to Hispanics," *Advertising Age,* January 5, 2004, p. 16.

15. Jane Hodges, "Newspapers Plug Along in Quest for Web Answer," *Advertising Age,* April 29, 1996, p. S-6.

Chapter 13

1. Leon Lazaroff, "Comcast Adopts Focused View," *Chicago Tribune,* March 20, 2004, Sec. 2, pp. 1, 8.

2. Mercedes M. Cardona, "Ad Watch," *Advertising Age,* March 15, 2004, p. 8.

3. Gary Levin, "Four Dynamics That Have Changed What We Watch," *USA Today,* February 10, 2004, p. B5.

4. Ibid.

5. "Radio Stations." <www.arbitron.com/downloads/radiotoday03.pdf>.

6. Melanie Wells, "Jean Pool: Wants Less Commercial Clutter on TV," *USA Today,* May 26, 1998, p. B3.

7. "Black Format Growth Trends," *Black Radio Today 2003 Edition,* Arbitron Inc.

8. "Radio Stations."

9. "Imperial Study, Radio vs. TV," *RadioAd,* White Paper No. 1, November 15, 2002.

10. Janet Stilson, "Radio Scraps for Its Ad Share," *Advertising Age,* February 2, 2004, p. 22.

Chapter 14

1. Joseph Jaffe, "The State of Online Creativity," *i.Intelligence,* Spring 2004, p. 18.

2. Bruce Horovitz, "AOL's Chat Rooms Opened to Advertisers," *USA Today,* 1996, p. B1.

3. Lee Hall, "The New Momentum," *i.Intelligence,* Spring 2004, p. 4.

4. "Link Up," *Link,* Vol. 2, No. 4, April 1997, p. 4; Hall, "The New Momentum," p. 6.

5. Allison Price Arden, "Letter," *i.Intelligence,* Spring 2004, p. 3.

6. "AdWatch," *Advertising Age,* April 26, 2004, p. 8; Jaffe, "The State of Online Creativity," p. 18.

7. "Pointroll Success Story," <pointroll.com/success/1800mattress.asp>.

8. Jeffrey H. Kessler, Internet Task Force Report, for CCH, Riverwoods, IL, 1994. Reprinted with permission.

9. Jon Swartz, "Yahoo Earnings Make Investors Say, 'Woo Hoo!'," *USA Today,* April 8, 2004, p. 3B.

10. Paul Davidson, "AOL to Offer Content to Non-Subscribers," *USA Today,* April 8, 2004, p. B1; Catherine Arnold, "Ads Front and Center," *Marketing News,* March 17, 2003, p. 3.

11. Steven Levy, "Bill and Al Get It Right," *Newsweek,* July 7, 1997, p. 80.

12. Jeffrey D. Neuburger and Jill Westmoreland, "Legal Link," *Silicon Alley Reporter,* September 1998, p. 76.

13. Tessa Wegert, "Pop-Up Ads, Part I: Good? Bad? Ugly?" <www.clickz.com>.

14. Bruce Horowitz, "Summit Will Be 'Defining Moment' of Net Advertising," *USA Today,* August 17, 1998, pp. B1-B2; Jean Halliday, "Automakers Embrace Net Ads," *Advertising Age,* July 14, 2003, p. 18.

15. Jean Halliday, "Case Study: Promo Drives Web Traffic for Hyundai," *Advertising Age,* July 14, 2003, p. 18.

16. Bill Barnhart, "Nothing But Net: A Commentary on the Impact of the Internet on Investor Relations," *Journal of Corporate Public Relations,* Vol. 7, 1996-97, pp. 16-17.

17. "The Accidental Superhighway," *The Economist,* July 1, 1995, pp. 3-4.

18. "A Multi-Take on Multitasking," *Advertising Age,* March 29, 2004, p. S-8.

19. Hairong Li, "Advertising Media," <www.admedia.org/>.

20. Jack Neff, "P&G Extends Online Custom Publishing," *Advertising Age,* March 22, 2004, p. 24.

21. Erin Stout, "Turning Web Leads into Online Sales," *Sales & Marketing Management,* September 2000, pp. 28-29.

22. Robert W. Ahrens and Quin Tian, "Who's Using Rich-Media," *USA Today,* November 29, 2003, p. 8B.

23. Stephanie Armour, "E-Mail 'a Blessing' for Business," *USA Today,* July 2, 1998, p. 1A.

24. "Global PR Effort Can Help Start-Ups Survive," *O'Dwyer's PR Services Report,* November 1995, p. 45.

25. "About the Nature and Future of Interactive Marketing," *Journal of Interactive Marketing,* Vol. 12, No. 1, 1998, p. 68.

26. "E-Mail Company Asked Not to Use the Word 'Spam,'" *The South Bend Tribune,* July 6, 1997, p. B3.

27. Jonathan Jackson, "E-mail Marketing," *eMarketer, Inc.,* <www.eMarketer.com>.

28. Jon Swartz, "Spam's Irritating Cousin, Spim, on the Loose," *USA Today,* March 1, 2004, p. B1.

29. Wegert, "Pop-Up Ads, Part I: Good? Bad? Ugly?"

30. Kate Fitzgerald, "Debate Grows over Net Data," *Advertising Age,* March 15, 2004, p. 4.

Chapter 15

1. Carla Johnson and Alyson Leatherman, "El Toro de Osborne: Advertising, Community, and Myth," *The Social Science Journal,* Vol. 42, No. 2, 2005, p. 135.
2. Lisa Sanders, "Gimme Shelter: New York Seeks Ad Sites," *Advertising Age,* April 5, 2004, p. 3; Mike Leidig, "Cows Become Latest Billboard," *Advertising Age,* October 14, 2002, p. 12.
3. "Ad Watch," *Advertising Age,* March 15, 2004, p. 8; TNS Media Intelligence/CMR; Michael Wilke, "Outdoor Woes: Gannett Could Suffer Layoffs," *Advertising Age,* August 19, 1996, p. 3; Bruce Horovitz, "Greyhound Turns Buses into Rolling Billboards," *USA Today,* July 2, 1997, p. B2.
4. Michael Wilke, "Outdoor Ads Entering Whole New Dimensions," *Advertising Age,* July 29, 1996, p. 20.
5. Johnson and Leatherman, "El Toro de Osborne."
6. Information provided by the Institute of Outdoor Advertising, 1991.
7. *Preference Building: The Dynamic World of Specialty Advertising,* Irving, TX: Specialty Advertising Association, 1988.
8. Seth Sutel, "Yellow Pages Still Profitable," *The South Bend Tribune,* August 12, 2003, pp. B7-B8.
9. Ibid.
10. "Breaking: Chrysler," *Advertising Age,* July 13, 1998, p. 40.
11. Carol Marie Cropper, "Fruit to Walls to Floor, Ads Are on the March," *The New York Times,* February 26, 1998, pp. A1, A8.
12. Stephanie Thompson, "Pringles Got Game—Right on the Chips," *Advertising Age,* April 5, 2004, p. 4.
13. "Unilever Launches Skippy Snack Bars," *Advertising Age,* March 1, 2004, p. 1.
14. "Happy Meals to Get New Look, Choices," *Chicago Tribune,* March 19, 2004, Sec. 3, p. 2.
15. James B. Arndorfer, "Miller Lite Promo by 'Dick': Scratch 'n' Sniff Labels," *Advertising Age,* April 27, 1998, p. 8.
16. Joshua Hammer and Corie Brown, "Licensed to Shill," *Newsweek,* December 15, 1997, p. 43.
17. Richard Lorant, "License to Shill?" *The South Bend Tribune,* December 5, 1997, p. B1.
18. Mercedes M. Cardona, "Home Depot Revamps Results," *Advertising Age,* November 24, 2003, pp. 1, 23.
19. Emma Hall, "Young Consumers Receptive to Movie Product Placement," *Advertising Age,* March 29, 2004, p. 8.
20. Lisa Sanders, "Revlon Launches Bond Line," *Advertising Age,* October 14, 2002, pp. 4, 55.
21. "Fruit Became the Ad Medium," *The World Journal,* October 11, 1997, p. B8.

22. "Motorcycle Firm Co-Opts Grey NZ to Life China Sales," *Media Asia,* February 13, 2004, p. 8.
23. Bill Keveney, "'Idol' Marketers Rolling up Their Sleeves," *USA Today,* February 2, 2004, p. D1.
24. Press Kit "It's Time to Get Connected," Fort Lee, NJ: MSNBC, 1997.

Chapter 16

1. Jane Hodges, "Neiman Marcus Is Looking Far East," *Advertising Age,* September 16, 1996, p. 16.
2. Cara Dipasquale, "Direct Marketing a Tale of Rapid Recovery," *Advertising Age,* September 9, 2002, p. 10.
3. Mercedes M. Cardona, "Qualified Cheer," *Advertising Age,* December 15, 2003, p. 8.
4. *Fact Book on Direct Response Marketing.* New York: Direct Marketing Association, 1982.
5. "Triple Play," *Advertising Age,* May 17, 2004, p. S-8.
6. Susan Jones, *Creative Strategy in Direct Marketing.* Lincolnwood, IL: NTC Business Books, 1991, pp. 9-12, 408.
7. Rob Jackson, "Breaking the Code: Maximizing Customer Value," *Direct,* August 1997, p. 57.
8. Paul Davidson, "Next on FTC's Hit List: Spyware," *USA Today,* April 19, 2004, p. 5B.
9. Edward C. Baig, "Targeted Ads Tied to Gmail's Super Space," *USA Today,* April 15, 2004, p. 6B.
10. "Information Privacy & Security," Federal Trade Commission, <http://www.ftc.gov/privacy/5/19/2004>.
11. Jones, *Creative Strategy in Direct Marketing,* p. 130.
12. *The Direct Marketing Association's Statistical Fact Book 2003.*
13. Ibid.
14. James Cox, "Catalogers Expand in Asia," *USA Today,* October 18, 1996, pp. 4B, 10B.
15. Hackett Best Practices' 2000 Book of Numbers–Call Center, The Hackett Group, ANS Werthink Company, *The Direct Marketing Association's Statistical Fact Book 2003,* p. 258.
16. Larry Nielson, "Do Not Call Legislation: Are You in Compliance?" *Insurance Journal,* November 3, 2003, <www.insurancejournal.com/5/19/2004>; Julie Vallese and Bill Mears, "Bush Signs 'Do-Not-Call' Bill into Law," CNN.com, <http://edition.cnn.com/2003/ALLPOLITICS/09/29/do.not.call>.
17. Jones, *Creative Strategy in Direct Marketing,* p. 214.
18. Ibid, p. 232.
19. Tom Pope, "Direct Merchandising Spurs New Revenues for Nonprofits," *Direct Marketing,* October 1996, pp. 1, 4.
20. Char Kosek, "Business-to-Business Grabs $51.7 Billion," *Advertising Age,* June 10, 1996, p. S-3.
21. "Direct Marketing Without Borders," presented at the Direct Marketing Education Foundation's Institute, Chicago, June 1, 1995.

22. Patrick Marketing Group Report. <www.pmgdirect.com>, 2002.

23. Laura Loro, "Mail Favorite Tool in Direct Marketing Circles," *Advertising Age,* June 10, 1996, p. S-16.

24. Maria Rosa Balzaretti, Kimberly Evard, Adam Von Ins, Hugh Williams, and Kevin Young, "African Americans: Lifestyles, Purchase Behaviors and Perceptions of Marketing Communication Tactics," Northwestern University Integrated Marketing Communication Program, February 27, 1995, unpublished.

25. "02-07 International Direct Marketing Ad Spending (Ranked by Level of 2002 Forecast; Millions of U.S. Dollars)," The DMA Report: Economic Impact—*U.S. Direct Marketing Today,* 2003.

26. David Reed, "DMers Well Placed to Utilize the Euro," *Direct,* February 1998.

27. Henry Heilbrunn, "Interactive Marketing in Europe," *Direct Marketing,* March 1998, pp. 58-59.

28. Matt Moore, "Spam in Europe Blamed on U.S.," *Marketing News,* June 23, 2003, p. 9.

29. Rebecca A. Fannin, "Internet Finds Its Audience Among Elite Latin Americans," *Ad Age International,* December 1997.

Chapter 17

1. Claire Atkinson, "Brawny Man Now a Metrosexual," *Advertising Age,* February 16, 2004, p. 8.

2. Betsy Spethmann, "Milk Promos Multiply in $30 Million Push," *PROMO Magazine,* May 20, 2004.

3. Richard Gibson, "At McDonald's, a Case of Mass Beaniemania," *The Wall Street Journal,* June 5, 1998, p. B1.

4. John J. Burnett, *Promotion Management,* Boston: Houghton Mifflin, 1993, p. 7.

5. Howard Schultz and Dori Jones Yang, *Pour Your Heart Into It,* New York: Hyperion Press, 1997, pp. 255-256.

6. "Shopper Friendly," *Advertising Age,* February 9, 2004, p. 43.

7. Don E. Schultz and Beth E. Barnes, *Strategic Advertising Campaigns,* Lincolnwood, IL: NTC Business Books, 1994, p. 229.

8. Kate Fitzgerald, "In-Store Media Ring Cash Register," *Advertising Age,* February 9, 2004, p. 43.

9. Martin Sloane, "Coupon Fraud Is a Serious Problem," *The South Bend Tribune,* June 16, 1997, p. D3.

10. Lorrie Grant, "Rebates Motivate Consumer Choices," *USA Today,* March 1, 2004, p. 6B.

11. William M. Bulkeley, "Rebates' Secret Appeal to Manufacturers: Few Consumers Actually Redeem Them," *The Wall Street Journal,* February 10, 1998.

12. Grant, "Rebates Motivate Consumer Choices," p. 6B.

13. Carole Fleck, "The Long Rebate Wait," *AARP Bulletin,* April 2004, p. 21.

14. Judann Pollack, "PM Readies $40 Mil-Plus Marlboro 'Ranch' Promo," *Advertising Age,* May 11, 1998, p. 8.

15. Greg Jaffe, "Sweepstakes Industry May Not Be a WINNER!" *The Wall Street Journal,* February 18, 1998, pp. B1, B16.

16. Tom Lowry, "New Yorkers, You May Have Won a $60 Legal Settlement," *USA Today,* August 24, 1998, p. 1A; Carol Krol, "Image Makeover," *Advertising Age,* July 13, 1998, p. 22.

17. "McDonald's Launches New Monopoly Promotion," *The South Bend Tribune,* October 14, 2003, p. B8.

18. "Woman's Name for New Soft Drink Is a Hit with Company," *The South Bend Tribune,* December 13, 2000, p. B7.

19. Mercedes M. Cardona, "Capitol One Sports Mascot Promotion," *Advertising Age,* October 14, 2002, p. 6.

20. Michelle Higgins, "Foul! Sports-Feat Contestants Trip over Rules," *The Wall Street Journal,* July 8, 1998, p. B1.

21. Alain D. Astous and Isabelle Jacob, "Understanding Consumer Reactions to Premium-Based Promotional Offers," *European Journal of Marketing,* Vol. 36, Nos. 11 & 12, 2002, pp. 1270-1286; P. Kotler and R. E. Turner, *Marketing Management,* Ninth Edition, Scarborough: Prentice-Hall Canada, 1998.

22. Carol Krol, "Hallmark Uses Loyalty Effort for Segmenting Customers," *Advertising Age,* February 1, 1999, p. 36.

Chapter 18

1. "Big Mac Invasion Forces France to Weigh Culture," *USA Today,* <www.usatoday.com/money/industries/food/2>.

2. Ibid.

3. Donald Spoto, *The Decline and Fall of the House of Windsor,* New York: Simon & Schuster, 1995, p. 298.

4. Donna Freydkin, "Celebs Try to Refurbish Their Reps," *USA Today,* April 8, 2004, p. 5D.

5. "Product Survival: Lessons of the Tylenol Terrorism," Washington, DC: Washington Business Information, 1982, pp. 11-17.

6. Jose Rivera, "The Case of TWA Flight #800: Uncovering New Challenges and Opportunities for Public Relations Practitioners on the Internet," *Journal of Integrated Communications,* Vol. VII, 1997-1998, p. 56; Lisa Brownlee, "TWA Cautiously Rolls out Campaign," *The Wall Street Journal,* September 6, 1996, p. B2.

7. Daniel Kadlec, "Not a Good Thing for Martha," *Time,* March 15, 2004, p. 66.

8. Dennis L. Wilcox, Phillip H. Ault, and Warren K. Agee, *Public Relations Strategies and Tactics,* Fifth Edition, New York: Longman, 1998, p. 12.

9. <Adage.com>, April 12, 2004.

10. Jonah Bloom, "Mixed Messages Muddy Mission, Effectiveness of PR," *Advertising Age,* March 1, 2004, p. 15.

11. Stephanie Thompson, "Frito-Lay Homes in on Health Workers," *Advertising Age,* February 23, 2004, p. 41.

12. Jennifer Nedeff, "The Bottom Line Beckons: Quantifying Measurement in Public Relations," *Journal of Corporate Public Relations,* Vol. VII, 1996-1997, p. 36.

13. Thompson, "Frito-Lay Homes in on Health Workers."

14. DeWayne Wickham, "More Professionalism Would Improve News," *USA Today,* July 7, 1998, p. 13A.

15. Geoffrey A. Fowler and Kimberly Song, "Investors' Push for Disclosure Fuels Growth of PR in China," *The Wall Street Journal,* May 20, 2004, pp. C1, C16.

16. David N. McArthur and Tom Griffin, "A Marketing Management View of Integrated Marketing Communications," *Journal of Advertising Research,* October 1997, p. 22.

17. Lisa Sanders, "Selling Scions with Forehead Ads," AdAge.com, April 7, 2004.

18. Skip Wollenberg, "New General Ready for Battle in Cola Wars," *The South Bend Tribune,* May 13, 1998, p. C8.

19. Emma Hall and Normandy Madden, "Ikea Courts Buyers with Offbeat Ideas," *Advertising Age,* April 12, 2004, p. 10.

20. Jean Halliday, "Audi's A4 Sedan Helps Propel Revival a Decade After Bad PR," *Advertising Age,* p. 3, July 29, 1996.

21. Caroline E. Mayer, "GMAC Agrees to Settle Racial-Bias Lawsuit," *The Detroit News,* <detnews.com>.

22. Rudolph Bush, "Chrysler Execs Tell of Slurs," *Chicago Tribune,* <blackvoices.com>.

23. Lorrie Grant, "UGG Boots a Fashion Kick," *USA Today,* <usatoday.com>2004.

24. Wilcox, Ault, and Agee, *Public Relations Strategies and Tactics,* p. 490.

25. Arundhati Parmar, "Jiminy Cricket! Sponsorship Deals for the Sport Grow in India," *Marketing News,* March 17, 2003, pp. 4-5.

26. Claire Atkinson, "Sponsors Star on Broadway," *Advertising Age,* February 23, 2004, p. 6.

27. Rich Thomaselli, "Nextel Antes up $70 Million to Leverage Nascar Alliance," *Advertising Age,* February 9, 2004, p. 8.

28. Bloom, "Mixed Messages Muddy Mission," p. 15.

29. Wilcox, Ault, and Agee, *Public Relations Strategies and Tactics,* p. 492.

30. Ellen Byron, "Cognac and a Splash of Controversy," *The Wall Street Journal,* April 29, 2004, p. B5.

Index

Page numbers followed by the letter "f" indicate figures; those followed by the letter "t" indicate tables.